Jerry Baker's

BUG OFF!

www.jerrybaker.com

Jerry Baker's Supermarket Super Gardens
Jerry Baker's Dear God...Please Help It Grow!
Secrets from the Jerry Baker Test Gardens
Jerry Baker's All American Lawns
Jerry Baker's Terrific Garden Tonics!
Jerry Baker's Backyard Problem Solver
Jerry Baker's Green Grass Magic
Jerry Baker's Great Green Book of Garden Secrets
Jerry Baker's Old-Time Gardening Wisdom

Jerry Baker's Backyard Birdscaping Bonanza
Jerry Baker's Backyard Bird Feeding Bonanza
Jerry Baker's Year-Round Bloomers
Jerry Baker's Flower Garden Problem Solver
Jerry Baker's Perfect Perennials!

Grandma Putt's Home Health Remedies
Natures Best Miracle Medicines
Jerry Baker's Supermarket Super Remedies
Jerry Baker's The New Healing Foods
Jerry Baker's Cut Your Health Care Bills in Half!
Jerry Baker's Amazing Antidotes
Jerry Baker's Anti-Pain Plan
Jerry Baker's Oddball Ointments, Powerful Potions
  & Fabulous Folk Remedies
Jerry Baker's Giant Book of Kitchen Counter Cures

Jerry Baker's Can The Clutter!
Jerry Baker's Cleaning Magic!
Jerry Baker's Homespun Magic
Grandma Putt's Old-Time Vinegar, Garlic, Baking Soda,
  and 101 More Problem Solvers
Jerry Baker's Supermarket Super Products!
Jerry Baker's It Pays to Be Cheap!

To order any of the above, or for more information on Jerry Baker's amazing home, health, and garden tips, tricks, and tonics, please write to:

Jerry Baker, P.O. Box 805
New Hudson, MI 48165

Or, visit Jerry Baker online at:

www.jerrybaker.com

Jerry Baker's

BUG OFF!

2,193 Super Secrets for Battling Bad Bugs...
Outfoxing Crafty Critters...
Evicting Voracious Varmints
and Much More!

by Jerry Baker,
America's Master Gardener®

Published by American Master Products, Inc.

Published by American Master Products, Inc. / Jerry Baker

Executive Editor: Kim Adam Gasior
Managing Editor: Cheryl Winters Tetreau
Writer: Vicki Webster
Copy Editor: Barbara McIntosh Webb
Interior Design and Layout: Sandy Freeman
Cover Design: Kitty Pierce Mace
Illustrator: Ron Hildebrand
Indexer: Nanette Bendyna

Publisher's Cataloging-in-Publication
(Provided by Quality Books, Inc.)

Baker, Jerry.
    Bug off! : 2,193 super secrets for battling bad bugs—
  outfoxing crafty critters— evicting voracious varmints and
  much more! / Jerry Baker, Kim Adam Gasior.
    p. cm.
    Includes index.
    ISBN 978-0–922433–96-4

  1. Insect pests—Control. I. Gasior, Kim Adam. II. Title

SB931.B325 2004   632'.7
                    QBI04–200052

Printed in the United States of America
2 4 6 8 10 9 7 5 3 1 softcover

INTRODUCTION

 As you can probably imagine, I get asked a lot of questions as I talk to folks from all around this great land of ours. And do you know what? The vast majority of those people's puzzling predicaments have to do with pesky pests—whether it's raccoons robbing the corn, slugs making a slimy mess of the flower beds, or some mysterious midnight marauder munching on every morsel in sight. Well, my friends, in these pages, you'll find answers to those critter concerns and a whole lot more!

We'll start off with the louts who lust after your lovely landscape. In the first three chapters, I'll reveal my tried-and-true tactics for battling the bad guys who trash your turf grass, terrorize your trees, and turn your showy shrubs into a hole-y shame. We'll also cover a couple of vile villains who don't care beans about your plants—they're out gunnin' for you! I'm talking about mosquitoes and fire ants, and I'll clue you in on my sure-fire strategies for putting them exactly where they belong: 6 feet under on Boot Hill!

Chapter 4 is just for show: your big, fat flower show, that is! Here, you'll find techniques that are guaranteed to protect your annuals, perennials, and bulbs from pests, both big and small. I'll share my super-simple secrets for saying sayonara to everything from all-but-invisible nematodes to big, beautiful (but bothersome) deer, and every size critter in between.

It's sad, but true, that more bad bugs target vegetables than any other kind of plant. Fortunately, though, I know plenty of ways to ensure that your harvest winds up in your kitchen, and not in the tummies of a bunch of greedy gluttons! Chapters 5, 6, and 7 are chock-full of my tips, tricks, and tonics that will put an end to your vegetable-villain vexations—including potent pest killers that are safe and super easy-to-use!

Of course, not all of the critters who make mischief in your yard are bad guys. In fact, some of them are your best pals (or maybe the pets of your friendly, but misguided neighbors). Still, that doesn't give them the right to dig up your lawn, flatten your flowers, or leave fragrant souvenirs anyplace they please! Well, take heart: Wherever Fido or Fluffy is frolicking, I'll tell you how to say, loud and clear, "Not here, my dear!" (See Chapter 1 for the lowdown on dogs, and Chapter 4 to keep cats from cuttin' their capers in your corners.)

Finally, in Chapter 8, we'll look at nine superstars who would love to join your army to fight the battle of the bugs. You'll learn all about recruitment strategies and enlistment bonuses for bats, birds, toads, and a half-dozen good-guy bugs who polish off more pesky pests than you can shake a draft card at. Then, once your fierce fighters are on board, all you have to do is sit back and cheer as they march on to victory!

So without further ado, let the battle begin!

CONTENTS

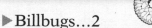

CHAPTER 3
SHRUB SPOILERS...76

CHAPTER 4
ANNUAL & PERENNIAL PLAGUERS...116

CHAPTER 1

LAWN
LOOTERS

When it comes to settin' off a house—and havin' a lot of summer fun—nothing beats a lawn full of lush, green, toe-ticklin' turf. And, as any lawn keeper knows, it can take a lot of time, money, and good old-fashioned elbow grease to keep that grass looking its best. So the last thing you need is to have it dug up or chewed to pieces by a bunch of pesky pests. Well, folks, you don't need to put up with those mischief-makin' trespassers. Here's a wheelbarrow load of ways to say, "Get out, and STAY OUT!"

← 1/4" – 3/4" →

1"

THIS IS THEIR LIFE

First, here's the good news: Billbugs usually produce only one generation of offspring per year. The adults come up out of the soil in spring to mate and (of course) eat your grass. The females lay their eggs in the soil. When they hatch in midsummer, the larvae burrow a little deeper into the ground and go to town on your grass roots. They chomp merrily away through the fall, then sleep through the winter in the soil. Come early spring, they wake up—still in grub form—and feed even more heavily before pupating and starting the cycle again.

ALSO ON THE MENU

Turf grass is the main item on the billbugs' menu, but on occasion, they'll wander into the veggie patch for a corn feast. If that happens at your place, launch an attack force of beneficial nematodes (see "Get 'Em While They're Young!", at right).

Many insects get up to no good only at one stage of their lives, but billbugs make a lifetime career of ruining your lawn. The grown-ups chew holes in grass blades, and their offspring eat the whole plant— roots, blades, and all. Small, distinct circles of brown or yellowish grass are a good clue that billbugs are at work. You'll know that for sure if the discolored turf pulls up in a mat, and the roots are covered with a light brown powder that looks like sawdust.

The culprits are easy to recognize. The larvae are white, legless grubs with bright, burnt-orange heads. The big guys are brown or black weevils, 1/4 to 3/4 inch long. (You'll sometimes see them strolling along sidewalks and driveways in early spring.) Like all weevils, they have a distinctive snout, or "bill," that gives them their name.

🍃 Get 'Em While They're Young!

While adult billbugs can make a mess of your lawn, grubs can destroy it. So close the restaurant early by investing in some beneficial nematodes. They'll boot the juvenile delinquents out the door, fast! It's a temporary remedy, though; for long-term control, you'll need a bigger bag of tricks. Read on for my top tips.

🍃 No Drain, Their Gain

Billbugs tend to zero in on lawns planted in poorly drained soil. If that's why they've targeted your turf, you've got several options for chasing the billbug blues away. Choosing the best one depends on where and how big the problem area is, how much time and money you want to spend on the solution, and your own taste in outdoor surroundings. Here are your choices:

▶ Improve the drainage in the trouble spots. This could be as simple as adding organic matter to the soil, or as complicated—and expensive—as calling in a landscaping contractor for a full-fledged overhaul.

▶ Replace the grass with perennial plants that take to damp soil.

▶ Forget growing anything in the problem area, and build a patio or deck instead.

▶ Go whole-hog and install a pond or a bog garden.

🍃 Call In the Superpowers

If you live where you can grow fescue or perennial rye-grass, you've got some powerful

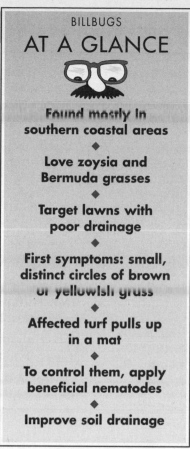

BILLBUGS
AT A GLANCE

Found mostly in southern coastal areas

◆

Love zoysia and Bermuda grasses

◆

Target lawns with poor drainage

◆

First symptoms: small, distinct circles of brown or yellowish grass

◆

Affected turf pulls up in a mat

◆

To control them, apply beneficial nematodes

◆

Improve soil drainage

help at your beck and call. Some varieties of both of these grasses are chock-full of microscopic fungi, called endophytes, that actually kill billbugs and a slew of other lawn pests, including armyworms, chinch bugs, and sod webworms. What's more, these endophytic grasses also have first-class disease resistance, drought tolerance, and all-around staying power. When you go to buy seed, though, here are two things you need to remember:

1. Each variety, and even each seed lot, has a different life expectancy and a different level of pest and disease resistance. So ask the folks at the garden center for the one that'll perform best in your yard.

2. The fungi inside the seeds are alive and ready to do battle, and you need to plant them before they go belly-up. So check the expiration date on the package—and don't let it sit around too long when you get it home!

🌿 Head 'Em Off

Once you've banished the billbugs, follow this routine to make your lawn one big unwelcome mat for the next generation:

Home on the Range

Billbugs

▶ Blast thatch and do everything you can to keep it at bay—it draws billbugs like peanuts attract squirrels! (See page 21 for my sure-fire thatch-removal plan.)

▶ Keep the soil enriched with organic matter, especially compost. Besides improving drainage, the "black gold" will supply important trace nutrients and help fend off diseases.

▶ Aerate your lawn so that water can penetrate deeply, and spray it once a month with my Aeration Tonic (at right). Billbugs *hate* a lawn with loose, airy soil!

▶ When you reseed, choose billbug-resistant grass varieties. Your Cooperative Extension Service can clue you in on the best ones for your region.

🌿 Hi, Hi, Birdie!

One of the surest ways to keep billbugs, and just about every other kind of insect pest, from trashing your lawn is to lay out the welcome mat for songbirds. They eat bad bugs by the barrelful, at both the adult and grub stages. For the full scoop on enticing winged warriors to your home, sweet home, see Chapter 8.

THUG BUSTER

Aeration Tonic

To keep your turf grass in the pink of health—and billbugs far away from it—aerate your lawn regularly with the help of this timely tonic.

1 cup of dishwashing liquid
1 cup of beer

Combine these two ingredients in your 20 gallon hose-end sprayer, and fill the balance of the sprayer jar with warm water. Then once a month during the growing season, spray your lawn with this tonic to the point of run-off.

THIS IS THEIR LIFE

Adult chinch bugs spend the winter in thatch or in the upper layers of the soil. In the North, they hibernate, but down South, they sometimes carry on in low gear right on through the winter. When the weather warms up, they crawl out of their hiding-holes, and for as long as the temperature allows, they feed, mate, and lay eggs. Each batch hatches in about two weeks, and the pin-head-sized nymphs mature in about a month. They live for another two months or so after that, eating and repro-ducing the whole time.

ALSO ON THE MENU

In addition to turf grasses, chinch bugs like to munch on corn, which—technically speaking—is a member of the grass family. To stop the tiny bugs from bugging your crop, use the flannel-sheet trick described in "How Cozy!" (see page 6).

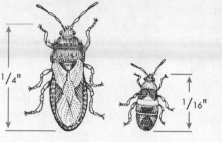

1/4" 1/16"

Both adults and nymphs suck the sap from grass blades and, at the same time, inject a poison that makes the plants go belly-up in a hurry. Your first clue that the suckers have arrived will be round, yellow patches that quickly turn brown and die. If chinch bugs have launched a major invasion, your next clue will be the odor: When you step on your lawn, you'll be hit with a scent that makes you want to hold your nose and run away! These guys are so small that you may need a magnifying glass to get a positive I.D., but here's what to look for: The nymphs are bright red with a white band across their backs. The grown-ups have dark brown bodies with a black triangle between white, folded wings.

Get 'Em While They're Hot!

Chinch bugs usually appear during dry spells, when the temperature is 70°F or above. They set up their first camps in the warmest, sunniest parts of your lawn—most often in the strips of grass along sidewalks or driveways, where reflected heat really cooks the turf. They spread out fast, so don't dawdle!

Just Testing

Both chinch bugs and drought stress cause look-alike yellow spots, so unless you've got a big bunch of bugs, you may not be able to detect them by smell. Before you launch your good-riddance campaign, perform this simple telltale test: Cut both ends off of a coffee can, and sink it 2 or 3 inches into the ground. Then, fill the can with soapy water, and wait 5 minutes or so. If there are chinch bugs crawling in the grass, they'll float to the surface.

🌿 How Cozy!

It's a cinch to send chinch bugs packin' from a small lawn, or just a few trouble spots. Here's how to do it: First, make a solution of 2 tablespoons of dish-washing liquid to 1 gallon of water, and pour it on the area. (I use a watering can to ensure good, even coverage.) Then, put a white flannel sheet or other soft, white cloth on top of the grass. Wait 15 or 20 minutes, then peek under the fabric. It should be teeming with chinch bugs who've crawled toward the surface to escape the soap. Gather up the cloth, and dunk it into a bucket filled with soapy

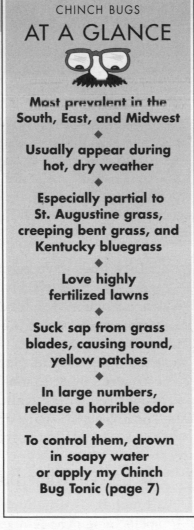

CHINCH BUGS
AT A GLANCE

Most prevalent in the South, East, and Midwest

◆

Usually appear during hot, dry weather

◆

Especially partial to St. Augustine grass, creeping bent grass, and Kentucky bluegrass

◆

Love highly fertilized lawns

◆

Suck sap from grass blades, causing round, yellow patches

◆

In large numbers, release a horrible odor

◆

To control them, drown in soapy water or apply my Chinch Bug Tonic (page 7)

water. Then, get out the hose, and spray your lawn thoroughly to remove the soap residue.

🌿 Make 'Em Sick

A fungus called *Beauvaria bassiana* makes chinch bugs too sick to reproduce. It works like a charm, and you can buy it from catalogs and at some big garden centers. There's only one catch: You won't see the results until the following year, so be patient.

🌿 And Don't Come Back!

Once you've cleared out the chinch bugs, show them a lawn they won't want to come back to. To be specific:

▶ Blast thatch (see page 21).

▶ Keep your lawn well watered.

▶ Avoid overfeeding your lawn.

🍃 Turn 'Em Off

Even if you grow St. Augustine grass, there is hope: Although chinch bugs go hog-wild for most kinds, there are a few varieties they don't like, including 'Floralawn', 'Floratam', and 'FX-10'. New, resistant types come out from time to time, so before you plant a new lawn, check with your Cooperative Extension Service for the latest and greatest version.

🍃 The Eyes Have It

A whole posse of good guys go gunnin' for chinch bugs, but the most gung-ho bounty hunters are big-eyed bugs. It's easy to post a reward: These guys go gaga for yarrow, goldenrod, Queen Anne's lace, and a whole slew of herbs, including fennel, dill, parsley, and cilantro. If you live down in Dixie, you've really got a sweet way to solve your chinch bug problems: Just plant some oleander, and the big-eyed bugs will beat a path to your yard!

But make sure you take a close look at the wanted poster: Chinch bugs and big-eyed bugs are almost dead ringers for each other. So, when you think you've spotted a crowd of chinch bugs, don't fire till you see the size of their eyes! (For the whole lowdown on big-eyed bugs and the chinch bug's other enemies, see Chapter 8.)

Home on the Range

Chinch Bugs

THUG BUSTER

Chinch Bug Tonic

If problem areas are too big for the flannel-sheet treatment in "How Cozy!" (see page 6), make up a batch of this potent brew.

1 cup of Murphy's Oil Soap®
3 cups of warm water
Gypsum

Combine the soap and water in a 20 gallon hose-end sprayer, and saturate your lawn. After it dries, apply gypsum to the bug-infested areas at the recommend rate.

THIS IS THEIR LIFE

Several times a year, male and female fire ants (both with wings) swarm out of the nest and into the air where, at 600 to 800 feet above the ground, they mate. The males die and fall back to earth. The females fly off to build nests and settle into their life's work: filling the world with fire ants. Over the course of a three-year life span (give or take), a fire ant queen lays thousands of eggs, and every few months, another batch of youngsters takes to the sky to start the process all over again.

ALSO ON THE MENU

In addition to attacking humans, pets, and other animals (sometimes with fatal results), they also dine on many kinds of plants. They love apples, corn, okra, potatoes, and strawberries, and they can girdle the trunks of young pecan and citrus trees. Wherever the ants are causing trouble, call on any or all of these tricks.

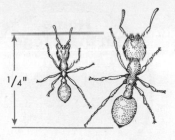

1/4"

The South is cursed with two kinds of imported fire ants, one red (*Solenopsis invicta*), and the other black (*S. richteri*). Both deliver a sting that would put any bee to shame, but the red devils have a couple of trump cards: a hearty appetite for any critter that moves, and an aggressive streak the size of Texas. What's more, they've stood up and said "boo" to just about every chemical pesticide known to man. In fact, like many other bugs, they've reacted to the poisonous onslaught by evolving into "super-bugs" that can fend off anything the folks in white lab coats send their way.

🖉 Seek and Ye Shall Destroy

By sight, it's hard to tell fire ants from the garden-variety picnic pests. To deliver death and destruction, you need to identify the nest. That can be tricky with a young colony; the most you'll see is a slight bump in the ground. There's no mistaking a mature mound, though: It's a rock-hard dome that's up to 1½ feet high and 2 feet in diameter—a disaster-in-waiting for any car or piece of machinery that runs over it. But that's only the tip of the fireberg. The excavation often extends 3 feet or more below the surface, and flitting around inside, there can be as many as a quarter of a million ill-tempered ants!

Fire ants will nest almost anywhere in the

great outdoors (fortunately, they don't venture inside the house). They prefer warm, sunny spots, and they *love* raised beds and compost piles.

🖋 If It's Any Consolation...

Even these villains have a good side: In the process of their feeding frenzy, they gobble up a lot of bad-guy bugs, including boll weevils, aphids, earwigs, corn earworms, and even fleas and ticks.

🖋 Death to the Queen(s)!

To wipe out a nest of fire ants, you need to kill the queen, or queens. That's all but impossible to do with poison bait, because the worker ants test all food before it reaches the boss's lips. Instead, your best option is to stage an ambush. For the surest— and safest— results, enlist a partner-in-crime for this escapade. Plan to attack early

Home on the Range

Fire Ants

in the morning, or on a cool, sunny day. That's when the queen is usually holding court near the top of the mound. Then:

1. Mix up a batch of my God-Sink-the-Queen Drench (below).

2. While the potion is simmering on the stove, put on gloves, a long-sleeved shirt, and long pants that are tucked into high boots. Have your partner do the same. If you want to be extra-safe, wear rubber boots that you've smeared with a sticky substance like petroleum jelly.

THUG BUSTER

God-Sink-the-Queen Drench

When fire ants are driving you up a wall, serve their boss lady this fatal cocktail.

4 cups of citrus peels
3 gallons of water

Toss the peels into a pot with the water, bring it to a boil, and let it simmer for about 10 minutes. Then pour the potion into the hole. (Be sure to follow the procedure described in "Death to the Queen(s)!" at left.) The boiling water will polish off any ants it reaches, and the citrus-oil fumes will send more to the gas chamber. Repeat the procedure every two or three days, until there's no sign of life in the mound.

Arm your partner with a long, sharp stick or metal rod (anything that's long, strong, and sharp on one end).

3. Take the potion from the stove and, together with your partner, tiptoe as softly as you can up to the mound—fire ants are super-sensitive to ground vibrations.

4. Have your partner poke the entrance hole with the stick.

5. *Immediately* pour the boiling solution into the hole. Then turn around, and run like the dickens!

Off with Their Heads!

Like all imported pests, fire ants arrived on our shores without a natural predator to their name. Back home, though, in Central America, they have a deadly enemy: the phorid fly. This hit-squad hero injects an egg into the ant's throat. When the maggot hatches, it moves into the ant's head. After a few weeks, the head falls off, and the maggot uses the hollowed-out skull for its own pupal chamber. (Yuck!) Even as I write this, pest-control honchos are working on importing phorid flies, so keep tabs on garden-supply catalogs, and stay in touch with your local Cooper-

ative Extension Service. Salvation may soon be at hand!

Call In the Pros

Dealing with a major fire ant invasion is no job for an amateur. If the villains are driving you to drink, call a pest-control operator who will use one of these two weapons:

▶ An insect growth regulator, such as abamectin

▶ Avermectin, a naturally occurring soil fungus that's lethal to fire ants

One word of caution: Don't let them talk you into anything more toxic—it'll only encourage the breeding of more super-ants!

If you've wound up on the wrong end of a fire ant, reach for Grandma Putt's favorite bee-sting remedy: a half-and-half solution of chlorine bleach and water. Applied within 15 minutes of the sting, it'll ease the pain and swelling. A paste made of meat tenderizer and water works, too. If the pain is severe, or spreads beyond the bitten spot, get to a doctor—pronto!

🍃 No More Mounds!

When it comes to stakin' their claim on nesting territory, fire ants are one determined crew! In some parts of the country, it's darn near impossible to keep them at bay. Still, there are ways to make your turf less inviting. Here are several.

▶ Forget about a compost pile. Instead, cook your supply in a commercial composting bin, and keep it raised a few inches off the ground.

▶ Don't grow anything in raised beds—it's like opening a low-cost housing development for fire ants.

▶ Cover paths and unpaved walkways with 2 or 3 inches of sand or pea gravel to keep the ants from tunneling in. Better yet, pave them!

🍃 Stick It to 'Em

If you already have enclosed, raised beds or big planters, wrap a sticky trap around the bottom portion of each one. (It's also good

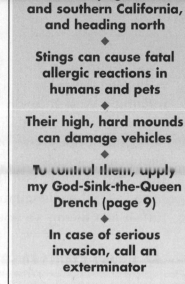

FIRE ANTS
AT A GLANCE

On the rampage in Texas and southern California, and heading north

◆

Stings can cause fatal allergic reactions in humans and pets

◆

Their high, hard mounds can damage vehicles

◆

To control them, apply my God-Sink-the-Queen Drench (page 9)

◆

In case of serious invasion, call an exterminator

extra protection for your compost bin.) To make the trap, just cut a strip of plastic sheet or flexible cardboard that's about 6 inches wide and long enough to reach around the container. Tack or tape the strip onto the container, then coat it with any sticky substance, such as petroleum jelly, spray adhesive, or Tanglefoot®. Just remember to keep the strip clear of "bridges" that the ants could scramble over, like twigs, leaves, or dead bugs.

🍃 Made in the Shade

Fire ants are sun worshipers, so the shadier your yard is, the less enticing it'll look to a house-hunting queen. If you're on the fire ants' hit list, do whatever you can to dim the lights: Plant trees and tall shrubs; build walls or fences; or grow vines on arbors and trellises. Of course, there is a risk that you'll have to replace your grass with shade-loving ground-covers—but for my money, that's a small price to pay for peace of mind, especially if you have children or pets on the scene.

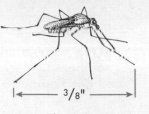

THIS IS THEIR LIFE

After sucking as much as four times her weight in blood, a female mosquito flies off in search of water on which to lay her eggs. Some species have particular preferences, such as ponds, tidal marshes, or swamps. Others will settle for anything that contains a little H_2O (preferably stagnant). Old tires are big favorites; but potholes, tin cans, and even footprints make dandy skeeter maternity wards. In a few short days, the eggs hatch, and the babies will spend the next two stages of their lives in the water, first as larvae (wrigglers), then as pupae (tumblers).

ALSO ON THE MENU

Female mosquitoes are out gunnin' for blood, *period!* The males just go around sippin' nectar from flowers; they have no desire to zero in on anybody, so they pose no threat to humans or pets.

Mosquitoes couldn't care less about your lawn they want to sink their chops into you and your four-footed pals! And, as we all know, these bloodsuckers can leave you with more than just itchy, red welts; they also transmit deadly diseases, including West Nile virus, yellow fever, encephalitis, and heartworm in dogs and cats. Like fire ants, mosquitoes have been so bombarded with chemical pesticides that they've grown immune to nearly all of them. But that doesn't mean you have to let the vile villains spoil your summertime fun. It just means ya gotta outwit 'em!

Power Plants to the Rescue!

A whole lot of plants repel mosquitoes. There's just one minor catch: Contrary to what you see in some magazine ads and catalog descriptions, you can't just plant them and expect the skeeters to flee in horror. You need to crush the leaves to release their volatile oils, then rub them on your skin. When you do that, you can expect to stay bite-free for a couple of hours. The most effective bug-control plants have one thing in common: a strong, citrusy scent that's pleasant to humans, but repugnant to mosquitoes and other insects. Here are some of my favorite anti-mosquito plants:

Lemon balm (*Melissa officinalis*)

Lemon basil (*Ocimum basilicum* 'Citriodorum')

Scented geraniums (*Pelargonium* 'Citrosa' and P. 'Citronella')

Lemon thyme (*Thymus* × *citriodorus*)

🌿 Close the Maternity Wards

To *really* control mosquitoes, you need to eliminate their breeding grounds. In your home landscape, that's really not as hard as it may sound. Here's your to-do list:

Ask Jerry

My husband wants to get one of those electric bug zappers to kill the mosquitoes in our yard. I've heard that they don't really work well, and I'm afraid that all it's going to zap is our peace and quiet. Am I right?

Yes and no. Those gadgets zap bugs all right—just about every kind *except* mosquitoes, including a whole lot of the good guys. That's because most of the zappers use light to attract their "prey," and mosquitoes don't care beans about light. Mosquitoes are out for blood, so they zero in on the smell of carbon dioxide, which mammals (including humans) give off. What you want is a machine like a Mosquito Deleto® that uses CO_2 to lure skeeters to their deaths—and quietly, too.

▶ Get rid of any debris that could hold water—like those old tires you keep meaning to take to the dump.

▶ Fill in potholes and any low-lying areas where rainwater collects.

▶ Change your pets' water at least once a day, and refill birdbaths every couple of days.

▶ Empty portable wading pools as soon as the kids are through using them. Then, turn them upside down or take them indoors.

▶ Keep rain barrels covered.

🌿 Go Fish!

If you have a pond or water garden, you probably don't want to drain it or cover it up, and you don't have to. Just stock it with goldfish, minnows, or guppies. They're all first-class skeeter eaters. If you're up to your ears in buzzers, though, go for the big guns: Call your Cooperative Extension Service, or a nursery that specializes in water gardens, and ask where you can get some *Gambusia*. These little fish never grow more than 2½ inches long, but they polish off so many mosquito larvae that in many parts of the country, fish hatcheries are breeding them just for that purpose. The only downside is that *Gambusia* can't live through the winter in cold climates. So if you live up North, you'll have to restock your pond every spring.

✎ Ring the Dinner Bell

Bats, frogs, toads, turtles, lizards, ants, praying mantises, spiders, dragonflies, and birds (especially purple martins) all eat mosquitoes. So lay out the welcome mat! (See Chapter 8 for helpful hints on encouraging hit-squad hospitality.)

✎ Bye, Bye, Baby

You probably can't eliminate every single low spot in your yard and garden, but you can make sure it doesn't

become a skeeter nursery. When you find a body of water that you can't empty, pour in one of these weapons:

▶ Oil (vegetable, mineral, or neem oil). It'll spread across the surface and smother the future vampires. (Even though mosquitoes spend their babyhoods in the water, they have to breathe air to survive.)

▶ Cold, old coffee. Forget the decaf, though: It's the caffeine that does the trick. When mosquito larvae are exposed to caffeine, they get so confused that they can't tell which end is up, and they drown!

▶ Bti (*Bacillus thuringiensis* var. *israelensis*). You can buy it in tablet form from garden-supply catalogs. It kills skeeters within 24 hours without harming any other critters. (Make sure you look for slow-release tablets like Mosquito Dunks™; some brands lose their effect after about three days, and you'll have to add more.)

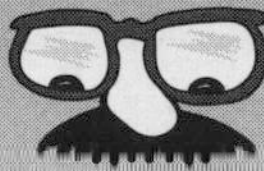

GRANDMA KNEW BEST

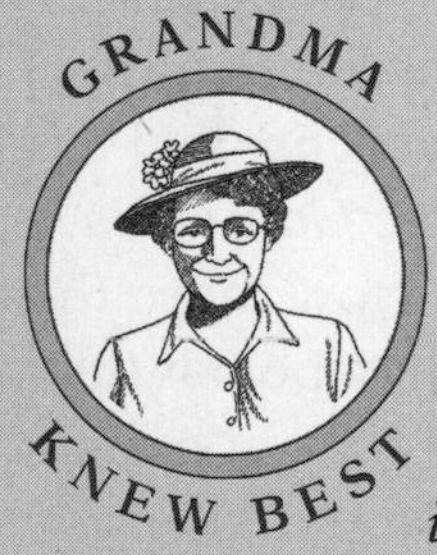

Grandma Putt had a dandy way to cut down on the mosquito population: She'd fill some old pans with water, add a few squirts of dishwashing liquid, and set them outside. When skeeters set down to lay their eggs, they couldn't get up again!

▶ Laginex®. It contains a naturally occurring water-mold fungus that kills mosquitoes (but nothing else) for three to four weeks.

Home on the Range

Mosquitoes

🍃 Don't Give Blood

When you invite friends to a barbecue, you want 'em to *have* dinner, not *be* dinner. Here's how to dine in peace:

▶ Set out an oscillating fan or two—mosquitoes don't like moving air.

▶ Toss a handful of sage, rosemary, or citrus peels on the coals. You'll keep the biters at bay and spice up the chow at the same time!

▶ Serve up a menu that includes a lot of fresh garlic, which seems to repel mosquitoes. And why not? After all, they *are* vampires!

▶ Before the guests show up, spray everything in your yard with Mosquito Lemon Aid (at right).

🍃 Cure for the Common Itch

Nothing takes the fun out of summer like a bunch of itchy mosquito bites. Well,

I don't know any way to *guarantee* that you'll never be bitten. But I can tell you two simple ways to nix the itch:

1. If the skeeter has just done her dirty work, dab the spot with a few drops of ammonia to head off the itch and swelling. Just make sure you use this trick *before* you start scratching. If the skin is already broken, the ammonia will deliver a sting that you won't soon forget!

2. When you're already scratching up a storm, reach for a bottle of antiseptic mouthwash. Moisten a tissue or cotton ball with it, hold it on the bite for about 15 seconds, and then kiss that itch good-bye.

THUG BUSTER

Mosquito Lemon Aid

There's nothing mosquitoes hate more than the scent of lemon. So what are you waiting for? Give 'em a whiff of this fragrant potion!

1 cup of lemon-scented ammonia
1 cup of lemon-scented dishwashing liquid

Put these ingredients into your 20 gallon hose-end sprayer, and hose down everything in your yard three times a week, preferably early in the morning or late in the evening.

FALL ARMYWORMS

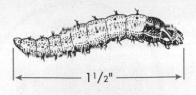

1¹/₂"

Although armyworms wander far and wide, they do the most damage in southern Florida and along the Gulf Coast. There, they produce six or more generations per year. In the rest of the country, only one generation appears, in late summer or early fall. Here's how the cycle works: In the spring, swarms of gray moths leave the South, fly northward, and lay eggs. Several weeks later, the caterpillars hatch, eat for two to four weeks, then burrow into the ground. In another two to four weeks, they emerge, head farther north, and lay their eggs, and the whole process begins again.

ALSO ON THE MENU

The fall armyworm targets turf grasses, especially Bermuda grass. Two close cousins, the common armyworm and the yellow-striped armyworm, conduct maneuvers in the vegetable patch.

These culprits got their name for a very good reason: They travel in groups, and in years when their population soars, they're like an invading army on the march, gobbling up every grass blade in their path. (A large horde can destroy a small lawn in a single night.) They generally strike in late summer or fall, leaving round, bald spots in the turf. A fall armyworm is a slightly hairy caterpillar that's about 1¹/₂ inches long, with a black head marked with a white Y. Three thin, yellowish white stripes stretch along the back from head to tail. On each side is a dark stripe and, below that, a wavy yellow line splotched with red. The main body color can be green, brown, or nearly black.

Call Up the Troops

To you, a regiment of armyworms looks like an invading horde; but to a whole lot of other critters, it's a first-rate smorgasbord. Songbirds, toads, and skunks gobble up all the armyworms they can find, and bats polish off the night-flying moths by the bucketload. If volunteers aren't showing up fast enough to solve your problem, high-tail it to your local garden center and pick up some hired guns: Two kinds of parasitic wasps, trichogramma and braconid, are lethal to armyworms—but harmless to humans and other animals.

Search and Destroy

If the invasion is too big for your defensive army to handle, don't despair. Just mix up a batch of my Caterpillar Killer Tonic (below). Then load up your sprayer jar, and let 'er rip! Remember, though: For this treatment to be effective, it has to make direct contact with the target. So make sure you stage your attack just after dusk, when the armyworms venture out to feed.

Home on the Range

Fall Armyworms

Bring On the Big B

Another armyworm assault tactic: Buy some Btk *(Bacillus thuringiensis* var. *kurstaki)*. This magic bullet is a bacteria that's poisonous to caterpillars, but nothing else. All you do is apply it to a plant (in this case, your grass), according to the directions on the package. Then, when the pesky pest chows down on the leaves, he gets a big mouthful of Btk at the same time. He may cling to life for a few more days, but one thing is sure: He soon won't be eating your lawn— or anything else! (Just remember to reapply the stuff after it rains.)

You Parasites!

When it comes to polishing off bad-guy bugs, parasitic nematodes are some of the handiest hired guns you can find. There are numerous species, each with its own roster of targets. In this case, the nematodes you want are *Neoaplectana carpocapsae*—they've been specially bred to polish off armyworms.

Regroup

Once you've turned the tide of battle, dig up the dead turf, and reseed with a grass that's resistant to armyworms. New varieties come on the market almost every year, so check with your Cooperative Extension Service to find the best type for your territory.

THUG BUSTER

Caterpillar Killer Tonic

This potent brew means death on contact to armyworms and any other cantankerous caterpillars.

¹/₂ lb. of wormwood leaves
2 tbsp. of Murphy's Oil Soap®
4 cups of water

Simmer the wormwood leaves in 2 cups of the water for 30 minutes. Strain, then add the Murphy's Oil Soap and the remaining 2 cups of water. Pour the solution into a 6 gallon hose-end sprayer, and saturate your lawn in the early evening, when armyworms (and other grass-munching caterpillars) come out to dine. Repeat this treatment until the varmints are history.

MOLE CRICKETS

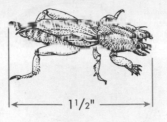

1¹/₂"

The mole cricket's life cycle varies a little according to the species (there are three, all from South America). In general, though, from April through June, females lay eggs in underground chambers that are 4 to 12 inches below the soil surface. In three weeks or so, the eggs hatch; soon afterwards, the parents die. The young'uns eat each other at first (talk about sibling rivalry!), but they soon graduate to munchin' on grass roots. From then on, all they do is eat and grow until winter, when they hibernate as either nymphs or adults. Here's the good news: They produce only one generation per year.

Although mole crickets dine primarily on grass, they sometimes eat vegetables, especially tomatoes and potatoes. Your best option: Use the "Seek and Destroy" plan (see page 19).

Like their namesakes, mole crickets tunnel through the soil, destroying large sections of lawn in the process. Normally, they go after the roots, and the result you see is turf "decorated" with irregular brown streaks, where the grass has died. On warm nights, though, when the soil is moist, the crickets venture above ground to munch on grass blades. These thugs pillage lawn grasses throughout the South, from the Atlantic Coast to Texas, where they go on the rampage from April to October. They look much like their above-ground cousins, except their heads are bigger and they have short, powerful front legs with shovel-like feet.

✍ Goin' Under

The surest way to end the crickets' excavation project is to go at 'em underground with one of these magic bullets:

▶ Bt (*Bacillus thuringiensis*)

▶ Predatory nematodes (specifically *Steinernema scapterisci*)

▶ A beneficial wasp by the name of Larra bicolor

▶ The Brazilian red-eyed fly, a.k.a. *Ormia depleta*

If you can't find your weapon of choice in a garden-supply catalog, call your local Cooperative Extension Service. Don't stop with this list, though. Ask about the best time to plan your attack (it can vary from one region to another, and from one year to the next), and whether any new biological controls have come on the market.

✐ Seek and Destroy

If your lawn is on the small side, or if you enjoy tiny-game hunting, this is your two-step, good-riddance game plan:

Step 1. Flush the area with a solution made of 3 tablespoons of lemon-scented dishwashing liquid per gallon of water. Within 2 or 3 minutes, the entire mole cricket population will rise to the surface.

Step 2. Let 'em have it with my Hot Bug Brew (at right).

Home on the Range

Mole Crickets

action, just saturate the turf with soapy water (3 tablespoons of unscented dishwashing liquid for each gallon of H_2O will do the trick), and the tasty tidbits will rise to the occasion—of their demise, that is!

✐ Blast That Thatch!

There's nothing mole crickets like better than a lawn with a nice, thick layer of thatch. So to keep the vile villains from darkening your doorstep again, follow my thatch-removal program starting on page 21.

✐ Seek and Let Others Destroy

If you'd rather not spend your time spraying, you're in luck: Unlike a lot of imported pests, mole crickets have more than their fair share of natural enemies. Ground beetles and assassin bugs go gunnin' for them right in their tunnels. And, when the foul felons come to the surface, they're sitting ducks for a whole boatload of insect eaters, including toads, snakes, raccoons, foxes, and birds. To get the above-ground crew into

Hot Bug Brew

This potent beverage will deal a death blow to mole crickets, maggots, flies, and any other bug that's buggin' your plants.

3 hot green peppers (canned or fresh)
3 medium cloves of garlic
1 small onion
1 tbsp. of dishwashing liquid
3 cups of water

Puree the peppers, garlic, and onion in a blender. Then pour the mixture into a jar, and add the dishwashing liquid and water. Let stand for 24 hours. Strain out the solids, pour the liquid into a spray bottle, and blast the mole crickets to kingdom come. **Note:** You probably won't get all the varmints on the first try, so you may need to repeat the process a few times.

THUG BUSTER

SOD WEBWORMS

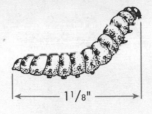

1⅛"

THIS IS THEIR LIFE

Sod webworm larvae spend the winter just under the soil surface, among the roots of grasses and weeds. At the first sign of warming weather, they wake up and chew on grass blades and roots until late spring, when they spin cocoons and pupate. A week or two later, they emerge as small, tan or gray moths that only live for a few days. The females fly at dusk, dropping eggs over the grass. In about a week, the eggs hatch, and life as they know it goes on.

ALSO ON THE MENU

Like many turf-grass pests, sod webworms also make a meal out of young corn plants. You can put an end to their garden-variety fun by letting them have it with Btk or my All-Season Clean-Up Tonic (see page 98).

When you mow your lawn in the early evening, do clouds of small moths rise up in front of your mower? If so, then their babies—sod webworms—are probably picnicking in your grass. The damage first appears as small dead patches (1 to 2 inches in diameter) in early spring. By July or August, there may be *big* dead patches. The worms are sleek, tan caterpillars with black spots on their backs and a beak-like projection on their heads. They do their dirty work at night, chewing off grass blades at the crown and pulling them into silk-lined tunnels in the ground to eat them. Sod webworms wander everywhere and eat any kind of grass, but their favorite stomping, er crawling, ground is America's heartland. And their idea of real dining pleasure is a lawn full of bent grass or Kentucky bluegrass, covered with a nice, thick layer of thatch.

🌿 Watch the Birdie!

A big flock of birds dining on your lawn is a good clue that sod webworms have arrived: Our fine feathered friends can't resist these tasty treats! Before you panic, though, confirm the diagnosis with the soup-can test starting on page 23. If you count 15 sod webworms to a can, get to work!

🌿 Get the Early Worm

Act fast: A big crowd of worms will polish off your lawn faster than you can say,

"Hey, that's my grass you're eating!" Here's the routine: First, mow your lawn, then spray it with my Aeration Tonic (see page 4) so that your weapon of choice can better penetrate the thatch layer. Then, let 'er rip with one of these big guns:

Home on the Range

Sod Webworms

▶ *Bacillus thuringiensis* var. *kurstaki* (commonly called Btk)

▶ My All-Season Clean-Up Tonic (see page 98)

Whichever weapon you use, you may need to repeat the process several times before you see results.

Thatch Blaster Tonic

THUG BUSTER

This excellent elixir will help keep your lawn free of nasty thatch all season long.

1 cup of beer or regular cola (not diet)
½ cup of dishwashing liquid
¼ cup of ammonia

Mix all of these ingredients in your 20 gallon hose-end sprayer. Fill the balance of the sprayer jar with water, and saturate the entire turf area starting in spring. Repeat once a month during the summer, when the grass is actively growing.

A Pretty Solution

Like most caterpillars, sod webworms have more natural enemies than the Pentagon has stars and bars. One of the most gung-ho of the bunch is the spined soldier beetle, and you can call up these troops simply by including permanent perennial beds in your yard. So what are you waiting for? Grab that shovel and go to it!

Now, about That Thatch...

No matter how many times you kill off the sod webworms in your lawn, more will show up to haunt you (along with just about every other pest and disease germ under the sun) until you rip up the welcome mat—the thatch. So get rid of the stuff with a dethatching rake, and dump it onto your compost pile. If your lawn is large, or the thatch layer is extra-thick, rent a power rake. (Your back will thank you!) Then, to keep the soil surface free and clear in the future:

▶ Wear golf spikes or aerating lawn sandals whenever you mow your lawn. That way, you'll break up the surface tension barrier between the soil and the blades of grass.

▶ Apply my Thatch Blaster Tonic (see page 21) once a month starting in spring, as soon as temperatures stay above 50°F.

▶ Don't overdo it: Feed only the amount recommended for your grass variety. Too much chow of any kind invites thatch, and other problems, too.

🌿 Just Say No

…to chemical fertilizers, that is. They're a prime cause of thatch buildup. Instead, put your lawn on a healthy, natural-food diet. You can either buy a commercial organic lawn food, or make your own using these simple ingredients:

▶ **For nitrogen:** bloodmeal, fish emulsion, manure

SOD WEBWORMS
AT A GLANCE

Most prevalent in the Midwest

◆

Partial to thatch-covered lawns, especially bent grass and Kentucky bluegrass

◆

Feed actively from the first sign of warm weather until late spring

◆

Damage first appears as 1- to 2-inch-diameter dead patches in early spring

◆

To control them, encourage birds or spray with my All-Season Clean-Up Tonic (page 98)

▶ **For phosphorus:** bonemeal, rock phosphate

▶ **For potassium:** greensand, wood ashes, seaweed

Just one word of caution: Grasses vary greatly in their appetite levels, and when it comes to fertilizer, more is not better. If you don't know how much food your turf needs per square foot—and particularly the amount of nitrogen—check with your local garden center or Cooperative Extension Service.

🌿 And Don't Forget!

Apply half an inch or so of finely sifted compost in spring and fall. It will supply important trace nutrients, improve the soil texture, and even help fend off nasty turf diseases.

WHITE GRUBS

THIS IS THEIR LIFE

In the summer, adult beetles lay eggs on grass blades. When the larvae hatch, they tunnel into the ground and start eating the roots, generally staying within 3 inches or so of the surface. As winter approaches, most species head deeper underground to hibernate. Come spring, they wake up and go on a brief eating binge before pupating. The adults emerge in late spring to mate and start the whole process over again.

ALSO ON THE MENU

White grubs also munch on flower and vegetable roots, but they rarely cause serious damage. If a few healthy plants suddenly wilt, poke through the soil nearby. If you find grubs, either drop the culprits in a bucket of soapy water, or just leave them lying on the surface where birds can have them for lunch.

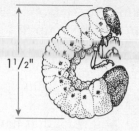

1½"

These pests are the larvae of many different beetles, including chater, Japanese, June (a.k.a. May), and Asiatic garden beetles. It's all but impossible to tell them apart: They all have fat, whitish bodies that tend to curl up into a C shape. They all do the same dirty work, too, eating the roots of your grass, and leaving you with a lawn full of irregular, brown patches that look burned. If you tug on one of the dead clumps, it'll come right up like a piece of loose carpet—often exposing the culprits in action. Grubs start feeding in early spring, and the damage becomes apparent at any time from late spring through early fall, usually during dry spells.

🌿 Another Clue

Many things can cause burned-looking patches in turf grass (see "Coulda Fooled Me" on page 30). You'll know you've got big-time grub trouble if skunks, moles, raccoons, or crows are paying frequent, damaging visits. They all think grubs are the tastiest snack a critter could ever ask for.

🌿 Soup's On!

A few grubs here and there won't eat you out of lawn and garden. In fact, like all "bad-guy" bugs, they're an important cog in the wheel of life.

The trouble comes when too many grubs start munchin' on the same chunk of turf. Here's a simple way to take a census: Cut both ends off of a soup can, and sink it into your lawn up to its rim. Then fill it close to the top with water. Repeat the process in several parts of your lawn, with the cans spaced about 10 feet apart. Wait 5 or 10 minutes, then count the grubs that have floated to the top of each can. That number will equal the number of grubs per square foot of lawn. If you've got 8 to 10 bodies per can, don't sweat it: Birds can keep that population under control without wrecking your lawn in the process. More than 10 grubs means you've got a major invasion on your hands, and you need to strike back—hard!

Ask Jerry

Grubs made such a mess of our lawn that we dug the whole thing up, and we're about to put in a new one. If we plant an endophytic grass, will we be safe from future grub attacks?

I'm afraid not. Endophytic grasses fend off insects that chew on the grass blades, but they're fair game for grubs and other root-eating pests. And adult beetles lay their eggs on any kind of turf grass, endophytic or otherwise. But depending on how you plan to use your new lawn, there may be a simple way to make it a no-grub zone: Instead of grass, plant groundcovers. (If you don't know what would work well in your area, check with some gardening neighbors, a nearby garden club, or your Cooperative Extension Service.) Come egg-laying time, beetles will make a beeline to somebody else's yard!

🌿 Take a Hike

This double-threat maneuver will ease your grub woes and aerate the turf at the same time. Just order a pair of spiked sandals from a garden-supply catalog.  When they arrive, strap 'em on, and stroll back and forth across your lawn. With every step you take, the spikes will skewer grubs galore. You won't get every single one, but you'll polish off enough to turn a big problem into a no-worry situation in no time at all.

🌿 Got Milk?

If you know the grubs in your lawn are baby Japanese beetles (because the grown-ups are chewin' the daylights out of your shrubs, flowers, and veggies), get some milky spore disease *(Bacillus popilliae)*, available in catalogs and many garden centers. All you do is sprinkle it onto your freshly mowed lawn according to the package directions, and it stays in the soil for years, killing baby grubs as soon as they hatch, but harming nothing else. Unfortunately, milky spore takes a few years to achieve its full effect, but once it gets up to speed, your grub woes will be gone for good.

Home on the Range

White Grubs

🌿 Take That!

For fast-acting relief, drench your turf with beneficial nematodes (available in catalogs and garden centers). These almost microscopic worms burrow into white grubs, reproduce, and at the same time, deliver a bacteria that kills the grubs, but no other critters. In order for the nematodes to do their job, you need to apply them in just the right way, so follow the instructions on the label to the letter. There's one down-

---

GRANDMA KNEW BEST

No matter what strategy you use against white grubs, it's important to attack while they're still small and vulnerable. The exact time frame varies, depending on who the grubs' parents are and what part of the country you live in. That may sound confusing, but there's a simple way to schedule D-Day. Just do what Grandma Putt did: Keep an eagle eye on your back-porch light. When you see a lot of beetles flitting around, makin' whoopie, you know it won't be long before your lawn's full of baby grubs. Wait five to six weeks, then choose your weapons, and charge! (Or, if you'd prefer a more exact approach to timing, call your closest Cooperative Extension Service and ask when the grubby action starts in your town. They should be able to help you.)

---

side to this method: The results are temporary, so you may have to repeat the maneuver the following spring.

🌿 Air 'Em Out

This grub-routing routine is the way to go when you're planning a new lawn, revamping an old one, or replacing turf grass with groundcovers, flower beds, or a vegetable garden. It's simple, too: Just cultivate the soil thoroughly, and you'll bring all the grubs to the surface, where birds will polish 'em off pronto. If you do your digging in spring or

Eat grass roots, causing irregular, burned-looking patches

◆

Damage can appear anytime from late spring through early fall

◆

Most obvious during dry spells

◆

Are the larvae of many kinds of beetles

◆

To control, apply beneficial nematodes or (for Japanese beetle grubs) milky spore disease

early fall, 3 to 4 inches is deep enough. Once the weather turns cool, though, the grubs head deeper; then, you'll need to till the soil from 4 to 8 inches deep.

🌿 Planned Un-Parenthood

Once you've got the grub population under control, you need to keep it from skyrocketing again. How? Grab the grown-ups *before* they have a chance to fill up the maternity wards—that's how! Start handpicking adult beetles early in the season, hang out traps, and encourage beetle-eating helpers like birds and toads. For more on useful predators, see Chapter 8. And for the full lowdown on Japanese beetles, see page 81.

THIS IS THEIR LIFE

...and yours. You gaze into a pair of big brown eyes, give a little scratch behind the ears, get a big, wet slurp in return, and presto—you've got yourself a true-blue pal. And while they are man's best friends, more often than not (especially when they're young), you get a little true-blue mischief.

ALSO ON THE MENU

Besides leaving unwelcome souvenirs on your lawn and digging holes looking for God-knows-what, some dogs love nothing better than trampling down your flowers to make cozy sleeping nests. You'll find solutions to those bedtime woes in this chapter, too (see "Holey Cow," on page 29). Or simply include rue (*Ruta graveolens*) or pot marigolds (*Calendula officinalis*) in your flower beds. Dogs hate 'em both!

They're our best friends, all right—but since when is friendship a license to ruin your yard? On a lawn, dog damage generally comes in one of two forms: yellow spots left on the grass, or holes dug in the turf. (By the way, the old wives' tale that female-dog urine is more potent than that of males isn't true. It causes more damage only because female dogs tend to urinate all at once, in one spot, while males generally spray a little here and a little there.)

🍂 Out, Out, Dang Spot!

When nature calls, dogs answer (after all, a smooth, green lawn is *our* invention, not theirs). The spots that occur are simply the result of too much of a good thing—namely, nitrogen and salts. The same brown, burned-looking patches would occur if you spilled fertilizer on the grass. If the deed has just been done, just turn on the hose, and flush the site thoroughly. After more than a day or so, though, follow this routine:

Step 1. Lightly sprinkle gypsum over and around each spot to dissolve accumulated salts.

Step 2. Overspray the lawn with 1 cup of baby shampoo or dishwashing liquid mixed with a gallon of water in a hand-held sprayer.

Step 3. One week later, overspray the turf with my Lawn Saver Tonic (see page 28).

🌿 Whoops! Too Late!

When the burned spots have been in place for a while, you have only one choice: Dig out the damaged turf, and flush the soil with plenty of water to dilute the salts and nitrogen. Then reseed or re-sod the renovated areas.

🌿 Damage Control

It's all but impossible to avoid dog spots altogether, but there are ways to minimize the damage. Among my favorites are:

▶ Go easy on the lawn food, and try to avoid chemical fertilizers entirely. They're loaded with highly concentrated nitrogen—a little more, courtesy of Rover doing his duty, is enough to push grass right over the edge.

▶ Reseed or overseed your lawn with fescue or perennial ryegrass. Both are resistant to

damage caused by dog urine. If neither of those will work where you live, at least steer clear of Bermuda grass and Kentucky bluegrass; they're the most sensitive turf types of all.

▶ Teach your dog to go where his offerings won't hurt anything. (My pup has his own private square of gravel behind the tool shed.)

▶ While he's learning to use his privy, and to keep neighborhood roamers at bay, spray my Doggone Dogs Tonic (page 29) on areas where Spot isn't welcome. This same technique

---

Lawn Saver Tonic

When bad things happen to good grass, reach for this liquid safety net.

THUG BUSTER

½ can of beer
½ can of regular cola (not diet)
½ cup of ammonia

Combine these ingredients in your 20 gallon hose-end sprayer. Then saturate your grass to the point of run-off.

---

will also keep your dog and any roving neighborhood canines from digging up your turf.

Altered States

A couple of nutritious food supplements seem to alter the chemistry of dog urine, making it less damaging to turf grass. What's more, they help repel fleas. What are these miracle workers? Brewer's yeast and garlic. You can add Yeast & Garlic Bits™ to Rover's daily treat menu, or simply sprinkle a little brewer's yeast on his food at dinnertime. **Note:** First check with your veterinarian for the right yeast or garlic dosage.

Holey Cow!

What do you do when Rover insists on digging holes in a newly seeded area, or maybe smack in the middle of your flower beds? Draw the line—fishing line, that is! Here's a simple technique that will help to keep the pooch out and the soil (and plants) in place:

Step 1: Push stakes into the soil, all around the edges of the place you want to protect. Then put more stakes in a row down the middle of the area. They should stand about 7 inches above the ground.

Step 2: Tie nylon fishing line to one of the stakes, about an inch from the top. Then, start weaving the line from stake to stake, across the mini-plot and back again. When you're finished, you'll have a big zigzag

THUG BUSTER

Doggone Dogs Tonic

Dogs may be man's best friends, but they sure as shootin' aren't the best pals your lawn ever had! Keep your pooch and other neighborhood dogs where they belong by dousing off-limits areas with this spicy concoction.

2 cloves of garlic, finely chopped
2 small onions, finely chopped
1 jalapeño pepper, finely chopped
1 tbsp. of hot sauce
1 tbsp. of chili powder
1 tbsp. of dishwashing liquid
1 qt. of warm water

Combine the garlic, onions, and pepper with the rest of the ingredients. Let the mixture sit and "marinate" for 24 hours, then strain it through cheesecloth or old pantyhose, and sprinkle it on any canine-problem areas. Repeat after each rain, and before long, the spot makers and hole diggers will get their kicks elsewhere.

pattern. Be sure to keep the openings big enough so you can step into them easily to plant or weed.

Once the pup gets tangled up in the net a time or two, he won't prance through that place again! One word of caution: If you use this trick in a flower bed, remember that once the plants come up, you won't be able to see the line—so when

Home on the Range

Dogs

you're working in the bed, be careful you don't get trapped yourself!

🌿 On the Rise

For reasons of their own, most dogs avoid raised beds. But planting your flowers on the up and up will do more than deter cavorting canines. It will also improve soil drainage, and plenty of pesky insect pests hate well-drained soil.

Coulda Fooled ME!

Before you blame a roving canine for the unsightly patches in your lawn, take a closer look. Plenty of things besides dog urine can cause very similar damage. Your problem could be thatch (see page 21 for my thatch-blasting techniques). Or it could be one of the culprits listed here. In each case, the only cure may be to dig up the dead grass, then reseed or re-sod. But knowing the cause will help you avoid future problems.

■ **Underground competition.** Tree roots and buried debris, such as rocks, chunks of wood, or even lost toys, prevent good root penetration. When roots can't reach into the soil for water, they—and

soon the grass blades—dry out. If the problem is tree roots, give up on grass and plant a less-thirsty groundcover. Otherwise, just get the obstacles out of the way, and you'll be good to go.

■ **Human error.** Gasoline, oil, and fertilizer spills cause dead, brown spots. So do mower blades that are dull or set too low, or a mower that's left running in one place. The solution: Be careful!

■ **Too much of a good thing.** Overfeeding gives turf grass more nitrogen than it can handle; overwatering leaches away essential nutrients. The way out of this one: Give your lawn the food and water it needs and no more!

THIS IS THEIR LIFE

Moles mate, give birth, and raise their babies deep inside their tunnels. (In fact, they almost never come to the surface if they can help it.) The females bear one litter of three to five babies per year, usually between March and June. The young'uns grow up fast, and live for two to three years.

ALSO ON THE MENU

Besides making a mess of lawns, moles tear up flower and vegetable gardens, and they can even damage the roots of very young trees and shrubs. Often, this territorial expansion comes just after you've freed your lawn of grubs, and the moles are searching frantically for food. But don't panic—just use the tips here, and the moles will soon move on.

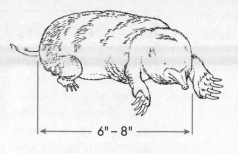

6" – 8"

If moles did their eating above ground instead of below, we'd probably award them the Nobel Prize for pest control! Every day, they eat close to their own body weight in grubs, beetles, and other bugs, and even a snail now and then. For us lawn-and-garden tenders, the problem is that as moles tunnel through the soil in search of dinner, they travel right through plants' roots, leaving them vulnerable to drought, diseases, and other pests. What's more, other critters, like mice and voles, who *do* eat plants, take full advantage of the free-and-clear subway system. Moles operate throughout the United States and southern Canada, and they have very

good taste in accommodations: They prefer loose, moist loam, a.k.a. ideal lawn and garden soil!

🌿 Scrub the Grubs

Nobody likes to hear this, but the only sure way to get moles out of your yard and *keep* 'em out is to banish their food supply—namely grubs. Over the long haul, milky spore disease (*Bacillus popilliae*) is your best bet, but you won't see the full results for several years. In the meantime, choose from the following bag of anti-mole tricks, and see page 23 for my grub-control tactics.

A Word to the Newly Grubless

If you've just gotten rid of the grubs in your yard, beware: Your mole problems could get worse for a while before they get better. That's because the little guys, suddenly finding themselves without their favorite food, will charge around your lawn frantically in search of dinner before they head for grubbier pastures.

see page 23

DID YOU KNOW?

Moles are not rodents, as a lot of folks think. They belong to the biological order Insectivora, which in scientific lingo means insect eaters. Rodents, including gophers, mice, rats, and voles, belong to the order Rodentia. (If *that* bit of trivia doesn't take you back to high school biology class, I don't know what will!)

Are You Sure?

Before you launch your attack on moles, make sure they're really the culprits. You *could* be entertaining a gaggle of gophers. Their tunnel systems look very similar. Here's how to read the telltale evidence:

▶ **Look at the mounds.** Moles leave simple, round piles of loose dirt at the entrances to their tunnels. Gophers make mounds that are crescent- or horseshoe-shaped.

▶ **Look at the damage.** Unlike moles, gophers do eat plants, and plenty of them. In fact, they cause a lot more trouble in flower and vegetable gardens than they do in your lawn. (See page 225 for my goodbye-gopher tactics.)

See page 225

Where, Oh, Where?

In their quest for food, moles dig a huge network of tunnels, but many of them are only used once. To find the active ones, step lightly on every tunnel you can see (you want to

THUG BUSTER

Move On, Moles Tonic

When you want to clear out a mole-tunnel system in a hurry, mix up a batch of this tonic, and let 'er rip!

1 cup of dishwashing liquid
1 cup of castor oil
2 tbsp. of alum, dissolved in hot water

Mix these ingredients in your 20 gallon hose-end sprayer, and saturate the problem areas.

disturb the underground opening, but not destroy it). Then use sticks, rocks, or brightly colored golf tees to mark the tramped-on runs. Two or three days later, go back and see which tunnels have popped back up—and saturate each one with my Move On, Moles Tonic (page 32).

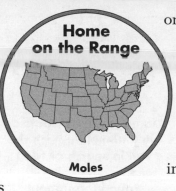

Home on the Range

Moles

or at least make the moles think you've done that. Get some ferret droppings from a zoo, pet shop, or ferret-owning friend, and sprinkle the stuff in and around the critters' holes. It'll make 'em scurry in a hurry!

Down the Hatch

When you find an open tunnel entrance, pop one of these anti-mole tools into the hole. Whichever one you choose, you might have to repeat it a few times, but eventually, the moles will give up and move on:

▶ A stick of Juicy Fruit® chewing gum and a partially crushed garlic clove

▶ Several scoops of used kitty litter

▶ A few squirts of pine-based household cleaner

▶ Half a cup or so of my Mole-Chaser Tonic (at right)

Call Out the Archenemy

Ferrets are first-class mole hunters. So set one loose—

Whoosh!

Moles are super sensitive to sounds and ground vibrations. Here's a colorful way to chase the critters: Get yourself a bunch of plastic toy pinwheels, and shove them into the ground at regular intervals. The whooshing sound will send the moles packing.

THUG BUSTER

Mole-Chaser Tonic

Moles will pack up and head outta town (or at least out of your yard) when they get a taste of this potent potion.

1½ tbsp. of hot sauce
1 tbsp. of dishwashing liquid
1 tsp. of chili powder
1 qt. of water

Mix all of these ingredients in a bucket, and pour a little of the mix into each mole hole. The little guys will get a taste they won't soon forget!

🍃 Bring 'Em Back Alive

Moles are solitary critters, and they try to keep a lot of space between themselves and their relatives. In fact, in mole terms, a major invasion consists of three or four little diggers per acre. Such low population density makes live trapping a dandy good-riddance method. Here's all there is to it:

Step 1. Find an active mole runway (see page 32), and dig a hole in it that's as deep as the height of a 3-pound coffee can standing up.

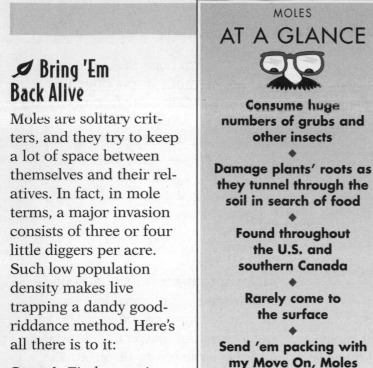

MOLES
AT A GLANCE

Consume huge numbers of grubs and other insects

◆

Damage plants' roots as they tunnel through the soil in search of food

◆

Found throughout the U.S. and southern Canada

◆

Rarely come to the surface

◆

Send 'em packing with my Move On, Moles Tonic (page 32)

Step 2. Set the can (without the lid) into the hole so that the open top of the can is level with the floor of the runway.

Step 3. Cover your excavation site at ground level with a board, so that no light gets in. As the moles scamper along inside the tunnel, they'll fall into the can and won't be able to climb out.

Step 4. Check your trap twice a day or so, and when you've got yourself a prisoner, cart him far, far away from your lawn and then let him go.

That's not all, folks!

These sometime-troublemakers can also get up to no good in your lawn:

APHIDS occasionally target shady, northern lawns, making the grass grow poorly and turn yellow-orange. Read all about aphids beginning on page 117.

CUTWORMS chew on grass crowns, where the blades meet the roots, leaving behind 1- or 2-inch-diameter spots of close-cropped dead turf. For the full story, see page 164.

CHAPTER 2

TREE
TRASHERS

You would think that a plant that's as big and strong as a tree could shrug off garden-variety pests without blinking an eye (er, a knot, maybe). But as we all know, even these giants have their share of multilegged troublemakers giving them grief. So, if your trees are plagued by pests, this chapter tells you how to say, loud and clear, "Go pick on somebody your own size!"

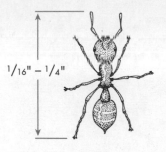

1/16" – 1/4"

Ants rarely damage trees, or any other plants. In fact, these tiny guys actually improve growing conditions for all plants. Besides breaking down organic matter into soil-building humus, they dig literally thousands of miles of little tunnels in the ground. And those openings allow free passage for water, nutrients, and earthworms. Ants also wage war on termites so they can take over their nests, and they prey on some of the peskiest pests around, including mealybugs, scale insects, cockroaches, and (for all you cotton farmers out there) boll weevils.

But, hey, nobody's perfect! Around the yard and garden, ants have two major flaws: They make first-class nuisances of themselves at picnics and barbecues, and (much worse) they "farm" sap-sucking insects like aphids, so that they can have a steady supply of the honeydew that the little monsters produce.

🍃 Hold On There!

Many species of ants sip nectar from flowers, pollinating the posies in the process and, in the case of peonies, helping the blossoms to open fully. So if you see the little guys in your garden and there's no sign of damage, just let them be. (Don't confuse regular, garden-variety ants with fire ants, though. Fire ants *do* eat plants—and plenty of them. For my best tips on battling those nasty villains, see the "Fire Ants" entry starting on page 8.)

THIS IS THEIR LIFE

About once a year, generally in summer or early fall, male and female ants (both winged at this stage) fly into the sky and mate. The males fall to earth, dead as doornails, while the females soar off to find nesting sites. Once each queen has chosen her realm, she builds her nest and lays an enormous number of eggs. These hatch into workers with only one mission in life: pampering the queen. And Her Majesty's only mission is to lay more eggs—thousands of them, each of which is pre-ordained to become either a sexless worker, a fertile male, or a fertile female, a.k.a. future queen.

ALSO ON THE MENU

Living plants are just about the only food that most ants don't normally eat. But they go hog-wild over anything sweet, whether it's the honey on your picnic table or the honeydew that sap-sucking insects leave on your trees and other plants.

🌿 Off to Work They Go

It's a frustrating sight all right: a line of ants, marching up the trunk of your tree to the aphid ranch in its branches. You might think that getting rid of the aphids would send the ants off to stickier pastures. Not so. Unless you fire those multilegged cowhands, er, bughands, they'll round up another herd in no time flat. But if you can keep the ants out of your tree for just a couple of months, good-guy bugs will take over, and your aphid woes will be history. Here's how to lock the gate to the old corral:

1. If necessary, prune your tree so that only the trunk is in contact with the ground.

2. Wrap a band of carpet tape or double-sided masking tape around the trunk. The tape won't harm the tree, but it will trap the ants as they try to scamper up it. Be sure to inspect the tape every few days, and remove any twigs, leaves, or other "bridges" that appear.

3. For added protection, sprinkle bonemeal or diatomaceous earth around the trunk. Ants won't cross the scratchy stuff.

🌿 Get 'Em on the March

What do you do about ants that are already up in the branches, or on the trunk? Simple: Spray the tree with my Lethal Weapon Tonic (below). It'll

THUG BUSTER

Lethal Weapon Tonic

If ants have turned your favorite tree into an aphid ranch, don't pull any punches. Reach for your trusty hose-end sprayer, and load it with this magic bullet.

3 tbsp. of garlic and onion juice*
3 tbsp. of skim milk
2 tbsp. of baby shampoo
1 tsp. of hot sauce
1 gal. of water

Mix all of these ingredients in a bucket, and pour the solution into a 20 gallon hose-end sprayer. Then spray your tree every 10 days until the aphids are lyin' 6 feet under on Boot Hill.

*To make garlic and onion juice, put 2 cloves of garlic, 2 medium onions, and 3 cups of water in a blender, and puree. Strain out the solids, and pour the remaining liquid into a jar. Use this mixture whenever it's called for in a Thug Buster. When you're done, bury the solids in your garden to repel aphids and other pesky pests.

wipe out the aphids and their midget minders at the same time.

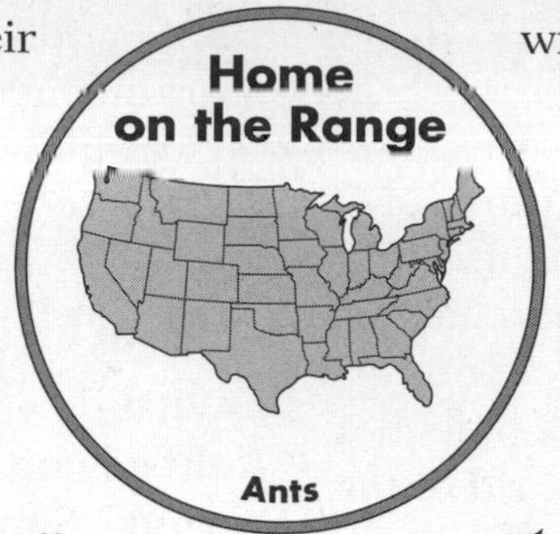

Gotcha!

To trap ants before they even get to the tree, use one of these no-fail tricks:

Home on the Range

Ants

▶ Set jars of sweet, sticky stuff like honey or sugar syrup in the troubled area. The ants will make a beeline to the dessert bar, fall in, and die happy.

▶ Put a piece of tape over the hole in the bottom of a flowerpot, and set the pot upside down on top of the anthill. When the ants come out of the hole, they'll scamper up the sides of the pot. Within a day, your trap should be so full of little scamperers that you can hardly see the sides. Then, just pick it up and dunk it into a bucket of boiling water.

The Two-Day Wonder

Trapping the workers will ease your ant troubles for a while. To get rid of a colony for good, though, you need to eliminate the driving force: the queen, who's hunkered down in her bunker doing nothing but churning out eggs by the thousands. And here's an easy way to do it: Just sprinkle instant grits on top of the anthill. The worker ants

will carry the grains into the nest, where they and Her Majesty will have a feast. Then the grains will swell up inside their little bodies. Within about 48 hours, the whole colony will be history.

Into the Drink

If you're fresh out of grits, reach for the old-time ant-control weapon: boiling water. Just scrape the top off of the mound, and quickly pour the water into the nest. And act

DID YOU KNOW?

What happens when a female mosquito lays eggs in a puddle that dries up before the youngsters hatch? Those eggs can just lie there, for years if necessary, until rain or other water starts the hatching action. So what has this sobering fact got to do with ants? Just this: The little guys gobble up millions of these stranded eggs long before they have a chance to become blood-thirsty skeeters. So before you send all of the ants packing from your yard, think again!

fast before the workers swarm all over the place! If the water reaches its target, the queen will be an instant goner, and any workers who survive will soon die of old age. Check back in a week or so; if the colony still shows signs of activity, treat 'em to another boiling-hot shower.

Anti-Ant Plants

Once you've got the ants out of your trees, keep them from coming back by planting tansy, spearmint, pennyroyal, or southernwood in the vicinity. (Ask for that last one by its scientific moniker, *Artemisia abrotanum*.) The little rascals will keep their distance from all of 'em!

Not in My House!

While most ants are happy as clams in the great outdoors, some prefer cozier quarters—like your home. Well, just

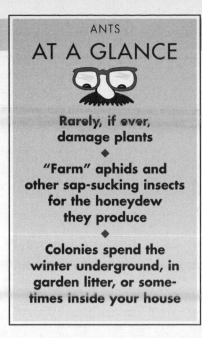

ANTS

AT A GLANCE

Rarely, if ever, damage plants

◆

"Farm" aphids and other sap-sucking insects for the honeydew they produce

◆

Colonies spend the winter underground, in garden litter, or sometimes inside your house

because they do good work in the garden doesn't mean you have to offer them hospitality in your kitchen! Just use any of these tricks to send them back where they belong (or, if all else fails, to the Great Ant Farm in the Sky):

▶ Lay sprigs of fresh mint where the little fellows are coming and going. The ants'll go back where they came from.

▶ For good measure, brew up a batch of strong mint tea and spray it on their pathways.

▶ For those persistent types who don't get the message, mix 1 teaspoon of boric acid with ⅓ cup of honey, put dabs of the mixture into bottle caps or on pieces of tape (sticky side up), and set the bait in ant-infested areas. Activity will cease in a hurry. (Be sure to keep these traps well out of reach of children and pets.)

BARK BEETLES

Believe it or not, trees that are under stress from drought, disease, or other woes give off a distinctive scent. Male bark beetles home in on that aroma and fly to the scene from miles around, like bargain hunters flocking to a going-out-of-business sale. Once the boys are on the scene, they release their own scent that invites the girls to the party. They fly in, and after the usual festivities, insect-style, they lay eggs within the bark or on the ends of cut branches. When the larvae hatch, they tunnel through the cadmium (the tissue just under the bark) to pupate. Then, all grown up, they exit through holes in the bark and fly away to start the cycle all over again in other trees.

Bark beetles attack many kinds of trees and shrubs, both deciduous and evergreen, but they don't bother any nonwoody plants.

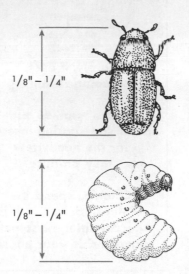

1/8" – 1/4"

1/8" – 1/4"

There are several different species of bark beetles, but they all look pretty much the same: They're dark, shiny, hard-shelled, and about the size of a grain of rice. The larvae are white, legless grubs about 1/4 inch long. They tunnel through and just under a tree's bark, cutting off the flow of nutrients. One of the most notorious of the bunch is the European elm bark beetle, which spreads the fungus that causes Dutch elm disease. If your trees have little holes in the bark with what looks like sawdust oozing out, or little projections that resemble toothpicks, think bark beetles. In more advanced cases, you may see drooping, yellowed branches or even girdled, dead trunks and limbs.

Bark beetles are attracted to trees that are diseased, dead, or under stress; but once they're in the neighborhood, they sometimes attack healthy trees, too.

First Response

At the first sign of trouble, prune off infested branches and burn them if that's allowed in your neighborhood; otherwise, cut up that wood and send it off with the trash. Don't get it anywhere near the compost pile, or before you know it, you'll have bark beetles all over the place. Then, give the tree a big dose of water and fertilizer. That will help it produce pitch or sap, which will ooze out through the beetles' holes, taking grubs with it. As for any adult beetles you find scampering around on the bark, give 'em what for with my Peppermint Soap Spray (below).

Home on the Range

Bark Beetles

🌿 Drink to Their Health

Drought stricken trees are prime targets for bark beetles. To help keep your personal forest off their radar screen, make sure the big guys get enough water. Most trees can handle short rainless periods just fine, but during prolonged dry spells, they sometimes need an extra drink or two. When you deliver that H_2O, soak the ground slowly and thoroughly from the trunk out to the far reaches of the branches (a.k.a. the drip line). Then mulch with compost or well-rotted manure to help conserve moisture.

🌿 Pickled Beetles

Once bark beetles have tunneled into a tree, no Thug Buster or even commercial insecticide can reach them. Fortunately, though, it's a snap to get 'em on the fly. The weapon: white vinegar. The vile villains throng to it in the same way they zero in on sick trees. (Maybe the odor is the same as a tree's distress signal.) Just set jars of the tangy stuff among your troubled trees, and the beetles will dive right in—and they won't get out alive. **Note:** This trick seems to work only with white distilled vinegar, not cider or any of the fancy flavored kinds.

Peppermint Soap Spray

This brew is a nightmare-come-true for hard-bodied insects like beetles. The secret weapon: peppermint. It cuts right through a bug's waxy shell, so the soap can get in and work its fatal magic.

2 tbsp. of dishwashing liquid
2 tsp. of peppermint oil
1 gal. of warm water

Mix the dishwashing liquid and water together, then stir in the peppermint oil. Pour the solution into a hand-held sprayer, take aim, and fire! Those beetles'll never know what hit 'em!

THUG BUSTER

Loosen Up

If bark beetles are targeting your trees, the reason could lie in the soil. When it's compacted, water, nutrients, and oxygen can't reach the tree's roots—leaving the poor plant as stressed out as you'd be if you couldn't get water, food, or air! To solve the problem, work organic matter, such as compost, into the soil as far down as you can without disturbing the roots. Then, reroute both foot and vehicle traffic (the prime cause of soil compaction). Install a foot path, and if that doesn't send a strong enough message, erect a barrier around the root zone.

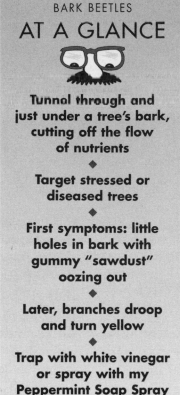

BARK BEETLES
AT A GLANCE

Tunnel through and just under a tree's bark, cutting off the flow of nutrients

◆

Target stressed or diseased trees

◆

First symptoms: little holes in bark with gummy "sawdust" oozing out

◆

Later, branches droop and turn yellow

◆

Trap with white vinegar or spray with my Peppermint Soap Spray (page 41)

Go Native

One of the simplest ways to prevent stress (and therefore, major problems with bark beetles and other bad-guy bugs) is to choose trees that grow naturally in your area. The same applies to any other kind of plant. If you're not sure what species are native to your neck of the woods, get in touch with your local Nature Conservancy office, native plant society, or Cooperative Extension Service.

CODLING MOTHS

THIS IS THEIR LIFE

Every spring at apple-blossom time, codling moths emerge from their cocoons and lay eggs on the leaves and later, on newly formed fruit. Depending on the temperature, the eggs hatch in one to three weeks, and the larvae eat their way into the core of the fruit, usually starting from the blossom end. They munch away for three to five weeks, then slither down the tree to pupate under loose bark or nearby plant litter. And then another generation of moths takes to the sky. In most parts of the country, this cycle repeats itself two or three times per year.

ALSO ON THE MENU

Unlike many fruit pests, codling moths don't bother bush or vine fruits. They tend to dine only on apple, crabapple, pear, quince, plum, and walnut trees.

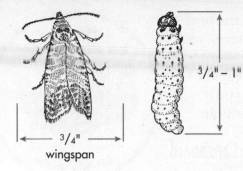

$3/4$" – 1"

$3/4$"
wingspan

These are the culprits responsible for the old joke that goes, "What's worse than biting into an apple and finding a worm? Finding half a worm!" Although codling moths are most famous for ruining apple harvests from coast to coast, they also target crabapple, pear, quince, plum, and walnut trees. You don't have to bite into the fruit to learn whether codling moths have paid a visit. Just look for a hole, usually at the base of the fruit, with blackish fecal matter inside.

Codling moths have a wingspan of about $3/4$ inch, and from a distance, they appear grayish brown. Up close, though, you can see that the wings have fine, coppery brown, wavy patterns, with chocolate brown tips on the forewings. The larvae are $3/4$- to 1-inch-long caterpillars, with a pink or whitish body and a dark brown head.

Start Early

At the first hint of warmth in the air, scrape off any rough bark from the lower 3 feet of the trunk. Underneath, you'll find cocoons filled with future codling moths. Pull off the cocoons, and drop them in a bucket of soapy water.

When the Fruit Falls

When the first infected fruit drops, pick up every single piece and destroy it. That way, you'll make a sizable dent in the next generation. Whatever you do, don't get that wormy fruit anywhere near the compost pile, or you'll soon have BIG trouble!

Home on the Range

Codling Moths

Catch 'Em in Cardboard

Control the next generation of codling moths by wrapping a band of corrugated cardboard around the tree trunk in early summer. Place the band about 3 feet off the ground. As the larvae crawl down the trunk to spin their cocoons, they'll be trapped in the corrugated board's nooks and crannys. Then, just peel it off and drop it into a bucket of soapy water.

Hands Off!

If you'd rather not get up close and personal with a bunch of squirming caterpillars, after you've trapped them on the cardboard, spray them with my Garden Cure-All Tonic (at right). Either way, when the creepy things are good and dead, toss 'em on the compost pile, cardboard and all.

Sweets for the Not-So-Sweet

Codling moths have a sweet tooth that rivals a 10-year-old's. So invite 'em over for dessert in the form of my "drink of death" traps. You want to make these in the spring, just as the blossoms on your trees are starting to open. All you need are some 1-gallon plastic milk jugs, and a solution that's made of 1 part

Garden Cure-All Tonic

When you need bad-guy bug relief pronto, mix up a batch of this fast-acting remedy.

4 cloves of garlic
1 small onion
1 small jalapeño pepper
1 tsp. of Murphy's Oil Soap®
1 tsp. of vegetable oil
Warm water

Pulverize the garlic, onion, and pepper in a blender, and let them steep in a quart of warm water for 2 hours. Strain the mixture through cheesecloth or pantyhose, and dilute the liquid with about 3 quarts of warm water. Add the Murphy's Oil Soap and vegetable oil, and pour the solution into a hand-held sprayer. Then take aim, and polish off the bugs that are buggin' you!

THUG BUSTER

molasses to 1 part vinegar (any kind will do). Pour 1 to 2 inches of solution into each jug, tie a cord around the handle, and hang the trap from a branch. The moths will belly up for a drink and die happy. Just one word of caution: Bees like sweet stuff, too, so if some of these good guys are on the scene, cover the opening with ⅛- to ¼-inch mesh screen.

✐ Rev Up Their Hormones

If you lack the time or the inclination to make your own fatal lures, buy some pheromone traps at the garden center. Just be sure you get the ones that are made to attract codling

moths. You don't want to attract pests that you don't have already!

✐ Hey, Woody!

A worm might be the last thing *you* want to find in an apple, but to a woodpecker, that little white menace is one tasty tidbit. If these helpful diners aren't hanging around your yard now, just hang some suet in your trees. Woody and his pals will flock to the free meal, and hang around to polish off the larvae for dessert. (For more on hiring birds for pest-control work, see Chapter 8.)

FRUIT FLIES

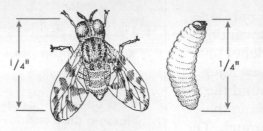

Usually in mid-to late June, adult flies lay eggs under the skin or around the stems of developing fruits and nuts (rather than on leaves, twigs, or fruit buds, as codling moths do). The larvae hatch in about a week, then burrow into the fruit, grow up inside, and eat their way out. They drop to the ground, pupate in the soil through the winter, and emerge as full-fledged flies the following spring. At least, that's the pattern up North, with only one generation of youngsters born each year. Down South, fruit flies often reproduce year-round.

In addition to tree-grown fruits, fruit flies also target blueberries and currants. In each case, your best control options are the same as they are for keeping the foul felons out of your fruit trees.

You may think of these villains as apple maggot flies because it's the younger generation that causes so much trouble in apple and crabapple trees. Closely related species go gunning for cherries, pears, plums, peaches, citrus, and walnuts. In most cases, fruits drop early and they're decayed, wormy, malformed, and chock-full of holes. Walnuts are a slightly different story. There, the critters go by the name of walnut husk flies, and their major villainy consists of stained shells; the nutmeats are generally left untouched.

Home on the Range

Fruit Flies

Regardless of type, adult fruit flies are about ¼ inch long, dark in color, with white or yellow stripes or spots. (Don't confuse these pests with the smaller vinegar flies that hover around rotting fruit.) The babies are the little white maggots that we all know and, um, love so well.

🍃 We'll Have a Ball!

Regardless of what kinds of fruit flies are after your trees, the most effective way to say "Good riddance!" is with sticky-ball traps. Walnut husk flies flock to green balls; all the others go gaga for red, even if the fruit they favor is some other color. (Go figure.) Garden centers and catalogs sell fine traps, but it's easy to make your own. Better yet, let the kids or grandkids do it—it's a great project for a rainy spring day. Here's all there is to it: Before the blossoms on your trees turn to fruit, go to the grocery store and buy some red apples with the stems still attached (or green ones if you're dealing with nut cases). Spray the apples with Tanglefoot® or another commercial adhesive, or coat them with petroleum jelly, and hang them in your trees. You'll need six to eight traps for a full-sized tree; for a dwarf version (less than 9 feet high), two traps should do the trick.

Before you know it, those orbs will be covered with flies that thought they'd found the perfect maternity ward. As the fruits fill up, cut them down

DID YOU KNOW?

Fruit flies sure are little, but they don't come close to winning the World's Tiniest Fly award. That honor goes to fairyflies, which are just one-fifth of a millimeter long. They actually lay their eggs inside the eggs of other insects, including a lot of the bad-bug brigade. (You can read about more good-guy bugs in Chapter 8.)

and replace them with new ones. By the time the tree-borne fruits appear, your fruit fly—and maggot—woes will be history, and you can take down your traps for good.

Get 'Em While They're Eating

Once the fruit falls from the tree, it doesn't take the maggots long to burrow into the soil and start pupating. So act fast! Pick up and destroy that spoiled stuff as soon as you spot it, from summer through fall. If you can't patrol your yard daily, at least make an inspection tour every other day.

Whoops—Missed a Few!

As a fallback measure, use an organic mulch around your fruit trees, or plant a dense groundcover. Either ploy will invite ground beetles and rove beetles to set up housekeeping, and they eat fruit fly maggots as well as the pupae.

GYPSY MOTHS

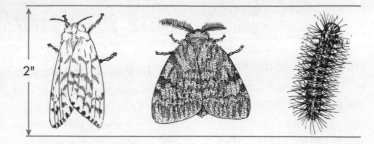

2"

Adults mate in late July or August, leaving the female so full of eggs that she can't fly. So she strolls up the tree trunk to lay the eggs in a single mass covered with hairs from her abdomen. The egg case remains stuck to the trunk through the winter; when the larvae hatch in the spring, they slither farther up into the branches and start munching. They don't always stay on their birth tree, though: The caterpillars often swing through the air on strands of silk to land on new greenery. In midsummer, they crawl back down, pupate in the bark, and emerge to launch a whole new generation.

If gypsy moths are dining on your trees, keep a close watch on your shrubs, too, because the foul felons sometimes target them as well. Your control options are the same as they are for trees.

Millions of acres of forest and countless backyard trees have fallen victim to these villains since they first sailed in from France in the late 1860s. Their port of entry was Boston, but as befits a critter with the name of gypsy, they've moved steadily west. And I do mean move. The females have even been known to lay their eggs on cars and trucks!

The adult females are white with dark markings and a wingspan of about 1³/₄ inches. The males are a little smaller and dark tan in color. The youngsters are dark, hairy caterpillars, about 2 inches long, with bright red and blue warts all over their bodies. They're the ones who do the dirty work—and plenty of it. They generally appear in midspring or early summer, and in large numbers, they can strip a tree bare of its leaves in no time flat. Any tree is fair game, but oaks and aspens are special favorites.

From Time to Time

If you're Johnny-on-the-spot, you can nip trouble in the bud. But you must be vigilant, because you've got only two windows of opportunity:

1. Beginning in midsummer, check your trees for mahogany-colored pupae. You'll most likely find them in cracks in the bark of the tree trunk.

2. From July onward, keep an eagle eye out for egg cases stuck to the bark. They're about 1 inch long and look like little suede pouches.

When you spot either form of these menaces-in-the-making, scrape it off the tree, pronto, and destroy it. There are numerous ways of doing that, but I've found that the old bucket of soapy water works as well as any.

Orange Aid

THUG BUSTER

You'll love the aroma of this citrusy spray—and you'll love its firepower even more. It'll deliver a death blow to any caterpillar who comes within shooting range of your spray gun. It also works like a charm on other soft-bodied insects, including whiteflies and aphids.

1 cup of chopped orange peels*
¼ cup of boiling water

Put the orange peels in a blender or food processor, and pour the boiling water over them. Liquefy, then let the mixture sit overnight at room temperature. Strain the slurry through cheesecloth, and pour the liquid into a hand-held sprayer. Fill the balance of the bottle with water, then take aim, and let 'er rip.

*Or substitute lemon, lime, or grapefruit peels.

It's a Wrap!

Even after the monsters have hatched, there's still time to head off trouble. In early spring, get a strip of burlap, about 1 foot wide and long enough to wrap around the tree trunk with a few inches of overlap. Tape the top edge of the burlap onto the tree to keep it in place, and tie a piece of twine around the strip at about the middle. Then strip off the tape, and fold the upper half of the burlap down over the twine so that it covers the lower half. As the caterpillars mosey up the trunk, they'll be caught in the fold. All you need to do is check your trap every day and dispose of the trapees. You can squash 'em, knock 'em off into a bucket of soapy water, or blitz 'em with my Orange Aid (at left)—it's your call.

Different Schedule, Different Culprit

Later in the summer, catch gypsy moth females headed for the maternity ward by wrapping a band of cardboard around the trunk, and coating it with Tanglefoot® or a spray adhesive. Just make sure to keep the trap free of twigs, leaves, or (yuck) dead bug bodies that the moths could use as bridges.

🍃 Boys' Night In

...the trap, that is. You can put a definite crimp in the gypsy moth population by hanging phero-mone traps in your trees beginning in early summer. That way, you'll catch the boy moths on their way to make whoopie with the girl moths.

🍃 Small Fry

When the larvae are small, you can polish them off with Btk (see page 98). Just get some at the garden center, and apply it according to the

Home on the Range

Gypsy Moths

instructions on the package. When the little gypsies get bigger, though, it takes a direct hit from a weapon like my Orange Aid (see page 49) to do them in.

🍃 Good Guys to the Rescue

Unlike many imported pests, gypsy moths have plenty of natural enemies here. Assassin bugs, spined soldier bugs, parasitic wasps, and tachinid flies all prey on the hairy caterpillars. So do shrews, deer mice, and some birds, including chickadees and tufted titmice. So call in the troops! (For good reading on some good guys, see Chapter 8.)

🍃 Keep in Touch

Scientists have devel-oped a new product called Gypchek that's made from a naturally occurring virus that kills gypsy moth larvae. It's not yet available commercially, but it is being used in some U.S. and state forests. It pays to follow the action, though, because eventually, you'll be able to buy the stuff. If the moth marauders are a major problem in your area, contact your local Coopera-

---

DID YOU KNOW?

The gypsy moth was actually brought to our shores on purpose. Frenchman Ettiene Trouvelot came to Massachusetts in 1852 to study native American silk-worms. In the late 1860s, M. Trouvelot visited France and returned with some gypsy moth egg cases. He installed them on trees behind his house, and when the larvae hatched, some of them escaped. The first outbreak occurred on M. Trouvelot's street in 1882, the same year he returned to live in France!

---

tive Extension Service or the USDA Forest Service's Forest Health Protection group for the latest news.

Don't Let 'Em See the U.S.A.

Gypsy moths are traveling through the country, and they're moving fast—thanks in large part to the females' wide-ranging taste in maternity wards. If you live in the East and you're headed west on a road trip, don't offer the pests a free ride. Inspect your vehicle and camping gear for egg cases. And if you're moving, before the van shows up at your door, do a thorough check on lawn furniture, outdoor play equipment, lawn mowers, hoses, and anything else that spends time outdoors.

Calling All Westerners!

Even if you've never seen a gypsy moth in your life, don't think you're home free. The way these monsters

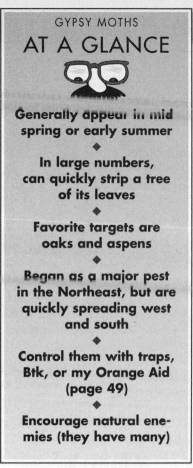

GYPSY MOTHS
AT A GLANCE

Generally appear in mid spring or early summer

◆

In large numbers, can quickly strip a tree of its leaves

◆

Favorite targets are oaks and aspens

◆

Began as a major pest in the Northeast, but are quickly spreading west and south

◆

Control them with traps, Btk, or my Orange Aid (page 49)

◆

Encourage natural enemies (they have many)

travel, they could appear on your doorstep at any minute. And once they get a toehold in a territory, there's almost no stopping them. So do yourself and your neighbors a favor: If you spot an unfamiliar moth or caterpillar, and it matches the description on page 48, catch it and put it in a jar. Then take it to the closest state or federal forest service office for a positive I.D.—so they can issue an all-points bulletin.

Friends in Low Places

Are chipmunks and voles driving you nuts with their destructive antics? Well, before you declare war on these two little mischief-makers, consider this: The little furballs just might be two of the best friends you (and your trees) could ask for, because both of them eat loads of gypsy moth caterpillars. And what's a few missing flower buds or a little chewed bark when you're gaining freedom from these fiendish French felons?

PLUM CURCULIOS

THIS IS THEIR LIFE

The grown-ups spend the winter in the soil or in fallen leaves and debris. Then right around apple blossom time, they come out of hibernation and start chewing the daylights out of leaves and buds. A week or two later, the females lay eggs inside the developing fruit. The larvae tunnel around inside for two to three weeks, then cut an exit hole in the fruit, drop to the ground, and burrow into the soil to pupate.

ALSO ON THE MENU

Like many fruit-tree pests, plum curculios also go bananas over blueberries. You can use the same arsenal of tricks you see on these pages, but there's an easier way to banish the berry-bush blues: Just plant blueberry varieties that ripen late in the season, after the crescent slicers are through laying their eggs.

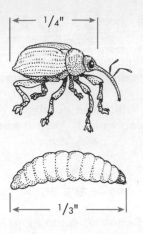

1/4"

1/3"

Don't let the name fool you. In addition to plums, these varmints target apples, apricots, cherries, peaches, and pears, and they're trouble at both the adult and larval stages. In each case, the fruit falls from the tree early and bears a distinctive calling card: a crescent-shaped slit in the skin, where the mama curculio has laid her eggs.

The adults are grayish brown weevils, about 1/4 inch long, with a long, curved snout, which is how they came by their alternate name, snout beetles. They chew holes in flower buds, blossoms, and green fruit. The kiddies, white, legless grubs about 1/3 inch long, tunnel their way through the fruit, leaving the insides brown and rotted.

🍃 Batter Up!

When they're disturbed, plum curculios curl up into a ball and drop to the ground, which gives you—or your favorite baseball slugger—a chance to take some batting practice. Here's all you need to do:

Step 1. When the first blossoms appear on your fruit tree, spread old sheets on the ground under the branches.

Step 2. Wrap a baseball bat or similar weapon in thick padding, and whack the tree limbs. When the curculios rain down, gather up the sheets and shake the varmints into a bucket of kerosene.

Step 3. Repeat the wack-and-shake process early every morning (when the curculios tend to be sluggish) for about six weeks.

🖊 Stick 'Em Up

Plum curculios are attracted to the color (or noncolor) white. So wrap white paper around the tree trunk and spray it with Tanglefoot® or coat it with petroleum jelly. The vile villains will zero right in on the paper—and stay there for good!

🖊 Then, for Good Measure...

On the theory that more is better, hang white sticky traps from your trees' branches. (Just be sure to take them down after three or four weeks, so you don't trap good bugs along with the bad.)

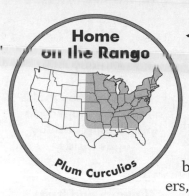

Home on the Rango

Plum Curculios

🖊 Serve 'Em Up

Curculios are a prime menu item for chickens, turkeys (both wild and domestic), and some of the prettiest songbirds around, including blue-birds, chickadees, flycatch-ers, and juncos. So invite the gang over for lunch! (For tips on issuing invitations, bird-style, see Chapter 8.)

THUG BUSTER

Beetle Juice

When beetles, weevils, or any other bugs are driving you to drink (or just increasing your consumption), round up a bunch of the culprits and whip 'em up into this potent potion.

½ cup of beetles (adults, larvae, or both, either dead or alive)
2 cups of water
1 tsp. of dishwashing liquid

Whirl the beetles and water in an old blender (one you'll *never* use again for human or pet food preparation). Strain the goop through cheesecloth, and mix in the dishwashing liquid. Pour the liquid into a 2-gallon bucket, and fill it the rest of the way with water. Drench the soil around the plant to kill hibernating adults and larvae in the ground. **Note:** To use the juice as a spray, pour ¼ cup of the strained, soapy mixture into a 1 gallon hand-held sprayer, and fill the rest of the jar with water. Spritz your plants from top to bottom, and make sure you coat both sides of the leaves.

Get 'Em While They're Down

In early spring, before the adult curculios emerge from their long winter's nap, cultivate the soil around your trees (being careful not to damage any roots). In the digging process, you'll kill many of the hibernating adults and pupating larvae. You'll also bring many to the surface, still living, where birds will quickly gobble them up. If you're not in the mood for that much digging, whip up a triple batch of my Beetle Juice (see page 53) and drench the soil around the tree. It'll kill 'em all!

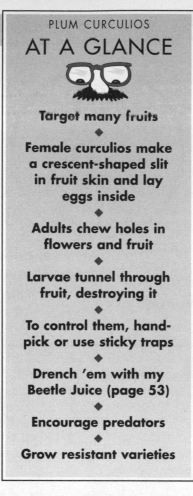

PLUM CURCULIOS
AT A GLANCE

Target many fruits

◆

Female curculios make a crescent-shaped slit in fruit skin and lay eggs inside

◆

Adults chew holes in flowers and fruit

◆

Larvae tunnel through fruit, destroying it

◆

To control them, hand-pick or use sticky traps

◆

Drench 'em with my Beetle Juice (page 53)

◆

Encourage predators

◆

Grow resistant varieties

light shines in, these fruit slicers will likely stay away in droves—they hate direct sun.

🍃 Join the Resistance

For the very best chance at giving curculios the cold shoulder, grow resistant varieties of your chosen fruit. To find the best ones for your region, check with your Cooperative Extension Service or a local nursery that specializes in fruit trees. Just bear in mind that "resistant" does not mean "home-free"; it simply means, in gardening lingo, that a plant is less likely to fall victim to a particular pest or disease.

🍃 Let There Be Light

If plum curculios insist on targeting your trees every year, the trouble could lie in your pruning (or lack thereof). If you keep the branches clipped to a nice, open pattern, so the

🍃 Hard-ly Their Style

If apples are the apple of your eye, look for the firm, crunchy types. Even when the variety isn't technically resistant, curculios tend not to bother with the fruit—probably because it's just too much trouble slicing into that hard flesh.

BAGWORMS

THIS IS THEIR LIFE

Eggs hatch around mid-spring, and the larvae immediately start feeding. They browse from branch to branch, crafting their sacks around them as they go, and only partially emerging to eat. In September, they attach the bags to branches with silk cords and then pupate. Unlike many bugs, which spend the whole winter pupating, these guys perform the task in a just a few days. The winged males emerge, track down the females, and mate inside the females' bags. The ladies lay eggs and promptly die, and the males flitter off to do the same.

ALSO ON THE MENU

Bagworms are true woody-plant generalists: As far as they're concerned, any tree or shrub in their geographic area is fair game. So you've got to watch and protect everything

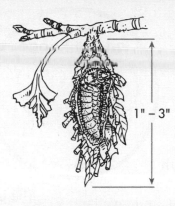

1" – 3"

The name says it all! In their stomping grounds, east of the Rocky Mountains, bagworms mosey around trees in bags that they make from leaf strips woven together with silk. Generally, the damage they do is more unsightly than harmful. Conifers look thinned out; on broad-leaved evergreens and deciduous trees, you'll notice striped or ragged foliage and, on all the victims, shaggy, carrot-shaped sacks hanging from branches. When the population soars, though, bagworms can defoliate a tree and kill it. Adult males are black, clear-winged moths with a wingspan of about 1 inch; the females are wingless. The larvae are slender, dark brown caterpillars, about $3/4$ to 1 inch long, with a white or yellow head.

🍃 Clip, Clip

The surest way to control bagworms is simply to get those sacks off of the trees and destroy them before the eggs hatch. (I just drop them into a

bucket of water laced with soap or alcohol.) To be on the safe side, do the job by late winter, because a sudden warm spell could trigger early hatching. Technique is important, too: Always cut the silk band that's holding the bag to the tree. If you pull on it, you're likely to damage or even break the branch—that silk is *strong* stuff!

🍃 The Young and Lifeless

If you've missed the start of hatching season, or if you'd rather not fuss with wormy bags, just reach for your trusty hose-end sprayer. Then fill it with either Btk (see page 98) or my Spiked Soap Spray (below), and give your stricken tree a good shower. There's just one catch: For either of these two magic bullets to work their best, you need to use them about two weeks after the larvae have hatched, while they're still young and tender. (Hatching time is generally in May and June, so plan your attack accordingly.)

Home on the Range

Bagworms

🍃 Good Guys to the Rescue— Maybe

Parasitic wasps prey on bag-worms, and pretty effectively, too. There's just one catch: Like the sprays mentioned above, these good bugs can only pol-ish off young larvae. So don't dawdle! Round up your waspish posse from a catalog or garden center, and release them while they still have time to get the job done. (If you're not sure about

timing, check with your Cooperative Extension Service.)

🍃 Into the Bag!

Once the worms are big-ger and tougher, you need some helpers who will go gunnin' for them right inside the bags. And who are these trusty sidekicks? Beneficial nematodes, that's who! You can find them at your local garden center and in plenty of cata-logs. (Not all species can handle this assignment, though, so read the label carefully to make sure you're getting the right kind.)

Spiked Soap Spray

THUG BUSTER

When you've got a tree-sized pest inva-sion on your hands, this simple soapy spray, spiked with alcohol, is just the remedy to reach for.

2 cups of dishwashing liquid
1 cup of isopropyl (rubbing) alcohol

Mix these ingredients in your 20 gallon hose-end sprayer, then saturate your bug-infested trees from top to bottom. If necessary, repeat the process once or twice at one-week intervals until the culprits are history.

🍃 Distract Their Attention

What if you're too late with your spraying campaign? Not to worry. You can get the varmints in September, when the boy moths wake up with just one thing on their minds: finding the girls. Your mission is to make sure they don't. In August, just buy some pheromone traps from a catalog or garden center, and hang them in your trees.

🍃 Shop with Care

If you're setting out to plant new trees, and bagworms are a serious problem in your area, think before you shop. In general, deciduous trees

will survive even a fairly heavy attack because (of course) they can grow a new crop of leaves the following year. Evergreens aren't so lucky. In particular, juniper, pine, arborvitae, and spruce tend to fare poorly. And Leyland cypress rarely recovers from a serious encounter with the baggy brigade.

THIS IS THEIR LIFE

Adult moths lay their eggs on tree trunks or in the soil within a few inches of the trunk. (Exact timing varies with the species, but it's always during the warm-weather months.) When the eggs hatch, the larvae tunnel into the tree to feed and over-winter until the following year. When transformation time comes, the pupae often push back through old tunnels to the bark surface, where they emerge as moths and leave the pupal skin behind. Regardless of species, there is only one generation per year.

ALSO ON THE MENU

Some of the clearwing youngsters target rhododendrons, and sometimes azaleas and mountain laurel. These go by the name of (surprise!) rhododendron borers, and you can deal with them the same way you polish off their tree-munching relatives.

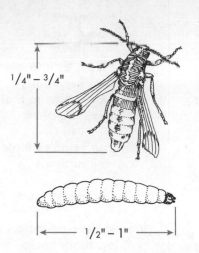

1/4" – 3/4"

1/2" – 1"

I f your tree appears weak and branches are dying back, start-ing 5 to 10 feet above the ground, suspect that you've got borers at work. You may also see holes in the bark, surrounded by rings of what looks like gummy sawdust; on poplars or birches, the bark may look roughened or bumpy. The cul-prits are the larvae of several species of clearwing moths. They eat their way through the bark and wood of many kinds of trees, leaving them less resistant to heat and drought, and prime targets for diseases. The youngsters all look the same: They're whitish caterpillars with dark heads. The grown-ups look more like wasps than moths, with translucent wings, black bodies, and markings that are either red, orange, or yellow.

🌿 Crochet, Anyone?

At the first sign of borer attack, stick a sturdy wire into each hole, and stir it around to kill the creeps. Grandma Putt used a crochet hook for this job, but a giant-sized paper clip, bent straight out, will work, too. Then spray my All-Season Clean-Up Tonic into the holes (see page 98).

🌿 The Squeamish Person's Alternative

If the thought of squashing borers makes you turn slightly green, get some parasitic nematodes and a garden syringe, and squirt the good guys into each hole, following the directions on the package.

Don't Touch That Stuff!

Whether you stick the borers or squirt 'em to death, don't scrape the gummy stuff off the tree trunk. It'll help seal the openings and prevent other pests and disease organisms from moving in.

Good News!

Healthy trees can generally defend themselves against borer attacks by drowning the villains in sap or oozing pitch to push them back out through their tunnels. You still have a job to do, though: First, prune off and destroy any affected branches. Then water and fertilize the victim to speed up the recovery process.

Dust 'Em Off

To keep ground-hatched larvae from crawling up the trunk, spread a wide band of diatomaceous earth around the tree. Dig it into the top few inches of soil, and sit back. Just remember to renew the supply after every rain.

Home on the Range

Borers

Different Strokes

Sticky bands on the tree trunk will catch the female moths as they saunter up the tree to lay their eggs (see "Stick 'Em Up" on page 53). To eliminate the male half of the equation, hang pheromone traps in your trees. Just make sure you get the kind that's designed to lure clearwing moths—you don't want to attract problems that you don't already have!

They're for the Birds

Given half a chance, birds eat borers by the bucketload. In particular, sapsuckers, flickers, and woodpeckers are genuine borer gluttons. So do

GRANDMA KNEW BEST

Grandma Putt had her own technique for keeping borers out of her fruit trees: She planted garlic in a circle all the way around the trunk. Take it from me, it works like a charm—but there is a catch: You have to plant the garlic at the same time you plant the tree.

your trees a favor and do everything you can to encourage these guys to hunker down on your turf. For the lowdown on winged warrior hospitality, see Chapter 8.

✐ To Their Health!

Like bark beetles (see page 40), borers' parents are attracted to trees that are not, shall we say, in the pink of health. So keep your personal forest in tip-top shape, and they'll be looking elsewhere for hospitality.

✐ Ashes, Ashes...

They'll all stay out. Here's a super-simple way to keep borers out of your trees and shrubs, too. Just mix wood ashes with enough water to make a paste, and spread it on the trunks up to a height of 2 feet

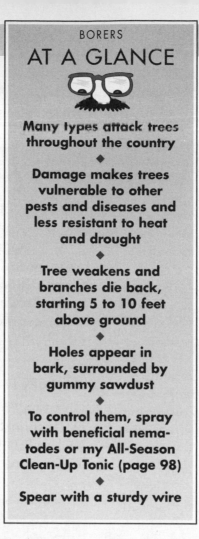

BORERS
AT A GLANCE

Many types attack trees throughout the country

◆

Damage makes trees vulnerable to other pests and diseases and less resistant to heat and drought

◆

Tree weakens and branches die back, starting 5 to 10 feet above ground

◆

Holes appear in bark, surrounded by gummy sawdust

◆

To control them, spray with beneficial nematodes or my All-Season Clean-Up Tonic (page 98)

◆

Spear with a sturdy wire

or so. Both female moths and newly hatched larvae will seek lodging someplace else.

✐ Put 'Em in Mothballs

Here's a trick from way back that works especially well on peach tree borers. In late summer, before the soil temperature drops below 60°F, bury mothballs or moth crystals in a circle about 1 inch deep and 1 to 2 inches out from the trunk. If the female hasn't laid her eggs, the odor will keep her away; if she's already done the job, the fumes will kill the larvae as they hatch. A word of warning: Don't use this technique if you have a dog or cat who might dig up the mothballs. They're just as toxic to our furry pals as they are to our crawling adversaries.

CANKERWORMS

THIS IS THEIR LIFE

Spring cankerworm moths emerge in early spring and lay round, gray-brown masses of eggs on tree branches just as leaves start appearing; the larvae hatch quickly and start munching right away. The fall moths perform the motherly role in (you guessed it!) the fall. The eggs stay on the tree through the winter, and hatch about the same time as their spring cousins. Feeding goes on for three to four weeks, and then the larvae drop to the ground and pupate in the soil, anywhere from 1 to 4 inches deep.

ALSO ON THE MENU

Spring and fall cankerworms also dine on many shrubs, and your best control options are the same as they are with trees. Several related species attack flowers but, fortunately for flower lovers, rarely do enough damage to notice.

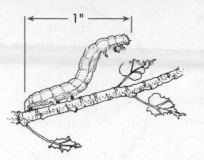

1"

Remember the old song that goes, "Inchworm, inchworm, measuring the daffodils..."? Well, the cankerworm is the critter in that song. The alternate name comes because, as the worm crawls along, its body humps up, leaving a roughly 1-inch gap between the front and back ends. Contrary to the song's lyrics, though, the inchworm's prime targets are not flowers, but trees—especially oak, linden, ash, apple, and elm. They chew both buds and foliage, sometimes stripping the leaves to mere skeletons. In addition to their destructive eating patterns, cankerworms have another annoying habit: spinning down from trees on silken cords to land on cars, people, and lawn furniture. Yuck!

Two of a Kind

There are two species of tree-munching cankerworms, spring and fall, but both kinds do their dirty work in spring and early summer. They look very similar, too. Either type can vary in color from pale greenish yellow to black or brown, sometimes with pale stripes along the body. So how do you tell the difference? Count the legs! Fall inchworms have three pairs of legs at both ends of their bodies; the spring variety only has two. Adult males are light gray moths with a wingspan of a little over an inch; females have fuzzy 1/2-inch-long bodies and no wings.

🍃 Hold Your Horses

The first principle of cankerworm management is "Don't panic!" These crawlers have more enemies than you can shake a ruler at. When you've got a crew of the good guys on the job, they nearly always keep the cankerworm population under control. The real champs at this job are both ground and soldier beetles, and some of my favorite songbirds, including bluebirds, chickadees, nuthatches, and titmice.

Home on the Range

Cankerworms

🍃 Wrap It Up

Of course, you don't need to hand all of the worm-control chores over to your flying and flittering allies. You can also protect your trees by wrapping sticky bands around the trunk, about 3 feet off the ground (see "Stick 'Em Up" on page 53). If you do the job in early spring, you'll trap female moths of both types as they saunter up the trunk.

🍃 Later On...

Before the next springtime rolls around, spray your trees with horticultural oil (available from garden centers and catalogs) or my Tree Protection Potion (below). Either oily blanket will prevent fall-laid eggs from hatching into leaf-munching caterpillars.

🍃 Whoops!

If something goes awry with your defense strategy, and the worms suddenly appear in large numbers, don't despair. Just spray the foliage with Btk or my Spiked Soap Spray (see page 56).

THUG BUSTER

Tree Protection Potion

Use this mild, but potent oil to keep insect eggs from hatching into tree-eating monsters.

1 cup of corn oil or olive oil
1 tbsp. of dishwashing liquid
1 gal. of water

Combine the ingredients together thoroughly, and pour the mixture into a hand-held sprayer. Shake well, and spray the trunk of your tree until it's well covered. (Shake the sprayer every now and then to keep the oil and water mixed.)

THIS IS THEIR LIFE

Eggs hatch in early spring, and the caterpillars munch for a month or so, sometimes moving from one leaf to another as they grow. They pupate within rolled leaves or in brownish silk cocoons stuck to the tree bark. They emerge, all grown up, in late June or July, and lay masses of eggs that overwinter on the bark.

ALSO ON THE MENU

In addition to trees, fruit-tree leaf rollers target deciduous shrubs, roses, and bramble fruits. Wherever you find those creeps, the same methods you see in this chapter will help you deal out death and destruction. Other types of leaf rollers go gunnin' for many annual flowers. You can read all about them in Chapter 4.

Don't be misled by the name. Although fruit-tree leaf rollers do attack fruit trees (they're especially partial to apples), they also go after just about any deciduous tree you care to name. The symptoms: leaves, buds, blossoms, or fruit filled with irregular holes, and some leaves rolled into tubes held together by silk webbing. The adults are golden brown, mottled moths about ¾ inch across; the young'uns are pale green caterpillars, ¾ to 1 inch long, with shiny black heads.

🌿 They're Bungee-Jumping!

When leaf rollers are disturbed, they wriggle like crazy and try to escape by dropping to the ground on strands of silk. That makes 'em easy game for the batting practice routine on page 52. (If you use this trick on shrubs and fruit bushes, though, just jostle the stems and branches gently; don't try to hit one over the left field wall!)

🌿 Don't Let 'Em Roll

To get your best shot at leaf rollers, you need to make your move before they roll up inside their leafy pupal chambers. If you're on the scene early, buy some Btk (see page 98), or whip up a batch of my Caterpillar Killer Tonic (see page 17), and let 'er rip!

🍃 The Backup Plan

If you miss attacking the pests before they're in their leafy chambers, your best tactic is to clip off the rolled-up leaves and destroy them, by either crushing or drowning in soapy water. Then, just toss 'em on the compost pile, leafy shrouds and all.

🍃 Don't Hatch on My Tree!

In the winter, scrape the egg masses off of the tree and give them the old soapy water treatment. If scraping's too much effort, smother the eggs with horticultural oil or my Tree Protection Potion (see page 62).

🍃 Don't Hatch II: The Sequel

You say you've got better things to do in the winter than freeze your fingers wielding a

Home on the Range

Fruit-Tree Leaf Rollers

scraper or hand-held sprayer? Don't worry: Trichogramma wasps can come to your aid. They think leaf-roller eggs are the tastiest meal this side of Joe's Diner. The almost-invisible (and nonstinging) wasps will mosey right on over if you grow plants with delicate flowers, such as parsley, tansy, coriander, dill, clover, or Queen Anne's lace. You can also buy trichogramma wasps in garden centers and catalogs, but don't waste your money: The species that are available commercially generally don't emerge until after the rollers' eggs have hatched.

DID YOU KNOW?

The moths that produce our tree-munching caterpillars average an inch or less across. But in the forests of Malaysia, they've got a real whopper on their hands: the Attacus Atlas moth, which has a wingspan of 8 inches!

🍃 It's Those Birds Again

Young leaf rollers are one more item on the songbirds' menu. For the full scoop on enticing these heroes to your yard and garden, see Chapter 8.

TENT CATERPILLARS

THIS IS THEIR LIFE

In midsummer, female moths crawl up tree trunks to lay masses of eggs on twigs. The eggs stay on the tree through the winter and hatch in early spring. Then the caterpillars mosey on over to the nearest branch crotch to spin their silken tent. They eat up a storm for five to eight weeks, and then pupate in white cocoons, either attached to the tree trunk or tucked into leaf litter on the ground. The grown-ups emerge in 10 days to continue the cycle.

ALSO ON THE MENU

Although tent caterpillars favor fruit trees above all other campgrounds, no woody plant is off-limits to these squatters. They'll also hunker down in just about any kind of shrub they come across. In general, they target deciduous shrubs more often than conifers, and they're especially partial to roses. Wherever you find them, you can close down the operation the same way you do in trees.

Like bagworms, tent caterpillars have housing accommodations that give them away every time. In this case, though, the dwelling is a gauzy tent where a whole crowd of the pests live together in early spring. They hunker down inside at night and during stormy weather; on balmy days, they venture out to devour huge numbers of leaves. Although these bugs will pitch their tents in many kinds of trees, they're most partial—and most damaging—to apple, peach, plum, and cherry trees.

The adults are gray-brown moths about 1½ inches across; the youngsters are brown, hairy, downright ugly caterpillars with stripes or spots of blue, red, orange, or white.

Give 'Em the Brush-Off

Thanks to their group living quarters, you can wipe out a whole colony of tent caterpillars in one fell swoop. You want to perform this maneuver in the early evening or on a cloudy day, when you know the creeps are at home. First, fasten an old, stiff brush, like a round hairbrush, to a long pole. (If you don't have an old brush handy, pound several nails into the end of a wooden stake, so the nails stick out horizontally.) Twirl the brush around inside the tent until the gauzy stuff clings to your brush. Then scrape it off into a fire or a bucket of soapy water. Any worms who escape will be fair game for birds and other predators, of whom they have many (see "The Ground Troops," on page 67).

Spray and Stick

For severe infestations, use this two-step plan:

Step 1. Spray your wormy troubles away with Btk or my Spiked Soap Spray (see page 56).

Step 2. In early summer, wrap sticky bands around your trees (see page 53) to catch any females who managed to escape the blitz and are fixing to stroll up the trunk.

Search and Destroy

During the fall and winter, inspect your trees for egg masses. They're shiny brown, sometimes with an orangey tinge, and often encircle branches and twigs. You may also find some on wooden outdoor furniture,

Home on the Range

Tent Caterpillars

DID YOU KNOW?

There's no doubt about it: Controlling tent caterpillars can be a bear of a job. And bears can do it, too. In fact, researchers at Minnesota's Department of Natural Resources found that black bears can eat as many as 25,000 tent caterpillars in a single day!

play equipment, or garden sheds. Scrape off the eggs or clip off the twigs, and destroy them.

Don't Panic!

When tent caterpillars go on a full-scale rampage—which tends to happen about every 10 years—they can strip a tree of its leaves from top to bottom in no time flat. It's a sorry sight, all right, but whatever you do, don't rush out with your chain saw! The good news is that even severely damaged trees usually survive a tent-caterpillar attack. You need to be patient, though, because full recovery can take up to two years. In the meantime, just keep the tree well fed, well watered, and as stress-free as possible.

One Fine Fly

Tachinid flies are some of the best friends a tree tender could ask for—especially if tent caterpillars are setting up camp in the neighborhood.

You might mistake a tachinid fly for a regular old housefly on steroids. But these good guys are not simply bigger versions of the old household nuisances. These friendly flyers don't eat the pests. Rather, they lay eggs on top of them, and when the maggots hatch, the caterpillars die.

So how do you entice these helpful mamas to your yard? Simply by growing some of the prettiest flowers I know of, including painted daisies (*Chrysanthemum coccineum*), pincushion flowers (*Scabiosa*),

cosmos, bachelor's buttons (*Centaurea cyanus*), bee balm (*Monarda*), purple coneflowers (*Echinacea*), blanket flowers (*Gaillardia pulchella*), and Swan River daisies (*Brachyscome iberidifolia*).

The Ground Troops

When it comes to doin' battle with tent caterpillars, your allies are not all in the sky. Ground beetles and spined soldier beetles both eat the wormy villains. You can read all about these two heroes, and some of their fellow good guys, in Chapter 8.

If you've got fruit or nut trees, you know how much trouble squirrels can be. In the blink of an eye, these clever acrobats can scurry off with your whole harvest—or empty the bird feeder that you've set up for your fine-feathered insect gobblers. They're also partial to tree sap, shoots, and buds, and the seed-bearing cones of conifer trees.

🍃 Aw, Nuts!

…or fruits or pinecones. Whatever the little thieves are swiping from your trees, these tactics will stop the action:

▶ Prune your trees so that the lowest branches are at least 6 feet above the ground. Then, about a foot below the lowest branch, circle the trunk with a 2-inch-wide piece of aluminum roof flashing. As the tree grows and the trunk increases in diameter, replace the flashing with a longer piece.

▶ Make sure the squirrels' target is 10 to 12 feet away from other trees, fences, or deck railings. That may mean pruning branches, or even removing trees or shrubs that serve as launching pads.

▶ Spray your trees with my Squirrel Beater Tonic (page 69). It works like magic on your shrubs, flowers, and vegetable plants, too.

THIS IS THEIR LIFE

There are a number of species of North American tree squirrels—the ones most of us do battle with in our yards. They build leafy nests in tree crotches or crevices and, depending on the species, the females have either one or two litters per year, of anywhere from two to five babies each. On average, they live 7 to 8 years in the wild and up to 20 years in captivity. And here's a neat piece of trivia: Once a female has mated with a particular male, she never has anything to do with him again!

ALSO ON THE MENU

Diets vary slightly from species to species, but the bottom line is that there's almost nothing a squirrel won't eat. They can even devour many poisonous plants and mushrooms, apparently without suffering so much as an upset stomach.

🍃 Down Under

Protecting your trees from squirrels is one thing. But what if their targets are the bulbs you've planted under the trees? Here's a trio of protection plans:

1. After you've planted your bulbs, lay chicken wire over the area, and cover it with a thin layer of soil. The foliage will grow up through the holes in the wire mesh, but the squirrels won't be able to dig up the bulbs, no matter how hard they try.

2. Once the plants come up, sprinkle pickling lime on them—squirrels hate the stuff!

3. Plant shade-loving annuals among your bulbs. That way, as the bulbs' foliage fades, the flowering plants will cover it up, making the squirrels less likely to find the underground tidbits.

🍃 Hiss-ss-ss

I can't think of anything that scares the daylights out of a squirrel more than a snake. If you happen to be a fancier of the slinky serpents, you might want to invite a few onto your turf. King snakes, rat snakes, gopher snakes, and boas are particularly talented at squirrel control. On the other hand, if you're anything like me, you'd rather walk barefoot across a hot barbecue grill than get within a hundred miles of a snake! In that case, fake it. Buy a few realistic replicas from a garden center or toy store, and scatter them around your yard. Just make sure you move them every day or so; otherwise, the little nut crunchers will catch on to your game and you'll be right back where you started.

Squirrel Beater Tonic

THUG BUSTER

To keep pesky squirrels from making off with your crop, spray your fruit and nut trees with this spicy potion.

2 tbsp. of cayenne pepper
2 tbsp. of hot sauce
2 tbsp. of chili powder
1 tbsp. of Murphy's Oil Soap®
1 qt. of warm water

Mix all of these ingredients together. Then pour the mixture into a hand-held sprayer, and coat your trees from top to bottom. Just make sure you rinse your fruit thoroughly before you bite into it, or you'll get a taste "treat" you won't soon forget!

WALKERS & STALKERS

🌿 Give 'Em a Whiff of Trouble

Snakes aren't the only diners who consider squirrels a blue-plate special. Just about any carnivore worth his choppers will gobble up these troublemakers. As with ravenous reptiles, you don't need to have a predator in residence; you only need to make the fur-balls *think* you've got one. The urine or feces of dogs, wolves, foxes, cats (both wild and domestic), and birds of prey will all send the little rascals scampering. So how do you find the fragrant stuff? Just ask around. Some garden centers and catalogs sell wolf and fox urine, and a wildlife refuge or rehabilitation shelter may supply you with many kinds of wild-critter waste. There's just one catch: You need to switch "brands" once in a while, or the squirrels will figure out that the big, bad wolf is nothing but a paper tiger.

🌿 This Restaurant Is Closed!

I've tried just about every kind of "squirrel-proof" bird feeder on

Home on the Range

Squirrels

the market, and take it from me: A squirrel who's really determined can break into any of 'em! That is, unless you do a little remodeling. These two tactics have worked for me:

1. Mount your feeder on a 4 × 4-inch wooden post about 5 feet off the ground. Then cover the post with strips of duct tape, run vertically. The squirrels' little feet will slip right off!

2. Hang your feeder from a rope or cable that's strung between two trees or posts. But before you attach it, cut the bottoms off some empty orange juice or soup cans, and thread them onto the rope. (Paint 'em green first if you want 'em to blend into the scenery.) Three or four cans on each side of the feeder should do the trick. Then sit back and have fun watching the squirrels doing a jig down the line!

Whichever technique you use, just make sure you put the feeder out of leaping distance from tree limbs, garage roofs, and other handy launching platforms.

> ## DID YOU KNOW?
>
> If you're going nuts keeping little tree squirrels from eating you out of house and garden, just be grateful that you don't live in Nepal or Southeast Asia. Those places are home to the Indian giant squirrel, a.k.a. ratufa, who can grow up to 3 feet long!

☙ Top o' the Mornin'!

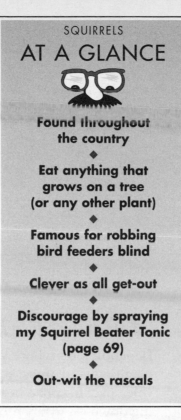

Here's another neat trick for keeping squirrels from taking food from your fine-feathered friends: Feed the birds early in the morning, when they're ready to hit the breakfast chow line, but while many squirrels are still snug in their beds. And go easy on the seed. You want to put out only as much as the birds will polish off in the morning. Then, by the time the squirrels straggle by in the afternoon, they'll find slim pickins. After a week or so of finding the cupboard bare, the furry fiends will seek hospitality elsewhere. (**Note:** The effectiveness of this ploy depends on what species of squirrels live in your area. Some types are most active late in the day; others, in the morning.)

☙ Make 'Em See Red

Unlikely as it may sound, squirrels often avoid the color red whenever they can. Scientists speculate that the

reason may be that in many places, squirrels and certain red-headed woodpeckers compete head-to-head for the same resources. And the woodpeckers' sharp beaks have taught the furry rascals not to be too pushy in claiming territory. I can't guarantee that the squirrels in your neighborhood are red-aphobic, but it can't hurt to test the theory. Try some of these simple measures to make them keep their distance:

▶ Buy a red bird feeder, or paint your current one red.

▶ Set out red lawn furniture.

▶ Hang red balloons or banners in your troubled trees.

▶ Plant beds of bright red flowers, or set containers of them on your deck. Even if they don't keep squirrels at bay, they're guaranteed to attract hummingbirds, and besides giving you hours of viewing pleasure, the hummers will polish off pecks of pesky pests. (Read more about winged warriors in Chapter 8.)

← 2³/₄" – 6" →

Voles are close cousins to mice. They look similar, but with rounder heads and shorter tails. Actually, they're very cute—but the damage they do is anything *but* cute. The pudgy little guys have a humongous appetite for any kind of plant material, and that includes the fruit, nuts, leaves, needles, or bark of any tree you can think of.

THIS IS THEIR LIFE

Unlike many rodents, voles munch by day and sleep by night. And they don't hibernate; they're active all year-round—in the bedroom as well as the dining room. It's not unusual for a single female vole to have four or five litters a year, with up to five young'uns in each litter.

ALSO ON THE MENU

Voles love munching on shrubs every bit as much as trees. They also venture into the flower garden to nibble on roots, and in the vegetable patch, they've been known to demolish whole crops of beans, peas, and potatoes. Wherever the marauding munchkins are meandering, treat them to the same spraying and trapping measures you use to protect your trees.

🍃 Don't Rush into Anything

Depending on where you live and what pests are plaguing your trees, you may not want to send voles packing: The hungry little guys love chowing down on gypsy moth caterpillars, and that's a good thing.

🍃 Check Their I.D.

Before you set out to banish the voles from your yard, make sure they're really the varmints who are damaging your plants. Your problem could be rabbits. To tell for sure, examine the evidence. When voles gnaw on tree bark, they leave a whole mess of uneven marks, in irregular patches and at varying angles. Rabbits, on the other hand, make less distinct, but more regular marks that are about $1/8 \times 3/8$ inch.

🍃 It's Scratchy-Clean

Voles generally do their tree damage in winter, when they scamper through mole runs and eat any roots they come across, or tunnel through the snow to chew on trunks. But I know a trick that will make the varmints pack up and spend the snowy season elsewhere: Just mix equal parts of diatomaceous earth and Bon Ami® cleansing powder, and sprinkle it around your trees, shrubs, and planting beds. For good measure, mix the same powdery duo with your fall lawn food. You'll make the voles vamoose and pep up the grass at the same time.

Home on the Range

Voles

Don't Bite Those Bulbs!

If you plant spring-flowering bulbs under your trees, make sure you give them extra protection—they're a vole's idea of a real gourmet treat. When you tuck the bulbs into the ground, sprinkle a teaspoon or so of Bon Ami® into each hole. The tiny gluttons will satisfy their appetites elsewhere.

Save Those Trees!

To protect your tender, young trees from those sharp, nasty teeth, use this one-two punch:

Step 1. Circle the trunks with hardware cloth or fine mesh wire from the ground up to above the typical snow line.

Step 2. Just before the snow flies, drench the area around your trees with my All-Purpose Pest Prevention Potion (below).

The Unwelcome Mat

Unless you've got a *very* determined crew of voles—or they've got no place else to go—disrupting their neighborhood should send them in search of cozier quarters. How do you do that?

All-Purpose Pest Prevention Potion

Voles, rabbits, and just about any other critter I can think of will run away when they get a whiff of this powerful potion.

1 cup of ammonia
1/2 cup of urine
1/2 cup of dishwashing liquid
1/4 cup of castor oil

Mix all of these ingredients in your 20 gallon hose-end sprayer. Then thoroughly saturate the area around each of your young trees (or anyplace else you don't want hungry varmints venturing).

THUG BUSTER

By depriving the tiny varmints of easy food and cover. For instance:

▶ Wage war on weeds.

▶ Keep your yard free of fallen leaves and other plant litter.

▶ Mow your lawn on a regular basis.

▶ Keep all mulches and groundcovers about a yard away from your tree trunks.

All in the Family

Mousetraps work just as well on voles as they do on mice. Bait them with apple slices (which voles prefer to peanut butter), and set them out among your trees. Just be sure to put the traps inside milk cartons or coffee cans, or cover them with "bridges" made of bricks or boards. Otherwise, you could catch birds, pets, or small, human fingers instead of voles. Keep checking, emptying, and refilling your traps until your bait no longer has any takers.

Drop In Anytime

If you prefer to trap your enemy alive, set out some 2- to 3-gallon buckets, and

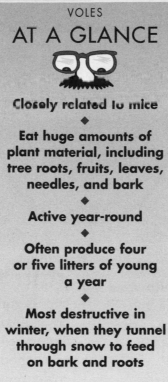

put a carrot or a slice of apple inside each one. The dexterous little guys will scamper up the side and leap in to get the goods, but they won't get out. Then all you have to do is find a place 5 or 6 miles away to release the prisoners.

Help on High

If you have a fair amount of land, one of the surest ways to keep voles under control is to ask owls and hawks to lend a hand, er, talon. Just remove some leaves from a branch of a large, tall tree to make a good landing area, or install a pole that's 15 to 20 feet tall, with perches on top. The raptors will swoop in and solve your rodent problems lickety-split. Just one word of warning: Don't try this trick if you let your cats or small dogs roam outdoors, or they could wind up in the big birds' claws!

Underground Resistance

When voles are tunneling into a confined area, such as a grove of dwarf fruit trees, a shrub border, or a flower or vegetable garden, your best defense is an underground "wall." That's not as complicated as it sounds: Just dig a trench that's 1 foot wide and 6 to 8 inches deep around the area that you want to protect. Then fill it to the top with crushed gravel or small pebbles. After one swipe with a claw, the little rascals will find other dining options.

🍃 Basket Cases

This trick won't work with trees or shrubs, but it will keep voles from demolishing a small garden. Just dig down to the appropriate planting depth for your plants, and lay a sheet of 1/2-inch wire mesh on the ground, with the edges turned down. Then set your plants into the bed and fill 'er up with soil. For spring-flowering bulbs, use a variation on the theme, and make a little wire-mesh basket for each clump of bulbs.

That's not all, folks!

Trees come under attack by many of the same pests that plague shrubs (see Chapter 3 for that roster). In addition, these culprits may get up to no good in your woods.

APHIDS suck juice from tree leaves, making them pucker, curl up, and turn yellow. For the full story, see page 117.

 BIRDS do far more good than harm around the yard and garden, but they have an unpleasant habit of snatching fruit from cherry trees. Read all about the wingers (good and mischievous) in Chapter 8.

DEER eat the buds and growing tips of small trees, and in the spring, bucks use larger trunks to scrape the velvet off their new antlers—scraping off bark in the process. Get the lowdown beginning on page 197.

 WHITE GRUBS (the larvae of June beetles) sometimes eat the roots of young fruit and nut trees. For the goods on grubs, see page 23.

CHAPTER 3

SHRUB
SPOILERS

For my money, shrubs are the best workhorses a homeowner could ask for. Besides giving your green scene visual pizzazz, they can divide space, block views, muffle noise, and attract hordes of insect-gobbling birds. For the most part, they're strong as horses, too, shrugging off problems that would topple lesser plants. Once in a while, though, shrubs come face to face with creepy critters. That's when they need your help. Armed with the timely tips in this chapter, you can be a first-class problem-solver!

BLACK VINE WEEVILS

THIS IS THEIR LIFE

The adults (all females; there are no male black vine weevils) appear in June, chow down for several weeks, then lay eggs in the soil around their host plants. About 10 days later, the grubby kids hatch, burrow into the roots, and start munching. And munching. When winter comes, they nod off to sleep, only to wake up in early spring to enjoy a brief, hearty breakfast. Then they pupate in the soil, and the process begins again. There is only one generation per year—thank goodness!

ALSO ON THE MENU

Black vine weevils live up to their middle name by targeting the queen of all vines, wisteria. They also go after many perennials, and they have a big-time taste for fruit plants, especially blackberries, blueberries, cranberries, and strawberries.

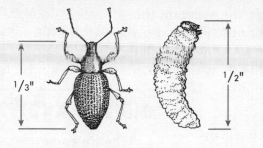

1/3"   1/2"

More than 1,000 species of weevils munch on shrubs and other plants, but almost none of the diners cause real trouble. Black vine weevils are one of the few exceptions. They target many shrubs, including rhododendrons, azaleas, hydrangeas, and yews, and they do their dastardly dirty work at both stages of their life cycle. The adults—brownish black, pear-shaped weevils about 1/3 inch long—dine at night, leaving scalloped margins along the edges of leaves. The youngsters' modus operandi is less obvious and a whole lot more dangerous. They chew the roots and the bark around the base of the plant, and the symptoms appear so gradually that you may not notice trouble until the victim is at death's door. Severely damaged plants grow slowly, then wilt and die. The culprits are C-shaped, creamy white grubs with brown heads and no legs.

🌿 Night Patrol

The secret to victory over these villains is to play to their weaknesses, and black vine weevils have two big ones: They can't fly, and they move very slowly. That leaves you with a very simple, three-step battle plan.

Step 1. As soon as you've made a positive I.D., gather your supplies. You'll need an old sheet, a bucket of water laced with about half a cup of alcohol, and a flashlight.

Step 2. Spread the sheet on the ground under the plagued plant. Then sit back and wait until nightfall, when the dirty devils come out to dine.

Step 3. Grab your flashlight, tiptoe up to your plant victim, and gently shake the branches. When the weevils tumble down onto the sheet, gather it up, and empty it into the bucket of water.

Repeat the process every few evenings until your shrub is a weevil-free zone.

 Not All Shook Up

For extra protection, or if shaking sheets just isn't your style, hit the rascals on the run—or in their case, a slow walk—with my Peppermint Soap Spray (see page 41). Again, you want to perform this maneuver at dusk or later, when you know the weevils are on the job. Cover all the leaf surfaces, because for this (or any other spray) to work, you need to score a direct hit. Spray again every three to five days for two weeks, and you will kiss your weevil woes good-bye.

The Blue Plate Special

Spiders, ground beetles, and birds of many kinds—especially chickens—will gleefully gobble grubs till the goats come home. To set the table for supper, gently cultivate the soil under your stricken shrubs, then ring the dinner bell! The same crew also dines on grown-up weevils; but in that case, you don't have to lift a finger—the sweet scent of bugs in the air will draw hungry helpers from near and far. (For more on putting useful predators to work in your garden, see Chapter 8.)

DID YOU KNOW?

When it comes to battling weevils and other bad-guy bugs, you couldn't find better allies than spiders. But the Reverend Dr. Thomas Mouffet, who lived in England in the sixteenth century, thought these multi-legged web spinners had uses that ranged far beyond pest control. In fact, the good doctor was convinced that eating live spiders could cure just about anything that ailed you, and he insisted that his young daughter, Patience, take her medicine like a soldier. No wonder the poor child became a world-famous arachnophobe! Over the years, though, the spelling of her last name was changed: You and I know Patience Mouffet as Little Miss Muffet.

🍃 Road Closures

To head off damage from next year's crew, close the road to the salad bar. In late May, before the adults emerge, smear the stems of your shrubs with petroleum jelly, Tanglefoot®, or another commercial adhesive. Check your traps every few days, scrape off any bodies, and replenish the sticky stuff if you need to.

🍃 Cleanliness Is Next to Pest-lessness

Like many other bad-guy bugs, weevils snuggle down in dead plants and leaf litter. So clip off and destroy all infested foliage the minute you spot it, and keep your planting beds free of debris, especially around the plants' crowns. You'll deprive a lot of trouble-makers of a happy home!

🍃 Say No to Weeds

When their appetite alarm goes off, weevils flock to certain kinds of weeds. Then, of course, once they're on the scene, they'll move on to other plants—like your favorite shrubs. To take your yard off of the list of fine dining establishments, say "No Way!"

Home on the Range

Black Vine Weevils

to these menu items:

▶ Bindweed (wild morning glory)

▶ Cocklebur

▶ Joe Pye weed

▶ Ragweed

▶ Thistle

🍃 Oooh...Too Late

If your stricken shrubs are dying, dig them up along with as much of the root system (and therefore, as many grubs) as possible, and destroy the whole shebang. Then leave the hole open for a few days so that birds can polish off any villains that you may have missed.

GRANDMA KNEW BEST

Grandma Putt had a neat trick for keeping black vine weevils away from her prize rhododendrons: She planted catnip among the plants. It worked like a charm, too! When those rhodies burst into bloom every spring, the whole neighborhood turned out to "ooh" and "aah" at the show.

🌿 Proceed with Caution

When you go to buy new shrubs, inspect the roots and bark very carefully. Weevil grubs sneak into countless gardens by way of potted nursery stock—and you don't want to go through that, um, adventure again.

🌿 Aw, Dry Up!

Vine weevil larvae thrive when the soil moisture is moderate to high in July and August. So keep their living quarters well drained and as dry as you can without harming your shrubs. Remove all but a thin layer of mulch, water only during prolonged dry spells, and make sure downspouts are not emptying onto your planting beds.

🌿 Give the Bugs a Bug

If the sight of your stricken shrubs is making you sick, return the favor:

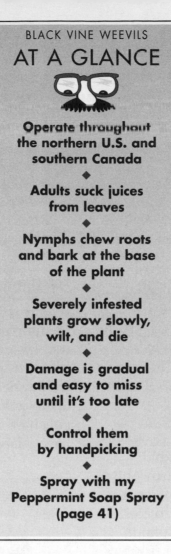

BLACK VINE WEEVILS
AT A GLANCE

Operate throughout the northern U.S. and southern Canada

◆

Adults suck juices from leaves

◆

Nymphs chew roots and bark at the base of the plant

◆

Severely infested plants grow slowly, wilt, and die

◆

Damage is gradual and easy to miss until it's too late

◆

Control them by handpicking

◆

Spray with my Peppermint Soap Spray (page 41)

Make the weevils sick. As a matter of fact, they'll be deathly sick soon after you spray them with Beauvaria bassiana, a natural fungus that kills adult vine weevils. You can find it in catalogs and in some garden centers.

🌿 Plant a Protection Crew

If black vine weevils are known troublemakers in your neighborhood, don't take chances: When you plant new shrubs in the spring, add beneficial nematodes to the soil at the same time. These nearly microscopic warriors will keep your new babies safe and sound. Remember, though, that you need to release good-guy nematodes at the right time and in the right way, or they can't do their job. So read the package directions carefully, and follow them to the letter!

JAPANESE BEETLES

Both adult Japanese beetles and the larvae live through the winter in the soil. The grubs spend about 10 months underground, wreaking havoc on turf grass (see page 23). They go dormant for about 10 days, then spend anywhere from 8 to 20 days pupating from grub to beetle. After gathering strength for a few days, the adults crawl to the surface and start terrorizing the neighborhood. After mating, the females burrow a few inches underground, lay their eggs, then rest for a couple of days before returning to work. Meanwhile, the eggs hatch in about two weeks, and another generation of greedy grubs is born.

Besides shrubs (especially roses), Japanese beetles have big-time appetites for raspberries, hollyhocks, and grapes. In truth, the gluttons will gobble up just about any plant they land on.

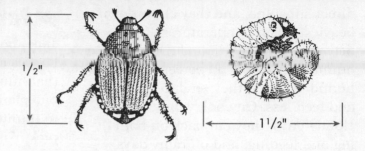

1/2"

1 1/2"

These unwelcome imports hit our shores in 1916, set up camp in open woods and meadows along the East Coast, and started right in, marching and munching. Now, Japanese beetles plague yards, gardens, parks, and golf courses everywhere east of the Mississippi River, and they're steadily moving west.

In early summer, the beetles appear from out of nowhere (or so it seems) and start eating their way through the garden. There's no chance of mistaken identity: Japanese beetles are about 1/2 inch long and 1/4 inch wide, and they're a dramatic, metallic copper color with green and white markings. (In fact, you'd have to call 'em downright pretty if it weren't for all the damage they cause.)

And, speaking of damage, once they start chowing down, there's almost no limit to their appetite. They'll turn buds and flowers to shreds and leaves to skeletons faster than you can say, "This restaurant's closed!" Fortunately, there are lots of ways to control these pesky pests—though it's not always easy.

🌿 Whether the Weather

For such heavy eaters, Japanese beetles have pretty definite ideas about good picnicking weather. They prefer to do their munching in direct sunshine, and they chow down heaviest when temperatures are between 83 and 95°F and the relative humidity is below 60 percent. In hot, humid weather, they tend to fly more and feed less. On cool, windy, or cloudy days, they cut back on both flying and feeding; and on rainy days, they just hole up and relax.

Ask Jerry

Help, Jerry! Something's chomping holes in some of my rose leaves. The holes are neat and clean, but they're all different shapes—round, oval, and even scalloped. Otherwise, the plants seem perky and healthy as can be. Who are the culprits, and how can I get rid of them?

The answer, my friend, is that your munchers are leaf-cutting bees. As to how to get rid of them—don't! These little guys can't harm your roses; they just do a little cosmetic damage to the leaves, and they do yeomen's work as pollinators of many garden plants. If the Swiss cheese leaves really bother you, just cut 'em off and toss 'em on the compost pile.

Pick a Peck

Talk about party animals! Japanese beetles are so bent on togetherness that hundreds of them will zero in on one plant and leave the bush right next to it untouched. That's why hand-pickin' is the surest way to get the critters off your shrubs—or any other plant. Timing is crucial, though: Always do your huntin' and pickin' in the morning or evening. At those times of day, when you knock 'em from their perches, they tend to drop straight down; at midday, when they're disturbed, they generally fly off. Here's my simple good-riddance method:

▶ Fill a wide bowl with water, and add a few drops of dishwashing liquid (just to break the surface tension).

▶ Hold the bowl under a beetle-infested branch and shake it gently; the pests will tumble into the soapy water and drown.

All Juiced Up

Japanese beetles enjoy chowing down on a lot of foods, but they have one very favorite drink: grape juice. So, invite the creeps over for a cocktail: Set a pan of soapy water on the ground about 25 feet from a plant you want to protect. In the center of the pan, stand an opened can of grape juice with a piece of window-screening over the top. The beetles will make a beeline for the juice and fall into the water, and that'll be all she wrote!

Munching Time Down South

As you know if you live down Dixie way, Japanese beetles love crape myrtle as much as they love roses—and maybe even more so. So here's a tip to make your handpicking chores easier: Keep your crape myrtle pruned low so that you won't have to reach as high. Also, the beetles will fall into your bowl of soapy water and not onto your head!

Powerful Plants

Geranium maculatum is a delicate-looking plant with pretty little pink flowers. To look at it, you'd never take it for a killer—but just put it where you've got Japanese beetle problems, and stand back. As if by magic, the shiny, pesky guys are drawn to this plant, and when they chow down on the leaves, they die! Other kinds of geraniums deliver a less potent punch:

Home on the Range

Japanese Beetles

Their leaf juices don't kill the munching pests, but they do knock the buggers out for 8 hours or so—thereby giving them less time to produce offspring.

You're Trapped!

Nowadays, garden centers and catalogs sell very effective Japanese beetle traps. In fact, to my way of thinking, they can be a little *too* effective. Because these gadgets are gener-

---

Hot Pepper Spray

THUG BUSTER

This hot toddy will say a loud, strong "Get lost!" to any Japanese beetle who starts to sink his chops into your shrubs (or any other plants). And recipes don't come any simpler than this one!

½ cup of dried cayenne peppers
½ cup of jalapeño peppers
1 gal. of water

Add the peppers to the water, bring it to a boil, and let it simmer for half an hour. (Make sure you keep the pan covered, or the peppery steam will make you cry a river of tears!) Let the mixture cool, then strain out the solids, pour the liquid into a spray bottle, and spritz your plagued plants from top to bottom. You'll have to repeat the process after every rain, but that's a small price to pay for a beetle-free summer!

---

ally baited with phero-mones (sex hormones), you wind up with beetles from all over town thronging to your yard for an X-rated party. If you'd rather not entertain that big a crowd (dead or alive), here's an easy alternative:

1. Make a funnel out of stiff, yellow construction paper. (Like most insects, Japanese beetles are drawn to the color yellow.)

2. Into a plastic bag, pour about ½ teaspoon of rose-, anise-, or fennel-scented essential oil (available at health food stores and craft shops).

3. Tape or staple the top of the bag to the bottom of the funnel.

4. Poke a hole through the top of the funnel, thread string or wire through the hole, and hang the trap downwind, about 25 feet away from your roses.

To the Rescue!

As tough as they are, Japanese beetles *do* have their share of enemies. Plenty

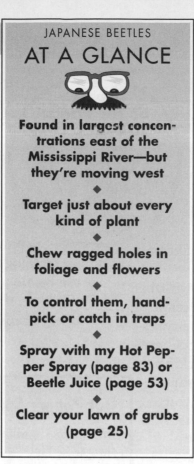

JAPANESE BEETLES
AT A GLANCE

Found in largest concentrations east of the Mississippi River—but they're moving west

◆

Target just about every kind of plant

◆

Chew ragged holes in foliage and flowers

◆

To control them, hand-pick or catch in traps

◆

Spray with my Hot Pepper Spray (page 83) or Beetle Juice (page 53)

◆

Clear your lawn of grubs (page 25)

of birds gobble them up. Two parasitic tachinid flies attack the adult beetles, and two good-guy wasps go after the larvae. See page 335 for tips on attracting good guys to your garden.

Grab the Grubs

To keep Japanese beetles from bugging your plants in the first place (or at least to greatly reduce their damage), put grub control at the top of your to-do list. For my surefire good-riddance routine, see Chapter 1.

Two for the Road

No matter how well you and your neighbors guard your territory, there are bound to be some beetles who fly in from who-knows-where. Here are two of the best ways I know of to make sure they don't hang around:

▶ Grow repellent plants among the beetles' targets. The villains flee from garlic, rue, tansy, larkspur, and white geraniums.

▶ Spray your shrubs with my Hot Pepper Spray (see page 83).

LACE BUGS

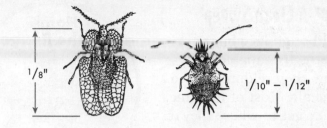

1/8"   1/10" – 1/12"

The exact life cycle varies slightly from one species to another. Generally, though, adult lace bugs lay clusters of eggs within the veins of leaves, and the nymphs hatch in late spring. They mature quickly—sucking sap the whole time—and start laying their own eggs. There are usually several generations per year, depending on the species and the local climate. Most lace bugs die when cold weather comes, leaving behind one last batch of eggs; but some species spend the winter snoozing under loose pieces of tree bark or in garden litter.

In addition to plaguing shrubs, lace bugs also attack trees, including sycamore, oak, and basswood. And, occasionally, they go after annuals, perennials, and vegetables. The same bag of tricks you use to save your shrubs will work with the other menu items, too.

Any of dozens of sap-sucking insects could go on a drinking binge on your shrubs, leaving behind foliage that is specked, splotched, or stippled with bleached-out spots. But lace bugs drop an additional calling card: hard, black spots of excrement on the undersides of leaves and sometimes flowers, too. In addition to sporting defaced plant parts, the victims lose their get-up-and-grow power and may bloom poorly. (Don't confuse lace *bugs* with lace*wings*, some of the greatest of the garden good guys. You can read all about them on page 336.)

There are several species of lace bugs, all of them host-specific, which means that each one attacks only one type of plant. All of the nogoodniks look pretty much alike: The adults are pale brown or whitish, about 1/8 inch long and boxy in shape, with lacy, transparent wings. The wingless nymphs are darker than the grown-ups, and are covered with spines.

🌿 Don't Dawdle!

Both adult lace bugs and their nasty nymphs target many shrubs, including azaleas, rhododendrons, cotoneasters, and ceanothus. The bad news is that heavy feeding may kill foliage and stems. The good news is that if you spring into action fast enough, you will save your plants.

A Clean Sweep

Although lace bugs are perfectly capable of flying, they seldom take to the air. Most of the time, they get to where they're going by just sidling sideways. That makes them perfect targets for one of my favorite good-riddance tools: your handy-dandy vacuum cleaner. Here's all you need to do: At the first sign of trouble, pluck off the stricken leaves and pack 'em off with the trash. Then, get out your wet/dry vacuum cleaner, fill the reservoir with about 2 inches of soapy water, and sweep those bugs off of the leaves and into the drink. If you don't have a wet/dry vacuum (a.k.a. Shop-Vac®), just use a regular, hand-held kind. In this case, of course, you want to run the cleaner dry and then empty the multi-legged contents into a bucket of soapy water.

Home on the Range

Lace Bugs

Broom Power

No vacuum cleaner handy? No problem! Just spread an old sheet or shower curtain on the ground under your afflicted shrub, and use a broom to sweep the lace bugs off their feet and onto the fabric. Then gather up the goods and dump the little thugs into a bucket of soapy water.

THUG BUSTER

Grandma Putt's Simple Soap Spray

This old-fashioned solution kills off lace bugs and just about any other soft-bodied insect you can name, including rose midges, mealybugs, thrips, and aphids.

½ bar of Fels Naptha® or Octagon® soap,*
    shredded
2 gal. of water

Add the soap to the water and heat, stirring, until the soap dissolves completely. Let the solution cool, then pour it into a hand-held sprayer, and let 'er rip. Test it on one plant first, though—and be sure to rinse it off of the plants after the bugs have bitten the dust, because lingering soap film can damage leaves.

*You'll find Fels Naptha and Octagon in either the bath soap or laundry section of your local supermarket.

Spray Your Troubles Away

If you prefer liquid cleaning, give the bugs a lethal shower in the form of Grandma Putt's Simple Soap Spray (page 86). And be sure to thoroughly coat the undersides of the leaves, because that's where the lacy little louses congregate.

One More Time

A year after using Grandma Putt's Simple Soap Spray (page 86), in early spring, spray the leaves again, but this time, use a light horticultural oil (available in garden centers and catalogs) or my Tree Protection Potion (see page 62). Either oily treatment will smother any eggs or emerging nymphs that have spent the winter on your shrubs.

Drink Up!

Lace bugs seem to target plants that aren't getting as much moisture as they should. So, if it's been a while since Mother Nature sent rain clouds scurrying by, haul out the garden hose and give your shrubs a good, long drink of H_2O. The best method is to

LACE BUGS
AT A GLANCE

Suck sap from leaves of shrubs, trees, and many other plants

◆

Leave black spots of excrement on the undersides of leaves and sometimes flowers

◆

Stricken plants grow weak and bloom poorly

◆

Nymphs hatch in late spring and continue feeding and breeding until cold weather hits

lay a soaker hose on the ground in loose circles, from the crown of the plant out to the drip line (the farthest reaches of the branches). Then turn on the water, and let it seep into the ground for about half an hour.

A Clean Shrub Is a Happy Shrub

Because many lace bugs spend the winter in dead leaves and other garden litter, here's a simple strategy for a bug-free spring: Do a thorough fall clean-up, and destroy any plant material that you suspect may be harboring lacy bad guys.

Location, Location, Location

Most lace bugs are die-hard sun worshipers. This is especially true of the species that target rhododendrons and azaleas. If your stricken shrubs are small enough to move, relocating them to shady sites should guarantee them safe passage for life. To protect bigger specimens, plant larger, fast-growing shrubs or trees where they'll block the midday sun, or erect walls, fences, or vine-covered trellises to do the same thing.

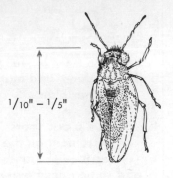

1/10" – 1/5"

Psyllids are close cousins to aphids, and they operate in a similar way, sucking the juices from plants' leaves. There are scads of species, each of which targets just one type of plant. The symptoms vary from plant to plant. For instance, on boxwood (the most common victim in the Northeast), the leaves curl up together over the growing tips, making the bush look as though it's covered with tiny cabbages. On other shrubs, you may notice leaves that are pitted, or covered with either white wax or a combination of honeydew and sooty mold (yuck!). If you look closely, you'll see that in each case, the new shoots are stunted, too. Fortunately, in most cases, the damage these suckers do is cosmetic. But that doesn't mean you have to put up with it—after all, shrubs are supposed to be *ornamental* plants!

🌿 Look Sharp

Psyllids' dirty work may be easy to spot, but you'll have to look *very* closely to see the culprits themselves. The adults could pass for the cicadas that accompanied Alice through the looking glass and shrank in the process. They're only 1/10 to 1/5 inch long and green or brownish, with antennae and clear wings that fold up into a triangular shape. When the little guys are disturbed, they leap straight up in the air—a habit that gave them their alias, jumping plant lice. The nymphs are flat, white, cottony blobs that seldom move at all.

THIS IS THEIR LIFE

The psyllid life cycle varies somewhat, depending on the species. Basically, though, it's the same old, simple story: They eat, grow up, eat some more, lay eggs, and eat still more. The cycle goes round and round as long as the weather holds out, with as many as half a dozen overlapping generations appearing each year. In warm climates, the pesky pests overwinter as adults; in colder territories, the grown-ups die after laying a final batch of eggs that will hatch in the spring.

ALSO ON THE MENU

Numerous species of psyllids attack trees, including pears, willows, and magnolias—and in warm climates, acacia, eucalyptus, eugenia, sweet bay, and yaupon. Just follow the action plan outlined here for shrubs, and your trees will soon be as good as gold.

🖊 Clip and Stick

At the first sign of trouble, clip off the affected foliage and destroy it (don't put it on the compost pile). Then, hang yellow sticky traps in your shrubs. That way, you'll learn how big the psyllid population is and therefore, what you need to do about it. (Of course, you'll also polish off some of the ornery bugs at the same time.) You can buy sticky traps from any garden center or cata-

Home on the Range

Psyllids

log, but I have a version that I like to use just for psyllids. Here's how to make your own supply—it's as easy as 1, 2, 3, 4:

1. Collect some 4-inch-diameter plastic lids from cottage cheese or yogurt containers, and poke a hole in each one. You'll need two or three traps for a large shrub; for a smaller bush, one will do just fine.

2. Spray them with bright yellow paint. (Psyllids seem to be especially

---

Coulda Fooled ME!

Even if your sticky traps are chock-full of what you think are psyllids, don't panic—at least not until you've examined the evidence under a strong magnifying glass. Those stuck-up bodies could be psocids, totally harmless insects that feed on fungi, including the sooty mold that grows on honeydew produced by bad-guy bugs. (Unlike ants, though, psocids don't farm the honeydew makers; they just gobble up the mold wherever they find it.) These two pests are almost dead ringers for each other, but you *can* tell them apart. Here's how:

■ **Check the neck.** A psocid's "neck" (the segment between the head and thorax) is narrower than a psyllid's.

■ **Scout out the mouth.** Psyllids have tubular mouthparts that are made for sucking; psocids, on the other hand, have chewing mouthparts.

■ **Recognize the response.** If you encounter the little guys while they're still alive, you can tell them apart by the response. Adult psyllids generally jump straight up when they're disturbed, while psocids fly or run away.

■ **Ask for I.D.** If you simply can't tell one tiny bug from another, catch a couple and take them to your Cooperative Extension Service or the entomology department at the closest university.

---

fond of Rust-Oleum® Yellow No. 659.)

3. When the paint has dried, thread a piece of wire or string through the hole, and coat the surface lightly with STP® motor oil additive. Why not something stickier? Because the STP is just tacky enough to snag the itty-bitty psyllids, but light enough that bees and other bigger, stronger good guys can escape if they venture a landing.

4. Hang the traps in your shrubs, and stand by for action.

Count and Respond

If your sticky traps show only a handful of psyllids, relax. The native species have plenty of natural parasites and other enemies, including lacewings, that will keep the population down to a harmless level, as long as you don't use pesticides. (For the lowdown on lacewings, see Chapter 8.) On the other hand, if there are so many buggy

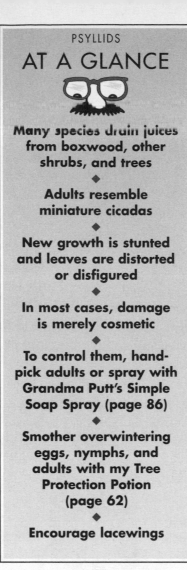

PSYLLIDS
AT A GLANCE

Many species drain juices from boxwood, other shrubs, and trees

◆

Adults resemble miniature cicadas

◆

New growth is stunted and leaves are distorted or disfigured

◆

In most cases, damage is merely cosmetic

◆

To control them, hand-pick adults or spray with Grandma Putt's Simple Soap Spray (page 86)

◆

Smother overwintering eggs, nymphs, and adults with my Tree Protection Potion (page 62)

◆

Encourage lacewings

bodies that you can hardly see the yellow paint on your yogurt tops (see "Clip and Stick," on page 89), you need to take action.

Smother Love

In late winter or early spring, give your shrubs a security blanket in the form of my Tree Protection Potion (see page 62). That way, you'll smother any hibernating adults, nymphs, or eggs, and your treasured plants should breeze through the growing season in fine fettle.

Simple Gifts

Bug-battling potions don't come much simpler, or more potent, than Grandma Putt's Simple Soap Spray (see page 86). To use this wonder weapon on psyllids, just spritz your shrubs from top to bottom, paying special attention to the undersides of leaves, where the tiny terrors tend to hang out. Repeat the process every two to three days until the vile villains are history.

RUST MITES

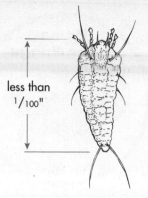

less than 1/100"

THIS IS THEIR LIFE

When it comes to reproducing, mites put rabbits to shame. In warmer climates or in protected places like greenhouses, a new generation can appear every three to seven days all year-round. In colder regions, rust mites generally start settling In for the winter by late August or early September. Eggs, nymphs, and adults spend the chilly season at the base of buds or in cracks in bark, then move into developing buds in the spring.

ALSO ON THE MENU

Besides plaguing just about any kind of shrub you care to name, rust mites target most ornamental trees, as well as apples, pears, citrus fruit, and tomatoes. In the case of the fruit, the damage appears as hard, brown, black, or gray scaly patterns on the skin. If the mite attack comes early in the season, fruit may drop or stop growing. Later on, mites cause mainly cosmetic damage.

Like their fellow mites (there are hundreds of species throughout the U.S.), rust mites are not insects; they're actually close relatives of spiders. Even compared with others of their kind, they're tiny—less than 1/100 inch long—so you'll never spot them without a strong magnifying glass. You can't miss the work they do, though. The itty-bitty monsters burrow into the undersides of leaves, stems, and flower buds to suck out the life-giving juices. At the same time, they inject a toxin that discolors the tissue. Generally, the first symptoms you see will be on the leaves: On deciduous shrubs and broad-leaved evergreens, afflicted foliage takes on a russet or bronze color; on conifers, the needles turn color and drop off. Eventually leaves, stems, and buds dry out and turn brown, and webbing may appear between various plant parts. If a massive invasion goes unchecked long enough, the plant weakens and may even die.

Too Darn Hot

Rust mite damage is usually most severe during mild weather. That's because when a heat wave strikes, rust mites lose some of their taste for socializing, and as a result, the populations decline a little.

Go Get 'Em, Tiger!

When the weather is to their liking, rust mites multiply with the speed of lightning, which means that a small problem can turn into a big one in

---

the blink of an eye. So when you spot trouble, don't put mite control on your to-do list—get after those munchkins NOW. First, though, because early mite damage can masquerade as disease or cultural problems, make sure you really do have these multi-legged marauders in your midst. Just hold a sheet of white paper under a branch and jostle the foliage. Then look at the paper. If it's full of tiny yellow or tan specks and some of them are moving, your shrub is hosting a squad of rust mites.

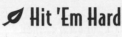

Home on the Range

Rust Mites

✔ Hit 'Em Hard

In the early stages, a good, hard blast of water will generally end your rust mite woes. So grab your garden hose, take aim, and fire! Repeat the procedure daily for three days, and if you're lucky, the mites will be history.

✔ Bigger Guns

If a series of heavy showers doesn't do the trick (see "Hit 'Em Hard," above), don't fret: You've got a whole arsenal of weapons at your disposal. Your best choices depend on the size of your shrubs (or trees) and what time of year you're setting out to do battle. For big shrubs that are already leafed out, whip up a batch of my Mite-Free Fruit Tree Formula (at left) and spray your troubles away. Don't let the name fool you: This stuff works like magic on any kind of shrub or tree, with or without fruit.

✔ One-Shot Wonder

If you'd rather spray once and be done with it, use my Go-Go Glue Trap. Just mix an 8-ounce bottle of white glue, such as Elmer's®, with 2 gallons of warm water. Pour the mixture into a hand-held sprayer, and spray all the twigs and leaves. The mites will be

---

THUG BUSTER

Mite-Free Fruit Tree Formula

Mites might be teeny, but they can do BIG damage to shrubs as well as fruit trees. When these pests attack, protect your prize plants with this easy recipe.

5 lb. of white flour
1 pt. of buttermilk
25 gal. of water

Mix the ingredients together, and keep the potion in a tightly closed garbage can. Stir before each use, and spray weekly until the mites are history.

92

caught in the glue, and when it dries, it'll flake off, taking the dead mites with it.

🍃 Security Blanket, Shrub-Style

In late winter, when your shrubs are dormant, smother the sleeping mites and their eggs with my Tree Protection Potion (see page 62) or horticultural oil from the garden center. Just one word of warning: Some commercial oils will discolor evergreen foliage. So, if you're treating either conifers or broad-leaved evergreens, read the label carefully. If it doesn't even mention color, keep shopping.

🍃 Don't Take Hitchhikers

Mites are big-time travelers. Not only do they move from one plant to another under their own steam, but they're also famous for hitching rides on transplants, birds, pets, and even your hands and tools. (If you're a bug, being nearly invisible does

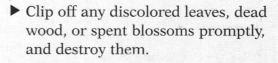

RUST MITES
AT A GLANCE

Suck juices from leaves and sometimes fruit skins

◆

Attack many shrubs and trees

◆

Afflicted foliage or fruit takes on a russet or bronzy color

◆

To control them, encourage or purchase native predatory mites

◆

Spray plants with my Mite-Free Fruit Tree Formula (page 92) during the growing season

◆

In late winter, use my Tree Protection Potion (page 62)

---

have its advantages!) So if you've had even minor mite trouble, do everything you can to keep the puny pests from spreading out. In particular, follow these anti-travel tips:

▶ When you're working with your plants, wash your hands now and then, and dip your tools in rubbing alcohol to kill any stowaways.

▶ Keep after weeds, and at the end of the growing season, remove all plant debris that could shelter mites for the winter.

▶ Clip off any discolored leaves, dead wood, or spent blossoms promptly, and destroy them.

▶ When you shop for new plants, examine them *very* carefully. If you see any signs of mites, take your business elsewhere.

▶ Spread plants out so they aren't touching each other. That won't guarantee their safety, but at least it will make them less-likely travel destinations.

THIS IS THEIR LIFE

Taxus bud mites spend the winter between the scales of buds. When spring arrives, they resume life as all mites know it: eating and reproducing. (Unlike insects, mites do not go through metamorphosis; instead, the females lay eggs that hatch into miniature versions of the adults.) In late summer, when the tiny terrors have drained the daylights out of their birth buds, they crawl to new ones and continue feeding until cold weather arrives, and they bed down again. There are many overlapping generations born each year, but the exact number varies with the climate.

ALSO ON THE MENU

Unlike most species of mites, the Taxus bud brigade targets only yews. But plenty of other mites go gunning for just about every plant under the sun. The tips in this section will help you battle many of them.

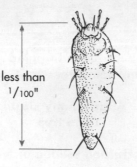

less than $^1/_{100}$"

Most mites are generalists, but these twerps specialize in one of the most popular shrubs in the country: yews (the genus *Taxus* in botanical lingo). You'll know that these pipsqueaks are plaguing your plants if the buds and growing tips are larger than normal and russet colored. You may also see tiny, pimple-like galls on the buds. If the invasion is light, the shoots and needles will grow, but they'll be distorted. In the case of heavy infestation, though, the buds generally die, and you'll see no new growth at all. Strangely enough, it's not the mites themselves that cause the physical damage—in spite of the fact that there can be as many as 1,000 of the teensy critters crammed into a single bud. Rather, the trouble comes from disease-causing organisms that invade the plant through the mites' feeding sites.

🍃 Prune, Prune, and Prune Some More!

Clip off distorted growth the minute you spot it, and destroy every last bit of it. Don't toss it on the compost pile, or before you know it, you'll have a mighty mite invasion on your hands—er, on your yews!

🍃 Get Down to Earth

Diatomaceous earth, that is. Mites can't stand the stuff. To keep the little suckers from making a return appearance on your yews, buy a sack of diatomaceous earth at the

garden center, pour some into an old talcum or baby-powder bottle, and sprinkle it onto each plant from top to bottom. If you find liquids easier to work with, mix 1 part earth to 3 parts water in a hand-held sprayer, and give your shrubs a thorough spritzing. When the water evaporates, the dust particles will linger on the foliage and the mites will stay away in droves! (For the lowdown on this sensational substance, see page 102.)

Home on the Range

Taxus Bud Mites

Faster!

In the unlikely event that the garden center is fresh out of diatomaceous earth, or if you just don't have time for an extra shopping trip, don't fret. Any of the following Thug Busters will send the minute marauders to kingdom come—and you're sure to find the ingredients you'll need in your pantry or at your local supermarket (where you have to go anyway):

▶ Mite-Free Fruit Tree Formula (see page 92).

▶ Rhubarb Pest-Repellent Tonic (see page 361).

▶ Mighty Fine Miticide (at right).

Preventive Medicine

If your yews tend to attract mites like carrots attract bunny rabbits, keep them safe and sound with this regimen. At the beginning of the growing season, mix up a batch of Grandma Putt's Simple Soap Spray (see page 86) and stir in a tablespoon of seaweed extract (available in any garden center). Three times, at two-week intervals, spray the potion on the undersides of all new growth. After that, for plants that seem especially vulnerable to mite attacks, spray once a month for the rest of the growing season.

Mighty Fine Miticide

This excellent elixir will eliminate mites and give your yews—or any other mite-plagued plants— a dose of some valuable nitrogen at the same time.

1 tbsp. of ammonia
1 tsp. of dishwashing liquid
2¹/₂ gal. of water

Mix these ingredients in a bucket, and pour the solution into a hand-held sprayer. Spray your afflicted plants every five days for three weeks. Then sit back and admire your pest-free greenery!

THUG BUSTER

Don't Spread the News

Like any other mites, the Taxus bud types spread out *fast*. If you've got a number of yews and only one or two are under attack, don't take chances: Dig up the victims and move them as far away as possible from their healthy cohorts. Or, if the non-targeted shrubs are smaller, move those.

Room to Roam

When you move your yews, or anytime that you plant new ones, be sure to site

TAXUS BUD MITES
AT A GLANCE

All-but-invisible orange or whitish mites target only yews

◆

They crawl between the scales of buds to suck the juices from tissue

◆

Resulting wounds usher in disease-causing organisms that distort new growth or halt it altogether

◆

Many overlapping generations appear each year

◆

To control them, clip off all affected foliage

◆

Encourage predators

◆

Dust plants with diatomaceous earth or spray with my Mighty Fine Miticide (page 95)

them so that their foliage doesn't touch. That way, mites will have a harder time leaping from one plant to another.

Your True-Blue Pals

As always, your best allies in the Taxus bud mite wars are the varmints' natural enemies. And they have many predators, including the crowd that gobbles up rust mites. These beneficials will flock to your aid if you don't kill them off by using pesticides in the rest of your garden. (You can read about a lot of good guys, including some world-class mite destroyers, in Chapter 8.)

FALL WEBWORMS

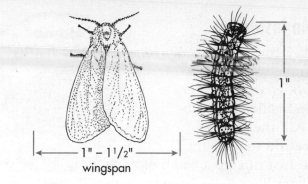

1" – 1¹/₂"
wingspan

1"

Adult moths appear in late spring or early summer and lay large masses of round eggs on the undersides of leaves. The larvae hatch in about 10 days and set about building tents to hide in as they eat. As the feeding range increases, so does the size of the tent, so that by the end of the summer, an infested shrub can be a real mess! As cold weather approaches, the caterpillars spin brown cocoons that you'll find attached to stems or tucked among leaf litter on the ground.

In addition to shrubs, fall webworms dine on trees, both fruit-bearing and ornamental. (In fact, the only trees they won't touch are conifers.) They do have their favorites, though, including apple, ash, oak, elm, maple, and willow. They also target wisteria and, now and again, some large perennials. Peonies are extra-special treats.

The term "fall" webworm is a slight misnomer. Generally, these pesky pests strike hardest in late summer. You'll find their gauzy nests on the outer ends of your shrubs' branches. (They look much like the nests of tent caterpillars, but those creepy guys build their domiciles in branch crotches, not at the tips.) Inside the webs, you'll see pale yellow or green caterpillars, about 1 inch long, busily turning leaves to skeletons. Fall webworms are not fussy eaters; they'll gladly gobble up the leaves of just about any shrub in your yard. (Roses are special favorites, though.) In most cases, the damage is mainly aesthetic, but a big gang of the villains can completely strip and kill even the largest of shrubs.

The parents of fall webworms are white moths, with a wingspan that measures 1 to 1¹/₂ inches, sometimes sporting black dots.

Cut 'Em Off at the Pass

For my money, the best way to halt a minor webworm attack is the classic technique of handpicking. Just cut out the nests, twiggy supports and all, and drop them into a bucket of soapy water. Then, give your shrubs a dose of my All-Season Clean-Up Tonic (see page 98).

An Inside Job

You say you'd prefer not to handle webs with a gang of wriggling caterpillars inside? No problem: Kill the creeps before you remove the nests. Just mix up a batch of my Caterpillar Killer Tonic (see page 17), and spray it into the gauzy tent. If you don't have the main ingredient—wormwood leaves—on hand, use my Orange Aid instead (see page 49). It'll deal the same death blow to the wily webworms.

Home on the Range

Fall Webworms

Don't Let 'Em Wake Up

During the fall, winter, and early spring, stroll around your yard with a bucket of soapy water in hand. Examine your shrubs carefully, and scout around on the ground beneath them. Then when you spot a cocoon, scrape it off the stem or scoop it up and drop it in the bucket.

Bacterial Warfare

Like all caterpillars, fall webworms fall dead when you spray them with Btk (*Bacillus thuringiensis* var. *kurstaki*). It's a naturally occurring bacterium that invades their digestive systems and kills them within 24 to 48 hours. If you're faced with a massive webworm invasion, or you have too many shrubs to handpick, Btk is the most effective weapon you could ask for. If you decide to use it, though, here are a few things to keep in mind:

▶ Btk kills *all* caterpillars, not just the rabble-rousing pests. So make sure you've got the right target. After all, you don't want to rub out a future butterfly!

THUG BUSTER

All-Season Clean-Up Tonic

This excellent elixir will kill lingering webworms and just about any other bad-guy bugs that mistake your yard for the local salad bar.

1 cup of dishwashing liquid
1 cup of antiseptic mouthwash
1 cup of tobacco tea*

Mix these ingredients in your 20 gallon hose-end sprayer, and saturate your plagued plants from top to bottom. Repeat as needed until the vile varmints vamoose for good, then apply it every two weeks in the evening for season-long control.

*To make tobacco tea, place half a handful of chewing tobacco in an old nylon stocking and soak it in a gallon of hot water until the mixture is dark brown.

▶ This stuff does not kill on contact; in order for it to work, the caterpillars need to eat it. Keep a close watch on your plants in spring and late summer, when caterpillars tend to be most active. Then, the minute you see the bad guys start munching, let 'er rip.

▶ You can buy Btk under several brand names, in liquid or powdered form. Both forms are equally effective; the only difference is in their staying power, both on the plants and in storage. The powder retains its lethal power for seven days after you apply it (presuming rain doesn't wash it off), and you can store it in its container for three to five years in a cool, dark place. The liquid version remains potent for just 24 hours on the plant, and it lasts one year on the shelf.

🖉 Btk Backup

If it's time to renew your Btk defenses and you're fresh out of the stuff, don't trek off to the garden center—whip up a batch yourself. Just gather up some of the webworms (dead or alive) that you've already sprayed with Btk, and follow the simple instructions on page 162.

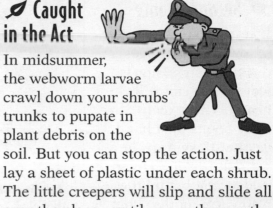

🖉 Caught in the Act

In midsummer, the webworm larvae crawl down your shrubs' trunks to pupate in plant debris on the soil. But you can stop the action. Just lay a sheet of plastic under each shrub. The little creepers will slip and slide all over the place—until you gather up the plastic and empty the squirming contents into a tub of soapy water.

GRANDMA KNEW BEST

Grandma Putt was a firm believer in the old saying "Cleanliness is next to Godliness." And for her, that meant outdoors as well as in. She knew that fall webworms and hordes of other pesky pests hibernate and multiply in dead plant debris, and she wasn't about to stand for that. Every time she went outdoors, she took her work gloves, clippers, and a big bucket. When she'd spy a plant part that was dead, diseased, or just didn't look right, she'd chop it off or scoop it up, and drop it into the bucket. Then she'd either burn the stuff or send it off with the weekly trash. Only plant material she knew was healthy and pest-free wound up in her compost pile.

Second Chance

If you miss that window of opportunity to get the youngsters, don't worry: You can still head off next year's baby boom. Just hang yellow sticky traps in your shrubs in early to midspring, before the webworm moths show up and start laying eggs. (See "Clip and Stick," on page 89.)

Wonder Wasps

When it comes to battling fall webworms, one of your best allies is a teeny wasp by the name of trichogramma. The little flitters lay their eggs inside the eggs of pest insects. Then, when the wasp egg hatches, the larva eats its host egg. To invite trichogramma wasps to hang out among your shrubs, just plant any flowers in the daisy or carrot families. Some of their favorites (and mine, too) are bee balm *(Monarda)*, coneflower *(Echinacea)*, marguerites *(Anthemis tinctoria)*, painted daisies *(Chrysanthemum coccineum)*, and yarrow *(Achillea millefolium)*.

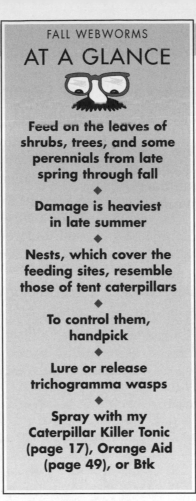

FALL WEBWORMS
AT A GLANCE

Feed on the leaves of shrubs, trees, and some perennials from late spring through fall

◆

Damage is heaviest in late summer

◆

Nests, which cover the feeding sites, resemble those of tent caterpillars

◆

To control them, handpick

◆

Lure or release trichogramma wasps

◆

Spray with my Caterpillar Killer Tonic (page 17), Orange Aid (page 49), or Btk

Big-Time Action

If fall webworms are coming at you left and right, don't wait for trichograma wasps to find your shrubs—buy a passel of them from a catalog or garden center. Then, release them in three batches, at two-week intervals, following the instructions on the package. You want to hit the webworms when they're most vulnerable, so if you're not sure about timing, check with a local nursery or your Cooperative Extension Service. They can clue you in on the best target dates in your area.

More Winged Warriors

When it comes to keeping the fall webworm population under control, trichogramma wasps are not your only allies. Robins and starlings eat legions of larvae, so invite them onto your turf (for hospitality hints, see Chapter 8). Better yet, if the webby munchers are driving you crazy, borrow a few chickens. They'll wipe out thousands in a couple of days!

THIS IS THEIR LIFE

Although the exact timing varies from one leaftier species to another, in general, adult moths lay their eggs on small twigs and branches in spring, just as the first leaves begin to expand. The larvae feed through the summer, then drop to the ground, where they spend the winter in plant litter and then emerge in spring.

ALSO ON THE MENU

Various species of leaftiers target an enormous range of trees, perennial plants, and vegetables. Apple and oak trees are big favorites, and so is the groundcover pachysandra. In the vegetable garden, one type of leaftier dines only on celery. Fortunately, the control measures you see here work right across the menu. **Note:** The leaftiers' close relatives, fruit-tree leaf rollers (see page 63) and leaf rollers (see page 178), inflict very similar damage.

1"

When your shrubs are entertaining a pack of these pests, there's no mistaking the evidence. You'll see brown, ragged foliage and, at the ends of branches, little green envelopes made of several leaves bound together with silken strands. Pop one open, and inside, you'll find a pale green or yellow caterpillar, about 1 inch long, munching away on an unopened bud or developing leaf. There are several species of leaftiers, but they all have the same modus operandi and lookalike parents: tiny gray or brown moths. The shrubby victims are azaleas, rhododendrons, and hydrangeas.

🍃 And the Loser Is...

If only a few leaftiers are making a mess of your shrubs, just clip off the envelopes and squash the rascals. Then, jot down the date you first noticed the nogoodniks so that next year, you can post a "Keep Out" sign in the form of my No Way! Garlic Spray (see page 102). Start spraying a few days before the leaves on your shrubs open up, and the little slimers will stay away in droves!

🍃 The Big Time

Big trouble calls for big guns. If your poor plants are sporting more envelopes than your local post office, rush off to the garden center and buy some Btk (*Bacillus thuringiensis* var. *kurstaki*). Then, spray the foliage from top to bottom once a week for three weeks according to the directions on the package. (For more about Btk, see page 98.)

🍂 Dust 'Em

If you can catch the leaftiers before they hole up in their leafy chambers, then diatomaceous earth, a sensational scratchy substance, will do them in faster than you can say "Priority Mail." Diatomaceous earth is a dust that's made from the fossilized remains of diatoms, one-celled sea critters that lived about 30 million years ago. Each tiny particle

Home on the Range

Leaftiers

has razor-sharp edges that puncture the skin of caterpillars and just about any other bad-guy bugs that come its way (or vice versa). The result: The vile villains die of dehydration. What's more, it won't hurt birds, even if they eat bugs that have been killed by the stuff. It won't harm earthworms, either; a substance on their skin protects them from the prickles.

You can buy diatomaceous earth from garden centers and catalogs. To use it as an anti-leaftier weapon, you have two choices:

1. Put the dust into an old talcum-powder can, and sprinkle it onto the leaves.

2. Mix it with water in a hand-held sprayer at a proportion of about 1 part earth to 3 parts H_2O. Then spritz the foliage from top to bottom. When the water evaporates, the dust particles will remain on the leaves to work their deadly magic.

Whichever method you use, though, you'll have to reapply the diatomaceous earth after each rain.

THUG BUSTER

No Way! Garlic Spray

Use this aromatic concoction to make your plants a no-munching zone for leaftiers and other garlic-phobic gallivanters. Because this repellent contains no soap, which can damage young, tender plant parts, it's safe to use even on brand-new buds.

1/2 cup of garlic, finely chopped*
2 cups of water

Mix the ingredients, then strain out the solids. Pour the liquid into a hand-held sprayer, and spray your plants once a week, paying special attention to new leaf and flower buds. Repeat after every rain.

*Or substitute onion or chives.

LILAC BORERS

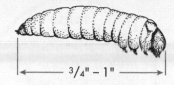

3/4" – 1"

As the name implies, these malicious marauders target one of the most beloved shrubs on the planet. In addition to lilacs, though, they feast on (rather, in) privet and other members of the olive family. The symptoms appear in late summer, generally after a very dry, hot spell, and most often in the crown and the first 3 feet of the stems. Both foliage and branch tips wilt, and at the tunneling site itself, the stem will be cracked and swollen, with broken bark and sagging branches. You'll also see two distinct holes: a rough-sided entrance and, above it, a smooth, round exit.

The vile villain itself is a creamy white, 3/4- to 1-inch-long caterpillar with a brown head. It's the larva of a clearwing moth that flies by day and closely resembles a wasp. The body color varies from yellow and black to orange and brown.

🌿 Don't Take This Lightly!

If your landscape includes any of the lilac borer's likely victims, watch those shrubs like a hawk! A massive invasion of borers can kill a plant faster than you can say, "There go the lilacs." But a series of lighter attacks is almost worse, because the damage will occur so gradually that you may not take action until it's too late. In particular, a lilac that becomes slowly weaker, more stressed, and riddled with borer holes is a prime target for a foul fungus called *Polyporus versicolor*. It appears as soft, multicolored hairs, and it destroys wood—fast.

THIS IS THEIR LIFE

Depending on the climate, adult moths emerge anywhere from March through June. They live for just a week, during which they mate and the females lay eggs at the base of lilac or privet trunks. Ten days to two weeks later, the larvae hatch and bore their way into the wood, where they munch and grow through the summer. They overwinter as partly grown larvae, pupate in tunnels under the bark, and fly out in spring to begin the cycle again. The good news: There is only one generation per year.

ALSO ON THE MENU

The lilac borer also targets ash trees, and in them, it goes by the name of (surprise!) ash borer. A close relative, the banded ash borer, also attacks ash trees, along with mountain ash and osmanthus. Numerous other clearwing-moth offspring terrorize a great many trees and shrubs (see Chapter 2).

Hooked One!

When you spot the first telltale symptoms mentioned on page 103, look for holes. Then, insert a hooked wire (like a crochet hook) into each one, pull out the culprit, and crush him. Or, if the thought of squishing borers makes you turn greener than your lilac leaves, drown the slimy things in a bucket of soapy

Home on the Range

Lilac Borers

water, and toss 'em on the compost pile. Whichever way you dispose of the perpetrators, follow up by spraying my All-Season Clean-Up Tonic (see page 98) to eliminate the disease-causing organisms that always ride in with borers.

Twists and Turns

Sometimes, lilac borers make such long, twisty tunnels that no wire will track them down. In that case, get some beneficial nematodes from a garden center or catalog and inject them into the hole according to the directions on the package. Then plug the opening with putty or chewing gum (well-chewed, of course). Just make sure you get the right kind of nematodes: You want the ones with the scientific name of *Steinernema carpocapsae*.

Catch 'Em on the Fly

You can put a serious dent in the borer population by keeping the boy and girl moths apart when it's time for their mating game. To do that, just get some pheromone traps from a garden center or cata-

THUG BUSTER

Homegrown Daisy Spray

If you grow painted daisies (*Chrysanthemum coccineum*), you've got the makings of one powerful pesticide. It'll deal a death blow to lilac borers and just about any other bad-guy bug you can think of. And the recipe couldn't be simpler.

⅛ cup of rubbing alcohol
1 cup of packed, fresh painted-daisy flower heads*

Pour the alcohol over the flower heads and let it sit overnight. Strain out the flowers, then store the extract in a sealed, labeled container. When you need it, mix the extract with 3 quarts of water, and pour the solution into a hand-held sprayer.

*If you don't grow painted daisies, look for them in the florist section of a large supermarket or, in the summertime, at your local farmers' market.

log and hang them in your lilacs in early spring. The males will hightail it to the traps, expecting some X-rated action, and bingo—end of party! (Just be sure you get traps made for clearwing moths, which are what lilac borers grow up to be.)

Whoops— Missed a Few

Most likely, your traps won't catch all of the moths. But don't worry—I have a backup plan. About 7 to 10 days after the first moth appears in one of your traps, start spraying your lilacs with my Homegrown Daisy Spray (page 104). Make three applications, at 14-day intervals, thoroughly saturating the stems from the ground up to about 4 feet, and reapply after each rain. Don't forget, because you need to keep the residue on the stems for the entire, short period after the eggs hatch and the larvae tunnel into the bark. (If you're not sure when the first moth flitted to its death, just start spraying one week after your lilacs come into full bloom.)

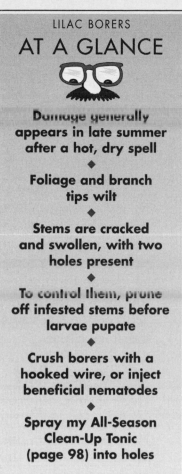

LILAC BORERS
AT A GLANCE

Damage generally appears in late summer after a hot, dry spell

◆

Foliage and branch tips wilt

◆

Stems are cracked and swollen, with two holes present

◆

To control them, prune off infested stems before larvae pupate

◆

Crush borers with a hooked wire, or inject beneficial nematodes

◆

Spray my All-Season Clean-Up Tonic (page 98) into holes

An Ounce of Prevention

Lilac borer invasions are easier to head off than they are to confront head-on. Here are some surefire ways to keep borers at bay:

▶ Make sure your shrubs get enough water during dry periods. Borers tend to bypass well-watered, stress-free plants.

▶ Each year, prune off the oldest, largest branches at ground level. This will keep your lilacs or privet healthier and, therefore, less vulnerable to attack—by borers or any other bad guys.

▶ Don't prune shrubs or trees during the time that clearwing moths are active. The cuts will be the equivalent of a sign that says "Borer Maternity Ward: Vacancy"!

▶ To deter young borers, "paint" the bottom 4 feet of your shrubs' stems with a half-and-half mixture of wood ashes and water. If your soil is very alkaline, substitute diatomaceous earth for the ashes.

ROSE SLUGS

THIS IS THEIR LIFE

In early spring, the female sawfly cuts a series of slits or pockets along the edges of rose leaves and deposits a single egg into each cavity. The rose slug larvae hatch around midspring, feed for several weeks, then pupate. Common and bristly rose slugs do their growing up in the soil, but the curled types tunnel into twigs to pupate. In the process, they kill the stems and create passageways for foul fungi.

ALSO ON THE MENU

There are more than half a dozen kinds of sawflies, and each is what scientists call "host specific." That simply means that each species lays its eggs only in a certain kind of plant. In this case, except for roses, all the targets are trees: cherry, pear, pine, alder, elm, and willow. And you can guard them all with the same tactics you'll read about in this section.

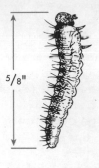

5/8"

These creepy guys look a little like the slimy slugs that slither along the ground, getting up to no good in cool, shady gardens. They're no relation, though. Real slugs are mollusks (snails without shells, so to speak). Rose slugs are the larvae of sawflies, wasp lookalikes that tunnel into rose leaves to lay their eggs. When the babies hatch, they start chewing their way through the foliage, and sometimes flower buds. The damage you see will be tissue partially chewed away between the leaf veins, leaving a sort of gauzy, translucent leaf.

Three of a Kind

Three species of rose slugs operate throughout the United States. The adult sawflies are dead ringers for each other, but the babies look as different as can be. Common rose slugs are about 1/2 inch long and yellow-green with an orange head. Bristly rose slugs are pale green, 5/8 inch or so long and, as the name implies, covered with short, bristle-like hairs. Curled rose slugs got their name for a good reason, too: They're generally found curled up like cutworms. They're pastel green with white spots on the abdomen, a yellow head, and black-rimmed eyes.

Help from Your Friends

Fortunately, sawflies have a lot of natural enemies, including birds, good-guy beetles, parasitic wasps, and even fatal viruses. These wonder workers will generally keep the population in check with no help from you, as long as you don't use pesticides in your yard. But even if something goes awry and you wind up with a baby boom on your hands, don't panic. There are plenty of easy ways to kiss 'em good-bye.

Home on the Range

Rose Slugs

about half a cup of alcohol. Whatever you do, though, don't touch the larvae with your bare hands. They're covered with a slimy substance that's highly irritating to human skin. (I keep a pair of barbecue tongs in the toolshed, just for bug-plucking purposes.)

What You See Is Not What You Get!

You might think that because rose slugs look a lot like caterpillars, you can do 'em in with the ultimate 'pillar killer, Btk. But appearances are often deceptive. Btk won't harm a bristle or a slime molecule on a rose slug's back. Neither will any chemical pesticide that you can buy in a garden center. So how do you keep the foul felons from defoliating your roses? Read on, my friend!

Give Them a Hand

In the case of a moderate rose slug visitation, just get out there and hand-pick them. Depending on your level of squeamishness, you can squash the tiny varmints by pinching them between your gloved thumb and finger, or simply clip off the leaves and drop them into a pail of water laced with

Blast 'Em Off

If a pair of barbecue tongs brings you too close for comfort, grab your garden hose, turn the nozzle on high, and fire away. Many of the slugs will be killed on contact, and any survivors will soon be gobbled up by predators on the ground.

GRANDMA KNEW BEST

Grandma Putt's roses were the toast of our neighborhood and blue-ribbon winners at every state fair I can remember. So she wasn't about to let rose slugs spoil the big show. Her simple secret: wood ashes. She sprinkled the stuff onto the leaves in early spring and again after every rain. It killed the vile villains on contact.

It's hard to believe that a critter as small as a mouse could actually destroy a big, healthy shrub, but it's true. These tiny tunnelers like nothing better than munching on roots and bark, sometimes girdling and killing the plants in the process. A few types, such as dormice, hibernate in the winter; but most species are active right through the year. In fact, most mouse-inflicted damage to shrubs and trees occurs between October and April, when the tiny twerps move into mole runs or else tunnel, unseen, through the snow. They may also spend the winter in mulch that you've spread around your shrubs to protect them from cold-weather damage. (Who's got the last laugh here?!)

In addition to the destruction caused by their chewing, some species of mice can transmit potentially deadly diseases, including hantavirus pulmonary syndrome (HPS). And in some parts of the country, deer mice are hosts of deer ticks, which cause Lyme disease.

🌿 Who's the Guilty Party?

Not sure what little critter is nibbling on your shrubs? Here's an easy way to find out: Just sprinkle white flour on the ground below your beleaguered plants. The next morning, check the telltale footprints. If you don't recognize them by sight, pull out your handy Audubon field guide, and make a positive I.D.

THIS IS THEIR LIFE

When you're as little and as basically helpless as a mouse, biological success depends on rapid reproduction. And have mice ever got that technique figured out! Depending on the species, a female mouse gives birth to as many as eight litters per year, with an average of six young'uns per litter. And here's the really sobering part: Each of those babies reaches sexual maturity in about a month. The good news is that most of them live only one to three years, tops.

ALSO ON THE MENU

Mice dine on any plant material they can sink their little choppers into, including trees, annual and perennial flowers, seeds, bulbs, vegetables, fruits, and the contents of your compost bin. And, we all know what trouble mice can cause in your house, garage, or garden shed! In this section, you'll find tips to rout the rodents, no matter where they're rambling!

🖋 Printed and Charged

If you'd like a more permanent footprint record, set an ink pad on a large, sturdy sheet of white paper, and surround the pad with a few kinds of tasty bait (for instance, chunky peanut butter, apple slices, and sunflower seeds). The culprit will mosey on over to get the goodies and leave solid evidence behind!

🖋 Time and Distance

These two simple steps will go a long way toward protecting your shrubs and trees from these mini marauders:

Step 1. When you mulch your shrubs, keep the material at least 6 inches away from the plants' trunks. That way, you'll deprive mice of one of their favorite hiding places.

Step 2. Before you mulch your shrubs for the winter, wait until the ground has frozen solid. So, even if the mice snuggle down in the cozy mulch blanket, they won't be able to tunnel into the soil.

🖋 Foiled Again!

Before winter sets in, wrap the trunks of your shrubs (or young trees) loosely in aluminum foil to a height of 18 inches to 2 feet. The glittering, rattling surface will send the gnawers looking for food elsewhere!

Ask Jerry

I tend a number of nesting boxes along a "bluebird trail" that runs through my town. Each box is fastened to the top of a 2-inch-diameter steel pipe. In the winter, when the birds are gone, deer mice climb right up the pipe and into the boxes. Besides smelling up the boxes with their nasty urine, we're concerned that they're spreading hantavirus to the birds (the disease is on the rise in our area). Do you have any ideas for keeping the mice out?

I sure have! Just detach each box, and slip a length of metal downspout over the pipe so that it rests on the ground and reaches up to an inch or so under the box. Then (of course) replace the box. When the mice try to climb the downspout, they won't be able to get their little paws around the wider downspout and will slide right off. (For more tips on keeping our feathered friends safe and sound, see Chapter 8.)

A Bedtime Safety Net

If aluminum foil isn't your idea of pleasing garden decor, guard your shrubs with a mini fence. Just circle your shrub bed, or the root zone of each plant, with fine mesh wire that extends 3 to 4 inches above the ground and 6 to 8 inches below. Then, for added protection, spray the entire area with my Hot Pepper Spray (see page 83)—it'll make the mice scram!

Make Mine Mint

As much as they dislike hot scents, mice also hate one cool one— namely mint. They'll flee if you plant it among your shrubs, but there's an easier way to put mint power to work in your yard. Just mix 2 tablespoons of peppermint extract or oil of peppermint in a gallon of warm water. Pour the solution into a hand-held sprayer, and thoroughly spritz the crown and lower stems of your shrubs. To pro-

Home on the Range

Mice

tect container plants, simply saturate a cotton ball in the oil or extract, and tuck it into the pot at the base of the plant (for large specimens, use two or three).

How Dry They Are

To you, a dryer sheet might smell like the freshest thing this side of a violet patch. But that strong, flowery scent sends mice scurrying. This go-away power lasts longer indoors (I use the sheets to safeguard the contents of my garden shed), but as a temporary measure, tie a few dryer sheets to the lower trunks of your shrubs. They'll keep mice and other small critters at bay at least until rain washes the aroma away.

Chocolate to the Rescue!

When mice are driving you crazy, indoors or out, use one of my favorite weapons. Just mix equal parts of flour and plaster of paris,

> ### DID YOU KNOW?
>
> The average mouse weighs little more than your electric bill, but in Central and South America, there's a rodent that can top the scales at 140 pounds! Fortunately, this critter, the capybara, is a gentle, mild-mannered soul who resembles a giant guinea pig. Capybaras love to swim. In fact, they spend so much time in the water that during the sixteenth century, the Vatican declared them to be fish and, therefore, fair game for eating during Lent.

and spoon the powder into jar lids or other shallow containers. Add a pinch or two of chocolate cookie crumbs or chocolate drink mix to each one, and stir it in. Then set out the bait where *only* mice can get to it (not children or pets), and put a saucer of water nearby. The mice, being bona fide chocoholics, will gobble up the bait and chase it with a swig of water. That will activate the plaster of paris, which will form a big, hard lump inside the critters' tummies. End of story!

Doin' the Mouser Mash

In a variation on the plaster of paris theme (see "Chocolate to the Rescue!", on page 110), set out shallow containers of instant mashed potato flakes, with a dish of water close at hand. The munchkins will eat the taters, drink the water, swell up, and die.

Trapping Technique 101

Folks have been trying for years to build a better mousetrap, but you still can't beat the old-fashioned snap trap, indoors or out. To get the very best results, stage a full-scale blitz. Rather

than setting out a few traps each night, invest in as many as your budget will allow, and set them out all at once. Repeat the process until your bait has no takers.

Trapping: The Sequel

My second favorite trap is a good old plastic bucket or wastebasket. Just set it upright near a shrub or other handy climbing device, and put your bait in the bottom. The mice will scramble up and over to the edge, jump in, and stay put. Unless you release them, they'll quickly die of starvation or be eaten by predators.

And Speaking of Bait...

If you ask half a dozen successful mouse catchers to name their favorite bait, chances are you'll get half a dozen answers. Well, just for the record, I've had the best results with these three:

▶ Chunky peanut butter

▶ Cucumber pieces with the rind left on

▶ Dryer lint (The tiny tykes covet the soft, fluffy stuff as nest-building material.)

THIS IS THEIR LIFE

Skunks are basically loners, getting together only in mating season, which runs from early February to the end of March. Then the males take off. From 61 to 69 days after conception, mama gives birth to mouse-sized babies, called kits. They're blind, deaf, and nearly hairless, but already sport their black-and-white color pattern. There may be as many as 10 in a litter, but the norm is 5 or 6. The youngsters hang around home for the first year, then take off to raise little stinkers of their own.

ALSO ON THE MENU

Although they do far more good than harm in the garden, skunks do enjoy forbidden fruit (mostly berries) when they can get it. And they're not above swiping a tasty ear of corn now and then. Use the tips in this section to send skunks packing.

If it weren't for that, um, *distinctive* aroma, gardeners would welcome skunks with open arms. These shy, gentle animals rarely eat plants. In fact, they consume huge quantities of a gardener's sworn enemies, including insects, their eggs, and larvae; slugs; mice; voles; baby rats; and—their favorite of favorites—grubs. Unfortunately, in their quest for dinner, they tend to run roughshod through shrub beds and lawns.

Skunks are adaptable and happy to live just about anywhere except desert areas. But they prefer underground burrows near the edges of woodlands or in bushy areas (like your shrub borders). And they often set up housekeeping in abandoned groundhog holes, old tree stumps, or that nice, cozy cranny under a porch.

This Diner's Closed!

The only sure way to send skunks packing for good is to eliminate their food supply, especially grubs. You can do that by following my grub-removal tactics in Chapter 1. The process takes time to work, though, so in the meantime, read on for my other tried-and-true ways to say, "Scram, skunk!"

Heed the Warning

Before you set out to clear your territory of skunks, here are a few things you ought to know:

▶ Contrary to what a lot of folks think, skunks

spray only as a last resort. When they're confronted by a human, or any other critter for that matter, they'd much rather flee than launch a fragrant attack.

Home on the Range

Skunks

▶ Like Roy Rogers and his cohorts, skunks honor the Code of the West: They give fair warning before they shoot. And the message is loud and clear. When he's cornered or feels threatened, a skunk will stiffen up his front legs, stomp them, and shuffle backward a little. He may also hiss and growl.

▶ When you've been issued that warning, just back off quickly and quietly, and the skunk may retreat, too. Otherwise, the little acrobat will throw his body over his head and—still facing you—let 'er rip.

The Hopeful News

Within 10 feet of their target, skunks are real sharpshooters. Between 10 and 20 feet, they're not so accurate. So, if you can make it that far before Pepe Le Pew pulls the "trigger," you may only get sprinkled. (See "But What about Me?" on page 115.)

Fence 'Em Out

Skunks rarely climb fences, which gives you an easy and attractive way to safeguard your territory. For the surest protection, use ¼-inch wire mesh that's 3 feet wide. Then, to keep the rascals from tunneling under, bend the bottom 6 inches outward at a 90° angle, and bury it at a depth of 6 inches. To disguise the 2 feet left above the ground, just tack it to a picket fence or other decorative yard accessory.

The Cover-Up

If you'd rather not erect a fence to keep skunks out, just cover your plant-

---

Skunk Odor-Out Tonic

When a skunk comes a-callin' and leaves some fragrant evidence behind, reach for this easy remedy.

1 cup of bleach or vinegar
1 tbsp. of dishwashing liquid
2½ gal. of warm water

Mix all of these ingredients in a bucket and thoroughly saturate walls, stairs, or anything else your local skunk has left his mark on. **Caution:** Use this tonic only on non-living things—not on pets, humans, or plants.

THUG BUSTER

---

ing bed's surface with hardware cloth. Make sure the openings are no larger than 1/4 inch square, and don't smooth it down flat. The more waves you leave in the surface, the less the critters' sensitive little feet will like it. To improve the appearance, you can spread a thin layer of soil or mulch over the metal. But be sure to keep it light so the little buggers can feel those sharp strands.

🌿 Two Can Play This Game

When a skunk first wanders onto your turf, intent on setting up housekeeping, a good spray of water can send him scurrying. Just grab your garden hose, stand at least 20 feet away from the trespasser, and blast away.

🌿 Glad Rags

When it comes to giving off aromas, skunks are the heavyweight champs of the world. And, for the most part, they can take what they dish out.

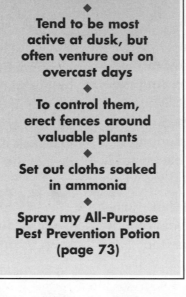

But there's one odor that'll send 'em packin' in a hurry—ammonia. So if the little guys are venturing where they're not wanted, soak some rags in the potent liquid, and hang them in the trouble spots. Or, if you don't want smelly rags lying around, keep skunks away by spraying your yard and everything in it with my All-Purpose Pest Prevention Potion (see page 73).

🌿 Anybody Home?

You've used all of the go-away tricks in your bag. Now how do you find out whether your little camper is still in his den? Simple: Just stuff newspaper into the entrance hole. If Mr. or Ms. Skunk is in residence, the paper will be shoved out within 24 hours. (I recommend using this technique around midday, when skunks are usually snoozing.)

🌿 Skunked!

When your dog tangles with the wrong end of a skunk, don't panic. Just saturate Fido with full-strength mouthwash, carefully avoiding his eyes and ears. Then wash him with a good dog shampoo, and rinse thoroughly. (If he's less than a year old, use a shampoo that's specially made for puppies.)

🖊 Skunked Again!

Fresh out of mouthwash to de-skunk your dog? Don't worry—this alternative formula is just as effective. Mix 1 quart of 3 percent hydrogen peroxide, ¼ cup of baking soda, and 1 teaspoon of liquid hand soap in a bucket. Then corral your pal and soak him thoroughly with the solution. Rinse well, and towel him dry. Presto—no more *eau de skunk*!

🖊 But What about Me?

If you or your youngsters get up close and personal with a skunk, use either of the two remedies above; they work as well on humans as they do on pets. As for your clothes, take them to the local laundromat and toss them in the washer with an alkaline detergent.

That's not all, folks!

Most of the insects and larger critters that target trees also go gunnin' for shrubs. You can read all about that brigade in Chapter 2. In addition, be on the lookout for these shrub-bothering varmints.

APHIDS, those all-around sap-suckers, drain the juices from shrubs' leaves, making them pucker, curl up, and turn yellow. For the full story, see page 117.

THRIPS chew and suck the daylights out of many shrubs, including roses, rhododendrons, and laurel. For the full story, see page 154.

CATERPILLARS of many kinds chomp on shrub foliage. You'll get the lowdown on them in Chapter 4.

DEER love nothing better than young, shrubby shoots. See page 197 for the details.

TICKS, those terrorizers of pets and people, often bed down in shrubs. See my anti-tick battle plan starting on page 157.

CHAPTER 4

ANNUAL & PERENNIAL PLAGUERS

■ just can't imagine life without flowers, and I'll bet you can't, either. A garden filled with a colorful mix of annuals, perennials, and bulbs is the best perker-upper a person could ask for. Flowering plants provide food and homes for hordes of good-guy bugs who return the favor by pollinating fruits and vegetables, and gobbling up the bad guys who are gunnin' for your trees, shrubs, veggies—and flowers. In this chapter, I'll give you the ammunition you need to send those pesky posy pests packin', pronto!

THIS IS THEIR LIFE

In cold regions, aphids hatch in May or June from eggs laid the previous fall. Then the females give birth to live nymphs every two weeks until the weather turns cold. The babies are born pregnant, and within a week, start delivering young'uns of their own. Some nymphs born late in the summer grow wings as they mature. Then they fly to trees and lay eggs that overwinter in the bark and hatch the following spring. In places where the weather stays mild all year, the pests just churn out one live litter after another.

ALSO ON THE MENU

Aphids attack just about any kind of plant under the sun, including turf grass. Your clues that they've arrived: The grass blades turn yellow-orange and grow poorly, and ant hills suddenly appear. Your mission: Mow your lawn, and spray it with my All-Season Clean-Up Tonic (see page 98).

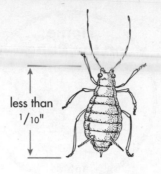

less than 1/10"

Anyone who's ever grown so much as a pot of petunias has come across these little suckers. You'll generally find them clustered on new growth, draining out the fluids and leaving the plants wilted, discolored, and stunted. As if that dastardly dirty work weren't enough, some aphids spread viral diseases as they move from one victim to the next.

North America is home to more than 1,300 species of aphids. Some of them target only one type of plant; others are less particular in their drinking habits. Aphids can be almost any color of the rainbow, but they're all tiny (less than 1/10 inch long), pear-shaped, and usually wingless, with soft bodies and mouths that can pierce right through even the toughest leaves and stems. Most species are smooth-bodied, but the kinds that attack trees have wooly coats that make them look like little cotton balls.

🌿 About That Honeydew...

Aphids are famous for the honeydew they produce, but have you ever wondered exactly what this substance is? I'll tell you: When aphids tap into a plant, they're after just one ingredient in the sap—nitrogen. Once their systems have extracted it, they secrete the excess liquid in the form of the sweet, sticky stuff that ants love so much. (See Chapter 2 for the lowdown on those little guys.)

Pray for Rain

A hard, driving rain will kill boatloads of aphids, and you won't have to lift a finger! If Mother Nature won't cooperate, give your plants a strong blast of water from the garden hose, making sure to spray the undersides of the leaves. Repeat two or three more times, every other day. And try to work in the morning, so the foliage has plenty of time to dry before nightfall. (Otherwise, you could end up swapping your aphid woes for fungus nightmares.)

Home on the Range

Aphids

Stronger Medicine

Sometimes, even a deluge doesn't wipe out all of the little sap-suckers. In that case, take care of any malicious malingerers with my Great-Guns Garlic Spray (below). I guarantee there won't be a live aphid left!

Old Yeller

Like many insects, aphids are drawn to the color yellow. When you're battling with the flying types, you can play this card to your advantage in two ways:

1. Hang yellow sticky traps on your plants (see page 89 for my versions specially designed for tiny bad guys).

2. Fill yellow plastic margarine tubs with soapy water, and set them on the ground near your plants. The felons will fly right into the drink and drown.

Nix the Nasty Side Effects

Anyplace you've got aphids at work, you face the threat of plant viruses. There is no cure for a viral disease, but there is a product that may prevent an outbreak. What is this wonder drug? Good old moo juice! Scientists have proven that milk helps protect plants against the nasty

THUG BUSTER

Great-Guns Garlic Spray

This fragrant concoction will halt an aphid invasion faster than you can say, "Please pass the dish soap!" In the process, it'll also kill any foul fungi that might be lingering on your plants, fixin' to cause dastardly diseases.

1 tbsp. of my Garlic Oil (page 119)
3 drops of dishwashing liquid
1 qt. of water

Mix these ingredients together in a blender, and pour the solution into a hand-held sprayer. Then take aim and fire. Within seconds, those bugs'll be history!

little organisms. Here's how you can put this germ-fighting power to work:

▶ Every time you empty a carton of milk, cream, or buttermilk, fill the container with water, shake it, and pour the contents onto one or two of your plants.

▶ Whenever you're working with aphid-plagued plants, keep a bowl handy that's filled with a half-and-half mixture of milk and water. Then every few minutes, dip your hands and tools into the mix.

🌿 The Intelligence Report

Once you've bid aphids bye-bye, I can tell you plenty of ways to keep them from launching another attack—and I will. But first, here's a dandy way to find out when they're grouping on your borders: Just plant either marigolds or nasturtiums on the perimeter of your yard. Aphids will flock to these two, easy-to-grow annuals before they'll touch any other flowers. If you find the pesky pests on your trap crop, your mission is two-fold:

1. Dig up the trap crop and destroy it.

2. Protect your other plants by implementing the aphid-avoidance measures in this section.

🌿 Turn 'Em Off

Aphids love nasturtiums and marigolds, but they hate other plants with equal passion. Include plenty of these winners in your garden, and even the suckers' favorite targets can rest easy:

▶ Basil ▶ Fennel

▶ Catnip ▶ Garlic

▶ Chives ▶ Mint

▶ Dill

THUG BUSTER

Garlic Oil

Keep a batch of this potent oil in the fridge, and you'll always have ammunition against aphids and other garden thugs.

1 bulb of garlic, minced
1 cup of vegetable oil

Mix the minced garlic and the oil, and pour into a glass jar with a tight lid. Put the jar in the refrigerator and "steep" the oil for a day or two. To see whether it's ready for action, open the lid and take a sniff. If the aroma is so strong that you take a step back, you're ready to roll. If the scent isn't so strong, mince half a bulb of garlic, mix it into the oil, and wait another day. Then strain out the solids and pour the oil into a fresh jar with a lid. Keep it in the fridge, and use it in any Thug Buster that calls for Garlic Oil.

Make 'Em See the Light

Spread aluminum foil, shiny side up, on the ground under your plants. The reflected light will scare the daylights out of the little suckers, and they'll take their soda straws elsewhere.

Yes, We Have Some Bananas

Aphids can't stand bananas. So, if you love these tasty fruits as much as I do, you've got a never-ending anti-aphid arsenal. Just lay the peels on the ground under your plants, and aphids will keep their distance. As an added bonus, these skins will break down (which they do with amazing speed) and enrich the soil with valuable potassium and phosphorus.

Go Easy on the N

A plant that's getting too much nitrogen (N) is a magnet for aphids and

APHIDS

AT A GLANCE

Suck the juices from plants, leaving them wilted, discolored, and stunted

◆

Often spread viruses

◆

Produce a sweet, sticky honeydew that attracts ants

◆

Reproduce prolifically as long as the weather stays mild

◆

To control them, use my Great-Guns Garlic Spray (page 118)

◆

In early stages, dislodge them with a blast of water

◆

Go easy on nitrogen fertilizers

◆

Encourage predators like ladybugs and lacewings (Chapter 8)

other sucking insects. So beware of N overload! In particular, avoid synthetic/chemical fertilizers, which deliver nutrients directly to plants' roots in highly concentrated form—making it a snap to serve up an overdose without even knowing it. Instead, use a natural/organic fertilizer, which adds essential nutrients to the soil, where they become available to the plants as they need them. You'll find some excellent brands in any garden center, or use my All-Purpose Organic Fertilizer (see page 243).

Ask for Help

Aphids have hordes of natural enemies, including aphid midges, big-eyed bugs, damselflies, hover fly larvae, snake flies, soldier beetles, and both adult and larval forms of lacewings and ladybugs. They'll all show up and start chowing down on the aphids as long as you don't use pesticides. (For more on the good guys, see Chapter 8.)

BLISTER BEETLES

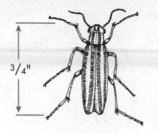

3/4"

1/4" – 1/2"

THIS IS THEIR LIFE

The life cycle varies somewhat, but in general, the adults lay eggs in midsummer in the same burrows where grasshoppers have already laid theirs. Of course, the young hoppers never see the light of day because the beetle bunch hatch first and settle in to a big, hearty hopper-egg breakfast. The grubs overwinter in the burrow, pupate in the spring, and emerge in the summer to continue the cycle.

ALSO ON THE MENU

Blister beetles can raise a royal ruckus in the vegetable garden. They're particularly partial to beans, beets, chard, spinach, tomatoes, eggplant, potatoes, and sweet potatoes. The same techniques used to protect your flowers will work with your edible crops, too. These beetles are also fond of many different shrubs—holly is an extra-special favorite—and every now and then, they munch on some trees.

When it comes to garden-variety dirty work, these bad boys are speed demons. A horde of the hellions can suddenly appear out of nowhere in midsummer and, before you even notice them, chew a whole garden bed to shreds—flowers and foliage both. There are many species of blister beetles, and they show up all over the country, but the ones that cause the most harm tend to haunt the East and Midwest. They're slender, about 3/4 inch long, and blackish or grayish, with soft, flexible wing covers that may have white stripes or margins. And, yes, these guys got their name for a very good reason: They exude a chemical called cantharidin that causes nasty (although not dangerous) burns or blisters if you touch them.

Now, are you ready for this? These disgusting demons actually give birth to good-guy youngsters. Blister beetle grubs gobble grasshopper eggs like there's no tomorrow!

🌿 The Choice Is Yours

If you live in a part of the country where grasshoppers are a real menace, you might want to tolerate blister beetles in the interest of keeping their young'uns on the job. On the other hand, if the blasted beetles are driving you batty, go get those grubs!

Frequently Fouled Flowers

Almost no flowering plant is safe from blister beetles, but there are some that draw them like magnets. If you live in a proven BB stomping ground, here are some plants that you might want to avoid:

Home on the Range

Blister Beetles

▶ Annual aster

▶ Calendula

▶ Chrysanthemum

▶ Clematis

▶ Dahlia

▶ Japanese anemone

▶ Phlox

▶ Zinnia

your pets and livestock. If you see symptoms such as colic, diarrhea, blood in the stool or urine, body tremors, or odd breathing patterns, call your veterinarian—*fast*!

Drop and Dunk

When blister beetles are disturbed in their dirty work, they tend to drop off of the plant. That makes them sitting ducks for the old brush-and-dunk trick. Just spread an old sheet on the ground under the victims, and jostle the plants. Then gather up the beetle-

Hold Your Horses

Although making skin contact with a blister beetle won't cause permanent harm to anyone (except in very rare instances), swallowing the foul things can be fatal—and has been to many critters, especially horses, who have gobbled them up by mistake when the beetles got into their hay. So, when the foul felons are on the fly in your neighborhood, keep a close watch on

Hooray-for-Horseradish Tonic

This tangy tonic is instant death to some of the vilest villains in gardendom, including blister beetles, aphids, Colorado potato beetles, whiteflies, and any caterpillar that ever crept down the pike.

THUG BUSTER

2 cups of cayenne pepper, finely chopped
1-inch piece of horseradish root, finely chopped*
3 qts. of water

Bring the water to a boil, add the pepper and horseradish, and let the mixture steep for an hour or so. Let it cool to room temperature, then strain out the solids. Pour the liquid into a hand-held sprayer, and blast those bugs to you-know-where!

*Or 2 tablespoons of bottled, pure horseradish.

filled fabric, and empty the contents into a tub of soapy water. Just make sure you and all your helpers wear the uniform of the day: long sleeves, long pants, socks, closed shoes, and gloves. You don't want to take any chances with these guys!

The Automated Approach

If you'd prefer to keep a little more distance between you and the beetles, haul out your wet/dry vacuum cleaner and fill the reservoir with a few inches of soapy water. Then attach the extra-long tube, and swoop those babies right off of your plants. (If you don't have a wet/dry vacuum cleaner, just use a regular hand-held model and empty the buggy contents into a tub of soapy water.)

Too Tangy to Tangle With

One of the tangiest taste treats on earth, good old horseradish, is lethal to blister beetles. So, if you want to maintain a *really* hands-off approach with the vile villains, mix up a batch of my Hooray-for-Horseradish Tonic (page 122), and spray your picked-on plants from stem to stern.

Well-Grounded

Blister beetles can't even stand horseradish when

DID YOU KNOW?

If a single example of every species of plant and animal on earth were lined up in a row, every fifth one would be a different kind of beetle, or *Coleoptera,* as they're known in scientific circles. Here are a few more trivial tidbits that you probably don't know about beetles:

- There are more than 350,000 species of beetles. That figure represents one-fourth of all the animal species on the planet.
- Half of those are in the weevil family, *Curculionidae* by name.
- Most beetles are entirely harmless, and many are big-time garden good guys.
- Beetles live in every part of the world except Antarctica.
- The smallest of the bunch is the featherwing beetle, which reaches less than 1/25 of an inch.
- Tied for largest are the Goliath and Hercules beetles, which can grow to 6 inches or more.

it's growing in the ground, so plant plenty of the pungent stuff among your annuals and perennials (and in the veggie patch, too). Fortunately, this zesty herb has foliage that's attractive enough to grace any flower bed. Horseradish is invasive, though, so unless you want to go into the condiment business, corral your tubers in bottomless pots that you've sunk into the ground. (A 3-pound coffee can is perfect for this job.)

Keep Out!

If you grow lots of annuals in a cutting garden, borrow this tactic from the vegetable patch: At egg-laying time in midsummer, put floating row covers over your plants. And be sure to bury the edges in the soil, so that the mama beetles can't get in to lay their eggs.

Sorry, Baby

If blister beetles are making a total wreck of your flowers, you probably don't care how many grasshopper eggs the young'uns are putting away. So, before you try other tactics, just till the top few inches of soil under your plants. You'll bring the grubs up to the surface, where you can polish them

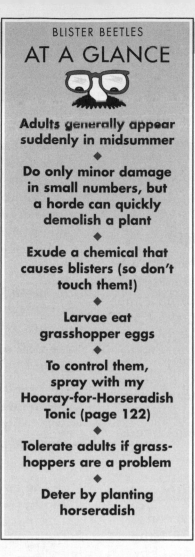

BLISTER BEETLES
AT A GLANCE

Adults generally appear suddenly in midsummer

◆

Do only minor damage in small numbers, but a horde can quickly demolish a plant

◆

Exude a chemical that causes blisters (so don't touch them!)

◆

Larvae eat grasshopper eggs

◆

To control them, spray with my Hooray-for-Horseradish Tonic (page 122)

◆

Tolerate adults if grasshoppers are a problem

◆

Deter by planting horseradish

off using any of the following methods:

▶ Wait for their enemies to eat them for lunch. You won't have to wait long—birds, toads, lizards, and many ground beetles all love these larvae! (For more about good guys, see Chapter 8.)

▶ Scoop up the grubs, and drop 'em in a bucket of soapy water.

▶ Collect about half a cup of grubs and whip up a batch of my Beetle Juice (see page 53). Then pour it on the soil. That'll be all she wrote!

▶ Buy some beneficial nematodes at the garden center, and apply them according to the directions on the package.

Hop to It

Once you've eliminated blister beetle grubs, chances are, you'll see a big leap in the grasshopper population. So don't delay! Hop on over to page 281 and read my tried-and-true techniques for giving grasshoppers the gate.

BULB MITES

THIS IS THEIR LIFE

Like all mites, the bulb-munching bunch reproduce like there's no tomorrow. A female bulb mite can lay 400 to 700 eggs at a time, with a new batch appearing every three to seven days. In colder regions, the egg factory shuts down for the winter, then cranks back up in the spring. But in warm climates or in greenhouses and sunrooms, the fun goes on all year-round.

ALSO ON THE MENU

In the vegetable garden, bulb mites target garlic, onions, and (are you ready for this?) ungerminated lettuce seeds. In each case, your only option is to destroy your plants and sow new crops in sterilized soil, or (better yet) in containers. But before you do that, put the lettuce seeds, onion sets, or garlic bulbs in a jar with about ¼ cup of diatomaceous earth, and shake it to coat those embryonic plants.

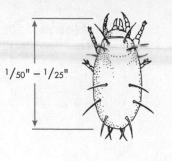

1/50" – 1/25"

Don't be misled by the name. While it's true that these almost-invisible terrors target mainly spring- and summer-flowering bulbs and bulb act-alikes (see "A Bulb by Any Other Name…" on page 127), bulb mites also attack fleshy-rooted perennials, such as daylilies and peonies. Above ground, be-mited plants are stunted and slow-growing. In the early stages, when you dig up the bulbs, you'll see large clusters of what look like tiny grains of white pepper. (You'll need a magnifying glass to see the actual critters, who grow only to about ¹/₂₅ inch at the most.) Later, corky, brown spots appear; these eventually turn to a dry, crumbly pulp. These mites almost never venture above ground. The one exception is in the case of lilies, where they sometimes move into the leaves and stems. Bulb mites are first drawn to damaged or rotting bulbs, but once they're on the scene, they quickly move to healthy ones—bringing foul fungi and bad bacteria with them.

✿ Travelin' On

It only stands to reason that with all these mites gathered on a single bulb, the food supply eventually runs out. So what happens then? Some of the mites enter a nonfeeding form called *heteromorphic deutonymph*, and just sit there until they can attach themselves to a visiting insect and be whisked away to a new life on another plant.

✑ Bite the Bullet

Unfortunately, when your bulbs are chock-full of these tiny terrors, you have only one option: Dig up the bulbs, and destroy them and the soil they were growing in. Whatever you do, don't throw them on the compost pile!

Home on the Range

Bulb Mites

✑ Early to Rise

The good news is that if you've caught the attack in its early stages, you can kill the pests and head off any further

damage. How? Just soak the bulbs for three to four hours in my Bug-Off Bulb Bath (below). Then, either move your bulb garden to fresh territory or solarize the infested soil before you plant new *or* treated bulbs. (See page 182 for my simple solarizing method.)

✑ Shopper, Beware

When you go to buy new bulbs, walk right past the ones that are packaged up in fancy boxes. There's no telling what might be inside. Instead, go straight to the bins filled with loose bulbs. Give each one the old eagle eye, and if you see any soft spots, dings, or nicks, take your business else-where. Even if mites aren't on the scene already, chances are they'll move into those damaged bulbs about 5 minutes after you put them in the ground—that is, if some other bad bug or foul fungus doesn't beat them to it!

✑ No Drain, Their Gain

Even a bulb that's in the pink of health will rot quickly if it's planted in poorly drained soil. So

THUG BUSTER

Bug-Off Bulb Bath

This spa treatment will help your spring- or summer-blooming bulbs fend off disease germs, as well as bulb mites and other pesky pests.

2 tsp. of baby shampoo
1 tsp. of antiseptic mouthwash
¼ tsp. of instant tea granules
2 gal. of hot water (120°F)

Mix these ingredients in a bucket. Then drop in your bulbs, and let them soak for 2 to 3 hours (longer for larger bulbs). And don't peel off the papery skins! The bulbs use them as a defense against pests. Then either plant the bulbs immediately or let them air-dry for several days before you store them—otherwise, rot could set in.

before you tuck your new campers into their beds, always add plenty of compost or leaf mold. If your home ground is so damp that nothing you can do will change it, grow your bulbs in containers.

Plant the Enemy

A predatory mite by the name of *Hypoaspis* attacks bulb mites in the soil. Just get a package of these handy helpers, and release them according to the directions on the package. If your local garden center doesn't stock *Hypoaspis*, your Cooperative Extension Service can probably direct you to a supplier, or just scout the Web via your favorite Internet search engine.

Handle with Care

Although bulbs look tough, they bruise easily, and bruises are open doors to bulb mites and other pesky pests and dastardly diseases. So, be extra careful when you're planting, digging up, or storing bulbs and when working the soil in their beds.

Smile for the Camera!

When bulbs' foliage dies down and your other flowering plants grow up, it's all but impossible to remember

GRANDMA KNEW BEST

When you dig up your tender bulbs in the fall, do what my Grandma Putt always did to make sure they got stored properly: Dust them with medicated baby powder or foot powder before tucking them away for the winter. That way, you'll fend off fungi and bacteria that you might not even notice in the spring—but bulb mites sure would!

where you planted the bulbs. So do what I do with spring- and summer-bloomers both: When the flowers burst forth, take a picture of each planting site. That way, you'll know exactly where *not* to sink your shovel later on, when you're working in the bed.

A Bulb by Any Other Name...

Technically speaking, a bulb is a swollen, underground stem with a bud in the center; wrapped around it are scale-like leaf bases that are chock-full of food. Tulips, daffodils, lilies, and onions are true bulbs. However, folks who sell or write about bulbs generally include three other plants that behave the same way—including entertaining the same pests—but are not *really* bulbs. This is the roster:

▶ **A corm** is similar to a bulb, but carries the bud on top. Every year, the old corm withers away, and a new one takes its place. Gladioli and crocuses are corms.

▶ **A tuber** is simply the swollen part of an underground stem. Tuberous begonias and cyclamen are tubers.

▶ **A tuberous root** is exactly that—a swollen root. In order to produce a plant, the root must have a piece of stem and at least one bud attached. Dahlias are an example of tuberous roots.

🍃 Some Like It Soggy

While it is true that most bulbs become mite magnets if they don't have near-perfect drainage, there are some exceptions. This trio all thrive in moist soil:

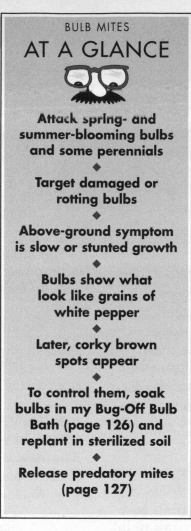

BULB MITES
AT A GLANCE

Attack spring- and summer-blooming bulbs and some perennials

◆

Target damaged or rotting bulbs

◆

Above-ground symptom is slow or stunted growth

◆

Bulbs show what look like grains of white pepper

◆

Later, corky brown spots appear

◆

To control them, soak bulbs in my Bug-Off Bulb Bath (page 126) and replant in sterilized soil

◆

Release predatory mites (page 127)

▶ **Camassia (*Camassia*).** Spikes of star-shaped flowers bloom in late spring, in shades of blue and white. Stems range from 14 to 36 inches tall, depending on the variety. These bulbs thrive even in heavy clay soil, but they do need full sun. Zones 5–8.

▶ **Checkered lilies (*Fritillaria meleagris*).** The flowers look like upside-down tulips on 12- to 15-inch stems, and they really are checkered, in either white or green against a base color that ranges from light purple to almost black. (There's also an all-white version called *F. meleagris* 'Alba'.) Checkered lilies bloom in midspring; they like shade, and soil that's evenly moist. Zones 4–8.

▶ **Snowdrops (*Galanthus*).** Bell-shaped white flowers bloom in very early spring on 4- to 10-inch stems. They prefer moist, shady sites, but will tolerate sun. Zones 3–8.

FLEA BEETLES

THIS IS THEIR LIFE

Adult flea beetles spend the winter in weeds and garden litter. At the first hint of warm weather, they wake up—hungry, of course. After eating for several weeks, the females lay tiny white eggs just under the soil at the base of target plants. About a week later, the larvae hatch, feed on roots for two to three weeks, then pupate. After another 12 days or so, they join their parents at the upstairs salad bar.

ALSO ON THE MENU

Flea beetles also bounce around in the vegetable garden. Most healthy plants can survive an attack and go on to produce a bumper harvest. The one exception is eggplant, which often doesn't recover. Here, your best bet is to cover the transplants with floating row covers when you set them into the garden, and keep them under wraps until the plants start to bloom.

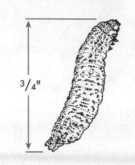

1/16" – 1/8"

3/4"

In early spring, just when the first flowers and veggies are poking their shoots above ground, flea beetles hop out of nowhere and start munching. Although a big crowd of the little monsters can kill a young plant, the real problem isn't so much the itty-bitty holes they chew in the leaves. It's the nasty and incurable diseases that they spread in the process (see "Nix the Nasty Side Effects" on page 118 for tips on battling bug-spread viruses). There are many species of flea beetles. They're all so tiny that you can hardly see them, but you'll know it when they're on your plants: Every time you go near them, they bounce up like tiny, black rubber balls.

🌿 The Nose Knows

Or does it? Flea beetles find their targets by scent, and most of the beetles are host-specific (which means they focus on a particular kind of plant). That gives you an easy way to keep the tiny twerps out of your flower garden: Forget beds, or even long swaths of only one kind of plant. Instead, go for a crazy-quilt mixture—the more, the merrier. Those itty-bitty beetles will be so confused by all of the different smells that they'll just give up and go elsewhere for dinner.

🌿 Wash 'Em Off

Flea beetles don't like water one little bit, so at the first sign of trouble, give your plants a good blast from the garden hose. If that doesn't do the trick, up the ante with Grandma Putt's Simple Soap Spray (see page 86) or, in case of severe invasion, my Tomato-Leaf Tonic (below).

Home on the Range

Flea Beetles

little louses leap to their death. Just set out either yellow sticky traps (see page 287) or shallow pans filled with cheap beer. Either way, the teeny-tiny terrors will die happy!

Play to Their Weaknesses

Flea beetles have two big weaknesses: beer and the color yellow. That gives you two easy options for making the

Up the Creek with a Paddle

If you get a real kick out of stalking tiny game, as I do, then foil flea beetles with my favorite low-tech weaponry: a pair of sticky paddles. Just get two 2-inch-wide wooden strips about 3 feet long, and staple a sheet of 10-by-12-inch cardboard (the color doesn't matter) to an end of each one to create paddles. Coat the paper with petroleum jelly, or spray it with a commercial stickum like Tanglefoot®, so it's good and gooey. Then, hold a paddle on each side of a beetle-ridden plant, and gently jiggle the plant with your foot. As the flea beetles leap off the leaves, they'll land on the paddles. Then just drop the beetle-encrusted paddles into the trash.

THUG BUSTER

Tomato-Leaf Tonic

Our ancestors thought tomatoes were poisonous, so they avoided them like the plague. Fortunately for us, flea beetles still do. Just spray your plants' leaves with this timely tonic, and kiss your flea-beetle battles good-bye!

2 cups of tomato leaves, chopped
1 qt. of water
¹/₂ tsp. of dishwashing liquid

Put the leaves and water in a pan, and bring the water to a simmer. Then turn off the heat, and let the mixture cool. Strain out the leaves, and add the dishwashing liquid to the water. Pour the solution into a hand-held sprayer, and spritz your plants from top to bottom. This potent potion also repels whiteflies, asparagus beetles, and cabbage-worms. (Like all repellent sprays, though, you need to reapply this tonic after every rain.)

🌿 Wonderful Woodies

Wormwood (*Artemisia absinthium*) and southernwood (*A. abrotanum*) are beautiful, gray-leaved perennials that add pizzazz to any flower garden, especially as a backdrop for colorful flowers. But these winners have more going for them than just good looks: They keep flea beetles away in mighty multitudes, so be sure to plant these handsome helpers in your garden.

🌿 How Catty Can You Get?

Flea beetles hate catnip as much as, if not more than, our feline friends love it. But you don't have to plant a patch of the invasive stuff to send the foul felons fleeing. Just steep a cup or so of dried leaves (available in pet stores, herb shops, and many supermarkets) in a quart of water for 10 minutes, and strain out the solids. Then pour the brew into a hand-held sprayer, and thoroughly spritz your plants. The foul felons will feed in farther fields.

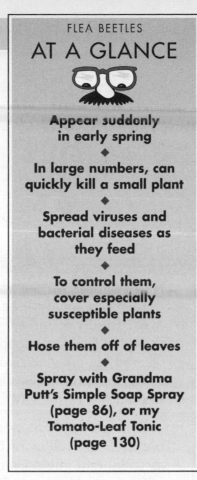

FLEA BEETLES
AT A GLANCE

Appear suddenly in early spring

◆

In large numbers, can quickly kill a small plant

◆

Spread viruses and bacterial diseases as they feed

◆

To control them, cover especially susceptible plants

◆

Hose them off of leaves

◆

Spray with Grandma Putt's Simple Soap Spray (page 86), or my Tomato-Leaf Tonic (page 130)

🌿 Keep Up Their Strength

Like many pesky pests, flea beetles tend to zero in on weak or stressed-out plants. So make sure your annuals and perennials get just the right amounts of food and water (not too much and not too little).

🌿 Homebodies at Heart

To say that a happy plant is a pest-free plant would be going a tad too far. But a plant that's growing in the conditions it likes best, including temperature range, soil type, rainfall, and light level, is likely to stand its ground against flea beetles and many other bad-guy bugs. So how do you find these happy campers? It's simple: Before you buy new plants or seeds, read the catalog descriptions carefully, peruse a regional gardening book, or (best of all) ask local gardeners what stands up best to pests in their yards. Don't struggle to make a home for whatever strikes your fancy in a catalog. That'll be an exercise in frustration for you—and a boon for flea beetles and their pals!

In late summer, Fraulein Four-line cuts a slit near the top of a bramble cane or a tender shoot of a tree or shrub. Inside, she deposits a cluster of eggs. The nymphs hatch in mid- to late spring, find their way to a choice target plant, and start right in sipping. It takes them about 30 days to mature into adult bugs that (of course) keep right on drinking for another month or so before laying eggs of their own, then dying. There is just one generation per year.

Four-lined plant bugs sink their mouths into just about every kind of plant, including vegetables, fruit bushes, and ornamental trees and shrubs. These bottomless pits even drain the juices from mint and basil, which send other pests scurrying. The good news is that the control options offered in the next few pages will work right across the menu.

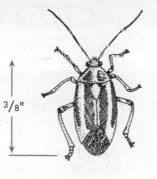

3/8"

These little demons (adults and nymphs both) operate by inserting their needle-sharp mouthparts into leaves and buds and sucking out the chlorophyll. Unless you see them, you could easily mistake the damage for a dastardly disease. The symptoms vary somewhat from one type of victim to another; but generally, in the early stages of an attack, you'll see discolored, usually round spots on young foliage. Later, the spots turn into depressions, followed by holes where the damaged tissue has dropped out. In most cases, these bugs attack the topmost leaves first and work their way down the plant.

The perpetrators of all this ugliness are soft-bodied bugs, yellow or bright yellow-green with—as you might guess from the name—four black stripes running down their backs. The tiny nymphs (just 1/12 inch long) look like brightly colored dots in shades of orange-yellow to red.

🖋 Know the Enemy

Four-lined plant bugs are often confused with their cousins, tarnished plant bugs. Their diets are similar, and so are their body shapes. But their coloration is different. Tarnished bugs have a mottled brown, yellow, and black pattern on their bodies that, from a distance, gives them the look of tarnished metal. The damage is different, too. When the tarnished troops are on the scene, you'll see distorted foliage or disbudded plants in early spring. (For the full scoop on these troublemakers, see Chapter 6.)

Tasty Treats

Home on the Rango

Four-Lined Plant Bugs

Almost no annuals or perennials are safe from these colorful cranksters, but some are more at risk than others. The four-lined four-star picks for good eatin' include chrysanthemums, coreopsis, dahlias, geraniums, lupine, morning glories, phlox, poppies, snapdragons, Shasta daisies, and zinnias.

The Whites of Their Eyes

Four-lined plant bugs are drawn to the color (or noncolor) white. To take advantage of that quirk, just gather up a bunch of tops from cottage cheese or sour cream cartons and coat them with petroleum jelly, or spray them with a commercial bug-trapping compound like Tanglefoot®. Then tuck these traps among the foliage of your troubled plants, and watch the little lined louses leap to their demise!

Spring into Action

In small numbers, four-lined plant bugs don't do much damage, and natural predators can keep the situation well in hand. But a big crowd of the felons can overwhelm their enemy forces and wipe out whole beds of plants. So keep a close watch on your flowers (and herbs, too) in May and June, and if the varmints start moving in, strike back fast. If you're Johnny-on-the-spot, they won't get more than a nibble or two. Well, hardly more.

Bug Away Spray

This timely tonic will issue a death warrant to four-lined plant bugs and other foul felons who are fussin' around with your favorite flowers (or any other plants).

1 cup of Murphy's Oil Soap®
1 cup of antiseptic mouthwash
1 cup of tobacco tea*

Mix these ingredients in a 20 gallon hose-end sprayer and soak your plants to the point of run-off.

*To make tobacco tea, wrap half a handful of chewing tobacco in an old nylon stocking and soak it in a gallon of hot water until the mixture is dark brown. Pour the liquid into a glass container with a tight lid for storage.

THUG BUSTER

Early Does It

Like a great many bugs (and a great many of us humans), the four-lined forces are a tad slow to get going in the morning. So, at the first sign of trouble, rouse yourself out of bed early, and get out there and handpick the pesky pests. I've found that the easiest way is to just brush them off the plants into a pail of soapy water.

A Clean Sweep

If you prefer a more automated approach, swoop the pests right off the foliage with a hand-held vacuum cleaner, then empty the contents into a bucket of soapy water. For plants that can handle slightly stronger suction, you can use a wet/dry vacuum cleaner with about 2 inches of soapy water in the reservoir.

DID YOU KNOW?

We tend to call any six-legged critter a "bug," but in reality, a true bug is a particular type of insect. The babies hatch from eggs, looking like miniature adults, and as they feed, they get bigger and bigger, molting their way to maturity. True bugs have sharp, beaklike mouthparts that they use to chew into leaves and suck out plant juices. In the process, they often inject a toxin that causes small dead patches to develop around the bites. Some true bugs, like four-lined plant bugs and squash bugs, are truly bad. But others, like assassin bugs, big-eyed bugs, and damsel bugs, are garden-variety heroes. You can read about some of these good guys in Chapter 8.

Liquid Alternatives

In the case of a massive invasion, collect about ½ cup of the four-liners, and blend them into a batch of my Beetle Juice (see page 53). Or, if you've got no time for whirling bugs in a blender, whip up a batch of my Bug Away Spray (see page 133). Then take aim with your hose-end sprayer, and fire away. Those bugs'll bite the dust!

That's It Egg-zactly

In fall and winter, inspect your shrubs, trees, and bramble bushes (including roses) very closely. If you see neat, clean slits near the tops of twigs or canes, you can bet there are eggs in there just biding their time until spring. Simply clip them off and drop them in a bucket of water laced with about a cup of rubbing alcohol. If you do a thorough de-egging job, you won't be facing any four-lined felons anytime soon!

They're Not Particular

Four-lined future mamas slice into a lot of weedy plants, too. Of course, you don't want to go scouting them for eggs—you want to wipe out those weeds entirely! Besides depriving four-lined bugs of their maternity wards, you'll be leaving no room at the inn for a lot of other bad-guy bugs.

All in the Family

Four-lined plant bugs have some big-time enemies among their own buggy clan, including big-eyed bugs, damsel bugs, and minute pirate bugs. The little pirates will flock to your aid if you plant yarrow or any kind of daisies. The other two good guys go gaga over any kind of low-growing groundcover that will give them shelter from their own enemies.

And Stay Out!

If four-lined plant bugs just can't get enough of your tasty plants, reach for either my Rhubarb Pest-Repellent Tonic (see page 361) or Bug Away Spray (see page 133). Both of these big guns say a loud, clear "Scram!" to some of the most persistent pests on the planet.

FOUR-LINED PLANT BUGS
AT A GLANCE

Both nymphs and adults drain chlorophyll from many plants

◆

Brown spots appear on foliage and later drop out, leaving small holes

◆

Usually, damage first appears in mid- to late spring

◆

Only one generation appears each year

◆

To control them, handpick and drown in soapy water

◆

Spray with my Hot Bug Brew (page 19)

THIS IS THEIR LIFE

There are many species of mealybugs, and their life cycles vary. Some types give birth to live young. In other species, the female lays eggs, which she carries in an ovisac (egg sac) until they hatch and scurry off to find feeding sites of their own. In cold-winter areas, there are usually one or two generations per year. In warmer climates, or in greenhouses, the little fiends crank out babies all year long.

ALSO ON THE MENU

Although in northern climes mealybugs are most famous for the damage they do in sunrooms and home greenhouses, they also target a wide range of outdoor plants of all types, including ivy, roses, apples, peaches, grapes, blueberries, and even potatoes. In warmer zones or in protected quarters, anything goes, but azaleas, hibiscus, and citrus trees of all sorts are prime targets.

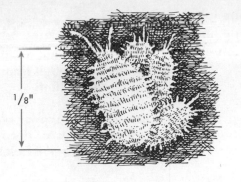

1/8"

These tiny suckers drain the juices from plants, making them lose their get-up-and-grow power. You'll most often see them massed on leaves or stems, looking like little piles of dirty cotton. They leave other clues to their presence, too, namely a white, fluffy wax lodged in leaf axils or between twining stems (their egg cases), and sticky, gooey honeydew on leaves and stems (see "Coulda Fooled Me," on page 137). Individually, they're soft-bodied, grayish or pinkish insects about 1/8 inch long or smaller.

A close relative, the root mealybug, targets the roots of container plants, both indoors and out. Its favorite victims are cacti and other succulents; but geraniums, ferns, fuchsias, and African violets are high-risk targets, too. When this underground menace is at work, you'll see a white, waxy powder covering the plant's roots and soil particles, as well as spying the bugs themselves.

🍃 One on One

If the plant is small, or you catch the invasion in its early stages, go head to head with the little pests. Just dab each one with a cotton swab dipped in rubbing alcohol, and it'll bite the dust instantly.

🍃 A Nice, Hot Shower

No patience for hand-to-bug combat? Just heat some water to between 120° and 150°F, pour it into a hand-held sprayer, and spritz your plants from top to bottom. You'll cook the little suckers in their tracks.

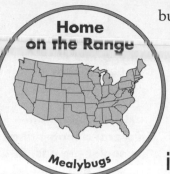

Home on the Range

Mealybugs

🍃 Heavier Fire Power

For heavier infestations, give the rascals a good dose of my Instant Insecticide (see page 152). But don't dawdle—you want to get the mealy-

bugs off of your plants before sooty mold has a chance to form on their honeydew (see "Coulda Fooled Me!", below).

🍃 Smoke Gets in Their Eyes

If you smoke or know someone who does, you can send mealybugs to the gas chamber with this simple trick. Just put a plastic bag over the bug-infested plant, and blow cigarette smoke into the bag, or have a smoker do the honors. Then quickly seal up

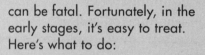

Coulda Fooled ME!

Your plant looks sick, all right. The leaves are covered with papery, black or dark gray patches that you can peel right off. It's sooty mold, and it develops on the honeydew produced by mealybugs and other sap-sucking insects. It occurs most often in hot, humid weather. Although it's a condition of the bugs' honeydew and not a plant disease, it can cause big-time trouble because it blocks the leaves' access to light, and sometimes clogs up the pores (*stomata* in scientific lingo) that let water and oxygen pass through the plant tissue. If it's left untreated long enough, it

can be fatal. Fortunately, in the early stages, it's easy to treat. Here's what to do:

■ **Wipe.** If there's not too much of it, just wipe the leaves gently with a cloth dipped in warm water.

■ **Spray.** For larger outbreaks, haul out the garden hose, and blast the plants with water.

■ **Spray again.** To get any malingering pests, spray again, this time with Grandma Putt's Simple Soap Spray (see page 86).

the bag. That's the end of the fuzzy bugs. This trick also works on other tiny terrors like aphids, whiteflies, and spider mites.

🍃 Out with the Old

When root mealybugs gang up on a container plant, whisk the victim out of its pot and give the roots a good, thorough washing in mild, soapy water. Just make sure you get *all* the soil off! Rinse them well, then repot the plant in fresh soil and a clean, new container. Then send the infested soil as far away from your plants as you can.

🍃 No Encore Performances

Before you reuse any pot that's hosted root mealybugs, wash it in a solution of 1 part household bleach to 8 parts hot water. And, just to play it extra-safe, use that container only for plants that are not root mealybug targets.

🍃 Hey, Lady!

Ladybugs *love* mealybugs. Generally, these superheroes will throng to your aid as long as you don't use

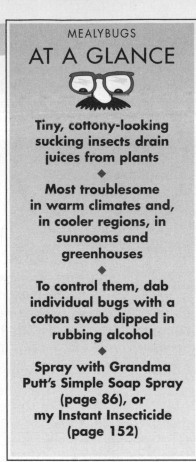

MEALYBUGS
AT A GLANCE

Tiny, cottony-looking sucking insects drain juices from plants

◆

Most troublesome in warm climates and, in cooler regions, in sunrooms and greenhouses

◆

To control them, dab individual bugs with a cotton swab dipped in rubbing alcohol

◆

Spray with Grandma Putt's Simple Soap Spray (page 86), or my Instant Insecticide (page 152)

pesticides. But if you have a greenhouse or sunroom, and mealybugs are coming out of the woodwork, er, glasswork, you might want to invest in a special type of ladybug known as the mealybug destroyer. The adults look just like any garden-variety ladybug, but the larvae resemble giant mealybugs. And both generations gobble up the little sap-suckers like there's no tomorrow. You can order these wonder workers from catalogs or over the Internet. Just type the scientific name into your favorite search engine. It's *Cryptolaemus montrouzieri*.

🍃 A Strong Bench

When it comes to winning the game against mealybugs, ladybugs aren't the only heavy hitters around. Green lacewings and predatory wasps will also play on your mealybug-busting team if you give them a chance. (See Chapter 8 for the lowdown on recruitment bonuses.)

ROSE CHAFERS

THIS IS THEIR LIFE

Adult chafers appear in late May through early June and mate almost instantly. Then they start right in eating and reproducing. The females lay two to three dozen eggs at a time, one batch after another, for about two weeks, usually in lawns or other grassy areas with sandy soil. The eggs hatch in about two weeks, and the larvae tunnel into the soil and start munching on roots. They spend the winter in the soil and emerge, all grown up, the following spring.

ALSO ON THE MENU

Except for roses and peonies, rose chafers love grapevines above all else. They're also partial to raspberries, strawberries, hydrangeas, and both ornamental and fruit trees. Among those last victims, apple, crabapple, cherry, and peach trees are special favorites. No matter where the chafers are dining, the tips here will help you close the restaurant.

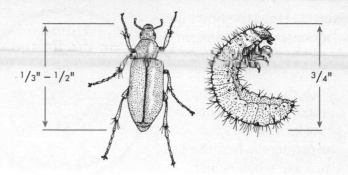

$1/3" - 1/2"$ $3/4"$

Don't let the name fool you: Rose chafers do attack their namesake plants, but they also target many others. In the flower garden, peonies, irises, dahlias, and hollyhocks are special favorites. The chafers' dirty work looks just like that of Japanese beetles, but once you've seen the culprits themselves, there's no chance of mistaken identity: Chafers are reddish brown, with black undersides and wings covered with thick, yellowish hairs. They're smaller than their Japanese cousins, too, and they have much longer legs. But if they're left unchecked, they're just as lethal.

Rose chafers appear suddenly in late spring or early summer, feast for three to four weeks, then vanish as quickly as they came. They cause major trouble only in years when their population skyrockets. But if you don't send 'em packin' pronto, they'll eat you out of house and garden!

🌿 Into the Drink

Rose chafers eat fast, but they move slowly, which makes 'em prime candidates for mass drowning. Here's all you need to do:

Step 1. Fill a wide bowl with water, and add in a few drops of dishwashing liquid (just to break the surface tension).

Step 2. Hold the bowl under a chafer-infested plant and jostle the foliage; the pests will tumble into the soapy water and drown. (This tactic works best on cool mornings, when the beetles are still sleepy.)

Home on the Range

Rose Chafers

A Taste of Their Own

In the case of a full-scale invasion, don't waste a minute: Blend those chafers into a batch of my Beetle Juice, and spray the plants from top to bottom. (See page 53 for the basic recipe.)

Swoosh!

Their slow, meandering gait also makes chafers great targets for your handy dandy wet/dry vacuum cleaner. Just fill the reservoir with an inch or two of soapy water, then reach out with the nozzle, and swoosh—those bugs will be history! To clean the pests off of more delicate plants, use a hand-held vacuum cleaner with more gentle suction.

Make 'Em Smell Trouble

If you spot the invasion in its early stages, just pick the chafers off the plants, drop them into a jar of soapy water, and screw on the lid. When you're sure the nogoodniks are dead, remove the lid and set the jar on the ground among your beleaguered plants. (The more soap-and-chafer-filled jars you come up with, the better.) The sight—or, more likely, smell—of their decomposing comrades will make the chafers go elsewhere for dinner.

All Juiced Up

If the thought of handling beetle bodies, dead or alive, makes you cringe, here's a more pleasant plan: Lure the chafers to their death with an aroma they can't resist—the ultrasweet smell of decaying fruit. Just fill some jars

GRANDMA KNEW BEST

Nowadays, every garden center sells floating row covers made from lightweight, spun fabric; but back in Grandma Putt's day, that sort of high-tech garden gear didn't exist. So when she wanted to keep rose chafers or other pesky pests away from her plants, she used old, sheer window curtains. I still keep a stash of them on hand for emergency coverup jobs.

about halfway with water, drop in some chunks of over-the-hill fruit (any kind will do), and set the jars on the ground among your plants. The hungry hordes will hurry on over for a snack, and fall right in.

Are Those Candy Canes I Smell?

If you'd prefer a weapon that appeals more to *your* sense of smell, just whip up a batch of my Peppermint Soap Spray (see page 41). Then take aim and fire. The peppermint will cut right through the chafers' hard shells, and they'll fall down dead.

Pull Up the Covers

Chafers strike at the peak of the blooming season, when the last thing you want to do is cover up your ornamental flower beds and rose bushes. But in a hardworking cutting garden or vegetable patch, it's a different story. There, your surest defense is to cover your plants with floating row covers at the first sign of the pesky pests.

Color Them Gone

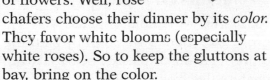

Most pesky pests prefer to munch on certain *kinds* of flowers. Well, rose chafers choose their dinner by its *color*. They favor white blooms (especially white roses). So to keep the gluttons at bay, bring on the color.

Ask Jerry

Every time I find white grubs in my lawn or flower beds, I compare them to pictures in books to see what kind they are—but they all look alike! Is there any way to tell the difference?

There is, but it takes a trained eye and a strong magnifying glass. You need to examine the anal opening, which is shaped differently in each type of grub. And I don't think you really want to do that—I know I sure don't! The same control methods work on all white grubs, but if you really want to know what you're dealing with, catch a few of the rascals, and put them in a jar of rubbing alcohol. Then take them to the entomology department of the closest university. The bug gurus there will give you a positive I.D.

Head 'Em Off

If your only rose chafer problems are in the flower garden, just dig down deep into the soil, where the babies (a.k.a. grubs) spend the winter. You'll expose the grubs to the elements—and to hungry birds. Bigger problems call for broader action: If the grubs have moved into your lawn, treat it with beneficial nematodes. (For the lowdown on white grubs, see Chapter 1.)

Call Out the Hired Guns

Beneficial nematodes will kill rose chafer grubs, or any other kind, in the blink of an eye. Timing is crucial, though: You need to apply the nematodes in spring or fall, when the larvae are in the upper layers of the soil. In the winter, they're down too deep for the good little guys to reach them.

Don't Cry Wolf

Many spiders are effective predators of rose chafers and other bad-guy beetles. So if you find these multilegged munchers in your flower garden, don't chase them away. Wolf spiders are especially good gobblers. They're ground dwellers, so you

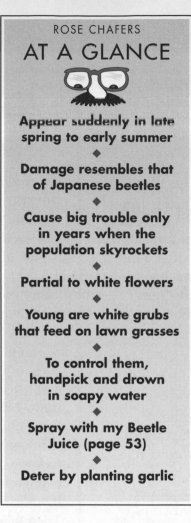
won't see them spinning webs as other spiders do. Instead, you'll probably find them snuggled under the mulch in your flower bed, or basking in the sun on the soil's surface. There are about 100 kinds of wolf spiders in North America, and they're all thin, long-legged (even for spiders), and dark-colored, with long, dark and pale stripes on their bodies.

The Resistance Movement

In a bad year, rose chafers can demolish a fruit crop; so if you're thinking of planting fruit trees, bramble fruits, or grape vines (all favorite menu items), look for resistant varieties. Your Cooperative Extension Service or a nursery that specializes in fruit plants can recommend good candidates for your area.

They'll Pass Right By

No matter what kind of plants you grow, give them protection by planting onions, garlic, or parsley nearby. Rose chafers flee from all of these.

SCALE

THIS IS THEIR LIFE

Some scale insects lay their eggs inside protective shells on leaves, stems, or twigs. Others deposit eggs mixed with white, waxy fibers that cling to the plant. When the eggs hatch, the tiny larvae, called crawlers, scamper around until they find feeding sites. Sometimes, they stay on their birth plant, but often they walk or get blown by the wind to a new one. Once they've grown up, mated, and settled in, most species never budge again. Outdoors in cool regions, there is one generation per year. Indoors, or in warm climates, breeding may go on all year long.

ALSO ON THE MENU

Almost no plant is off-limits to scale. Various species attack shrubs, trees, fruit plants, and sometimes even vegetables. With the tips in the next few pages, you can get the suckers wherever they're dining.

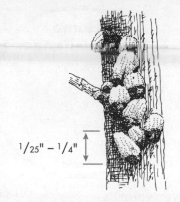

1/25" – 1/4"

Scale insects are most famous for sucking sap from plants in greenhouses and on windowsills, but they can get up to just as much mischief outdoors in the flower garden. When you see little waxy shells (a.k.a. scales) on stems and leaves, you'll know that underneath these protective covers, the tiny insects are hard at work. As their job progresses, yellow spots will appear on foliage, and leaves may drop off. Eventually, the whole plant turns sickly and stunted.

Like other sap-suckers, scale insects leave another bit of nastiness behind: a sugary sap called honeydew that attracts nuisance pests like ants and bees. Even worse, though, the sweet, sticky stuff is a breeding ground for a fungus called sooty mold, which clogs plants' pores and prevents air and water from passing through. Left untreated, it can cause more damage than the pests themselves (see "Coulda Fooled Me," on page 137).

✐ Too Bad, But…

When scale insects gang up on annual flowers, your best bet is to dig those plants out of the ground, or pull them out of their pots and destroy them—*yesterday!* (Don't even think of throwing them on the compost pile.) Otherwise, before you know it, your whole garden could look like a shell collection. Then, just to be safe, wash any containers the victims were growing in, using a solution of 1 part household bleach to 8 parts hot water.

🌿 Clip and Toss

Cut off infested stems of bulbs and perennials (even if it means chopping the whole plant to the ground), and send the trimmings off with the trash. If parts of the plant seem unscathed by scale, it's okay to leave them, but cover your bets by spraying the leaves and stems every three days for two weeks with my Super Scale Spray (below). It'll kill any of the critters that you might have overlooked.

🌿 Ah! That's the Rub!

Rubbing alcohol is instant death to scale insects. If you catch the invasion

Home on the Range

Scale

in the *very* early stages, all you need to do is dip a cotton ball or swab in rubbing alcohol and dab each pesky pest separately.

🌿 Test First

Before you use my Super Scale Spray (below) or any other alcohol spray on an entire plant, test it on a few leaves. Then wait 24 hours, and check for damage. Some plants are supersensitive to alcohol, and if you act too quickly, you could end up killing the pests *and* the victim!

🌿 Strike Oil

Oil will slither right into a scale's shell and smother the tiny bug and any eggs that may be waiting to hatch. You can buy horticultural oil at any garden center, but there's no need to bother: Just mix up a batch of my Oil's-Well-That-Ends-Well Mix (see page 361), and spray your scale-stricken plants from top to bottom. This terrific tonic works at any time of year, weather permitting (see "Whether the Weather," on page 145), but it's an especially effective preventive medicine for deciduous trees and shrubs.

THUG BUSTER

Super Scale Spray

This double-barreled potion works two ways: The soap kills the unprotected scale babies (a.k.a. crawlers), and the alcohol cuts right through the grown-ups' waxy shells.

1 cup of rubbing alcohol
1 tbsp. of dishwashing liquid
1 qt. of water

Mix these ingredients in a hand-held sprayer, and treat your scale-stricken plants every three days for two weeks. The scale will sail off into the sunset.

Just apply it in late winter, when the plants are still dormant and the bugs are sound asleep. They'll never wake up!

🍃 Whether the Weather

Oil-based sprays, like my Oil's-Well-That-Ends-Well Mix (see page 361), are potent weapons in the fight against scale and scads of other bad-guy bugs. The only problem is that in hot, humid weather, they can burn plant tissues, sometimes with fatal results. So how do you know when it's safe to spray? Just remember this rule: Anytime the temperature (in degrees Fahrenheit) plus the relative humidity equals 140 or above, either use a Thug Buster with no oil in it or wait for a cooler, drier day.

🍃 An A-Peeling Solution

This simple scale-icide is gentle enough for almost any plant, and you don't even have to check the temperature. I call it my Go-Go Glue Trap, and here's all you need to do: Just mix an 8-ounce bottle of white glue, such as

SCALE
AT A GLANCE

Sap-sucking insects attack just about every kind of plant

◆

Drain juices from foliage, leaving plants weakened and often stunted

◆

Secrete honeydew, on which sooty mold often forms

◆

To control them, dab individual scale insects with rubbing alcohol

◆

Use my Go-Go Glue Trap (below) for larger infestations

◆

Kill newly hatched larvae with my Hot Bug Brew (page 19)

Elmer's®, with 2 gallons of warm water. Pour the mixture into a hand-held sprayer, and spray all the stems and leaves of your plagued plant. The scale will be caught in the glue, and when it dries, it'll flake right off, taking the scale with it.

🍃 They're Not Crawlin' Anymore!

The minute they hatch, baby scale insects start scampering all over the place. That's when you can put a big dent in the future population with this simple trick. Just put rings of double-faced tape around several of your shrub's branches. (Fold over a little tab at the end so you can pull it off easily.) As little hatchlings bounce around, they'll be caught on the sticky stuff. Check your mini-traps every couple of days (you'll see what look like specks of gray dust), and replace them.

Your little tape traps won't catch all the crawlers (there are zillions of 'em), so it's good to have a backup plan. The best one I know of is my Hot Bug Brew (see page 19). It'll give those babies a spicy send-off to you-know-where!

SPIDER MITES

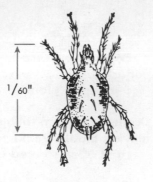

1/60"

The life cycle varies some-what depend-ing on the species, but like all mites, the spider mites reproduce with the speed of light (or so it seems). In general, adults spend the winter under loose tree bark or garden litter, or in cracks in the soil. In the spring, they emerge and the females lay eggs that hatch in five to seven days, grow up in a flash, and lay more eggs. Depending on the weather, there may be as many as 10 overlapping generations per year.

Many kinds of mites attack trees and shrubs (see Rust Mites in Chap-ter 3), and spider mites terrorize the vegetable garden. The same tricks you see in this section will save your food crops, too. And here's one more tip: If you grow tomatoes (and who doesn't?), plant plenty of radishes among them—the spider mites will spin their webs elsewhere.

These all-but-invisible spider relatives suck juices from plants, causing them to look dull and unhealthy and lose their get-up-and-grow power. In the case of severe attacks, which usually occur in hot, dry weather, the victims often die. You can't see the little varmints without a strong magnifying glass, but you can't miss their trail of clues. You'll see what looks like angel hair clinging to leaves and stems, and foliage that's pale, wilted, or covered with yellow-ish specks. If you want even more evidence, just hold a piece of white paper under your stricken plant and jostle a leaf or stem. Down will tumble what look like specks of dust or pepper—and they'll be moving.

Because spider mites are some of the most common garden pests in the world, they've long been bombarded by chemical pesticides. As a result, they've become immune to many of them.

🌿 Don't Give 'Em an Aphrodisiac

Nearly all of the plants that suffer from severe spider mite attacks have one thing in common: They've been repeatedly sprayed with chemical pesticides of one kind or another. The result? First, these potent potions kill off the mites' natural enemies, of which they have many (see page 148). Second (and this is sobering, folks), scientific studies show that not only have mites become immune to many pesticides, but when they're exposed to some of these chemicals, namely carbaryl and parathion, they reproduce even faster than usual! That's why you should stick to homemade repellents like the ones in this section.

Home on the Range

Spider Mites

Brrrr!

Once spider mites get a toe-hold, they can be the dickens to get rid of, so don't waste any time. Haul out the garden hose, and give the tiny tykes a cold shower. (Do the job early in the morning, before the sun has a chance to heat up the hose.) Or, if your plants are small, just fill a hand-held sprayer with ice water, and let 'er rip.

Water the Ground, Too

During dry spells, or if you live in an arid part of the country, sprinkle water on dirt pathways and other bare ground to keep dust to a minimum. There's nothing spider mites love more than dry, dusty spots, so this will help keep the population down.

Beyond H₂O

If the invasion has progressed beyond the blast-'em-off stage, don't worry: You have plenty of mighty anti-mite options to choose from. One of the best is my Go-Go Glue Trap (see "An A-Peeling Solution," on page 145).

Two for the Money

My Amazing Ammonia Antidote (below) gives you two good things for the price of one. Not only does it kill spider mites on contact, but it also delivers a mild dose of nitrogen to your plants. So what are you waiting for? Mix up a batch, and have at it!

THUG BUSTER

Amazing Ammonia Antidote

This fabulous formula is a powerful mite killer and mild fertilizer all rolled into one.

1 tsp. of dishwashing liquid
2 tsp. of ammonia
2 gal. of water

Mix these ingredients together, and pour the solution into a hand-held sprayer. Spray your beleaguered plants every five days for three weeks, and you'll moan over mites no more!

✍ Blast!

When the tiny terrors are draining the life from your plants, my Mite-Free Fruit Tree Formula (see page 92) will stop them in their tracks. It's harmless to most good guys, but don't take any chances: Before you pull the trigger on your sprayer, make sure that only spider mites are within firing range.

✍ Mitey Fine Eatin'

Many birds—and hordes of good-guy bugs, including ladybugs, damsel bugs, big-eyed bugs, and firefly larvae (a.k.a. glowworms)—eat spider mites. All you need to do to invite the gang to dinner is provide food and shelter in the form of annuals, perennials, trees, and

shrubs. (For more about the good guys, see Chapter 8.)

✍ Mighty Mites

Like their bad-guy cousins, predatory mites are so tiny that you can hardly see them without a magnifying glass. But the damage they do to spider mites is anything *but* tiny. Unlike most beneficial insects, predatory mites are not easy to lure to your garden, so if you need their help, buy a posse of 'em. Some kinds are hardy and will stay on and reproduce anywhere; others survive winter only in the South. Catalogs and garden centers generally sell a mixture of types, so no matter where you live, you're almost guaranteed to have their protection year after year.

SPITTLEBUGS

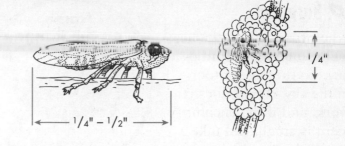

In early summer, if your plants' stems suddenly sport what look globs of spit, there's no mistaking the crude culprits: spittlebugs. These little guys with big, bad manners spew out a frothy mass of foam to protect themselves while they suck the sap from your plants. Eventually, the tiny greenish or yellowish suckers grow up to become small brown, black, or tan insects called froghoppers. Aside from producing crude offspring, froghoppers are harmless and so shy that you'll probably never notice them. The nymphs are another story. While they'll never make the Most Unwanted List of garden villains, their sucking sprees can stunt the growth of plants and reduce the size of flowers and fruit (see "Also on the Menu," at left), and leaves often become wrinkled and darker than usual. But aside from all that, who wants that disgusting spit all over a flower garden? Not me, that's for sure!

Now You See 'Em, Now You Don't

Have you noticed that some years, there are so many spittlebugs around that your plants seem to be taking a bubblebath, and other years, there's hardly a speck of foam anywhere? Well, there's a reason for that: Spittlebugs are closely related to cicadas, and big population swings tend to run in the family.

🍃 Surprise!

A quick blast from the hose will usually send spittle-bugs to the big spittoon in the sky. If that doesn't work, and if the encampment is small, just take a damp cloth and wipe away the frothy stuff, bugs and all.

🍃 A Stronger Message

If that gentle hint doesn't send the rascals packing, spritz your spat-upon plants with Grandma Putt's Simple Soap Spray (see page 86). Make three applications, every three to five days,

Home on the Range

Spittlebugs

and those baby hoppers will soon be history.

🍃 Declare War on Weeds

Spittlebugs tend to target gardens that are bordered by weedy fields or that (heaven forbid!) have become invaded by weeds. So pull up those unlovely plants—especially ones close to your flower beds. To rout really stubborn so-and-so's, mix up a batch of my Weed Wipeout (at left) and let 'em have it. Just be careful not to get the stuff on any of your precious posies!

🍃 An Inside Job

When you're spraying tonics in close quarters like a flower bed, it can be tricky to saturate weeds without getting any of the fatal fluid on plants that you want to keep. But here's an easy way to put the killing power where you want it: First, cut the bottom off of a 1- or 2-liter soda bottle (but save the cap). Then sink the bottle into the soil over your target weed, shove your sprayer nozzle into the bottle neck, and let 'er rip. Finally, screw the cap back on the bottle, and walk away. In a week or so, check back. The weed should be dead as a doornail, but if it's not, give it another blast.

THUG BUSTER

Weed Wipeout

When you've got weeds that won't take no for an answer, knock 'em flat on their backs with this potent potion.

1 tbsp. of gin
1 tbsp. of vinegar
1 tsp. of dishwashing liquid
1 qt. of very warm water

Mix all of these ingredients, and pour the solution into a hand-held sprayer. Then drench the weeds to the point of run-off, taking care not to spray any nearby plants.

STRAWBERRY ROOT WEEVILS

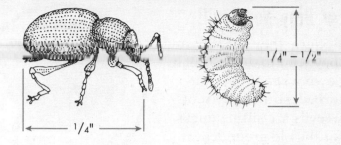

THIS IS THEIR LIFE

Most strawberry root weevil larvae overwinter in the soil, pupate in early spring, and emerge in mid- to late spring. Starting about two weeks later, they deposit eggs around the bases of plants. (All strawberry root weevils are female, so there's no dating-and-mating game to kick off the season.) In high summer—late July and early August in most places—the larvae hatch and start eating. In cold climates, they generally close up shop in early fall, but in milder regions, they often eat right through the winter.

ALSO ON THE MENU

Besides their namesake crop, strawberry root weevils attack the foliage, blossoms, and fruit of raspberries, grapes, apples, and peaches. They also hanker after arborvitae, pine, and spruce seedlings, and they love munching on mint, a plant that sends many other pests packing.

These evil weevils are notorious for the dirty work they do to strawberry plants, but they're just as likely to go after your perennial flowers. They operate on both ends of a plant: The larvae bore into the roots and crowns to feed, and the adults munch on foliage and flowers. They're especially partial to plants with large leaves, or big, many-petaled blooms, such coral bells (*Heuchera*), coreopsis, and all kinds of daisies. It's easy to tell when they've been dining—you'll see half-moon shapes bitten out around the edges. Like other weevils, the grown-ups do their feasting at night. By day, they snooze on the ground, snuggled up in dead leaves and other garden litter.

The adults are shiny, black, hard-shelled weevils, also known as snout beetles. The youngsters are legless grubs with white bodies and brown heads.

Aren't You a Little Early?

Although most strawberry root weevils drop dead at the end of the growing season, some spend the winter in plant debris or other sheltered spots. Then, when they wake up in the spring, they start right in munching. So don't be surprised if you see those half-moon cutouts on your plants much sooner than you expected.

✍ Drop, You Devil!

Because they can't fly, and they tend to drop straight down when they're disturbed, strawberry root weevils are sitting ducks for the old groundcover trick. Just spread an old sheet or other piece of fabric on the ground under your plants. Then, 2 or 3 hours after dark, when the weevils are enjoying a leisurely dinner, go out and jostle the foliage. When the rascals come tumbling down, gather up the cloth and dump the contents into a tub of soapy water.

Home on the Range

Strawberry Root Weevils

✍ Two-Timing Traps

If a nocturnal hunting trip is not your style, the time-honored sticky trap is an easy alternative. Just put bands of cardboard around the stems of your plants, and coat them with petroleum jelly or a commercial stickum like Tanglefoot®. Make sure the bands fit snugly, so the critters can't duck under them. Depending on your timing, you'll

get the weevils on their way up the plant in the evening, or strolling back down in the morning.

✍ Don't Delay— Spray Today

Tonight, rather. When the weevils are on the warpath and there's no time for making traps, arm yourself with a flashlight and a hand-held sprayer filled with my Instant Insecticide (below). Then go out there and get 'em!

✍ Keep It Clean

Strawberry root weevils make themselves right at home in dead plant material of all kinds. So whenever you

---

Instant Insecticide

When there's no time to fumble with fancy formulas, mix up this potent pest potion.* It's instant death to almost any bad bug in the book.

**1 cup of rubbing alcohol
1 tsp. of vegetable oil
1 qt. of water**

Mix all of the ingredients in a hand-held sprayer, take aim, and give each pest a direct hit.

*See "Test First," on page 144.

THUG BUSTER

---

go out to your flower garden, carry along a pair of clippers and a brown paper bag. Then the minute you spot a dead, damaged, or just plain odd-looking plant part, clip it off and drop it into the bag—before it has a chance to fall on the ground and become a weevil motel. When you're through with your rounds, you have two choices: If the stuff that you've collected is healthy, toss it, bag and all, on the compost pile. But if there's any sign of pesky pests or dastardly diseases, dump it into a bucket of soapy water, or send it off with the trash collector.

Wave Good-bye to Weeds

Weeds are prime breeding grounds for weevils and other bad guys. So keep after them with your whacker and your puller. And for really tough customers, reach for my Weed Wipeout (see page 150).

Your Hit Parade

A whole lot of good guys are champing at the bit to get at the strawberry root weevils in your yard. The hit squad includes spiders and a bunch of birds, including bluebirds, warblers, and wrens. For the lowdown on hit-squad hospitality, see Chapter 8.

Bought and Paid For

A paid protection plan is close at hand. Just get a batch of beneficial nematodes from a garden center or catalog, and release them into the soil according to the directions on the package. They'll get the baby weevils before they even wake up.

STRAWBERRY ROOT WEEVILS

AT A GLANCE

Target many kinds of perennials, especially those with large leaves or flowers

◆

Adults eat foliage and flowers at night; by day, they sleep in garden debris on the ground

◆

Larvae bore into roots and crowns to feed

◆

To control them, handpick adults or use sticky traps

◆

Apply beneficial nematodes to kill grubs

◆

Spray with my Instant Insecticide (page 152)

Adult thrips cut slits in plants and deposit eggs inside. The nymphs hatch within days, feed for a week or two, and start laying eggs of their own. Because some kinds of thrips can reproduce without mating, a small annoyance can become a big headache fast! In cold climates, the action stops in the fall with a final batch of eggs that overwinter on the plant. In warm regions, though, the fun just goes on and on.

ALSO ON THE MENU

Although flower thrips comprise the biggest segment of the population, various species attack roses (especially white ones), shrubs, and even cacti. In the vegetable garden, tomatoes, beans, peas, and onions are high-risk targets, but no plant is really safe. You can discourage the little suckers, though: Just hose off the leaves of your crops every three days—thrips hate moisture.

1/50" – 1/25"

If you were to look at a thrip under a microscope, you'd see a black or brown insect with two pairs of heavily fringed wings. The nymphs are creamy yellow and wingless. If you *don't* look at a thrip under a microscope, you'll probably never see one. But you can't miss seeing the evidence of their dastardly deeds. These tiny terrors operate by scraping away a plant's tissue, and then sucking sap from the wound. Damaged leaves take on a silvery sheen. Afflicted flower buds either never open, or unfold covered with odd-colored streaks and speckles. Severe infestations weaken plants and stunt their growth. But wait—that's not all! Some species of thrips spread viruses, and when that happens, there are no happy endings. What's more, because they're so tiny, the vile villains can get into tight places, where sprays can't get to them.

Wicked on White

Flower thrips will go after any annual or perennial in the bed, but they have a special hankering for white flowers. And they love big, lush blooms, like delphiniums, mums, hollyhocks, peonies, and daylilies.

Sing the Blues

Despite their fondness for white flowers, thrips make a beeline to blue traps (go figure). So glue pieces of blue paper to cardboard, spray them with STP® motor-oil additive, and hang or prop them among your plagued posies. Why not use a more potent adhesive? Because the STP is sticky enough to catch the tiny thrips, but light enough that bees and other bigger, stronger good guys can flitter off if they land on the traps.

Home on the Range

Thrips

🌿 Just to Be Sure

If you suspect that thrips are picnicking on your posies, but you want confirm the diagnosis, try this trick. Pluck off a damaged flower, and shake it over a piece of white paper. If tiny, dark specks rain down, and they hit the paper moving, you've fingered your bad guys.

🌿 Clip and Blast

At the first sign of an invasion, clip off the thrip-infested plant parts, and dunk them in soapy water to kill the creeps. Then send any lingering louses flying with a good blast from the garden hose.

So Long, Sucker Spray

This fabulous formula is just the ticket for tiny insects, like thrips and aphids, that are too small for you to handpick and whirl in a blender all by themselves.

THUG BUSTER

2 cups of thrip-infested flowers or leaves*
2 cups of warm water plus 1 gal. of water
Cheesecloth

Put the plant parts in an old blender, and whirl 'em with the 2 cups of warm water (tiny bugs and all). Strain the goop through cheesecloth, dilute with 1 gallon of water, and pour the juice into a hand-held sprayer. Then spray your plants from top to bottom, on both sides of leaves and stems, and along all runners. Repeat the treatment after rain. If you have any extra juice, freeze it right away before bacteria can get a toehold. Be sure to label it clearly—you don't want to have this stuff for dinner! Two notes of caution: Once you've used a blender to make this spray, don't use it again for either human or pet food preparation—ever! And don't make this spray (or any other) from mosquitoes, ticks, or other blood-sucking insects that transmit human and animal diseases.

*Substitute whatever pests are sucking the life out of your plants.

✎ The Blues Revisited

Don't want to fuss with all that sticky stuff? No problem! Just gather some blue containers, like the ones margarine and some chip dips come in, and fill them with soapy water. Then set them on the ground among your plants, and the thrips will fly right in.

✎ Enough Is Enough!

When you've tried everything, and throngs of thriving thrips just keep coming, it's time to cut the mustard—or whatever plants the thugs are ganging up on. To be specific, cut off about 2 cups' worth of damaged flowers and/or leaves. Then, stop the invading hordes dead in their tracks with my So Long, Sucker Spray (see page 155). It's a nightmare come true for thrips, aphids, and other little pests that suck the life out of their victims.

✎ End of Story

To put an end to the thrips' trips once and for all, enlist their enemies. Hordes of helpful predators are itchin'

THRIPS
AT A GLANCE

All but-invisible insects suck sap from foliage and flowers

◆

Afflicted leaves take on a silvery sheen

◆

Flowers either fail to open or unfold covered with odd-colored streaks and speckles

◆

Spread viruses

◆

To control them, catch with blue sticky traps

◆

Spray with my So Long, Sucker Spray (page 155)

◆

Encourage predators

to eat up these tiny, tasty treats. The potential dinner party includes ladybugs, lacewings, damsel bugs, minute pirate bugs, and hover flies, to name just a few. (For more about good guys, see Chapter 8.)

✎ And One More Thing

Anytime thrips have been on the scene, there's a chance that a virus outbreak will follow. So keep an eye out for leaves that are cupped, puckered, or covered with yellow and light green splotches, streaks, and mottled patterns. And in the meantime, cover your bases by giving your plants my Flower and Foliage Flu Shot (see page 361). I have to admit that this drug is still in the experimental stages, but scientists in California have found that juices squeezed from sweet green pepper plants can protect other plants from viruses. At this stage, I can't absolutely guarantee it'll work, but it's worth a shot (sorry, I couldn't resist). For more virus prevention tips, see "Nix the Nasty Side Effects," on page 118.

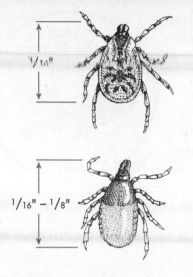

Ticks are actually giant mites, members of the biological order *Acarina*—and the only mites that can be identified without the aid of a microscope. Like female mosquitoes, ticks live on one food alone: blood. Unlike their biting buddies, though, ticks don't restrict their diet to the mammal contingent; some species go gunnin' for reptiles, amphibians, and birds. And, of course, during the dining process, they often spread dreaded diseases like Rocky Mountain spotted fever, Colorado tick fever, and Lyme disease.

Because ticks can't fly, hop, run, or even walk quickly, they spend most of their lives on or near the ground. Then, as dinnertime approaches, they climb up onto a taller plant, fence, or wall, and wait for a suitable target to saunter by. When the right vibrations or smells say, "This is a good one!", they reach out with their front legs and grab on.

🌿 Take That, Ticks!

Because ticks can't fly, they don't leap out at their victims, or zoom at them from the air the way mosquitoes do. Instead, these terrible terrorizers operate in a more subtle way. They just sit there on plants or grasses, and when a human or a four-legged critter brushes by, they

THIS IS THEIR LIFE

There are thousands of species of ticks, but all fall into two categories: hard and soft. (The dog tick shown at top right and the deer tick below it are both hard.) Mating takes place on the body of the host animal (yuck!). Then the female falls to the ground and lays her eggs. Generally, on the hard-tick side of the family, the male dies soon after mating; the female lays a single batch of 10,000 or more eggs, then dies. The softies of both sexes live long enough for several blood feasts, with the female laying from 20 to 50 eggs after each meal. The larvae hatch anywhere from two weeks to several months later.

ALSO ON THE MENU

Although ticks hang out on plants, they don't harm a single one. They live on one food alone: the blood of vertebrates like you, me, our four-footed pals, deer, and deer mice.

simply reach out and cling to whatever they can grab onto—be it fur, clothes, or bare skin. When you're off on a picnic or a hike, they're hard to avoid. Your only defense is to use a tick repellent on yourself and your furry companions. But if ticks have taken up residence on your own turf, kill 'em dead with my Toodle-oo, Tick Spray (below).

Home on the Range

Ticks

Toodle-oo, Tick Spray

THUG BUSTER

Ticks can make life miserable for both humans and pets. If these germ-totin' terrors are hanging out in your flowers or ornamental grasses, cook their geese with this spray. (The rubbing alcohol is the secret weapon here: It penetrates the rascals' protective, waxy covering so the soap can get in to do its deadly work.) Just make sure you wait until evening to blast the culprits; otherwise, the combination of sunshine and alcohol will burn your plants.

1 tbsp. of Ivory® liquid soap
1 gal. of rainwater or soft tap water
2 cups of rubbing alcohol

Mix the Ivory liquid with the water in a 6 gallon hose-end sprayer jar, then add the alcohol. With the nozzle pressure turned on high, spray your plants from top to bottom—and make sure you get under all the leaves. Repeat whenever necessary.

Nix 'Em in the Nest

Deer ticks spend their growing-up time on deer mice, which gives you a great way to rub out the vile villains—and turn some potential trash into treasure at the same time. All you need is lint from the clothes dryer, empty toilet-paper rolls, and a pet shampoo that contains a flea- and tick-killer called permethrin. Once you've gathered your supplies, just soak the dryer lint in the shampoo, and push a small wad into each cardboard tube. Then set the things out in brushy areas or other sheltered spots where the deer mice are likely to find them. The mice will take the fuzzy stuff home to line their nests, and the freeloading ticks will be history!

Warm and Low-down

I know that giving your yard a crew cut is not the way to a lush, healthy crop of turf grass. But it *is* a surefire way to destroy a lot of ticks—and to keep more from moving in. So, if tick-borne diseases are on the rise where you live, move your mower blade to its lowest setting, and trim away!

Ah—Smell the Vapor!

The same mentholated rub that opens up your breathing passages when you have a chest cold is a terrific tick repellent. Just smooth the stuff onto your skin, and you can head for the great outdoors without a care.

I Grew It Myself!

Two of the most effective tick repellents I know of are these beautiful, easy-to-grow herbs. In each case, just dry the leaves, and grind them up in a blender. Then, rub the powder into your pets' fur, and sprinkle it around in their (and your) outdoor play spaces:

▶ **Rosemary** (*Rosmarinus officinalis*), an evergreen shrub with pale blue flowers and grayish, scented foliage. It's hardy only in the warmest parts of the country (USDA Zones 8–10). In colder territory, grow it in a pot. It'll be happy as a clam on your deck all summer long, then sail through the winter in a sunny window.

▶ **Pennyroyal** (*Mentha pulegium*), a small-leaved, low-growing perennial that makes a terrific groundcover for shady spots. It has spikes of fragrant lavender flowers, and it's hardy from Zones 4–10.

GRANDMA KNEW BEST

Anytime my pup and I were headin' for a walk in the woods, Grandma Putt would spray us both with a mixture she made from 1 tablespoon of Dr. Bronner's Liquid Soap in peppermint (available from catalogs, in country stores, and online) and 1 cup of water. To try this at home, just mix the soap and water in a hand-held sprayer, and spritz your clothes, your skin, and Rover's fur. (Make sure you don't get any in his eyes or yours; it won't do any permanent harm, but it will sting.) I still use it, and it always reminds me of candy canes on a Christmas tree!

Just Doodlin'

If you live in the South or Southwest, you may have a dandy tick destroyer right on your doorstep. The doodlebug, a.k.a. ant lion, is related to the lacewing (see page 336); but in the adult stage, it looks more like a dragonfly. The larvae have a comical habit of walking backwards. Comical, that is, unless you happen to be a tick or an ant (hence the name ant lion). These little guys actually make pits in the sand where they wait patiently until a tick or ant saunters by. Then, bingo—ambush! You can urge ant lions to join your team by providing their favorite surroundings: a sheltered spot in dry, sandy soil.

Tick Removal: A Review Course

Conventional wisdom used to call for dabbing a tick with rubbing alcohol, oil, petroleum jelly, or some other substance before removing the foul thing. Well, forget that. Now we know that such pretreatment only causes the varmint to regurgitate germs into the victim's skin. Instead, this is the routine to follow, whether you're de-ticking a human or a pet:

Step 1. Grasp the tick's head, as close to your patient's skin as possible, with curved forceps or tweezers. (If you must use your fingers, cover them with several layers of tissue or a handkerchief or, better yet, wear latex gloves—*never* touch a tick with your bare hands!)

Step 2. Pull up with a smooth, steady motion. Jerking or twisting could cause pieces of the tick to break off

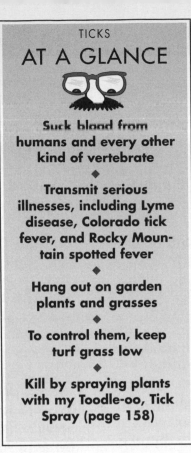

TICKS

AT A GLANCE

Suck blood from humans and every other kind of vertebrate

◆

Transmit serious illnesses, including Lyme disease, Colorado tick fever, and Rocky Mountain spotted fever

◆

Hang out on garden plants and grasses

◆

To control them, keep turf grass low

◆

Kill by spraying plants with my Toodle-oo, Tick Spray (page 158)

and stay in the skin.

Step 3. Drop the tick into a container of rubbing alcohol, or flush it down the toilet. Don't crush it; you could spread disease organisms that may be present in the body fluids.

Step 4. Disinfect the wound with rubbing alcohol, and wash your hands with soap and hot water.

Get Help

Tick removal is not major surgery, but there are times when you need medical help. In any of the following instances, get to a doctor or veterinarian, pronto:

▶ The tick's body slides out, but the head stays behind. It may take a small incision to finish the job.

▶ The victim starts showing signs of infection.

▶ You know the culprit was a deer tick, and you live in Lyme-disease territory.

▶ You experience any of these symptoms: fever, rash, stiff neck, or pain or swelling in your joints.

THIS IS THEIR LIFE

With so many different kinds of moths and butterflies producing caterpillars, details vary enormously. The basics are the same, though. Female butterflies or moths lay eggs that hatch into caterpillars (the larvae). These often change color as they grow and shed their skin. When it's time to pupate, the caterpillar forms a chrysalis (cocoon) to protect it as it changes into its adult form. Then presto—the butterfly or moth emerges and finds a mate, and the whole process starts again.

ALSO ON THE MENU

I can't think of a single plant that some caterpillar doesn't eat. For instance, parsleyworms, the larvae of swallowtail butterflies, eat only members of the Umbelliferae family, which includes dill, carrots, and Queen Anne's lace. Other caterpillars, such as fall webworms, will eat just about any plant under the sun.

1"

Across this great land of ours, there are more kinds of caterpillars than you can shake a butterfly net at. They come in all sizes, shapes, and colors. Some grow up to be drab moths; others turn into butterflies that look like jewels on the wing. Although most caterpillars are harmless to humans and other critters, a handful of them deliver a sting that would put any bee to shame. But all caterpillars have one thing in common: They eat the foliage of plants, and a *lot* of it! Throughout this book, you'll find my best tactics for dealing with specific types of caterpillars, ranging from tomato hornworms to gypsy moth larvae. But in this section, I'll give you a roundup of general tips on keeping your garden safe from these crafty critters—without dealing a death blow to some of nature's most gorgeous creations.

🍃 Do Your Homework

Buy a good field guide to butterflies, and learn to recognize the caterpillars that will turn into living works of art. That way, you won't wipe out a beautiful good guy by mistake. By the way, besides adding their good looks to your garden decor, the colorful wingers help pollinate your posies—and loads of fruits and vegetables, too.

🍃 Handle with Care—Maybe

Young caterpillars are delicate and easy to damage. That's good news if you're out gunnin' for munching marauders. But it means that when you need to move a baby butterfly from one plant to another, you need to proceed with caution. Don't pick it up with your hands; instead, use a soft brush, and gently set the youngster down on a sturdy leaf of another plant. And never touch a good caterpillar when it's molting or pupating, because they're especially fragile at those stages.

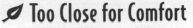

Home on the Range

Caterpillars

🍃 Too Close for Comfort

For some folks, even tongs' length away is closer than they want to get to a caterpillar. If you're one of those squeamish types, don't worry. You've got plenty of other options, including my Caterpillar Killer Tonic (see page 17), Ashes-to-Ashes Milkshake (see

🍃 Ouch!

Saddleback caterpillars are notorious for their stinging power. To my way of thinking, they're one of the ugliest caterpillars on the planet, too. They're light brown with a bright green, white-trimmed patch that resembles a saddle blanket thrown over their back. And scattered over their bodies are sharp projections with needlelike spines. If you encounter these guys, as you likely will if you grow cannas or hibiscus—two of their favorite foods—don't touch them with your bare hands. Instead, pick them off with tongs and wear gloves and a long-sleeved shirt.

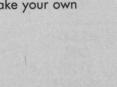

THUG BUSTER

Homemade Btk

When caterpillars are crawling out of the woodwork and you're fresh out of Btk, don't waste time running to the garden center for a new supply. Instead, make your own with this simple recipe.

1 cup of Btk victims*
2 cups of milk
Water

Mash the caterpillars slightly with an old fork, or chop them coarsely in a blender (one that you never plan to use again for human or pet food). Put them in a tight-lidded glass jar with the milk, and let it stand at room temperature for three days, well out of reach of children or pets. Strain out the solids, and add enough water to make a gallon of liquid. Then pour the solution into a hand-held sprayer, and go kill those 'pillars!

*Caterpillars that have been sprayed with Btk and are dead or dying.

page 176), and Btk *(Bacillus thuringiensis var. kurstaki)*. You can read more about this wonder-working bacterium on page 98. And see my Homemade Btk recipe (page 162).

✒ Wait!

Btk *(Bacillus thuringiensis var. kurstaki)* is a powerful weapon to have in your anticaterpillar arsenal, but to get the biggest bang for your buck, you need to apply the stuff at just the right time. As tempting as it is to go after the crafty crawlers when they're still tiny, don't do it. Chances are, they won't be able to eat enough Btk to kill them. Instead, wait until they get just big enough to chew a hole through a leaf. At that stage, they'll be able to gobble up a lethal dose of the bacteria, but they won't have had time to do a major demolition job on your plants.

✒ Halt!

If you see a bad-guy caterpillar strolling around with what look like grains of rice stuck to his back, don't

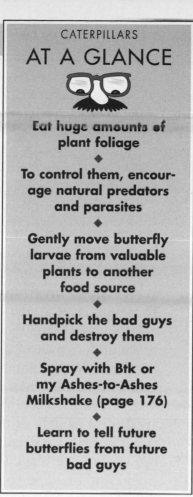

CATERPILLARS
AT A GLANCE

Eat huge amounts of plant foliage

◆

To control them, encourage natural predators and parasites

◆

Gently move butterfly larvae from valuable plants to another food source

◆

Handpick the bad guys and destroy them

◆

Spray with Btk or my Ashes-to-Ashes Milkshake (page 176)

◆

Learn to tell future butterflies from future bad guys

waste your time or your Thug Buster ingredients on him—he'll soon be dead. Those little white things are either egg cases or cocoons of a native parasite that lives on caterpillars (there are many, in every region of the country). So just lift that doomed critter gently (see "Handle with Care—Maybe" on page 161) and take him to a patch of weeds or a plant that can tolerate a few nibbles. That way, the parasites can continue their life cycle and rub out your garden-variety adversaries.

✒ Get a Glow On

When fireflies are flickering over your flower garden at night, count your lucky stars: Their babies, a.k.a. glow-worms, eat tons of small caterpillars. But that's not the entire roster of helpful munchers. Toads, birds, and lots of good-guy beetles also think caterpillars are the ultimate fine-dining experience.

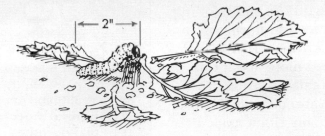

It's always disappointing to see your flowers after some pesky pest has run roughshod through the garden. But coming face to face with the results of a cutworm invasion can break your heart. These menaces attack new seedlings and young transplants, slicing them off at ground level. They strike under cover of darkness, and they work fast. A flower garden that was on the brink of a beautiful career when you went to bed could be a total wreck by morning. The culprits themselves are almost as ugly as their dirty deeds. They're fat, soft, bristly caterpillars that range from brown, gray, or black to red and greenish white. If you find one and you want a positive I.D., poke it lightly with a stick. If it curls up in a ball, it's a cutworm. The parents of these vile villains are many species of small, dark moths that are about 3/4 inch across.

🌿 The Offensive Line

Cutworms are the worst enemies that a bed of seedlings or small transplants ever had! Fortunately, these foul felons have enemies, too, and some of the deadliest are birds, toads, tachinid flies, and parasitic wasps. (Don't worry: These wasps don't sting!) All of these top guns love to hang out in flower gardens. If more than a few of your babies are being felled, chances are that the

THIS IS THEIR LIFE

Several different species of cutworms often share the same garden space, but their life cycles are the same: In the spring, adult moths lay teeny white eggs in the soil or in garden litter. By day, the cutworms snooze under a leaf or tucked into the soil. At night, they venture out to dine on whatever plants they can find. The feeding rampage lasts for several weeks before the gluttons burrow into the soil to pupate and emerge, all grown up, to lay their own eggs. The cycle continues as long as the warm weather lasts.

ALSO ON THE MENU

Cutworms perform planticide in the vegetable garden, too, and they sometimes target lawns. You can protect your veggies using the same methods that work for flowers. When the creeps invade your lawn, strike back hard with the routine on page 167.

good guy/bad guy balance has gotten out of whack. Here's my simple, two-part solution:

Part 1. Read before you spray. Even some pesticides (including my Thug Busters) that won't hurt humans or larger critters can kill off good-guy bugs along with the bad ones. And that'll leave you with more problems than you started with!

Home on the Range

Cutworms

Part 2. Keep your posse happy. Tachinid flies and parasitic wasps are drawn to any pollen- and nectar-packed plants, but they go gaga over dill, yarrow, sweet alyssum, and cosmos. For more tips on enticing pest-eating critters to your garden, see page 335.

Get 'Em on the Wing

Keep in mind that cutworms are vulnerable beyond the caterpillar stage. The adult moths have enemies, too. For example, bats eat them by the bucketful. (You can read more about these high flyers in Chapter 8.)

Don't Tempt Fate

Even with an army of good guys on your side, don't take any chances: Head off the varmints at the pass by putting a small barrier around each seedling. I sink my mini corrals 2 inches into the ground with about 3 inches showing above. Collars made from any of these materials will give young plants first-rate protection from chomping cutworms:

▶ Aluminum foil

▶ Cardboard rolls from wrapping paper, toilet paper, or paper towels

▶ Corrugated plastic or metal drain tile

GRANDMA KNEW BEST

The parents of cutworms are dark-colored moths that will never win any beauty contests. In Grandma Putt's day, folks called 'em millers (maybe because of the flour-like dusting on their wings). They flit around after dark, and light draws them like a magnet. Grandma lured them to their death with this old-time trick: Fill a wide, flat pan with milk and set it in the garden. Beside it, place a lighted lantern so that it shines on the milk. The moths will zero in on the glowing target, fall into the milk, and drown.

- ▶ Linoleum or vinyl flooring strips
- ▶ Mailing tubes
- ▶ Metal cans with both ends removed
- ▶ Paper or plastic cups with the bottoms cut out

🍃 Moving On

Once your seedlings have outgrown their collars (see "Don't Tempt Fate," on page 165), sprinkle a scratchy substance on the soil around each plant. The cutworms won't slink across anything that prickles their skin. These are some of my favorite rib-ticklers:

- ▶ Chicken manure (dried)
- ▶ Clay cat litter (unscented)
- ▶ Crushed eggshells
- ▶ Diatomaceous earth
- ▶ Hair (human or pet)
- ▶ Pine needles
- ▶ Shredded oak leaves
- ▶ Wood ashes (don't use where you have a toad on garden duty; wood ashes are highly toxic to the little guys)

🍃 Keep It Up

Because new batches of cutworms come along every few weeks, your garden is never really out of the woods. Once plants are past the seedling stage, the culprits aren't likely to cause fatal damage, but they'll still make a nuisance of themselves. They'll also turn into moths and lay next year's supply of cutworm eggs. So don't just sit there—trap the villains, and bring 'em back dead! In the evening, set out boards, cabbage leaves, grapefruit halves, or potatoes in your flower beds (or your vegetable garden). The next morning, the traps will be full of cutworms. You can

---

THUG BUSTER

Squeaky Clean Tonic

This is a more powerful version of my All-Season Clean-Up Tonic (see page 98), and it deals a mighty blow to cutworms and other bad guys who are buggin' your lawn.

1 cup of antiseptic mouthwash
1 cup of tobacco tea*
1 cup of chamomile tea
1 cup of urine
½ cup of Murphy's Oil Soap®
½ cup of lemon-scented dishwashing liquid

Mix all of these ingredients in a large bucket. Then pour the solution into your 20 gallon hose-end sprayer, and apply it to your lawn, flowers, or vegetable garden to the point of run-off.

*For the recipe, see "Winterizing Tonic" on page 207.

---

squash the creeps, burn them, or dump them into hot, soapy water. It's your call.

Dig It All

When you till the soil for a new flower or vegetable garden, you'll automatically bring cutworms up close to the surface. And that gives you a chance to wipe out hundreds of the rascals with no effort at all. Before you sow your seeds or set in your transplants, just let the beds sit for a few days. And keep your binoculars and your Audubon field guide close at hand, because before you know it, robins, meadowlarks, blue jays, and blackbirds will zoom in and pick that plot clean as a whistle.

Turn 'Em Off

After your fine feathered friends have gobbled up exposed cutworms, you need to fend off new waves of egg-laying moths. To do that, just plant plenty of onions, garlic, and tansy among your flowers or vegetables. Cutworm moths *hate* the pungent stuff!

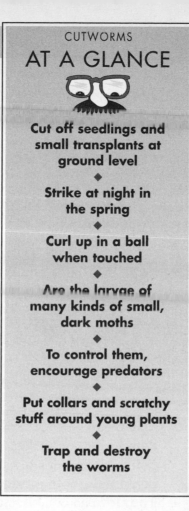

CUTWORMS
AT A GLANCE

Cut off seedlings and small transplants at ground level

◆

Strike at night in the spring

◆

Curl up in a ball when touched

◆

Are the larvae of many kinds of small, dark moths

◆

To control them, encourage predators

◆

Put collars and scratchy stuff around young plants

◆

Trap and destroy the worms

When They Louse Up Your Lawn

In spring and summer, cutworms can make a royal mess of your lawn by munching on the crowns, where the grass blades meet the roots. Here are your best options for cutworm control, lawn-style:

▶ Mix 3 tablespoons of dishwashing liquid with 1 gallon of water, and pour it on the troubled spots. The soap will bring the cutworms to the surface, where hungry birds will get them.

▶ If you don't want to wait for the birds, spray the turf with my Squeaky Clean Tonic (see page 166).

▶ Apply beneficial nematodes to the soil. Read the package instructions carefully—for the nematodes to work, they need to reach the scene at exactly the right time.

▶ If cutworms are making your life miserable, and you live in warm-season grass territory, you may want to replace your turf with either zoysia or Bermuda grass.

FOLIAR NEMATODES

Microscopic

THIS IS THEIR LIFE

Foliar felons are closely related to root-knot nematodes, but the leaf looters reproduce inside the foliage and stems of plants. The exact reproduction details vary from one species to another, but the basics are the same: Once the females lay eggs and youngsters hatch, they mature in two to four weeks (sooner in warm weather) and start laying eggs of their own. As a result, a single affected leaf will be home to multiple generations of nematodes.

ALSO ON THE MENU

For the most part, foliar nematodes confine their crimes to annual and perennial flowers, but they also attack strawberries. And an especially nasty type invades the foliage, bulbs, and seeds of onions and their close relatives. Afflicted plants will be stunted and swollen, with a soft, mealy texture that eventually leads to rot.

Yellow, geometric-shaped patches in leaves, especially lower ones, point to the early work of foliar nematodes. As these microscopic roundworms attack tissue between the veins, they make triangles, semicircles, and other shapes that start out yellow, then turn brown. Eventually, the whole leaf turns brown or black and dies. Often, these invisible thugs are inside their host plant all year, but you won't know about it until a period of damp weather strikes in late summer or fall. Foliar nematodes invade many annuals and perennials, both outdoors and in greenhouses. They love asters, chrysanthemums, dahlias, penstemons, zinnias, and primroses. And in recent years, they've become one of the biggest pests of one of America's favorite plants: hostas.

Just Testing

If you suspect the presence of foliar nematodes, perform this test: Hold a damaged leaf underwater in a bowl, and tear it. Leave it there for 24 hours, then examine the water with a strong magnifying lens (one that's at least 10× magnification). If the little worms are on the scene, you'll see what look like glistening, white threads swimming through the water.

This Year's Loss

When the nematodes' victims are zinnias or other annuals, don't hesitate for a minute: Dig up those plants, along with any plant litter or damp mulch that's on the ground under them. Then bundle up the whole shebang in plastic bags, seal them up tight, and send them off with the trash collector.

Home on the Range

Foliar Nematodes

Cut and Toss

With badly infested perennial plants, your best bet is the same as it is with annuals: Bite the bullet and bid those babies bye-bye. But in the earlier stages of an attack, you have many other options. At the first sign of trouble, cut off all the infested leaves and stems and destroy them, or send them off with the trash collector. And be sure to pick up any dead leaves that you see on the ground—foliar nematodes can live for a year or more in dry, dead foliage and then spring into action when water hits them.

Soap It to 'Em

After you've removed the plagued plant parts, spray the remaining foliage and any nearby plants with my Citrusy Soap Spray (below). It's a beefed-up version of Grandma Putt's Simple Soap Spray (see page 86), designed to go after really tough customers like foliar nematodes. Or, if the wily worms have you so tired out that you're not up to home cooking, look for a commercial product called

Citrusy Soap Spray

This potent insecticidal soap will go after extra-hard-to-kill pests like foliar nematodes and hard-shelled beetles. The secret lies in the super penetrating power of the citrus oil.

THUG BUSTER

½ bar of Fels Naptha® or Octagon® soap,* shredded
2 gal. of water
1 tbsp. of orange or lemon essential oil

Add the soap to the water and heat, stirring, until the soap dissolves completely. Let the solution cool, mix in the essential oil, then pour it into a hand-held mist sprayer and let 'er rip. Test it on one plant first, though—and be sure to rinse it off after the bugs have bitten the dust.

*You'll find Fels Naptha and Octagon in either the bath soap or laundry section of your supermarket.

ZeroTol™, a hydrogen dioxide spray that many nurseries use to combat foliar nematodes. (Ask for it at a nursery that specializes in hostas, or search for it by name on the Internet.)

🍃 They're in Hot Water Now!

A two-step bathing process will kill nematodes in the crown of a plant. It's a tricky process because temperature and timing are crucial. But if the stricken plant is a rare, expensive gem or a treasured heirloom, I say go for it! First, dig up the victim, or take it out of its pot. Then follow this routine (after you've removed all of the infested foliage, of course):

Step 1. Soak the crown in hot water (120° to 140°F—no hotter!) for 10 minutes. Monitor the temperature continuously, and don't leave the plant in the bath any longer than 10 minutes, or you could kill it. To play it safe, use a stopwatch.

Step 2. Remove the plant from the hot water, and immediately plunge

---

FOLIAR NEMATODES
AT A GLANCE

Microscopic worms attack leaf tissue of many perennials and some annuals

◆

Symptoms first appear as geometric-shaped patches on leaves

◆

Eventually, the leaf turns brown or black and dies

◆

To control them, remove and destroy infested foliage

◆

Spray with Citrusy Soap Spray (page 169)

◆

Destroy badly infested annuals

◆

Soak crowns of perennials in hot water

---

it into a bucket of cold tap water. Leave it there just long enough to cool down, but no longer than 5 minutes.

Step 3. Drain the plant, and immediately put it in a container with fresh potting soil. After it's back on its roots again, you can plant it in the ground if you like. **Note:** You'll have the best chance of success with this treatment if you do the job in early spring, just as the plant is about to break dormancy.

🍃 Aw, Dry Up!

Foliar nematodes move from one plant to another in drops of water. If your plants happen to be in a greenhouse or under a porch roof, that gives you a simple way to keep the population from spreading: Always water the soil of your plants, never the foliage, and keep the containers far enough apart so that moisture can't travel from one plant to another. Outdoors, use a soaker hose in your flower beds, and try to space your plants so that their leaves don't touch.

GERANIUM BUDWORMS

THIS IS THEIR LIFE

Moths lay their eggs on host plants, and when the baby caterpillars hatch, they tunnel into flower buds and start eating. Sometimes, they stay inside the bud; other times, they chew their way out and continue chomping on mature flowers and foliage. This whole feeding frenzy lasts for about three weeks before the worms pupate in the soil or in dried-up flower buds. The moths die when cold weather strikes, but pupae can live through the winter inside dead buds and emerge in spring, ready to launch a new generation.

ALSO ON THE MENU

Geranium budworms also target roses. And in the South, they attack both smoking tobacco and its ornamental cousin, *nicotiana*. Sometimes, they also tunnel into impatiens, petunias, ageratum, marigolds, and sweet peas. In the vegetable garden, they go after tomatoes and peas.

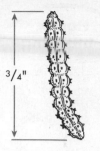

3/4"

Like many bad-guy bugs, these guys have a name that doesn't exactly follow full-disclosure guidelines. As their name suggests, they do attack geraniums (*Pelargonium* spp.), but they also go after petunias, impatiens, ageratum, nicotiana, and occasionally, other annuals. The second part of the name is also a partial truth: The creeps do burrow into flower buds, where they eat the insides. As a result, the empty buds just dry up, or the flowers open tattered and full of holes. But they don't stop with the buds. They also munch on fully opened flowers, and once in a while, on leaves, dropping tiny black fecal pellets as they move along.

The critters themselves are striped caterpillars, about 3/4 inch long, and tan, reddish, or greenish. They're the offspring of a light green moth with a 1 1/2-inch wingspan that has lighter-colored bands across its wings.

Fair-Weather Fiends

Geranium budworms can show up just about anywhere in the country. But they're most common—and do the most damage—where winters are mild. So if you've recently moved to a balmy clime, look out!

Seek and Destroy

When you see dried-up buds or tattered flowers on these critters' favorite plants, clip them off and drop them in a pail of soapy water. You can bet bucks to blooms that there's a bug holed up inside.

🌿 Fire When They're Ready

My Caterpillar Killer Tonic (see page 17) will kill the creeps in a flash. Timing is crucial, though: You *must* take aim and fire immediately after the eggs hatch; once the caterpillars slither into the flower buds, they're home free.

🌿 What? No Wormwood?

If you're fresh out of fresh wormwood, the main ingredient in my Caterpillar Killer Tonic (see page 17), don't panic—you have other spraying options. Whip up a batch of my Orange Aid (see page 49), or run down to the garden center for some Btk (*Bacillus thuringiensis* var. *kurstaki*). For the full lowdown on this wonder drug, see page 98. Just remember that no matter what spray you use, it will work only *before* the caterpillars burrow into the buds.

🌿 Fall Is for Housecleaning

At the end of summer, dig up and destroy any raggedy-looking plants that could be

Home on the Range

Geranium Budworms

harboring next year's crop of eggs. Then, for good measure, hose down your garden with my Knock-'Em-Dead Insect Spray (below). It'll polish off any lingering caterpillars and other bad guys that might be hanging around.

🌿 Don't Give 'Em Shelter

If you live in a cold climate, and you take your geraniums or impatiens indoors for the winter, repot them in fresh soil and fresh containers first. Otherwise, you could be giving shelter to next year's crop of budworms. When

THUG BUSTER

Knock-'Em-Dead Insect Spray

This potent mixture will deal a death blow to geranium bud-worms and other bad-guy bugs.

**6 cloves of garlic, finely chopped
1 small onion, finely chopped
1 tbsp. of cayenne pepper
1 tbsp. of dishwashing liquid
1 qt. of warm water**

Mix all of these ingredients, and let the mixture sit overnight. Strain out the solids, pour the liquid into a hand-held sprayer, and knock those pesky pests good and dead!

you remove the plants from their pots, get all of the soil off of the roots. Then swish them in soapy water and rinse them well before you tuck them into their new homes.

Bat's a Good Thing

Geranium budworm moths do their flying and mating at night, so to keep the population well in hand, invite some bats to hang out at your place. But if they don't get all the moths, don't worry. Other good guys go after geranium budworms during different stages of their lives. Tiny trichogramma wasps lay their eggs inside the budworms' eggs, destroying them in the process. And lacewing larvae gobble up newly hatched budworms. (See Chapter 8 for more about good guys.)

Moonstruck

You can entice both trichogramma wasps and lacewing larvae to your garden by planting a mixture of nectar-rich flowers. For this mission, I'd suggest buying a supply from a garden center or catalog. That way, you can take advantage of the budworms' maternity schedule: They lay most of their eggs during the first week after the full moon. Here's your battle plan:

► During the first week after the full moon, release the wasps so they can polish off the budworms' new eggs.

► One week later, release the lacewing larvae so they can eat any caterpillars that survived the wasps' advances.

So Just What Are These Rich Flowers?

Confused about how to tell a nectar-rich flower from its less-well-off relations? Well, here's a clue: Look at a vase full of cut flowers. If you spot one that's dropped a lot of pollen on the table, you've found a winner! But don't plant just one kind; the trick in luring trichogramma wasps, lacewings, and hordes of other good guys to your turf is to give them a whole smorgasbord of plants that bloom at different times. For the lowdown on hit-squad hospitality, see Chapter 8.

DID YOU KNOW?

If you can hearken back to high-school health class, you may recall that we human beings have 792 distinct muscles in our bodies. What your teacher probably didn't tell you, though, is that a lowly caterpillar has upwards of 4,000 separate muscles in its body! I wonder, do all of them ache after a long day in the garden?

✿ Buyer Beware

Geranium budworms often breed year-round in greenhouses, even up north. So, when you go to shop for plants, examine them very carefully. If you see any sign of leaf or bud damage, take your business elsewhere.

✿ Just Hangin' Around

If you love hanging baskets filled with ivy geraniums as much as I do, I've got some good news: Geranium budworms won't touch the gorgeous things. So plant 'em to your heart's content!

✿ But Wait! There's More

Budworms also keep their distance from scented geraniums. Although these are also part of the *Pelargonium* clan, they have smaller, more delicate blooms than their flashier cousins. But what they lack in visual pizzazz, they more than make up for in nose appeal—with the added element of surprise. The leaves deliver aromas

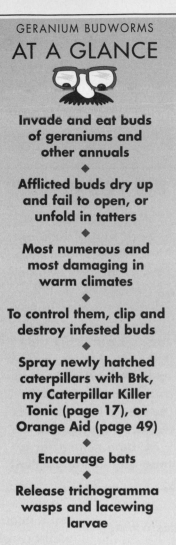

GERANIUM BUDWORMS
AT A GLANCE

Invade and eat buds of geraniums and other annuals

◆

Afflicted buds dry up and fail to open, or unfold in tatters

◆

Most numerous and most damaging in warm climates

◆

To control them, clip and destroy infested buds

◆

Spray newly hatched caterpillars with Btk, my Caterpillar Killer Tonic (page 17), or Orange Aid (page 49)

◆

Encourage bats

◆

Release trichogramma wasps and lacewing larvae

that are anything *but* what you'd expect from a geranium. Here's a half-dozen of my favorites varieties:

▶ **Apple** (*Pelargonium odoratissimum*)

▶ **Lemon** (*P. crispum*)

▶ **Lime** (*P. nervosum*)

▶ **Nutmeg** (*P.* × *fragrans*)

▶ **Peppermint** (*P. tomentosum*)

▶ **Rose** (*P. capitatum*)

✿ But I Want Petunias

Then you're in luck. Although no *Petunia* that I know of is resistant to geranium budworms, one of its relatives, *Calibrachoa* (a.k.a. million bells), stands right up and says "Boo!" to the crawlers. Million bells look just like small petunias and come in the same brilliant color range. They're tender perennials, which means that you can keep them out year-round in warm climates (Zone 9 and higher), and treat them as annuals elsewhere.

IRIS BORERS

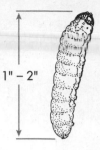

1" – 2"

In early summer, if you see dark or water-soaked spots or streaks on young iris leaves, it means only one thing: Iris borers are hard at work, and chargin' for the rhizomes—if they're not already there. You may also notice pinholes in the leaves, or ragged chew marks along the edges. Flower buds, especially the ones at the tops of the stalks, may look chewed upon. And, chances are, the whole shebang will be slimy. Yuck! By midsummer, damaged foliage turns yellow, wilts, and may be loose and rotted at the crown. When you dig up the rhizomes, you'll see holes that—depending on how long the borers have been there—may be filled with foul-smelling rot.

The characters responsible for all this ugliness are large, pinkish, grublike caterpillars with brown heads. They are the larvae of a short-lived, dark-colored night-flying moth.

🌿 Head Off Trouble

In very early spring, pull off all dead iris leaves that you find, and destroy them or send them off with the trash collector. That way, you'll wipe out any borer eggs that huddled there for the winter.

🌿 Oh, Joy!

In the happy (but unlikely) event that you catch the larvae just as they hatch in the spring, give 'em a lethal dose of my Ashes-to-Ashes Milkshake (see page 176). At this baby stage, the creeps are slim and greenish.

THIS IS THEIR LIFE

Adult moths emerge from the soil in August and September, mate, and deposit eggs on dead iris leaves or nearby plant debris. When the eggs hatch in April or early May, the larvae crawl up onto the new leaves and drill tiny holes a few inches above the soil surface. Then they crawl in and start chomping. By midsummer, they invade the rhizomes, and eat 'em alive from the inside out. Once the larvae are in the soil, they pupate. Between August and September, they emerge as adult moths to start the whole process over again.

ALSO ON THE MENU

Iris borers attack only irises. The tall, bearded (a.k.a. German) types are their favorite victims, with Louisiana iris a close second. Other kinds of borers tunnel into the stalks of several annual and perennial flowers, including cosmos, zinnias, dahlias, and delphiniums.

Squeeze Hard

Once the borers have drilled into a leaf or flower stalk, no spray will touch them, but you can pinch 'em to death. Just take each leaf between your fingers, and squeeze hard, from the base up. When you hear a "pop," you'll know that a borer has bitten the dust.

Bite and Cut

If the thought of squashing makes you squeamish, bite the bullet, and cut off the whole fan of leaves. Then drop it into a bucket of soapy water to kill the borers. You'll lose this year's big flower show, but you'll save the rhizome from invasion.

Dig and Poke

In midsummer—the normal time for dividing irises—dig up the rhizomes and look for tunnels. When you see one, poke a wire into it, and you'll hook the borer. (There's only one borer per rhizome, though droves of 'em may haunt the leaves.)

Home on the Range

Iris Borers

Soak and Plant

After you've de-bored the rhizome, dip it in a solution of 1 part household bleach to 3 parts water, then let it dry. While it's drying, prepare the planting hole by scraping out a few inches of the soil, adding an equal amount of compost, and mixing it in. Once the rhizome is dry, it's ready for replanting.

Fewer Flyers

Birds will happily eat all of the iris borers they can catch. The trouble is, the little 'pillars move so fast that the

---

Ashes-to-Ashes Milkshake

This milky beverage will bid bye-bye to all kinds of caterpillars and some of the meanest, toughest pests around, including weevils, cucumber beetles, and stalk borers.

**1 tbsp. of wood ashes
1 cup of sour milk or buttermilk
Water**

Mix the wood ashes in 1 quart of water, and let it sit overnight. Strain out the solids, stir the sour milk or buttermilk into the remaining liquid, and add 3 quarts of water. Pour the solution into a hand-held sprayer, and zap the pesky pests.

THUG BUSTER

176

ANNUAL & PERENNIAL PLAGUERS

wingers can't get many of them. But there is a dandy way to cut down on next year's borer population: Just invite some bats over to your place to polish off the egg-laying moths. (For the lowdown on these and other good guys, see Chapter 8.)

Can't Win 'Em All

Bats eat a *lot* of moths, but even they can't get every single one. So entice some parasitic wasps to set up camp at your place. They'll lay their eggs in the borers' eggs, and that'll be all she wrote. Lure the tiny (nonstinging) buzzers with flowers that are rich in pollen and nectar. Cosmos, gayfeather *(Liatris)*, bee balm *(Monarda)*, and daisies are all winners. See Chapter 8 for

more about good guys, and more flowers that say, "Come 'n' get it!"

Don't Give 'Em a Home

For reasons of their own, iris borers don't care for what, to my way of thinking, is one of the prettiest plants on the planet: Siberian iris. It's also one of the hardiest and trouble-free perennials you could ask for. It grows to about 4 feet tall, depending on the variety, and has narrow, grasslike leaves and big,

beardless flowers in just about every color of the rainbow. So do yourself a favor and cater to the borers' bad taste in housing accommodations!

THIS IS THEIR LIFE

The life cycle varies from one species to another, but in general, adult moths emerge in early spring and lay eggs on the undersides of leaves. When the eggs hatch, the baby caterpillars stroll to a leaf, roll up inside it, and get on with their business. Most species pupate inside their leafy chambers, and pop out a week or so later to start the process all over again.

ALSO ON THE MENU

Besides going on a roll in the flower garden, strawberry leaf rollers attack (surprise!) strawberries, often with disastrous results. Many other species of leaf rollers attack trees, deciduous shrubs, roses, and bramble fruits. (You can read about one type, fruit-tree leaf rollers, in Chapter 2.) Wherever you find the creeps, the same methods you see in these pages will help you deal with their destruction.

1" – 2"

Many species of caterpillars plague annual and perennial plants by rolling up the leaves and binding them with silken threads to form a cozy shelter, then proceeding to nest, feed, or pupate inside. Most often, the leafy shelter encloses developing buds that the pesky pests munch on, but they'll also nibble leaves, mature flowers, and fruit. Some of these villains, such as the strawberry leaf roller (don't let the name fool you), target many types of annual and perennial plants. Others, like the canna leaf roller, specialize in a single target. In most cases, damage is mainly cosmetic; but severe attacks can kill plants, especially if they're under stress or in less than the pink of health.

Leaf rollers' parents are moths of various sizes and colors. Except for laying eggs that turn into rude offspring, they're all perfectly harmless.

🌿 Learn All about 'Em

Although all leaf rollers perform the same kinds of dirty tricks, their timing and targets vary greatly from one part of the country to another. So, especially if you're new to an area, or you've just taken up gardening, get in touch with flower-growing neighbors, your local garden club, or the closest Cooperative Extension Service. They can clue you in on what kind of troublemakers you can expect, and when they might come a-callin'.

✿ Cut!

The minute you spot the telltale rolled-up leaves, clip them off and drop them into a pail of soapy water to kill the caterpillars. Or, seal them up in a plastic bag, and send them off with the trash collector—it's your call. Just don't toss the things on the compost pile. Then give your plants a good drink of my Compost Tea (below). It'll keep them strong, healthy, and better able to fend off future leaf roller attacks (or any other kind).

Home on the Range

Leaf Rollers

they'll come on their own if you give them some parsley-family plants, such as dill, yarrow, or Queen Anne's lace, and—of course—don't use pesticides.

✿ Winged Warriors Times Two

Birds will polish off all the leaf roller caterpillars they can get their beaks on. But there's just one hitch: The wingers can snatch the crawlers only before they roll up inside their leafy chambers. So cover your bases

✿ Cut Again

In the fall, cut off all dead or dying leaves, along with all plant litter on the ground. Then get rid of the whole shebang, because it could be harboring next spring's crop of eggs.

✿ Lay It On

While some parasitic wasps lay their eggs inside the eggs of their victims, the ichneumonid wasp lays hers on top of many kinds of caterpillars, including strawberry leaf rollers. You can buy these good guys from catalogs, but

THUG BUSTER

Compost Tea

This health-giving potion dishes up a well-balanced supply of all the essential nutrients your plants need, keeping them healthy, perky, and better able to fend off all kinds of pesky pests—and dastardly diseases, too.

1½ gal. of fresh compost
Burlap sack
10-gal. bucket with lid
4½ gal. of warm water

Scoop the compost into a burlap sack, tie it closed, and put it in a 10-gallon bucket with the water. Cover, and let it steep for three to seven days. Then pour the liquid into a hand-held sprayer, and spritz your plants every two to three weeks.

and invite some bats to bunk at your place. They'll gobble up hordes of the adult moths before they've even laid their eggs.

🍃 A Kitchen Cupboard Cure

Before you expect the leaf roller eggs to hatch, dust the leaves of your plants with flour. On their way to the big roll-up, the baby caterpillars will eat the stuff, swell up, and die. In theory, Btk *(Bacillus thuringiensis* var. *kurstaki)* will do 'em in at this stage, too, but the tiny terrors might not eat enough of the powder to get a lethal dose.

LEAF ROLLERS
AT A GLANCE

Larvae of many species of moths roll up plants' leaves to make shelters for nesting, feeding, or pupating

◆

Attack a variety of annuals and perennials

◆

Generally, damage is only cosmetic, but severe infestations can kill plants

◆

To control them, dust leaves with flour to deter caterpillars

◆

Spray newly hatched caterpillars with Btk or my Orange Aid (page 49)

◆

Encourage predators and parasites

🍃 Surprise!

If you happen to spot the leaf roller youngsters, let 'em have it with my Orange Aid (see page 49) or Caterpillar Killer Tonic (see page 17). Either potent potion will kill them on contact.

🍃 Beat the Buds

To keep spring-laid eggs from hatching, spray your plants with my Oil's-Well-That-Ends-Well Mix (see page 361). And remember two crucial points: Do the job before any buds break out, and make sure you coat the underside of every single leaf, because that's where you'll find the eggs.

THIS IS THEIR LIFE

An adult root-knot nematode lays anywhere from 300 to 3,000 eggs in one jellylike mass near the roots of a plant. They hatch in about a month to carry on the family tradition of demolishing plants and reproducing their species. In cold climates, nematodes gear down for the winter, but in warm regions, they carry on business as usual all year long.

ALSO ON THE MENU

Various species of nematodes attack every type of plant under the sun, both above- and below-ground (see Foliar Nematodes on page 168). Some target flowers, while others go in for lawns, shrubs, trees, or vegetables. Like many pesky pests, these teeny terrors tend to cause a lot more trouble in warm climates. But wherever you live, and whatever the worms' victims are, the tips in the next few pages will equip you to win the battle.

Microscopic

When your plants are sickly, turning yellow, and wilting—and they don't spring back to life when you water them—the trouble could stem from a number of pests or diseases. But when you dig up the plants and find the roots all covered with galls that you can't break off, it means just one thing: You've got root-knot nematodes at work. If you looked at one of these all-but-invisible thugs under a microscope, you'd see a tiny, segmented worm, pointed at both ends. The worm uses its front-end point to invade a plant's roots and, at the same time, inject cells with a chemical that makes them swell up like balloons. The giant cells multiply and show up on the roots as small galls that you can't break off.

🍃 Warm-Weather Warning

Root-knot nematodes can wreak havoc all over the country, but they cause the most trouble in warm, sandy soils of coastal regions. They're especially menacing in the sunny South, where the soil is so teeming with them that it's all but impossible to wipe them out entirely. Still, there are many ways to coexist with the minute monsters, wherever you find them.

Search and Destroy

In almost every case, when nematodes attack your annuals or perennials, your only option is to dig up the afflicted plants and destroy them. (Don't put them on the compost pile!) Then set about preventing future trouble by following the helpful hints in this section.

Target: Tubers

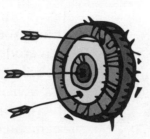

When the vile villains attack tuberous-rooted plants like dahlias and tuberous begonias, you're in luck (so to speak): In this case, you can usually save your plants. At the end of the growing season, when you dig up the tuberous roots, look closely for galls or knots. If you find any, kill their makers by soaking the tubers for 30 minutes in hot (120°F) water. The following spring, replant in fresh, sterilized soil.

Carry No Passengers

Root-knot nematodes seldom travel more than a few feet from their hatching place—unless you give them a ride to a new home. So after you've been working in soil that's a known—or even suspected—nematode stomping ground, hose off your tools, and dip them in a bucket of water with a cup or so of bleach added to it. If you've had your hands in the soil, dunk your gloves in the bucket, too.

Solar Power: Cleaner Soil in 7 Simple Steps

When root-knot nematodes are causing big-time trouble, you need to take big-time action. By solarizing your soil (heating it up to 150°F or so), you can kill not only nematodes, but also foul fungi and the larvae of many bad-guy bugs. For this process to work, you and ol' Sol need to get cookin' during the hottest part of the year, which in most places is July and August. Here's the routine:

Step 1. Dig up a plot of soil that's about 10 feet square.

THUG BUSTER

No Mo' Nematodes Tonic

This simple elixir will polish off nasty nematodes lickety-split.

1 can of beer
1 cup of molasses

Mix these ingredients in your 20 gallon hose-end sprayer, and thoroughly soak any area where the nematodes are doin' their dirty work.

Step 2. Lay on a 1- to 2-inch layer of fresh manure, and work it in well. Because solarization kills off most seeds, this is a good chance to use up weedy manure.

Step 3. Rake the soil into planting beds or rows.

Step 4. Water well, then let everything settle overnight.

Step 5. Cover the plot with a sheet of clear, 3- to 6-mil plastic, and pile soil around the edges to keep it in place. Patch any holes or tears that you find. Make sure the cover has some slack in it so it can puff up (instead of blowing away or even bursting) when the heat starts rising.

Step 6. Wait about six weeks—longer if the weather's cool.

Step 7. Take off the cover, water, and plant with confidence. Just don't do any cultivating, or you'll bring up untreated soil—nematodes, fungi, and all.

🍃 Give 'Em a Drink

Solarizing is one way to nix nasty nematodes, but it's not the *only* way. One of the simplest ways I know of to get rid of the tiny

Home on the Range

Root-Knot Nematodes

knot-makers is to serve 'em a drink of my No Mo' Nematodes Tonic (page 182). It'll deliver a real knockout punch!

🍃 Bring On the Enemy

A whole lot of underground good guys eat a substance called chitin, which happens to be what nematode eggs are covered with. Compost and manure contain lots of these tiny warriors. But when you need help in a hurry, load up your soil with chitin-rich things like eggshells, seafood meal, and shrimp hulls. Chitin

---

GRANDMA KNEW BEST

Grandma Putt had a sweet way to stop nematodes in their tracks: She just dug a little sugar into the soil (5 pounds for every 50 feet of planting area). The little louses gobbled the stuff up—and it choked 'em to death! One caution, though: Don't use this trick more than once on the same piece of land, because sugar will also kill beneficial organisms in the soil, and then you'll really be in trouble!

---

eaters from near and far will show up to feast on the free lunch you've given them—and then start right in on the nematode eggs.

More Water, Please!

Even some of the nematodes' favorite targets can carry on business as usual in enemy territory, but they'll need more water than they normally do. So keep your hose handy, and mulch your beds with a thick layer of compost. Besides keeping more moisture in the soil and smothering weeds, it'll add nematode enemies to the soil.

Super Spears

If you eat asparagus, you've got an A-1 nematode chaser at hand. Every time you finish cooking some of the scrumptious spears, let the water cool down, then pour it onto the soil around your trouble-prone plants. Nematodes can't stand asparagus juice!

Mighty Marvelous Marigolds

One of the best ways I know to stop root-knot nematodes in their tracks is to plant French marigolds *(Tagetes patula)* in your stricken beds. When they start to flower, till them under, and plant everything else you're hankering to grow. Unfortunately, marigold medicine is not a miracle cure: The effect wears off in about a year. Then you'll have to do it all over again.

ROOT-KNOT NEMATODES

AT A GLANCE

Microscopic worms enter roots and inject a toxic chemical

◆

Afflicted plants look sickly, turn yellow, and wilt

◆

Roots are misshapen and covered with galls that won't break off

◆

Most menacing in warm, sandy soils in the South

◆

To control them, plant resistant varieties

◆

Solarize soil

◆

Spray my No Mo' Nematodes Tonic (page 182)

THIS IS THEIR LIFE

In scientific terms, slugs and snails are hermaphroditic, which means that each and every one has both male and female sex organs. They do mate, but then both partners lay masses of small, gelatinous eggs in pockets of soft soil. Depending on the species, the hatchlings take anywhere from a few months to several years to reach maturity. Then they carry on the cycle, laying eggs as often as six times a year. Where winters are cold, slugs and snails hibernate in the soil; but in mild areas, they keep right on going all year-round.

ALSO ON THE MENU

Slugs and snails have hearty appetites for just about anything that grows in a garden. But their favorites are leafy green vegetables. There *is* one category of plants that the slimers won't touch—herbs with stiff, highly aromatic foliage, such as rosemary, sage, and lavender.

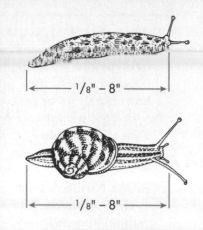

$^1/_8$" – 8"

$^1/_8$" – 8"

When slugs or snails have been slinking through your flowers, there's no mistaking the evidence. Both slobs chew ragged holes in leaves and flowers, often completely devouring seedlings and young transplants, and leaving behind disgusting trails of silvery slime. Slugs and snails are not insects; they're mollusks, closely related to shellfish like clams and oysters. The only real difference between the two villains is that a snail has a shell, and a slug does not. This dastardly duo can show up anywhere, but they appear most frequently and cause the most damage in cool, damp gardens. Almost no plant is safe from their sharp jaws, but in the flower garden, marigolds, hostas, and delphiniums are high-risk targets.

🍃 Home Improvement

A slug's idea of heaven on earth is a flower garden that's cool, shady, and moist. If those words pretty well describe your territory, then you're probably up to your ears in 'em. But two simple steps could reduce the population considerably. First, do whatever you can to let in more sunshine. For instance, remove or prune trees, replace solid fences with lattice panels, or paint walls and fences white so they reflect more light. Second, grow your plants in raised beds. The soil will drain quickly, and slugs don't like well-drained soil one little bit!

🍃 Snag a Sack of Slugs

For my money, the most effective way to clear slugs and snails out of a flower garden is to stage a hunting expedition shortly after dusk, when the slimers come out to feed. Just rally some pals, or hire a few youngsters, and arm each one with a pair of tongs, a bucket filled with your choice of poisons (see "The Fatal Dose," below), and orders to snatch 'em up and drop 'em in the drink.

🍃 Tried-and-True Traps

If a-hunting you'd rather not go, trap the twerps instead. In the evening, set citrus rinds, cabbage leaves, or potato chunks among your plants. In the morning, scoop up the traps, slugs and all, and send 'em to their doom.

🍃 The Fatal Dose

No matter what method you use to catch slugs and

DID YOU KNOW?

Contrary to popular belief, the giant banana slugs of the Pacific Northwest cause almost no trouble to anyone. In fact, these colorful guys are some of Ma Nature's best recycling wizards. They slither around the woods, gobbling up dead leaves and other forest debris, and they rarely venture into home gardens. (As the name "banana" implies, these slugs are often yellow, although they may be other colors, including mottled shades of red, orange, or brown.)

snails, you can send them to their just rewards by dropping them into a bucket of water laced with a cup or so of any of these lethal ingredients:

- ▶ Alcohol (rubbing)
- ▶ Ammonia
- ▶ Baking soda
- ▶ Epsom salts
- ▶ Pine cleaner
- ▶ Salt
- ▶ Soapy water
- ▶ Vinegar

🍃 Put Your Weeds to Work

Is your lawn sporting a few patches of quack-grass? If so, don't dig it up—at least not all of it. Scientists at the U.S. Department of Agriculture have proven that this perennial weed (known as *Agropyron repens*) kills slugs, without harming any other critters. To put these magical powers to work, just cut off the grass blades, and let them dry out in the sun. Then chop them into small pieces and sprinkle them in a thin layer around your mature plants. Just be aware that fresh

    ANNUAL & PERENNIAL PLAGUERS

quackgrass—or an overdose of the dry stuff—can damage some plants. So make sure the blades are completely dry, keep the layer light, and test it on a few plants of each kind that you want to protect before you mulch your whole garden.

Home on the Range

Slugs & Snails

For the Younger Crowd

To protect seedlings and tender new transplants from slugs, I recommend a more aggressive protection plan. To guard these youngsters, entice the slugs to their death with a batch of my Quack-Up Slug Cookies (below). Or, bury shallow cans up to their rims in the soil, and pour in about 1 inch of grape juice, cheap beer, or a solution made from 1 pound of brown sugar and ½ package of dry baker's yeast in 1 gallon of warm water. (If you have dogs or cats on the scene, use widemouthed pint bottles instead of cans; that way, Fido or Fluffy can't lap up the stuff.)

If It Feels Bad, Use It

For centuries, folks have been keeping slugs and snails at bay by surrounding their plants with scratchy stuff that prickles, or even slices the slimers' skin when they slink over it. And that strategy still works today. Just select your substance, and spread it around. Some of the best and easiest to come by are ground-up eggshells, sharp sand, diatomaceous earth, wood ashes, shredded oak leaves, pine or hemlock needles, and coffee grounds.

THUG BUSTER

Quack-Up Slug Cookies

Slugs will think it's time to party when they get a beer-scented whiff of these tasty treats. But after a couple of bites, they'll have a killer of a hangover!

**1 part dried quackgrass blades, finely chopped
1 part wheat bran*
1 can of beer**

Mix the quackgrass and bran in a bowl, then slowly add the beer, stirring until the mixture has the consistency of cookie dough. Run the dough through a meat grinder, or chop it into small bits (roughly ⅛ to ¼ inch thick). Let the "cookies" air-dry overnight, sprinkle them on the ground among your plants, and let the good times roll!

*Available in supermarkets and health-food stores.

🍂 Stopped by the Copper

A copper mini-fence is a classic device for keeping slugs out of a flower bed. When the critters try to slither over the barrier, something in the metal reacts with the slime on the slugs' bodies, and bingo: End of story! Before you erect your own fence, though, peruse this list of pointers:

▶ Don't buy a ready-made fence—it'll cost you a small fortune. Instead, visit an auto-wrecking establishment, and ask for some old copper radiator strips. You'll get 'em for next to nothing.

▶ Make sure you get all the slugs out of the bed before you put up your barrier. Otherwise, the varmints will be trapped inside, and boy, will they have fun!

▶ Keep your little fence clean. Once a coat of tarnish builds up on the copper, it won't deliver a charge,

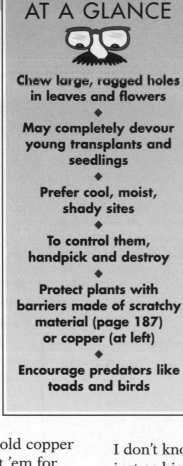

SLUGS & SNAILS

AT A GLANCE

Chew large, ragged holes in leaves and flowers

◆

May completely devour young transplants and seedlings

◆

Prefer cool, moist, shady sites

◆

To control them, handpick and destroy

◆

Protect plants with barriers made of scratchy material (page 187) or copper (at left)

◆

Encourage predators like toads and birds

and the slimers will slink right over it.

🍂 A Princely Meal

To you, slugs might be a royal pain in the grass, but to a lot of other critters, they're a delicacy fit for a king. Well, actually, make that fit for ducks, toads, birds, lizards, ground beetles, and plenty of other aristocratic good guys. (See Chapter 8 for more on satisfying these high-class customers.)

🍂 Egg 'Em On

I don't know about you, but I still get just as big a kick out of watching lightning bugs flit around the yard as I did when I was a little tyke. But now I know those twinklers are good for a lot more than entertainment value: Their young'uns, a.k.a. glowworms, polish off slews of slugs. It takes no special effort to attract fireflies; they'll find their way to your yard as long as you don't use pesticides, which will kill them off in a flash.

THIS IS THEIR LIFE

Scenario Number 1: A cute, fluffy kitten looks at you and says, "Meow," and you're hooked. You take her home, and she finds her true calling in life: running your household—and occasionally venturing into the garden for a romp in the flower beds.

Scenario Number 2: You've asked the neighbors time and again to keep their cats at home, but the felonious felines are still running rampant in your yard.

ALSO ON THE MENU

Cunning cats cut their capers all over the yard and garden. That nice, fluffy soil in the shrub border makes a dandy litter box, for instance. And when you planted that young sapling, you did intend it to be kitty's new scratching post, didn't you? In the next few pages, you'll find solutions that will stop Fluffy and Puffy in their tracks, no matter where they're on the rampage.

Cats are a lot of fun to have around the house, all right—I can't imagine being without one! They even do a good deed in the garden now and then by keeping the rodent population under control. Unfortunately, though, a gentle, playful kitty can turn into a menacing marauder in the blink of an eye, turning your flower beds into her own private privy, eating or trampling your plants or, worst of all, gunning for the winged warriors at your bird feeder. Of course, it's as easy as pie to keep your own cat from raising a ruckus in the garden—just keep her indoors. But policing the neighbors' free-roaming felines can be more of a challenge, so read on!

🌿 Super-Simple Sprays

When wandering tomcats leave your garden smelling anything *but* flowery, relief is as close as your kitchen cupboard. Just fill a hand-held sprayer with either straight vinegar or a half-and-half solution of pine cleaner and water, and regularly spritz the places where the boys are leaving their marks. The scent of either potion will confuse and repel the rascals. Just one word of caution: Both of these fabulous fluids can kill plants, so use them only on nonliving things—or on weeds.

🌿 All Dug Up!

If you venture out to your flower garden some morning and find a bunch of newly planted posies just lying there beside their holes, suspect a roving cat. Some frisky felines have an annoying habit of digging up young plants, for no good reason that I can see. What to do? Just tuck the youngsters back into their holes and give them a good dose of my Compost Tea (see page 179) to get them growing on the right root again. Then, to keep Fluffy from trying that trick again, turn up the heat with my Hit-the-Trail Mix (page 191). She'll turn tail and run when she gets a whiff of this extra-spicy elixir—and so will just about any other critter that has a nose to sniff with!

Home on the Range

Cats

When a family of pest-controlling birds sets up nestkeeping in your favorite tree, the last thing you need is a feline felon snagging them for dinner. So how do you keep the little chirpers safe and sound? Just do what Grandma Putt did: Plant a climbing rose at the base of the tree on the sunny side, and train the thorny canes up the trunk. Puffy will dine elsewhere.

A More Permanent Solution

No matter how potent a smelly repellent is, you'll have to renew it now and then, as wind, rain, and your garden hose dilute its firepower. Fortunately, there's a longer-lasting solution to your feline frustrations. First, plant seeds of a low-growing groundcover, like creeping thyme or sweet alyssum, around the perimeter of your flower bed. Then on top of the newly seeded soil, lay 2- to 3-foot-wide strips of chicken wire. When the plants grow up, they'll cover the flat fencing, so you'll hardly notice it. But when Puffy's paws touch that sharp wire, she'll be outta there!

Temporary Cover

No cat worth her weight in catnip can resist a nice, fluffy bed of freshly tilled soil—like the one where you've planted your annual seeds. Protect those future flowers by covering the soil with thorny canes cut from rosebushes or bramble fruits.

Don't Touch Those Birds!

You can use that same invisible fence (see "A More Permanent Solution," above) at the base of bird feeders and nesting boxes. Just make sure that those shelters are well out of leaping range of tree limbs, porch overhangs, or other handy platforms. Otherwise, the agile assassins won't even notice your fence!

🌿 A Flashy Solution

Because cats can jump and climb like nobody's business, it's all but impossible to build a vertical fence that'll keep them out. But this clever alternative will foil 'em fast—and it's as easy as 1,2,3. Here's all you need to do:

Step 1. Fill empty 2-liter soda bottles half full of water, and add a few drops of bleach, just to keep smelly algae from growing.

Step 2. Put two or three long, thin strips of aluminum foil into each bottle.

Step 3. Set the bottles every few feet around the area you want to protect.

The constantly changing reflections from the foil will scare the daylights out of any cat who comes prancing onto your turf.

🌿 Turn 'Em On or Turn 'Em Off

If you'd rather plant your protection, here's a duo of dandy choices for keeping ornery cats away from your flowers:

▶ Install a big bed of catnip as far away from your flower garden as your lot size allows. Most likely, the rascals will have so much fun rolling around in it that they won't give a second thought to your annual and perennial posies.

▶ Include rue in your planting scheme. It's an easy-to-grow perennial herb with beautiful, blue-green leaves, small, greenish yellow flowers, and decorative brown seedheads that look great tucked into wreaths and swags. Best of all, though, it makes felines flee, fast!

THUG BUSTER

Hit-the-Trail Mix

When cats are cuttin' capers in your flower beds or gunnin' for your fine feathered friends, put up a "Keep Out!" sign in the form of this zesty potion.

4 tbsp. of dry mustard
3 tbsp. of cayenne pepper
2 tbsp. of chili powder
2 tbsp. of cloves
1 tbsp. of hot sauce
2 qts. of warm water

Mix all of the ingredients, and sprinkle the solution around the perimeter of your yard, or anyplace where Puffy isn't welcome. She'll get her kicks elsewhere!

That Is Not Your Litter Box!

All across the country these days, more and more folks are doing their gardening in containers. And, judging from the letters in my mailbag, about 80 percent of them share a common problem: Cats who mistake the big pots for their personal bathrooms. Well, here's a trio of ways to say, "Take your potty break elsewhere!"

1. Plant low-growing groundcovers at the base of potted trees and shrubs. You'll spiff up the container scheme and keep Fluffy out at the same time.

2. Saturate some cotton balls in lemon-oil furniture polish, and tuck them into the pots. Kitty won't like the smell one bit! One ball will work for a small container; for larger ones, use two or three.

3. Cover the soil surface with aluminum foil, and spread a thin layer

CATS AT A GLANCE

Use beds and containers as litter boxes

◆

Roll around in flower beds, flattening the flowers in the process

◆

Eat plants, indoors and out (sometimes with nasty results to their tummies)

◆

Attack birds in feeders and nesting boxes

◆

To control them, keep your own cats indoors, and discourage roving felines with my Hit-the-Trail Mix (page 191)

of mulch on top. When Fluffy leaps into the pot to do her business, the rustling sound and strange feel will make her hop right out again.

Chow Time

Many cats may be perfectly content to use their own litter boxes—but they think your container garden is Joe's Diner. What do you do in that case? Give the frisky feline something better to munch on! Most cats prefer wheat or oat grass to garden-variety flowers, paws down. Just get some seed from a garden center, and sow it in a flat or pot that blends with your decor. When the grass comes up, set the container where Fluffy can get at it easily. She'll give your posies the cold shoulder. **Note:** When you bring your tender plants indoors for the winter, grow your guard grass on a sunny windowsill, and move it out to its duty station when it's a few inches high.

THIS IS THEIR LIFE

Chipmunks are born blind and hairless, in underground dens. They stay there for six to eight weeks, then emerge to romp and play like carefree tots for close to four months. Then it's time for serious business: mating and starting the cycle all over again. The number of generations per year varies, but generally, there are just one to three babies per litter.

ALSO ON THE MENU

Aside from their shenanigans in the flower garden, chipmunks can get up to major mischief in the vegetable patch. At planting time, they excavate newly planted seeds, especially those of cucumbers, melons, corn, and squash. Later in the season, they come back to sample whatever veggies they can find—and strawberries, too. They also love to peel the bark from shrubs and young trees.

4" – 7"

Chip 'n' Dale didn't become superstars by accident. Not only are chipmunks the cutest critters that ever came down the pike, but they're also smart, curious, and as acrobatic as the Flying Wallendas—in short, they've got everything it takes to succeed in Tinseltown! In real life, though, these adorable little rodents can be giant pains in the grass. They dig up seeds and bulbs, sometimes because they're hungry, but just as often because they've seen you at work and want to know what treasure you've just buried. When the plants come up, these guys are first in line to nibble on the new shoots and, later, to sample the buds. And as if that weren't enough mischief, their bird-feeder heists would put the wiliest squirrel to shame.

Not So Fast

If you live in gypsy moth territory (see page 48), don't be so quick to put chipmunks on your unwanted list. These little guys eat hordes of the moths' vicious larvae, and having them mess with a few bulbs or flower buds is a small price to pay for gaining freedom from terroristic moths!

They Just Popped Out!

If you plant spring-blooming bulbs, you've probably had this experience at least once: You spend hours tucking your bulbs into bed for the winter, and the next morning, you find them on the ground, right beside their holes, but looking

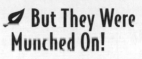
Home on the Range

Chipmunks

untouched by tooth or claw. Chip 'n' Dale strike again! How can I be so sure? Because any other critter would have munched on those bulbs or run off with them. But chipmunks operate differently. These little guys are very territorial, they have a terrific sense of smell, and they're curious as all get-out. (Often, they have no intention of eating the bulbs; they just want to get a good sniff.) In the course of planting, you transferred your scent to the bulbs, then popped 'em into the ground—thereby invading some chipmunk's territory. So naturally, the little fella *had* to investigate!

So What to Do?

Before you resort to more time-consuming measures to save your overturned bulbs, try this simple trick that (kooky as it sounds) has worked like a charm for me: Pop the bulbs back into their holes. Then, lay a bedsheet over the planting bed, and set a few rocks on top to weight it down. Leave it in place for three or four days, then take it off. By then, your scent will have faded, and I'll bet you dollars to daffodils that Chip or Dale won't bother those bulbs again!

But They Were Munched On!

Sometimes, chipmunks *do* actually eat bulbs, or at least chew on them. If your dug-up treasures have chunks missing, toss 'em on the compost pile and try again. But before you tuck the new bulbs into their holes, dust them with baby powder or scented talcum powder. The chipmunks and every other four-footed bulb thief in your yard will take one sniff and say, "None for me, thanks!"

The Tips Have Toppled

…into the chipmunks' tummies. When the little rascals are eating the buds and fresh, new shoots of your flowers, it takes more than scented powder to stop them. It takes a jolt to the mouth like the one my Hot Bite Spray (page 195) delivers. So don't delay: Mix up a batch, and go save your posies!

Save Those Seeds!

To keep the little bandits from swiping your flower and vegetable seeds, lay a sheet of hardware cloth or old window screen over the seedbed. Just make sure you take it off at the first sign of little green shoots poking up through the soil.

A Bloody Good Idea!

When chipmunks are having a field day in your flower garden, bloodmeal sprinkled on the ground will send 'em scurrying. There's just one problem: When it rains, the powder goes right into the soil. Having to replace the stuff is bad enough, but if it happens too often, all that bloodmeal can give the plants an overdose of nitrogen. Fortunately, there's a simple solution to that dilemma: Sink soup cans or plastic cups into the soil among your plants. Then fill each container with a mixture of 1 part bloodmeal to 2 parts water. (Stop about an inch from the top to leave room for rainwater.) As the solution evaporates, add more. The result: long-term 'munk relief with no nitrogen side effects. **Note:** Bloodmeal discourages other critters, too, including deer, skunks, ground-hogs, and rabbits.

THUG BUSTER

Hot Bite Spray

When chipmunks or other furry felons are feeding on your flower-ing plants, whip up a batch of this timely tonic.

3 tbsp. of cayenne pepper
2 cups of hot water
1 tbsp. of hot sauce
1 tbsp. of ammonia
1 tbsp. of baby shampoo

Mix the cayenne pepper with the hot water in a bot-tle, and shake well. Let the mixture sit overnight, then pour off the liquid without disturbing the sediment at the bottom. Mix the liquid with the other ingredients in a hand-held sprayer. Keep a batch on hand, especially when tender shoots and new buds are forming, and spritz the plants as often as you can to keep them hot, hot, **hot!** No critter who tastes the stuff will come back for a second bite!

Give 'Em the Hair of the Dog

Or the cat. Every time you brush Fido or Fluffy, sprin-kle their hair around the chipmunks' stomping grounds. The 'munks will high-tail it for safer pas-tures. Of course, feces or urine from a dog or cat will scare the daylights out of the little striped scoundrels, too, but I don't recommend it for use around flowers or vegetables. Aside from the, um, distinctive aroma, either substance can spread germs and burn tender plants.

🌿 A Dose of Real Danger

The chipmunk population will plummet pronto if a hawk or an owl takes up residence in your yard. To encourage the big birds, set up roosting platforms on high poles, or remove leaves from a branch of a tall tree to make a good landing area. Whatever you do, though, don't lay out the welcome mat for *any* birds of prey if you let cats or small dogs roam your yard. The ravenous raptors will snatch them up before you can say, "Gone with the Wind."

🌿 Movin' On

If the chipmunk population is bordering on the ridiculous, it is possible to live-trap them and move them deep into the woods. Just get a 5-by-5-by-

CHIPMUNKS
AT A GLANCE

Dig up freshly planted bulbs and large seeds, sometimes to eat, and sometimes just for kicks

◆

Nibble young shoots, flowers, vegetables, and fruits

◆

Raid bird feeders

◆

Strip bark from shrubs and young trees

◆

Eat gypsy moth larvae (nobody's *all* bad)

◆

To control them, cover seed and bulb beds

◆

Deter with bloodmeal and my Hot Bite Spray (page 195)

15-inch box trap at a hardware store, set it in a sheltered spot near the critters' stomping grounds, and cover it with leafy twigs. As for bait, any of these will lure 'em right in:

▶ Cereal

▶ Corn

▶ Molasses on crackers or whole wheat toast

▶ Peanut butter

▶ Rolled oats

▶ Sunflower seed

▶ Unroasted peanuts

Just two sobering notes: Studies show that the vast majority of trapped-and-transported animals do not survive in their new neighborhoods, so this method is not as kind as we old softies like to think it is. Also, trapping and relocating any kind of wildlife (yes, even chipmunks) is illegal in some states, so before you do anything, check with your state's Department of Fish and Wildlife or your local animal control officer.

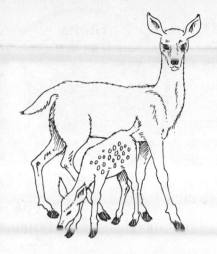

There are three species of deer in the United States: white-tails, found throughout most of the country; mule deer, which live primarily west of the Mississippi River; and blacktails, which roam the coastal areas of California, Oregon, Washington, and Alaska. All three types prefer the same kind of habitat—the edges of wooded areas, where they can find a wide variety of food and cozy shelter (in other words, modern suburbia). Regardless of species, deer mate in the autumn, and the following spring, each doe gives birth to one or, more frequently, two fawns. The babies stay close to mama until the following year, and then go off on their own.

What deer eat on any given day depends on how hungry they are, what goodies are available, and even individual taste. The bottom line is that almost no plant is safe.

Of all the letters in my mailbag, most of the cries for help concern these beautiful, brown-eyed bruisers. And it's no wonder. Within hours, a few hungry deer can munch their way through your entire flower garden—or any other kind of garden, for that matter. Even if you don't see them, or their little hoof prints, it's easy to tell when the Bambi Brigade has been on the scene: You'll see ragged cuts on the chewed-off stems. That's because deer have no incisor teeth in their upper jaws, so rather than slice through their food, they tear it from the plant.

In some parts of the country, homeowners have another reason for keeping deer at bay: They are targets of deer ticks, the infamous carriers of Lyme disease. (You can read all about those little monsters beginning on page 157.)

🌱 Double Whammy

I've got a whole lot of tricks up my sleeve for deterring deer, but I have to admit that the only surefire way to keep them out of your garden is to put up a fence. Or, better yet, two fences that are at least 5 feet high and 4 feet apart. The reason: Deer can jump high, and they can jump far, but they can't do both at the same time.

Zap Goes the Wire

I call this the "gotcha" fence. It lures deer with the smell of peanut butter. Then, when they reach out for a bite, they get a light, but unwelcome zap on the nose or tongue. Try it—they won't like it! Here's what you need to do:

1. Attach insulators to 4-foot metal stakes.

2. Pound a stake into the ground at each corner of your garden and about 10 feet apart along the sides and ends.

3. String a line of 50-pound-tension hot wire from post to post at the top.

4. Run the wire into an electrical source—either your regular house current or a battery-charged generating unit.

5. Spread peanut butter all along the wire.

6. Turn on the electric current.

7. Watch the deer come running when they get a whiff of that peanut butter. And take a good, long look, because you won't see them coming back anytime soon!

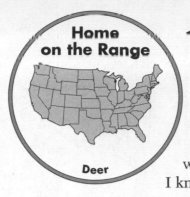

Home on the Range

Deer

A Greener Way to Go

If you lack the time, the inclination, or the budget to corral your garden with any artificial barrier, try one of these pseudo-fences. They've both worked well for some folks I know:

▶ **The not-worth-the-bother fence.** Surround your garden with a triple-thick hedge of tall shrubs or bushy trees that deer don't like. Unless they're *really* hungry, they'll probably go elsewhere rather than plunge through to your flowers. Good plant choices include these people-pleasers: barberry (*Berberis*), box elder (*Acer negundo*), butterfly bush (*Buddleia*), holly (*Ilex*), juniper (*Juniperus*), and mountain laurel (*Kalmia latifolia*).

▶ **The bountiful-banquet fence.** This fence takes the opposite tack: Install a triple-thick hedge of plants that deer go bonkers over. They'll flock to it and (if the gods are with us) leave your posies in peace. These are good candidates: American arborvitae (*Thuja occidentalis*), buckeye (*Aesculus californica*), European mountain ash (*Sorbus aucuparia*), Fraser fir (*Abies fraseri*), Korean lilac (*Syringa patula*), and rhododendron (*Rhododendron* spp.).

🌿 It's a Washout

One classic deer-chasing tip is to tuck deodorant soap, smelly old socks, pouches of baby powder, or other aromatic stuff among your target plants. It works, too, unless the deer are on the brink of starvation. There's just one drawback: Rain or snow will wash away the scent (and in the case of soap, the whole she-bang). So, before you hang up your deter-rents, put each one in a mini garage. Here's how to do it:

1. Tuck your deterrent of choice into an old pantyhose toe, or a mesh onion bag, and tie the pouch closed with a string.

2. Poke a hole in the bottom of a 12-ounce foam or waxed-paper drink cup. (Or use an old plastic flower-pot that has a drainage hole.)

3. Tuck the pouch into the cup, pull the string through the hole, and tie it into a loop. Fasten the loop to the branch of a tree, shrub, or sturdy annual or perennial, and you're good to go. Your smell-emitters should keep their deer-chasing power for about a year, right through rain, sleet, snow, or dark of night!

> ### DID YOU KNOW?
> At last count, there were about 25 million deer in the United States. That's more than the human populations of Illinois and Pennsylvania combined!

🌿 Spray Your Woes Away

Deer don't like the odor of rotten eggs any more than you and I do. And here's a super-simple way to deliver this aromatic unwelcome mat: Just dissolve two well-beaten eggs and 2 teaspoons of beef broth in 1 gallon of water. Let the mixture sit for two days, or until it smells really potent. Then pour it into a hand-held sprayer, and spritz the plants on the edge of your flower garden.

🌿 Urine for Trouble

No deer worth his antlers will venture onto territory where he smells a major predator like a cougar, wolf, or coyote. You probably don't want to invite any of those critters onto your turf to guard your geraniums, but you can make the deer think you have. How? Just crank up your favorite Internet search engine, and type in "predator urine." Up will pop scads of sites where you can buy the stuff. Order a bottle, and sprinkle it around the perimeter of your yard. You won't even notice the odor, but the Bambi Brigade sure will!

No matter what kind of deer-repelling tactics you use, you must change your routine periodically. Deer are creatures of habit, and they quickly get used to just about anything in their day-to-day world that doesn't gobble them up—including a cougar who leaves his scent on the ground, but never appears.

Too Good to Be True?

Believe it or not, there are plants that will send deer scooting off to friendlier pastures, at least much of the time. Castor-oil plant is a guaranteed deer-chaser. But it's also highly poisonous to humans and other animals, so you need to use it with caution. These are safe options:

- ▶ Catnip
- ▶ Chives
- ▶ Garlic
- ▶ Lavender
- ▶ Onions
- ▶ Spearmint
- ▶ Thyme
- ▶ Yarrow

No Guarantees, But...

Deer-resistant does not mean deer-*proof*, but most of the time, in most parts of the country, deer will leave

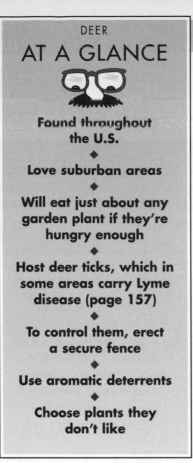

DEER

AT A GLANCE

Found throughout the U.S.

◆

Love suburban areas

◆

Will eat just about any garden plant if they're hungry enough

◆

Host deer ticks, which in some areas carry Lyme disease (page 157)

◆

To control them, erect a secure fence

◆

Use aromatic deterrents

◆

Choose plants they don't like

these winners standing. This is just a short list; to find other likely candidates for your garden, consult your Cooperative Extension Service, a comprehensive regional garden book, or (best of all) gardening neighbors:

Annuals: ageratum (*Ageratum houstonianum*), garden verbena (*Verbena × hybrida*), ice plant (*Mesembryanthemum crystallinum*), pincushion flower (*Scabiosa atropurpurea*), snapdragon (*Antirrhinum majus*), zinnia (*Zinnia*)

Perennials: bellflower (*Campanula*), common bleeding heart (*Dicentra spectabilis*), delphinium (*Delphinium*), foxglove (*Digitalis*), iris (*Iris*), peony (*Paeonia*)

Bulbs: common snowdrop (*Galanthus nivalis*), crocus (*Crocus*), crown imperial (*Fritillaria imperialis*), daffodils (*Narcissus*), glory of the snow (*Chionodoxa*), Siberian squill (*Scilla siberica*)

That's not all, folks!

Many of the bugs and other bad guys that get their kicks in the vegetable garden also run roughshod through beds of annuals and perennials (and bulbs, too). See Chapters 5 through 7 for that crafty crew. In addition, be on the lookout for these rascals:

DOGS just love to bury their bones and chew toys in flower beds, or trample the plants down into cozy napping nests. And, of course, the boys lift a leg toward the stems now and again. In Chapter 1, you'll find plenty of ways to say, "Not here, Pal!"

FIRE ANTS nibble flowering plants now and then—in addition to being darn unpleasant to have around the yard! You can put out their fire with the helpful hints in Chapter 1.

JAPANESE BEETLES can rip a flower garden to shreds if you turn your back for 10

minutes. The tactics in Chapter 3 will end their funfest fast!

MOLES can tunnel right through flower beds in their quest for grubs or other underground goodies. You'll also find the lowdown on these lowlifes starting on page 31.

SQUIRRELS love to munch on flower buds and bulbs. For the full story on these nutty guys, see page 68.

VOLES venture into the flower garden, too. Chapter 2 is the place to read all about them.

CHAPTER 5

ROOT-CROP
RAIDERS

For my money, plants that have their eatin' parts below ground are some of the tastiest treats around, especially when you harvest them at their small, sweet stage. Root crops are a hardy lot, too. But they do have their share of enemies, ranging from wily worms that wiggle their way into the roots, to crafty critters who steal the whole plant before your very eyes. And that's where this chapter comes in. It's loaded with my secrets for guarding your underground gems from troublemakers, both big and small.

CARROT RUST FLIES

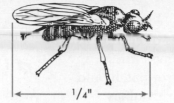

1/4"

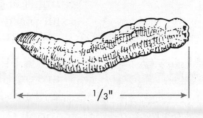

1/3"

THIS IS THEIR LIFE

Generally, adult flies emerge from mid-April to May and lay eggs in plants' crowns or in the soil at their base. Within days, the eggs hatch, and the larvae tunnel through the crown to the roots. They feast (and I do mean *feast*) for three to four weeks, then pupate in the soil. There are two or three generations each year, with the pupae of the last one spending the winter snuggled in the soil. Unfortunately, once your crop has been attacked, all you can do is pull up the plants and destroy them.

ALSO ON THE MENU

These vile villains also venture into the herb garden to munch on that branch of the carrot clan, including angelica, caraway, cilantro, dill, fennel, lovage, and parsley. You can protect your herbs by using the same tactics that give your veggies safe passage.

These foul felons flew in from Europe about a century ago, and they've been causing more trouble with every passing year. As their name implies, carrot rust flies attack carrot-family vegetables, including parsnips, celery, celariac, Florence fennel, and of course, their namesake crop. These sneaks do their dirty work below the soil surface, so unless the plants are badly infested, you may not notice that anything's amiss until harvest time. Then, when you pull up the roots, you'll find them riddled with rust-colored tunnels (which is how the varmints got their name). If you pay close attention, though, you will see early warning signs. First, your plants will wilt because their injured roots can't take up enough water. As the damage progresses, the plants will become dwarfed, and rot may set in around the crowns.

Home on the Range

Carrot Rust Flies

The terrible tunnelers are yellowish white maggots about 1/3 inch long. Their parents are small black flies, a shade under 1/4 inch long, with yellow hairs and yellow heads and legs.

🌿 Eat Up, Guys!

Ground beetles eat scads of carrot rust fly eggs and larvae. So invite these good guys into your carrot patch, and you can all but kiss your troubles

good-bye. For more on these garden-variety heroes, see Chapter 8.

🌿 Clean and Dig

At the end of the growing season, clear out all plant debris. Then till the soil to bring up maggots that are on the brink of pupating. Birds will zero in on the wrigglers and help themselves to lunch. They won't get 'em all, but they will greatly reduce the population.

🌿 Stick 'Em Up

Carrot rust flies are attracted to anything that's yellow-orange. So make a bunch of sticky traps in that color. Just glue yellow-orange paper to wooden boards or pieces of heavy cardboard, and attach each one to a wooden stake. Then coat the boards with petroleum jelly or spray them with a commercial stickum such as Tanglefoot®, and stick your traps into the soil among your carrot-family plants. The flies will flit over to investigate, and that'll be the end of their egg-laying careers!

🌿 Cover Your Bases

Even if you decide to put out yellow-orange boards (see "Stick 'Em Up," above), don't just stand there and wait for the flies to flock to them. If you see

Ask Jerry

Lately, I've been reading a lot about plants that repel insects. Is this stuff really on the up-and-up, or just a bunch of old-time superstitions? And if it is for real, what can I plant to get rid of carrot rust flies?

To answer your first question, I wouldn't rely on repellent plants as my sole means of pest control, but, yes, they sure do work—provided you choose the right ones. In the case of carrot rust flies, because they navigate by smell, you want to use a mixture of highly scented plants that will mask the odors of their targets. Some of the most effective flight-control-system cloggers I know of are pennyroyal, rosemary, sage, wormwood, black salsify, and all of the onion family, including chives, garlic, and ornamental alliums.

any flies flittin' around your garden, let 'em have it with my Great-Guns Garlic Spray (see page 118).

Cover Your Plants

If you live where carrot rust flies are a major problem, your surest defense is a full-scale coverup. Just drive stakes into the soil all around your target plants, and lay cheesecloth, old sheer window curtains, or commercial row covers on top. Make sure the stakes are an inch or so taller than the plants' mature foliage. For most varieties of carrots, that's anywhere from 18 to 24 inches—but check the seed packet or catalog description to be certain.

Wonderful Wood Ashes

If you sprinkle wood ashes on the ground among your carrot-family plants, carrot rust flies won't even

CARROT RUST FLIES
AT A GLANCE

Larvae tunnel into the roots of carrot-family plants
◆
Above ground, plants wilt and become dwarfed
◆
Rot may set in at the crown
◆
To control them, pull up and destroy affected plants
◆
Catch adults with sticky traps
◆
Spray with my Great-Guns Garlic Spray (page 118)
◆
Surround plants with wood ashes to discourage egg-laying
◆
Use row covers

think of laying their eggs there. The downside, of course, is that you'll need to collect a big supply of ashes to use in the spring, so you might have to spend a lot of winter evenings snuggled up in front of a roaring fire. Oh, well! It's a tough job, but when it comes to saving your carrot crop, no sacrifice is too great. Right?

The Resistance Movement

Plant breeders have developed many carrot varieties that are resistant to rust flies. So if the malevolent munchers are a problem in your area, read catalog blurbs and seed packet descriptions carefully to make sure you're getting a carrot that's got the right stuff. New kinds come out almost every year, but one of the best is 'Fly Away'. Its secret? It contains less of the odiferous chemical that draws the adult flies to their target.

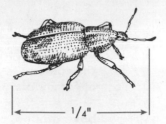
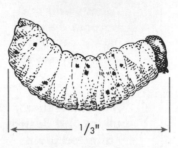

1/4"

1/3"

Adult weevils spend the winter in garden litter, weeds, or tall grass. They emerge in spring—generally in May—and lay eggs in the crowns of their target plants. (All weevils are females that produce fertile eggs without the need for male assistance.) The larvae hatch quickly, bore into the stems, and head downward toward the roots. By late June, they've reached the bottom and are snuggled into their pupal chambers. They break out a couple of weeks later, ready to launch a second generation. Fortunately, even in warm climates, there are only two generations per year.

The wily weevils target any plant that's related to carrots, including the herbs angelica, caraway, lovage, cilantro, parsley, fennel, and dill. On the wild side, they munch on wild parsnip, wild anise, and Queen Anne's lace.

These pesky pests primarily plague plants of their namesake family, which also includes parsnips, celery, celariac, and the little-known, but very tasty vegetable, Florence fennel—not to be confused with the herb fennel, which is also a member of the clan (see "Also on the Menu," at left). And they branch out a little: One of their prime targets is chard, which isn't even remotely related to the carrot clan (it's a kissin' cousin to beets).

Both generations of these demons deal out dastardly destruction. The adult weevils chew the top growth until there's nothing left but stems and the ribs of leaves. Meanwhile, below ground, their babies tunnel through the roots. The grown-ups are about 1/4 inch long and dark brown to bronze, with a long snout and a hard shell (like all weevils). The larvae are dingy white grubs with a brown head and no legs.

A Quick Pick-Me-Up

Carrot weevils eat fast, but they move slowly—and, they don't fly. That makes 'em a snap to pick up with a wet/dry vacuum cleaner. Just fill the reservoir with an inch or two of soapy water, and have at it. Or use a hand-held vacuum, and dump the buggy contents into a bucket of soapy water.

Brush and Blend

Their slow-movin' style gives you another dandy way to wipe out weevils: Just brush about half a cup of weevils into a container, and whir them up into a batch of my Beetle Juice (see page 53). Then mosey on out to the garden with your hand-held sprayer, and fire away. You'll kill 'em by the droves. If the thought of running a bunch of bugs through a blender makes you turn as orange as your carrots, don't worry: My Peppermint Soap Spray (see page 41) will do the trick, too.

Home on the Range

Carrot Weevils

Good-bye, Grubs

To send the grubs packin', get some beneficial nematodes at the garden center, and release them according to the directions on the package. These tiny good guys will solve your weevil woes, lickety-split.

Sorry, No Vacancy!

To head off damage next year, do a super-thorough fall clean-up. That way, you'll deprive the adult weevils of their winter sleeping quarters. Besides clearing

out garden debris, be sure to mow down tall grasses and weeds. Then, for good measure, treat your garden to a bedtime drink of my Winterizing Tonic (below). It'll zap any hiding weevils.

Harvest Early and Often

The longer carrots stay in the ground, the more prone they are to attack. So pull up those roots as soon as you deem them big enough to eat. You'll be fending off the weevil woes, and getting your crop at its tastiest, too!

Winterizing Tonic

To stop trouble before it starts, give bad-guy bugs a fatal drink of this bedtime beverage.

1 cup of Murphy's Oil Soap®
1 cup of tobacco tea*
1 cup of antiseptic mouthwash

Mix these ingredients in a 20 gallon hose-end sprayer, filling the balance of the jar with warm water. Then, after you've done your fall clean-up, saturate your carrot patch and the rest of your lawn and garden, too. Come spring, your plants will be pest-free and rarin' to grow!

*To make tobacco tea, place half a handful of chewing tobacco in an old nylon stocking and soak it in a gallon of hot water until the mixture is dark brown.

THUG BUSTER

THIS IS THEIR LIFE

Adult beetles spend the winter several inches under the soil, emerge in early spring, and get right down to their life's work: eating leaves and laying eggs. In fact, over the course of her five- to six-week life span, a female Colorado potato beetle lays up to 1,000 eggs, usually in batches of several hundred at a time. They hatch in about a week, the larvae eat like crazy for two to three weeks, and then they pupate in the soil. Then 5 to 10 days later, they appear again, all grown up and ready to carry on the family business.

ALSO ON THE MENU

Colorado potato beetles mainly plague members of the Solanaceae family, which includes the bugs' namesake crop, as well as tomatoes, tomatillos, peppers, and eggplant. But every now and then, they wander into the ol' cabbage patch for a nibble or two.

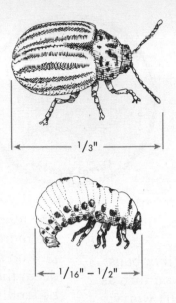

1/3"

1/16" – 1/2"

There are plenty of bad bugs with more varied targets than these pesky pests, but I can't think of a single one that can cause more destruction. A big gang of Colorado potato beetles can defoliate a plant faster than you can say, "Rocky Mountain high." Even when they don't completely strip the leaves, their feeding frenzies commonly kill young plants, and reduce the yield of mature ones. The only good thing about these vile villains is that there isn't a chance in the world of mistaken identity. The adults are rounded, shiny, yellowish orange beetles with 10 black stripes running the length of their back, and black spots on the thorax. The larvae are dark orange, humpbacked grubs with a double row of spots along each side. And both generations eat as though the restaurant were going to close in 5 minutes.

🌿 Get 'Em on Their Way to Breakfast

The first batch of adult spud beetles emerges in the spring, when the soil temperature hits the mid-50°F mark. When they wake up from their long winter's nap, they're groggy and too weak to fly—so they have to walk to breakfast. And that gives you a simple way to close the buffet line: In the fall or very early spring, dig a trench around their target plants, with the sides vertical or steeply sloping (at least 15°). Then line the trench with plastic. The nogoodniks will get as far as the trench and fall in. And, thanks to the slippery plastic, they can't get out. Not alive, that is. Before you know it, they'll be in the stomachs of some hungry birds.

Home on the Range

Colorado Potato Beetles

Give 'Em the Shakes

If it's too late for preventive measures, spread some old sheets or shower curtains on the ground under your plants. Then brush the leaves with a broom to send adults, larvae, and eggs tumbling down. Gather up the whole shebang, and dump the varmints into soapy water.

Pop Goes the Beetle

Here's a bye-bye, beetle, trick that couldn't be simpler: Just sprinkle

DID YOU KNOW?

Like many big-time bad bugs, Colorado potato beetles have been bombarded over the years with every chemical pesticide the folks in white lab coats could cook up. The result? Not only have the hooligans spread far and wide from their original home in the high-mountain meadows, but they've also become resistant to most pesticides. But that doesn't mean you have to put up with their shenanigans—it just means you need to outsmart the creeps!

cornmeal or wheat bran on the leaves of your plants. When the beetles eat the stuff, it'll expand inside their tummies, and they'll explode.

Take That, You Thugs!

You say you'd rather spray than sprinkle? No problem: Any of my beetle-battling Thug Busters will send the Colorado crowd to the big spud farm in the sky. Which recipe is best for you? Why, the one you've got the ingredients for in your kitchen cupboards, of course! Here's a trio of terrific options:

▶ Homegrown Daisy Spray (see page 104)

▶ Instant Insecticide (see page 152)

▶ Peppermint Soap Spray (see page 41)

Not This Time

Whatever you do, don't use my Beetle Juice (see page 53) against Colorado potato beetles. Something in their body fluids can be toxic to potato-family plants, and you could wind up trading one crop problem for another!

Bye-bye, Babies

If you reach the crime scene within the first week or so after the potato beetle larvae hatch, you can wipe 'em out with *Bt tenebrionis*, one of the many varieites of Bt *(Bacillus thuringiensis)*—and the only one that works on Colorado potato beetles. You'll find it in catalogs and garden centers under one of three trade names: Novodor®, M-Trak®, or Raven®.

Rally the Troops

Missed your window of opportunity? Don't panic. Plenty of good guys are on your side. Native parasitic wasps can put a serious dent in the spud beetle population. And assassin bugs, ground beetles, ladybugs, and stinkbugs love sinking their choppers into grownup beetles and larvae of any age. So do some of the prettiest songbirds around, including bluebirds, Baltimore orioles, purple finches, robins, cardinals, grosbeaks, chickadees, and juncos.

What's That Smell?

Because Colorado potato beetles find their targets by smell, you have some powerful weapons in your arsenal. One of the most potent is my Wild Mustard Tea (below). The tangy scent of mustard will mask the aroma of the 'tater plants, and the beetles won't even know they're near their favorite restaurant.

Longer-Lasting Protection

Although my Wild Mustard Tea (below) will give you instant protection for your plants, it has one drawback: Like

Wild Mustard Tea

Potato beetles, cabbage moths, and cabbage loopers will give your garden a wide berth if you spray your plants with this tangy tea.

4 whole cloves
1 handful of wild mustard leaves
1 clove of garlic
1 cup of boiling water

Steep the first three ingredients in the boiling water for 10 minutes. Let the elixir cool, then pour it into a handheld sprayer, and let 'er rip!

THUG BUSTER

any other odiferous repellent, it has to be re-applied after every rain. So, to deliver a standing noninvitation to the spud beetles, plant highly scented flowers and herbs among your potato-family crops. Marigolds, catnip, coriander (cilantro), tansy, and basil will all make the dastardly diners do their munching elsewhere.

On the Fast Track

You can avoid a whole lot of trouble by harvesting your spuds when they're small, or by growing varieties that mature early, before the beetle population peaks. There are many good ones, but some of the best are 'Caribe', 'Sunrise', Charlotte', 'Bison', and 'Yukon Gold'. A good catalog or your Cooperative Extension Service can clue you in on other winners that will perform well in your area.

What the Pros Know

Take a tip from organic potato farmers, and mulch your spud patch with wheat or rye straw. It works in two ways to ease the beetle blues: First, it somehow keeps many of the villains from finding the field in the first place. Second, that thick blanket provides a cozy shelter for good-guy bugs, so any beetles that do show up are quickly eaten by predators, such as ground beetles, ladybugs, and lacewings.

That's Wild!

Some wild potatoes contain a chemical called *leptine* that the beetles don't like, and some folks are breeding these wildlings with commercial spuds in hopes of developing a truly resistant variety. So keep checking catalogs and garden magazines for the big announcement. In the meantime, two old standbys, 'Sequoia' and 'Katahdin', offer some resistance to the thugs.

LEAFHOPPERS

Generally, adult leafhoppers spend the winter in garden debris or among weeds, and emerge in spring at about the time leaves start appearing on trees. Females lay eggs inside stems or leaves of plants. The nymphs hatch in 10 to 14 days, then eat and grow for several weeks before mating and laying eggs of their own. Most species produce from two to five generations per year.

Leafhoppers attack just about every edible plant under the sun, but potatoes, beets, celery, tomatoes, and vine crops are all targets. Grapes and roses figure high on the hit list, too, as do many annuals and perennials, especially annual asters, baby's breath, coreopsis, cosmos, dahlias, marigolds, nasturtiums, petunias, poppies, roses, salvias, and zinnias.

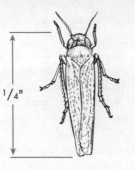

1/4"

There are many species of these jumping jacks, and their targets vary. But they all have the same modus operandi: Both adults and nymphs puncture plant tissues and suck out the juices, generally from the undersides of leaves. In the process, they inject saliva, leaving foliage mottled with white or yellow spots. Eventually, leaves shrivel up and drop, plants weaken, and growth is stunted. One species, the potato leafhopper, causes a condition called tipburn or hopperburn on potatoes, beans, rhubarb, and eggplant. Leaf edges curl up, turn yellow or brown, and die. In most cases, you'll still get a harvest, but the yield may be reduced. And, as if that weren't trouble enough, some leafhoppers also spread viruses and other plant diseases.

Depending on the species, leafhoppers range in color from a drab green that blends right in with foliage to vibrant patterns of red, green, and blue. But they're all tiny (about 1/4 inch long) and wedge-shaped. The wingless nymphs are a tad smaller.

Give 'Em a Wet Welcome

At the first sign of leafhoppers, reach for the garden hose, and blast the pesky pests off of your plants. Any culprits who aren't killed instantly will be so stunned that they'll be sitting ducks for hungry birds. Chickadees, sparrows, swallows, titmice, purple finches, and wrens all eat leafhoppers.

Strong Medicine

When pesky pests are just munching on leaves, making a few holes here and there, you can afford to cut the rascals some slack. (After all, you can't have good guys in your garden if you don't have bad guys for them to eat.) But when you're dealing with creeps like leafhoppers, who spread dastardly diseases, it's a whole 'nother story. If a hard, cold shower doesn't clean 'em off of your plants, whip up a batch of my Lethal Leafhopper Spray (below), and blast the vile villains to the back of beyond!

Your Heroes

After you've got the current crisis well in hand, avoid future trouble by inviting the leafhoppers' enemies onto your turf. Parasitic wasps attack the hoppers, and legions of good-guy bugs gobble 'em up. Green lacewings, assassin bugs, bug-eyed bugs, damselflies, and syrphid flies will all throng to your aid, if you don't use pesticides. (For more about hit-squad hospitality, see Chapter 8.)

Home on the Range

Leafhoppers

The Big Cover-Up

Good guy bugs provide solid protection against leafhoppers, but they're generally not out in full force until the weather warms up in late spring. So, right after planting, cover your crops with old, sheer curtains or commercial row covers. And be sure to seal the edges to the ground with rocks or wood strips so that the horrible hoppers can't sneak under the big top.

Foul Up Their Radar

To protect plants that you don't want to cover up, spread aluminum foil, shiny side up, on the soil in the bed. Light reflecting off the foil will foul up

---

Lethal Leafhopper Spray

Even hard-to-get bugs like leafhoppers will kick the bucket when you hit 'em hard with this stuff.

THUG BUSTER

½ cup of liquor (any kind will do)
2 tbsp. of dishwashing liquid
1 gal. of warm water

Mix all of these ingredients together, and pour the solution into a spray bottle. Then saturate your plants from top to bottom, especially the undersides of leaves, where leafhoppers love to hide.

---

the hoppers' navigational systems, so they won't be able to identify their target.

Color Them Yellow

Besides carrying viruses from plant to plant, some leafhoppers spread a disease called aster yellows. It strikes in early summer and spreads over a variety of vegetables, flowers, and non-woody fruit plants. The symptoms are just plain weird. First, plants' leaves turn yellow along the veins, then pale all over, with brown edges. Too many leaves emerge on a stem, and they're all yellow, spindly, and longer than they should be. Scraggly bunches of stems, like witches' broom, spring out of nowhere. Plants are stunted. If flowers appear at all, they're a sickly yellow-green, and oddly deformed. Although leafhoppers spread the disease, it's actually caused by a tiny nogoodnik called a mycoplasma-like organism, a.k.a. MLO. In size and behavior, it's somewhere between a virus and a bacterium.

Unfortunately, there is no cure, so if

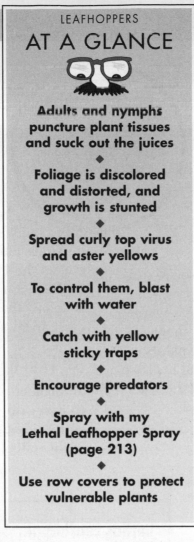

LEAFHOPPERS

AT A GLANCE

Adults and nymphs puncture plant tissues and suck out the juices

◆

Foliage is discolored and distorted, and growth is stunted

◆

Spread curly top virus and aster yellows

◆

To control them, blast with water

◆

Catch with yellow sticky traps

◆

Encourage predators

◆

Spray with my Lethal Leafhopper Spray (page 213)

◆

Use row covers to protect vulnerable plants

this stuff rears its ugly head in your garden, just dig up the victims. It's okay to put them in the compost pile, but don't let them touch any healthy plants on the way, because the MLO also spreads by plant-to-plant contact.

Protection That's Made in the Shade

Leafhoppers hate moisture and shade, so if you grow shade-loving flowers, or vegetables that can thrive in less than full sun (such as lettuce, peas, spinach, or chard), do whatever you can to dim the lights. For instance, position plants closer together (so that their leaves shade the ground), erect a fence, or grow tall shrubs to block direct sunlight.

Sunnier Outlooks

Screening out ol' Sol is not the only way to say, "No leafhoppers need apply." Just plant geraniums or ornamental perennial grasses among your high-risk targets. Then leafhoppers won't come anywhere near the place!

ONION MAGGOTS

THIS IS THEIR LIFE

Flies overwinter as pupae that look like little grains of wheat in the soil or garden litter. Adults emerge anywhere from mid-May to late July and lay eggs at the base of target plants. A week later, the maggots hatch, tunnel into the bulbs, and feast for two to three weeks. They pupate in the soil close by, then in a week or two, they pop out and start the process all over again. There are usually two generations each year.

ALSO ON THE MENU

Although onion maggots (known as *Delia antiqua* in scientific circles) attack only their namesake family, their close relatives, cabbage maggots (*D. radicum*), go gunnin' for the underground parts of the entire Brassica clan (see page 253).

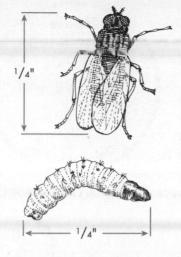

1/4"

1/4"

These malicious marauders have a very specific hit list: They target only radishes and members of the onion family, which includes leeks, shallots, chives, and garlic. But boy, do they ever hit hard! Over the course of its short babyhood, a single maggot can kill more than a dozen seedlings. They do their dirty work by burrowing into the bulb, munching all the way. Young plants generally die quickly. Older plants often survive the maggots' attack, but die soon from diseases that enter through the feeding sites. Sometimes, maggots attack just before harvest, leaving no telltale signs, and the victims end up rotting in storage.

These voracious villains are white, blunt-ended maggots about 1/4 inch long. Their parents are brown, hairy, humpbacked flies, about half the size of houseflies. Aside from giving birth to juvenile delinquents, they're entirely harmless.

✒ First Response

Unfortunately, once the maggots have invaded your crop, your only option is to pull up the plants and toss 'em on the compost pile. (Don't worry about spreading trouble; the slimeballs can't survive the winter in the pile.)

Take That!

To get rid of malingering maggots, drench your patch with my Hot Bug Brew (see page 19). Then, get some beneficial nematodes at the garden center, and apply them according to the directions on the package. They'll polish off any muggers remaining underground.

Home on the Range

Onion Maggots

No Babies on Board

Like a whole lot of pesky pests, onion maggot flies flee fast from wood ashes. So stoke up a roaring fire, grill a few steaks and potatoes, and toast some marshmallows. (I know, it's a big sacrifice, but think of your onions.) The next morning, when the ashes have cooled, spread them on the soil around the maggots' targets. If there's no time for fire building, trot off to the garden center and buy some diatomaceous earth. It'll issue the same "Keep Out" message.

Next Year...

foil the felons by planting your onions and radishes in a different place. Then, remove the soil from the former site and replace it with a fresh supply, laced with plenty of compost. After

that, rotate your crops every other year.

Mug the Muggers

Birds, toads, spiders, and ground beetles all feast on onion maggots. So invite them over to take up residence. To find out how, see Chapter 8.

Time Enough

An old-time technique for protecting onions from maggots is to plant a big bed of radishes (their favorite food) nearby. It works, too: The squirts throng to the radishes and leave the onions alone. But what if you want radishes for eatin', not for sacrificial

GRANDMA KNEW BEST

If you're a big tea drinker, reach for Grandma Putt's favorite anti-maggot weapon: used tea leaves. She saved 'em up all winter long, then worked 'em into the soil before she planted her onions and radishes. It worked like a charm! (Teabags'll do the trick too; the paper coverings dissolve lickety-split.)

guard duty? Just use a little fancy footwork, and try one of these maggot-thwarting techniques:

▶ **Plant early.** If you can get a mature crop by June 1, you'll be all but certain of beating the maggots to the punch.

▶ **Plant 'em and forget 'em.** Sow a midseason crop, and let 'em go to seed. After the seeds mature, till the plants into the ground. Before you know it, seedlings will come up willynilly, and produce radishes well into the fall. By then, the maggots will have turned into moths and flown the coop!

Get 'Em Outta There!

At the end of the growing season, make sure you get *all* of your onions

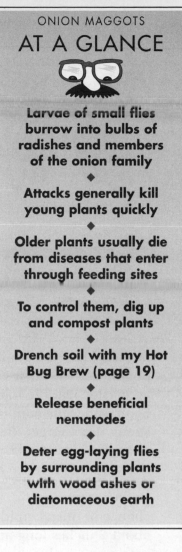

ONION MAGGOTS
AT A GLANCE

Larvae of small flies burrow into bulbs of radishes and members of the onion family

◆

Attacks generally kill young plants quickly

◆

Older plants usually die from diseases that enter through feeding sites

◆

To control them, dig up and compost plants

◆

Drench soil with my Hot Bug Brew (page 19)

◆

Release beneficial nematodes

◆

Deter egg-laying flies by surrounding plants with wood ashes or diatomaceous earth

(healthy or otherwise) out of the ground. That way, you'll deprive any hibernating maggots of their winter food supply.

In the Pink

Maggots' entry sites provide open doors for the onion clan's own family disease, pink root. It's a fungus disease that stunts roots and turns them pink or red. It strikes commercial onion fields far more than home gardens, and it shows up in bulb onions and scallions more than it does in leeks, chives, or garlic. But if the nasty stuff does head your way, pull up and destroy the infected plants, *pronto*. Don't throw them on the compost pile! And don't plant any onion crop in that spot for at least six years, because that's how long this fungus can survive in the soil.

PARSLEYWORMS

Female swallowtails lay their eggs on the tips of host plants, usually one at a time. Each one hatches into a tiny larva that starts right in eating, and growing into a big, colorful caterpillar—shedding its skin several times in the process. When it reaches full size, the critter attaches itself to a plant stem, rests a spell, and then sheds another layer of skin to form its pupal chamber, or chrysalis. Inside this cozy, papery-looking shelter, the caterpillar becomes a butterfly. There are several generations each year.

As the name implies, parsleyworms go for parsley in a big way. But they also love the carrot clan, including angelica, caraway, lovage, cilantro, fennel, dill, anise, yarrow, Queen Anne's lace, wild parsnip, and wild anise.

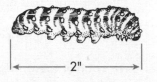

2⁵/₈" – 3¹/₂"

2"

Scads of major garden-variety pests grow up to be entirely harmless, but (unless you're an entomologist) boring insects. Then there's the parsleyworm—a pesky caterpillar that grows up to be a drop-dead gorgeous swallowtail butterfly. Like all of their kind, the adults sip nectar from flowers, pollinating the posies in the process. But the youngsters eat the foliage of every carrot-family plant under the sun, often leaving nothing but the stems. They target the top growth of carrots, parsnips, celery, celariac, and the little-known, but yummy Florence fennel.

When you spot one of these guys, there's no chance of mistaken identity. Parsleyworms are about 2 inches long and light, yellowish green, with a yellow, black-dotted band across each body segment. When they're disturbed, or threatened by a predator, they shoot out a pair of orange horns and give off a rank odor; but don't let the big act scare you: Parsleyworms are paper tigers.

What's in a Name?

A number of closely related caterpillars go by the name of parsleyworm. They all get up to the same mischief, and they look almost identical, but they're the larvae of several closely related swallowtail butterflies. Eastern black swallowtails cover all of the territory from the Atlantic Coast to the Rocky Mountains. West of the Rockies, the parsleyworm parental roster includes the western black swallowtail, desert swallowtail, anise swallowtail, and the official insect of the Beaver State, the Oregon swallowtail. All of these jewels-on-the-wing share a similar color scheme—black and yellow, accented with dabs of blue and orange—but each pattern is a little different. So, what are you waiting for? Get yourself a full-color field guide, grab your binoculars, and go spot some butterflies!

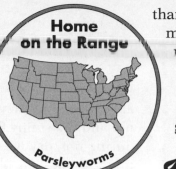

Home on the Range

Parsleyworms

Good News and Bad News

When you or I see a parsleyworm, we might think, "Ah! A future butterfly!" But a lot of hungry critters just think, "Dinner!" Baltimore orioles, barn swallows, bluebirds, kinglets, flycatchers, and chickadees all chow down on parsleyworms. So do toads, snakes, and all of the insects that prey on other kinds of caterpillars (see page 161). The bad news, of course, is that thanks to these gluttons, far fewer butterflies take wing to decorate your air space. The good news is that thanks to these helpful munchers, parsleyworms rarely survive in great enough numbers to do major damage to your plants. (For more about good guys, see Chapter 8.)

Oh, Well

If you find a parsleyworm with what look like grains of rice all over its back, just let it be, because its days are numbered. The little white things are the egg cases of parisitic wasps, and in no time flat, they'll hatch and kill the caterpiller. You'll lose a pretty butterfly, but you'll gain allies in the fight against a lot of other bad-guy bugs.

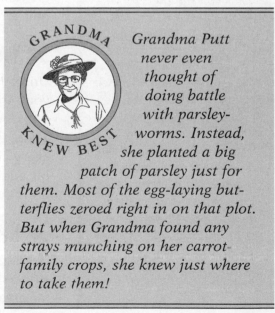

Grandma Putt never even thought of doing battle with parsleyworms. Instead, she planted a big patch of parsley just for them. Most of the egg-laying butterflies zeroed right in on that plot. But when Grandma found any strays munching on her carrot-family crops, she knew just where to take them!

GRANDMA KNEW BEST

POTATO TUBERWORMS

In the spring, female moths deposit eggs, one at a time, on rough plant surfaces, such as the undersides of leaves, or the eyes of potatoes that are left lying on the ground after harvest. But they're also attracted to spuds in storage, or to the sacks or boxes that they're stashed in. The eggs hatch in three to six days, and the larvae start right in tunneling. A week or so later, they pupate in the soil, or in garden litter. In six to nine days, new moths emerge to continue the saga.

ALSO ON THE MENU

Although potato tuberworms most often strike their namesake crop, they attack any member of the Solanaceae family, which includes tomatoes, tomatillos, peppers, and eggplant. They usually just go for the plants' leaves and stems. The one exception is tomatoes, where they burrow into both foliage and fruits.

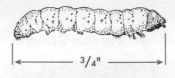

3/4"

These minute monsters can show up anywhere that potato-family (Solanaceae) crops are grown, but they appear most often in California and the sunny South. They tend to attack during hot, dry weather, and at first glance, you might think your plants just need a good drink, because they've up and wilted. If you look closer, though, you'll see tunnels in the leaves and stems, along with pink webbing at the entrance holes. When you dig up the spuds, you'll find holes bored right through the eyes of the tubers, with pink webbing around the openings.

The tunneling terrors themselves are little worms with dark brown heads and bodies that may be white, green, pink, yellow, or purplish. The parents of these juvenile delinquents are grayish brown moths with a wingspan of about half an inch.

Your Mission: Total Destruction

Unfortunately, once tuberworms have moved into your spuds, or any other plants, you have only one option: Dig up the victims and destroy them. Then, do a thorough cleanup. Make sure you get every single potato out of the ground, and clear off and destroy all the vines, where eggs are no doubt waiting to hatch.

Next Time

Next spring (or in the fall, if the worms have ruined your spring crop), plant your potatoes as far away as possible from the scene of the crime.

After that, rotate your crops every year, and to keep both the worms and egg-laying moths from invading your spuds, take these simple precautions:

Home on the Range

Potato Tuberworms

▶ Always keep at least 2 inches of soil over the tubers as they're developing.

▶ Water regularly, and use an organic mulch to retain moisture. (If cracks develop in the soil, moths or worms may sneak through them to invade tubers far underground.)

▶ Renew the mulch when it thins out, and in midsummer, spray it with my Mulch Moisturizer Tonic (below).

Let There Be Light

Tuberworm moths generally flit around at dawn and dusk, and they're attracted to light. So, wipe out throngs of the wingers with this simple trick: Just fill a pail or 3-pound coffee can with water, and add about a tablespoon of vegetable oil. Put it in your garden, and set up a light over the can, about a foot above the rim. The moths will zero in on the light, plunge into the drink, and drown.

Safe Storage

If you store your spuds in a root cellar, or even on the back porch, try to keep the temperature below 50°F, and put a screen over the storage area, so moths can't sneak in to lay their eggs.

Leave Those Leaves Alone!

All that advice is well and good for potatoes, but what about the tuberworms' other targets? Just cover the leaves with Btk (see page 98) or my Homegrown Daisy Spray (see page 104). The vile villains will never know what hit 'em!

Mulch Moisturizer Tonic

THUG BUSTER

Serve up this tasty drink in midsummer to keep your organic mulch fresh as a daisy, your plants happy as clams—and potato tuberworms absolutely miserable!

1 can of regular cola (not diet)
1/2 cup of ammonia
1/2 cup of antiseptic mouthwash
1/2 cup of baby shampoo

Mix these ingredients in your 20 gallon hose-end sprayer, and give your mulch security blanket a nice long, cool drink.

WIREWORMS

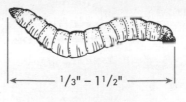

1/3" – 1 1/2"

A s pests go, wire worms rank among the most underrated. That's because the damage they do, tunneling into the plants' roots, closely resembles the dirty work of many other underground pests. When these live wires are on the scene, your first clue may come when your plants lose their get-up-and-grow power. Eventually, they wilt and may die. If you dig up affected root crops (one of the wireworms' favorite meals), you'll see obvious signs of an eating binge, and most likely, foul fungi will be finishing the destruction that the wireworms started. These unholy terrors cause the most trouble in poorly drained soil, or in garden plots that have been recently converted from turf grass.

The munching marauders themselves are jointed, hardshelled worms with three pairs of tiny legs directly behind their heads. Depending on the species, and their age, wireworms measure anywhere from 1/3 to 1 1/2 inches long, and range from yellow to dark brown.

Home on the Range

Wireworms

🌿 Click, Click, Click!

The parents of wireworms are several species of small, slender, brown or black beetles with broad stripes or grooves running the length of their

THIS IS THEIR LIFE

Adult beetles spend the winter underground, and lay eggs in the soil in early spring. Anywhere from 3 to 10 days later, the larvae hatch and immediately start munching on roots, tubers, seeds, or underground stems. They stay close to the surface from spring through fall, then head deeper into the soil for the winter, sometimes going as far as 10 inches underground. Some species of wireworms mature in a single year; others feed for two to six years before pupating.

ALSO ON THE MENU

Besides tunneling into potatoes, carrots, beets, sweet potatoes, and other root crops, wireworms attack the roots and seeds of just about every vegetable and garden fruit under the sun. Corn, snap beans, peas, lettuce, muskmelons, and strawberries are prime targets. They also munch on many bulbs, corms, and perennials.

wing covers. The critters have a tendency to roll over on their backs, and in the process of flipping themselves right-side up—which can take several tries—they make a clicking sound. Hence their common name: click beetles. Some types nibble on plant leaves, but so lightly that you'll probably never notice the damage. Their only claim to real infamy is their obnoxious offspring.

Tater Traps

Regardless of what targets the wily worms are after, this simple trick will wipe 'em out. Spear chunks of potato on sticks that are about 8 inches long, and bury them so that about 3 inches of the stick shows above ground. Then, every day or two, pull up the tater bits, toss 'em in a pail of soapy water to kill the worms, and add 'em to the compost pile.

Give 'Em a Taste of Their Own

To wipe out your current crop of wireworms, and keep more from moving in, collect a half cup or so of the worms, and whip up a batch of my Beetle Juice (see page 53). (You might want to double or even triple the recipe.) Then drench the soil around your infested plants and spray the stems and crowns thoroughly. Bingo—end of story!

Why Work?

Too busy to spend your time trapping and spraying? Just trot down to the garden center, or crank up your favorite online garden catalog, and order

Ask Jerry

I've just started a new vegetable garden, and wireworms are eating everything in sight! Do you have any big-time tricks up your sleeve?

I sure have! My Can o' Worms Traps are just the ticket for clearing out a major invasion. First, gather up some large, empty juice or coffee cans, and punch a lot of medium-sized nail holes in the sides. Fill the cans about halfway with cut-up potatoes or carrots, then bury them so that the tops are just above ground. Cover the openings with small boards, then toss a little mulch on top. Once or twice a week, pull up the cans, empty the contents into a bucket of soapy water, then toss the wormy liquid on the compost pile. Re-bait your traps, and you're back in business!

some beneficial nematodes. Then release them into the soil according to the directions on the package. They'll put an end to your wireworm woes in no time flat!

Sweet Success

To polish off the grown-up crowd, drizzle corn syrup, honey, or molasses on fence posts or thick wooden stakes. Then, when the beetles fly in to sip the syrup, pick 'em off and drop 'em into soapy water. Whatever you do, though, don't lace the sweet bait with poison: It'll kill the click beetles all right, but it'll also kill honeybees, butterflies, and other good-guy bugs who show up for a snack.

An Ounce of Prevention

Wireworms cause the most trouble in gardens that have been converted from turf grass within the past couple of years. So if you're thinking about replacing part of your lawn with food crops or flowers, dig your future beds in late summer or early fall. Then turn the soil over once a week for four to six

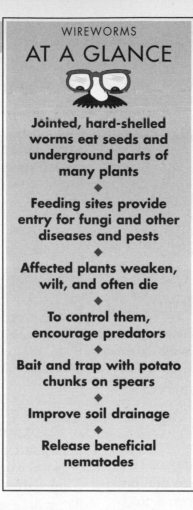

WIREWORMS
AT A GLANCE

Jointed, hard-shelled worms eat seeds and underground parts of many plants

◆

Feeding sites provide entry for fungi and other diseases and pests

◆

Affected plants weaken, wilt, and often die

◆

To control them, encourage predators

◆

Bait and trap with potato chunks on spears

◆

Improve soil drainage

◆

Release beneficial nematodes

weeks. That way, you'll bring the wireworms up to the surface, where birds can get at 'em. If the winged warriors don't get all of the pesky pests, don't fret, because the wireworm population is at its peak just after you strip off the sod. Over three to four years, the numbers dwindle, as long the land stays in cultivation. So just be patient!

Does the Colonel Know This?

If you're lucky enough to know someone who has chickens, invite a few of the cluckers over for lunch, and turn 'em loose on your freshly tilled plot. They'll clear out the entire wireworm population—along with cutworms and whatever other bad guys they can get their beaks around. (Trust me on this one, folks; I've tried it more than once, thanks to a neighbor who has some very sociable pet hens, and it works like magic!)

THIS IS THEIR LIFE

Female gophers give birth to 1 to 10 babies per litter, but the average is 3 to 4. Within about six weeks, Mom kicks them out to fend for themselves. About a year later, they reach maturity and start their own families. In cold climates, gophers produce just one litter per year, generally between March and June; but in balmy places, breeding can go on year-round.

ALSO ON THE MENU

Gophers are gluttons, pure and simple. Root vegetables rank near the top of their most-wanted list, but they also go gaga for tomatoes, peppers, squash, melons, cucumbers, and (are you ready for this?) garlic, which most pests won't touch. And they just love to munch on tulips, lilies, dahlias, hollyhocks, and the roots of fruit trees and grape vines.

Evidence of gophers is sometimes mistaken for that of moles, because the two little critters share the same simple approach to life: Dig it, man! Both of these terrific tunnelers spend their lives underground, never venturing to the surface if they can help it. But there, the similarities end. Moles eat only grubs and other insects; any damage they do to plants is a byproduct of their enthusiasm for the chase. (You can read all about these rascals in Chapter 1.) Gophers, on the other hand, are rodents who eat nothing *but* plants, and plenty of them. They're not subtle about it, either. When one of these guys is at work, you'll see no telltale signs of below-ground nibbling, such as limp stems or yellowing foliage. Instead, a plant that's growing great guns one minute will keel over onto its side the next—or even be pulled into the ground, lock, stock, and leaf tips!

Goin' for the Green

There are 33 different species of gophers in the U.S. They range in length from 6 to 12 inches, and in weight from 8 ounces to a full pound. They have external pouches on their cheeks, where they store their booty as they travel along—and travel they *do*, far and deep, in their quest for food and warm, cozy lodgings. In fact, a lone gopher can tunnel as far as 300 feet in a single night. Gophers have long, sharp claws to dig with, sensitive whiskers that help them navigate through their dark tunnels, and lips that close behind their incisor teeth—so that no soil goes into their tummies along with those tasty roots, shoots, and tubers. Gophers perambulate throughout the country, but they tend to cause the most trouble in the stretch from Indiana west to the Pacific Ocean.

Home on the Range

Gophers

Who's There?

Because defending your territory from gophers is no easy task, before you do anything, make sure it's gophers who've come a-callin', and not moles or ground squirrels. You can tell by

simply eyeballing the tunnel entrances. At a gopher's front door, you'll see a U- or crescent-shaped mound of moist soil that looks as though it's been sifted. Moles make round mounds at their entrance holes, and ground squirrels leave no kicked-up soil at all. (You can read all about moles in Chapter 1; for the lowdown on ground squirrels, see page 229.)

Do It Now!

Once you've got a positive I.D., act fast, because a single tunnel can turn into a maze the size of the New York subway system faster than you can say, "Take the A-Train." Before you even start contemplating longer-term measures, soak some sponges or old T-shirts in ammonia, and stuff one into each hole. Then seal them all up. Those G-men will dig out in a hurry! Next, mix up a batch of my Gopher-Go Tonic (page 227) and dribble it around your garden. That way, when the little varmints pop up out of their tunnels, they'll quickly take off for less aromatic quarters.

Different Strokes

No ammonia on hand? Don't worry. Plenty of other scents make gophers pack up and head outta town (or at

> **GRANDMA KNEW BEST**
>
> *Back in Grandma Putt's day, folks sent gophers packin' by putting fish heads in their burrows. The little guys couldn't stand the smell, so they got outta Dodge fast. If you try this trick, just be aware that although you will get rid of the gophers, you just might wind up entertaining a different crowd of equally unwelcome critters who are attracted to the stench.*

least out of your yard). Whichever one you use, there are two keys to success: Wear gloves so you don't transfer your scent to the repellent, and seal all the entrance holes you can find, so the tunnel gets good and smelly. Here are some of the best, easy-to-come-by odor emitters:

▶ Juicy Fruit® gum

▶ Rotting garbage

▶ Used cat litter

▶ Paper towels soaked in rancid oil

▶ Dog or cat hair

Highway Patrol

One of the most effective gopher chasers is as close as the trunk of your car—or the nearest auto parts store. What is it? A highway-emergency flare! Just cut through the "candle" with a sharp knife (not a saw), then dig into the tunnel, and sprinkle the contents (powdered sulfur) inside. Close up the entrance, as well as any exit holes that you've been able to find. The more airtight the tunnel system is, the more eager the gophers will be to

vacate the premises. Keep up your efforts until new mounds no longer appear. Then you'll know the no-goodniks have gone for good!

To Fence or Not to Fence

If your yard has more gophers than Georgia has peaches, you might be tempted to surround the whole plot with a mostly underground fence. Will it keep the rascals out? It might, in some parts of the country, but don't bet the family farm on it! Gopher tunnels have been reported as deep as 6½ feet, and there's no telling how far down the little diggers can go if they set their minds to it.

If you decide to go with a fence, use wire mesh with openings that are

---

Gopher-Go Tonic

When gophers just won't give up, reach for this remarkable recipe.

THUG BUSTER

4 tbsp. of castor oil
4 tbsp. of dishwashing liquid
4 tbsp. of urine
½ cup of warm water
2 gal. of warm water

Combine the oil, dishwashing liquid, and urine in ½ cup of warm water, then stir the solution into 2 gallons of warm water. Pour the mixture over any problem areas, and the gophers will gallop away!

---

no bigger than 1/4 inch across. Leave 6 to 12 inches above ground (gophers rarely strike from the surface), and extend the barrier as far below as your will to dig and budget allow; but I'd recommend no less than 2½ feet.

Bottoms Up

The most effective (and affordable) anti-gopher "fence" is 1/2-inch galvanized wire mesh lining the bottom and sides of each planting hole, or the entire bed if it's small enough. Lay the screen about 2 feet under the surface, and make sure it covers the sides all the way up to a few inches above the soil surface. Don't leave any gaps, because these little contortionists can squeeze through even the teeniest openings.

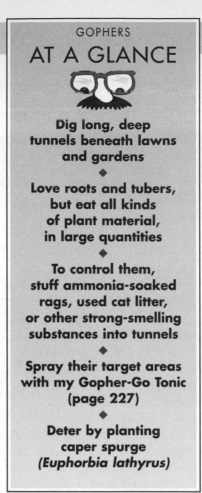

Splurge on Spurge

When gophers are gobbling up your garden, buy as much caper spurge *(Euphorbia lathyrus)* as you can afford. Then plant it all around the perimeter of your garden. The roots produce an acrid, milky juice that gophers can't stand. One whiff, and they'll find another dining establishment!

Sound 'Em Out

Like a lot of critters, gophers are very sensitive to sound vibrations. To use that fact to your advantage, just gather up six or eight empty glass bottles and half-bury them, top ends up, in a line near the gophers' hangouts. When the wind passes over them, it'll let out a scary noise that'll make the little guys scurry in a hurry.

There are 19 different species of ground squirrels in North America. Some of them just go about their business, in the southwestern deserts or the Alaskan tundra, playing their role in Mother Nature's food chain. But other ground squirrels are major pains-in-the-grass to homeowners, farmers, and golf-course greenskeepers from Maine to California. Besides gobbling up huge quantities of garden plants and farm crops, they leave the ground riddled with holes that trip up people, pets, and livestock.

Even ground squirrels have their good side, though. For one thing, they consume huge helpings of weed seeds, insect eggs, and insects, including caterpillars, grasshoppers, beetles, ants, and crickets. Some species even go gunnin' for smaller mammals, like mice, voles, and moles. What's more, in their quest for food and housing, the little diggers create miles of tunnels that help aerate the soil.

🍃 Just for the Record

The critter shown above is a California ground squirrel, one of the most destructive of the bunch. These voracious vegetarians roam parks, suburban yards, and farm fields all along the west coast, from Mexico north to Washington state.

🍃 Go Get 'Em, Guys!

Ground squirrels have hordes of enemies who help keep the population under control. Your

THIS IS THEIR LIFE

Most ground squirrels give birth to one litter of three to eight babies a year, usually in the spring. They grow up fast, live for an average of two to three years, and devote the whole time to their digging, eating, mating, and sleeping. Even within species, hibernation patterns vary. Some ground squirrels bed down in their dens from mid-October through April. Others scamper around during the mild months, hibernate through the worst part of winter, and lay low during the brutal heat of summer. As Mr. Gershwin said, it's nice work if you can get it!

ALSO ON THE MENU

The specific menu varies, depending on the species, territory, and time of year. But all ground squirrels have a humongous appetite for the roots, bulbs, stems, flowers, and seeds of just about any kind of plant under the sun.

allies in the fight against these greedy gluttons include badgers, snakes, coyotes, foxes, and bobcats. You probably don't want to invite all of those guys into your yard, but you can make the squirrels think you have. Just get some predator urine from a garden center or catalog, and pour it around the perimeter of your yard, or wher-

Home on the Range

Ground Squirrels

ever the voracious varmints are venturing.

🍃 Thanks, Rover!

Dogs put the fear of God into ground squirrels—and with good reason. You may not want the family pooch chowing down on these wild, possibly disease-carrying, animals. But Rover can still come to your aid. Just scoop up some of his droppings, and toss them into the squirrels' entrance holes. The little guys will run for their lives.

🍃 Brrr!

One of the most potent ground-squirrel evictors I know of is dry ice. Pick up a sack of the frigid stuff at the store, and scoop a cup or so into every tunnel entrance you can find. Then seal each one. The cold fumes will drive the little diggers outta town *fast!*

🍃 A Two-Timing Fence

Unlike gophers, who grab plants from under the soil surface, ground squirrels attack from above *and* below. And that means that

THUG BUSTER

Go-Go, Ground Squirrels Tonic

Ground squirrels don't often take "No!" for an answer, but when their tongues touch this firey brew, they usually go looking for a cooler dinner.

6 habanero chili peppers*
1 tsp. of dishwashing liquid
3 gal. of water

Puree the peppers in a blender with about 1 cup of the water. Strain out the solids, add the rest of the water, and stir in the dishwashing liquid. Pour the solution into a hand-held sprayer, and spray the ground all around the squirrels' target plants. Spray the plants, too, but *only* after testing a few leaves, because this hot stuff could burn them. (And the peppers *will* burn your skin, so wear rubber gloves when you're working with them!)

*Available in some specialty markets, or in catalogs that specialize in southwestern and Mexican food.

to fully protect your plants, you need to fence the critters out from both directions. Here's what to do:

1. Lay a sheet of ½-inch wire mesh about 2 feet below the surface, with the sides bent and extending up to ground level.

2. Erect a 6-foot-high, or higher, fence around the perimeter of your garden. Any material will work, as long as there are no openings bigger than ½ inch wide.

3. Attach a 24-inch-wide band of sheet metal to the top of the fence. When the little guys try to scamper up, they'll slide right back down.

Till 'Til the Cows Come Home

Or 'til the squirrels go away. I know this isn't what you want to hear, but once ground squirrels stake their claim to your turf, sometimes the only way to clear 'em out is to till up their (rather, your) territory until the whole tunnel system is destroyed. You may have to do the job several

times before the message really sinks in, but eventually, they'll give up and go elsewhere.

Take That!

I have to admit that ground squirrels (especially the California bunch) are some of the toughest customers I've ever had to contend with. Most taste and odor repellents that send other felons fleeing have no effect at all on these guys. The exception is my Go-Go, Ground Squirrels Tonic (page 230). I can't guarantee that even this hot toddy will work 100 percent of the time, but unless the gluttons have nothing else to eat, it will save your favorite plants from their clutches. The secret is in the habanero chilis— the hottest kind you can buy, with a whopping 200,000 to 350,000 Scoville heat units (the gauge by which chili-pepper heat is measured). Just as a comparison, pequin chili peppers, just one rung down on the four-alarm ladder, have 35,000 to 40,000 Scoville heat units.

GROUND SQUIRRELS
AT A GLANCE

Target yards, gardens, and farm crops throughout the country

◆

Consume huge quantities of plant material of all types

◆

Also eat weeds, insects, and smaller mammals, such as mice, moles, and voles

◆

To control them, fill their tunnels with dry ice or predator urine

◆

Protect prize plants with above- and below-ground fences

◆

Deter with my Go-Go, Ground Squirrels Tonic (page 230)

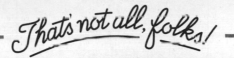

That's not all, folks!

Most of the pesky pests that plague annual and perennial flowers also run roughshod through the vegetable garden. You'll find tactics for fighting those felons in Chapter 4. Also, troublemakers that target vegetables in one category tend to strike other kinds, too. So, if your visiting villain isn't covered in this chapter, you'll find him in chapters 6 or 7. In addition, you may find these critters raising a ruckus among your root crops:

MOLE CRICKETS run roughshod through the South, dining mostly on turf grasses, but they also nibble on potatoes and tomatoes now and then. Read all the details starting on page 18.

MOLES don't eat plants, but they often tear through vegetable gardens in their quest for

grubs and other insects—destroying roots in the process. For the full story, see page 31.

VOLES, on the other hand, do eat plants, and plenty of them. For the lowdown on these lowlifes, check out page 72.

CHAPTER 6

LEAF-CROP
LOUSES

The fanciest salad bar in town can't equal the taste of tender, young greens picked fresh from your own garden—as you very well know, if you've ever grown so much as a windowbox of lettuce. Unfortunately, a whole lot of furry felons and bad-guy bugs love leaf crops, too, and they'll spare no effort to get at the goods. But you don't have to share your bounty with those greedy gobblers! Whether they're striking from the air, on the ground, or from deep in the soil, you'll find your battle plan in this chapter.

THIS IS THEIR LIFE

In the autumn or early spring, depending on the species, females lay clusters of 20 to 60 smooth, pearly-white eggs in a chamber 2 to 3 inches below ground. Then—and this is a great rarity in the insect world—mama tends the nest until the youngsters hatch and go through their first molt. After that, they go off to fend for themselves, just as other bugs do. By late fall, they've matured, gone underground, and laid eggs of their own.

ALSO ON THE MENU

Earwigs love lettuce, but they'll also munch on other leafy greens and numerous vegetables. They're especially fond of bean and beet seedlings, celery, potatoes, and strawberries. In the cornfield, they chew the tassels and blossoms, thereby reducing kernel set. In the flower garden, dahlias, zinnias, marigolds, roses, hollyhocks, and daylilies are high on the hit list.

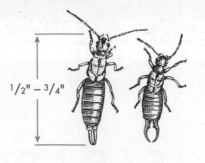

1/2" – 3/4"

Suddenly finding yourself up close and personal with one of these guys is enough to give you a good shock—if not a bad dream! Earwigs are slender and reddish brown with small, nearly useless wings, and (this is the nightmarish part) vicious-looking pincers on their rear end. On the males, this apparatus is curved and resembles a pair of miniature ice tongs. The females' pincers are smaller and straight, and fit neatly together. Both genders can deliver a painful pinch if you provoke them, but contrary to the old superstition (see "Did You Know?", on page 235), earwigs don't go looking for trouble. In fact, much of the time, they're garden-variety good guys, who help turn dead plant material into valuable humus and wipe out bad-guy bugs, such as aphids, fleas, and grubs. Sometimes, though, the critters go on the rampage and chew the daylights out of living roots, leaves, and flowers. Left unchecked, they can demolish a bed of seedlings, and they're especially fond of tender, young leaf crops. And here's the strange part: Whether earwigs take on the role of hero or villain seems to vary from one garden to another, and sometimes from one year to the next.

🍃 Look Before You Shoot

You say you've seen scads of earwigs in your garden *and* your leaf crops are full of ragged holes?

Well, don't jump to conclusions! Maybe because of their menacing looks, these little guys often take the blame for damage done by other leaf-chewing insects. Before you take to the battlefield, go out after dark with a flashlight and examine your beleaguered plants. If a crowd of ear-wigs scurry away from the light, go after 'em with the tactics in this section. But if your beam disturbs the dinner hour of some other demons, you can bet bucks to beetles that your resident earwigs are your allies in the pest-control wars. So just leave 'em alone to get on with their work.

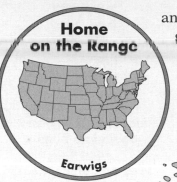

Home on the Range

Earwigs

ants. They're among the few garden-variety heroes who go gunnin' for the foul felons. (Just for the record, the others are ground beetles, mites, and spiders.)

🍃 Welcome, Firefighters!

If you live in one of the Sunbelt states, you might want to let earwigs share your turf even if they *are* nibbling on your future salad. Why? Because they're on your side in the fight against fire

DID YOU KNOW?

Earwigs got their name from a ludicrous—and gruesome—superstition. Centuries ago in Europe, folks believed that the insects crawled into sleeping people's ears and from there, bored into their brains. Yuck! Like many odd beliefs, this one (at least the first part of it) might have had a *tiny* basis in fact, because back then, most of the common folk slept on mats on the floor, where they were fair game for all kinds of bugs. As for the brain tunneling, it was baloney then, and it's baloney now!

🍃 What a Jarring Surprise!

Like many bugs, earwigs have a sweet tooth the size of Tipperary. So invite them over for a "jar," as our Irish friends like to say. Just pour about half an inch of molasses into some glass jars, then add enough water to reach about three-quarters of the way up. Stir until the water and molasses are thoroughly mixed, and set the beverages among your troubled plants. The earwigs will drop in for a drink, and they'll stay there long after the pub closes!

🌿 Smell That Bacon

Wondering what to do with all that bacon grease after your Sunday brunch? Just drop dollops of the stuff into shallow containers, like jar lids or cat-food cans, and set them around your garden. Earwigs will flock to the stuff. Then all you'll need to do is pick up the traps and dump them into a bucket of soapy water.

🌿 This Is a Stickup!

If you have an ornamental kitchen garden, or you're simply a natural-born Anglophile, this tip's for you. For eons, English gardeners have trapped earwigs by stuffing moss into small, clay flowerpots and hanging them upside down on sticks that they've pounded into the ground, with the rim of the pot an inch or two above the soil surface. If you don't have any moss on hand, dampened

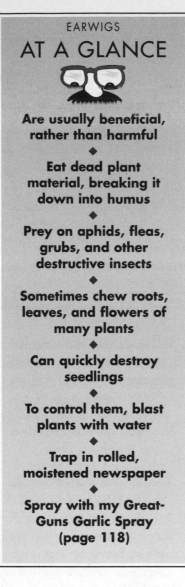

EARWIGS
AT A GLANCE

Are usually beneficial, rather than harmful

◆

Eat dead plant material, breaking it down into humus

◆

Prey on aphids, fleas, grubs, and other destructive insects

◆

Sometimes chew roots, leaves, and flowers of many plants

◆

Can quickly destroy seedlings

◆

To control them, blast plants with water

◆

Trap in rolled, moistened newspaper

◆

Spray with my Great-Guns Garlic Spray (page 118)

wads of newspaper will work just as well (even if it's not the London *Telegraph*).

🌿 It's News to Me

Earwigs feed by night. During the day, they hide in damp, shady places. To give them their dream home (and their final resting place), loosely roll up several sheets of newspaper, dampen the tube, and set it in a shady spot. During the day, hordes of earwigs will crawl inside. As evening approaches, before the critters mosey out for dinner, unroll the papers over a tub of soapy water. Or, simply toss the whole shebang on the compost pile and pour a bucket of hot, soapy water on top.

🌿 Soap's On

In the case of an all-out invasion, let the rascals have it with my Great-Guns Garlic Spray (see page 118).

HARLEQUIN BUGS

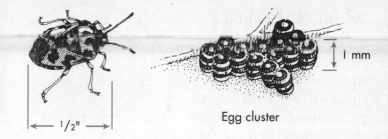

Egg cluster

1 mm

1/2"

THIS IS THEIR LIFE

In cool climates, adult harlequin bugs spend the winter among plant debris. They emerge in early spring, and females start depositing clusters of eggs on the undersides of leaves. They hatch from 4 to 29 days later, depending on the temperature, and the nymphs start right in eating. Four to nine weeks later, they mate and continue the cycle.

ALSO ON THE MENU

Harlequin bugs cause the most damage to cabbage and related vegetables, including broccoli, cauliflower, collards, kale, Brussels sprouts, horseradish, turnips, and watercress. They also target the clan's weeds, such as wild mustard, shepherd's purse, and peppergrass. When cole crops are not on the menu, they'll settle for tomatoes, potatoes, eggplant, okra, beans, asparagus, beets, or, on occasion, sunflowers and chrysanthemums.

These sap-suckers crossed the border from their home in Mexico shortly after the Civil War. Since then, they've spread across the country from coast to coast, but they rarely cause much trouble north of Colorado and Pennsylvania. When harlequin bugs have arrived in your garden, they're as easy to spot as a piñata at a party. The adults are shield-shaped, true bugs (see "Did You Know," on page 134) with black bodies and bright red, orange, or yellow markings. The nymphs are just as colorful, but slightly smaller, wingless, and oval. Both generations stick their needle-sharp mouthparts into leaves and stems of cabbage-family crops and drain out the life-giving juices. The damage first appears as irregular, cloudy spots around the puncture wounds. Young plants usually wilt, turn brown, and eventually die. Older plants can generally survive a moderate attack, but their growth is stunted.

🌿 You Stinker!

Whatever method you use to control harlequin bugs, be aware that they'll probably strike back by firing off a foul odor. So wear gloves and long sleeves to avoid getting the smelly stuff on your skin, and whatever you do, don't crush the critters. If you do, you'll *really* want a clothespin for your nose!

🌿 Oh, No You Don't!

If live up North and you're on the scene in early spring when the bugs wake up, you've got a great chance to head off any damage. Just get out there and whisk the rascals off the plants, and drown them in soapy water. You can either do the job by hand or use a vacuum cleaner, but be quick about it. Remember, you've only got two weeks or so before the eggs start arriving.

🌿 Double Your Pleasure

If you miss your window of opportunity, don't worry. It just means you've got two targets: grown-up bugs *and* their unhatched offspring. Simply scrape the eggs off of the leaves and into the bucket along with the adults, or clip off the leaves and drop them into the drink.

🌿 Take That!

In the case of a major invasion, or if you simply don't want to get too close to the odiferous invaders, let 'em have it with my Safe-and-Sound Pesticide (at right). It's lethal to harlequin bugs and a lot of other pesky

Home on the Range

Harlequin Bugs

pests, but it's so safe that you could eat it. But you probably don't want to, so rinse your greens thoroughly before you toss 'em into your salad bowl!

🌿 Trapped!

If you have the room, plant a trap crop of mustard or turnips. The hellacious harlequins will zero in on those tasty treats, and ignore your other cole crops—at least for the most part. There's just one catch: The minute you see the thugs land on the lure crop, you need to throw old sheets over the plants, pull 'em up out of the ground, and toss 'em,

THUG BUSTER

Safe-and-Sound Pesticide

Looking for a bad-bug killer that you know is harmless? Look no further! This one comes right out of your kitchen cupboard, but it's lethal to some of the peskiest pests that ever came down the pike.

⅓ cup of vegetable oil (any kind will do)
1 tsp. of baking soda
1 cup of water

Mix the oil and baking soda together. Then combine 2 teaspoons of the mixture with the cup of water in a hand-held sprayer, and go get those bad guys!

bugs and all, into a big bucket of soapy water.

Cleaning Time

At the end of the growing season, plow your cabbage-family crops under the ground or pull them all up and compost them. And clear out any other plant debris where the bugs could possibly spend the winter.

Help from Your Friends

For long-term control, lay out the welcome mat for assassin

Colorful true bugs suck sap from stems and leaves

◆

Are most damaging in the South

◆

Young plants frequently die; older ones generally survive, but growth is stunted

◆

To control them, handpick adults, nymphs, and eggs

◆

Encourage predators

◆

Spray with my Safe-and-Sound Pesticide (page 238)

bugs, damsel bugs, and native parasitic wasps. They all target harlequin bugs and their eggs, too. (You can read all about these good guys in Chapter 8.)

Resist!

When you're shopping for seeds, read the catalog descriptions carefully, and choose leaf-crop varieties that are resistant to harlequin bugs. There are scads of tasty ones, including 'Early Jersey Wakefield' cabbage, 'Green Blaze' collards, 'Snowball' cauliflower, and 'Cherry Belle' radishes—just to name a handful.

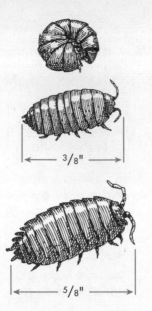

3/8"

5/8"

A female pillbug or sowbug lays anywhere from 7 to 200 eggs in (believe it or not) a pouch on the underside of her body. Three to seven weeks later, the babies hatch. They stay in their cozy pocket for six to eight weeks, then go off on their own. There may be one or two generations per year, and individuals live for up to three years.

Pillbugs and sowbugs stick close to the ground in their quest for food. Although their idea of real gourmet chow is dead plant parts, when these bugs get desperate, young seedlings of any kind become prime targets. So do melons, strawberries, cucumbers, and squashes that happen to touch the soil (especially if they've begun to rot). And on rare occasions, the crusty critters nibble on the leaves or low-hanging flowers of impatiens, violets, and other ornamentals.

Pillbugs, and their kissin' cousins, sowbugs, aren't really bugs at all; they're tiny crustaceans—closely related to shrimp, crayfish, and lobsters. Although these little crawlers look very similar, there are a couple of telltale differences. Both have seven legs and hard, segmented bodies. But sowbugs are a little bigger, flatter, and lighter gray than pillbugs, and they have two tail-like appendages on their rear ends. And, rather than roll up when they're disturbed, sowbugs simply run away.

Most of the time, these little critters turn up their noses (so to speak) at living plants. Instead, they feed on dead plant material, breaking it down into rich, fertile soil. You could think of them as earthworms with legs. Once in a while, though, the population explodes, and there's not enough dead stuff to go around. That's when trouble strikes: The hungry hoards sink their chops into tender, young leaf crops and plenty of other plants, besides.

🌿 Don't Shoot Your Pals

Like earwigs (see page 234), pillbugs and sowbugs are often saddled with blame that they don't really deserve. The reason: Because the little crustaceans need moisture to survive, they frequently crawl into holes that slugs and other pests have already chewed in fruits, vegetables, or succulent leaves.

So before you launch an all-out attack, do some garden-variety detective work and make sure you know who the real villain is.

Send 'Em Back to Work

Pillbugs and sowbugs find their true calling in the compost pile, where they can pig out on your fruit and veggie scraps, grass clippings, and fallen leaves. So when you find the little guys munching on living plants, just set out halved cantaloupe rinds among their targets, or tuck cabbage leaves, potato peelings, or corncobs under up-turned flowerpots. Every few days, check your traps, and relocate the prisoners to the compost pile. If you don't have a compost pile, just dig a hole in the ground and bury the traps in a place that's far away from your garden.

Going Up

To keep the hungry hordes away from your melons and squashes, prop each plant up on a coffee can, upside-down berry basket, or similar lifting device. Besides keeping the pillbugs and sowbugs at bay,

Home on the Range

Pillbugs & Sowbugs

you'll fend off a multitude of other pesky pests and dastardly diseases.

Goin' to the Dogs

Pillbugs and sowbugs love dry dog food. Could this mean they have an identity crisis? Who cares? Just ask Rover to lend you some kibble, and sprinkle the stuff all over your garden beds. The crusty crustaceans will chow down on the dog chow and leave your plants in peace.

Turn 'Em Off

To protect seedlings and new transplants, sprinkle lime or diatomaceous earth on the soil in their bed, or spray the ground with my Pop Off, Pillbugs Tonic (below).

THUG BUSTER

Pop Off, Pillbugs Tonic

This simple solution will send pillbugs and sowbugs searching elsewhere for supper.

3 medium-sized onions
1 qt. of water

Puree the onions and water in a blender or food processor, and strain out the solids. Then pour the liquid into a hand-held sprayer, and spritz the soil around any plants that need protection from these crafty crustaceans.

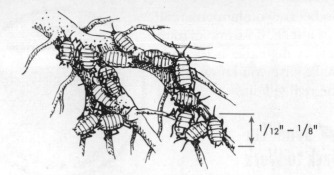

1/12" – 1/8"

The life cycle varies depending on the species and climate. Generally, though, in cold regions, aphids hatch in May or June from eggs laid the previous fall. Like their above-ground cousins, root aphids are born pregnant, and within a week, they start giving birth to live youngsters. As winter approaches, some species grow wings and fly off to lay a final batch of eggs in trees, weeds, or garden litter. Others deposit their eggs in the soil. In places where the weather stays mild all year long, the pests just churn out one live litter after another.

ALSO ON THE MENU

Root aphids love lettuce roots, but various species of the little gluttons go gunnin' for just about any type of plant you can think of. In the vegetable garden, corn, beets, and squash are high-risk targets. So are bulbs, corms, and tubers of all types (especially dahlias).

When your lettuce or other greens wilt during sunny weather, even though you know they're getting plenty of water, you could be entertaining a crowd of root aphids. These tiny suckers are kissin' cousins to the aphids that drain sap from leaves and flowers (see Chapter 4), but they do their dirty deeds underground, where you can't see them. If their shenanigans go on unchecked, plants lose their get-up-and-grow power, and may eventually die. Plenty of pests and diseases cause these same symptoms, so to confirm the diagnosis, pull up one of the victims. If root aphids are at work, you'll see a white, fluffy or powdery wax on the roots and soil. The critters themselves are tiny, pear-shaped insects, usually dirty cream in color, but sometimes bluish green.

🌿 Act Fast

If you reach the crime scene early, you can probably save your plants and bring in a decent harvest. As soon as you've made a positive I.D., drench the soil with my Orange Aid (see page 49), or Nix 'Em with Nicotine Tea (see page 259). These potions' key ingredients, citrus oil and nicotine, respectively, are lethal to root aphids.

🌿 Hi, Sweetie

When there's no time for home cookin', just sprinkle about ¼ cup of sugar around each plant, and water it into the soil. If the sweet stuff doesn't wipe out all of the rooting rascals, it'll at least put a big dent in the population.

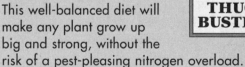

Home on the Range

Root Aphids

🌿 How Dry It Is

At the end of the growing season, clear out all dead plants and other debris where aphid eggs could be waiting to hatch. In the spring, try to replant in fresh territory. If that's not possible, till your plot to bring any lurking eggs up to the surface, and let the soil dry out thoroughly before you sow seed or set in transplants. Any eggs that are not gobbled up by predators will die of dehydration.

🌿 Hold the N

Root aphids zero right in on plants that are getting too much nitrogen. So go easy on the Big N! In particular, avoid synthetic/chemical fertilizers, which deliver nutrients directly to plants' roots in highly concentrated form— making it a snap to serve up an overdose without even knowing it. Instead, use a natural/organic fertilizer, which adds essential nutrients to the soil, where they become available to the plants as they need them. You'll find some excellent brands in any garden center, or use my All-Purpose Organic Fertilizer (below).

🌿 Look Sharp

Root aphids thrive in many nurseries and greenhouses. So before you bring home any container-grown plants, give them the old eagle eye. If you see symptoms of root aphids on the roots or soil, it's best to take your shopping list elsewhere.

THUG BUSTER

All-Purpose Organic Fertilizer

This well-balanced diet will make any plant grow up big and strong, without the risk of a pest-pleasing nitrogen overload.

5 parts seaweed meal
3 parts granite dust
1 part dehydrated manure
1 part bonemeal

Combine these ingredients in a bucket, then side-dress your plants with the mixture, and water it in well. Serve it up two or three times during the growing season.

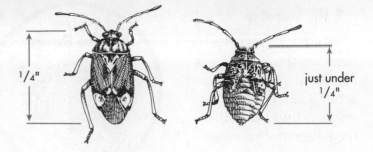

THIS IS THEIR LIFE

Adults spend the winter in dead leaves and other plant litter. In early spring, they wake up, go on a brief eating binge, and then begin laying eggs in stems and flowers. The youngsters hatch in about 10 days, and usually stay right on their birth plants until they become full-fledged bugs, three to four weeks later. There may be as many as five overlapping generations per year, with the reproduction schedule speeding up as temperatures rise. So by late summer, a really plagued garden can resemble a freeway at rush hour.

ALSO ON THE MENU

Any kind of herbaceous (nonwoody) plant is fair game for these vile villains. They love leafy greens, but any other vegetable suits them fine, too. Strawberries are big-time favorites. They also target perennial flowers, and they go gunnin' for a handful of annuals.

Like all true bugs (see "Did You Know," on page 134), these tarnished types, a.k.a. lygus bugs, do their dirty work by piercing and sucking sap from their victims. In the process, the bugs inject a toxic saliva, which results in leaves, shoots, and flowers that are pinched, scarred, and distorted. Fruits such as strawberries and tomatoes grow smaller than normal, with dark, sunken patches. Afflicted plants wilt, growth is stunted, and in severe cases, the victims die.

You probably won't catch these demons at their dastardly deeds, because they're both tiny (about ¼ inch long) and shy. The moment they sense a disturbance, they fly away or drop down out of sight. But here's what to look for: The adults are oval, with a mottled brown, yellow, and black pattern on their bodies that, from a distance, gives them the look of tarnished metal. The wingless nymphs have a similar shape, but are yellow-green.

🌿 A Clean Sweep

When tarnished plant bugs are eating everything in sight, do what organic strawberry farmers do: Vacuum the pesky pests right off your plants. The pros use a fancy machine, but you can just put an inch or two of soapy water in the reservoir of your wet/dry vacuum cleaner, and get out there and sweep those beds! Then pour the suds, bugs and all, onto the compost pile. Or use a hand-held model, and empty the squirmy contents into a bucket of soapy water.

Home on the Range

Tarnished Plant Bugs

or shower curtains on the ground under your plants, and sweep the foliage lightly with a broom. The bugs will rain on down. Then gather up the fabric, and dump the bugs into a tub of soapy water.

✿ Give 'Em the Brush-Off

If you do more than your share of vacuuming indoors, use the old brush-off trick instead. Just spread old sheets

✿ It's a Whiteout

Unlike most insects, which zero in on anything yellow, tarnished plant bugs

Coulda Fooled ME!

Here's the scenario: Your plants' leaves develop spots, turn color, curl up, or fall off. Or growing tips are damaged, maturity is delayed, and yield is reduced. Or maybe the poor things wilt or even keel over and die. The problem could be a pesky pest or dastardly disease. But it just might be *phytotoxicity.* This nasty condition is caused by pesticides. Synthetic chemicals are the most damaging, but even plant-based products like pyrethrin and rhotenone can cause big-time trouble. So can good old-fashioned soap, if you use it too often. Although phytotoxicity can strike any plant, seedlings and young transplants are most at risk.

Fortunately, the tips, tricks, and mild-mannered tonics in this book will fend off

pests a good 99 percent of the time—without giving you more problems than you had to begin with. When you do reach for one of my more potent Thug Busters (especially any that contain soap), follow these guidelines:

■ **Aim carefully.** Be sure to keep the solution away from the plants' growing tips.

■ **Wash it off.** A few hours after you spray, give your plants a good hosing to remove any soap residue.

■ **Walk on the mild side.** Don't use more soap than a recipe calls for. A stronger solution is no more effective at killing pests, and it can cause major damage to your plants.

are drawn to the color (or noncolor) white. So your solution couldn't be simpler: Coat pieces of white cardboard with petroleum jelly or a commercial adhesive, then hang or stand the traps among your troubled crops.

Sorry, Daisy!

You can often lure tarnished plant bugs to their doom by planting a trap crop of Shasta daisies. When the white flowers burst into bloom, the bugs will make a beeline to the beauties. Then all you need to do is grit your teeth and destroy the whole patch. I toss sheets over the infested plants, pull them up by the roots, and empty them into a big pot of soapy water.

Cover 'Em Up—Maybe

Floating row covers will keep your plants safe and sound from tarnished plant bugs and other kinds, too. But because the tarnished terrors feast and reproduce all summer long, you'll have to keep the covers on throughout the growing season. That works just fine for leaf or root crops. But if you're

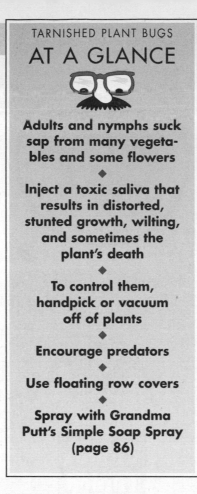

TARNISHED PLANT BUGS
AT A GLANCE

Adults and nymphs suck sap from many vegetables and some flowers

◆

Inject a toxic saliva that results in distorted, stunted growth, wilting, and sometimes the plant's death

◆

To control them, handpick or vacuum off of plants

◆

Encourage predators

◆

Use floating row covers

◆

Spray with Grandma Putt's Simple Soap Spray (page 86)

growing fruiters, such as corn, squash, or tomatoes, take the toppers off as soon as flowers appear, and then use other ways to keep the bad guys at bay. Otherwise, birds and good-guy bugs can't get in to pollinate the blossoms, and you'll have no crop at all.

Spray Your Troubles Away

In the case of an all-out invasion, mix up a batch of Grandma Putt's Simple Soap Spray (see page 86), and let the louses have it. Or, in really dire cases, collect half a cup of the villains, use them in my Beetle Juice (see page 53), and kill 'em with their own kind.

Bring On the Bugs

For long-term protection, put out the welcome mat for big-eyed bugs, minute pirate bugs, and damsel bugs. If you plant low-growing groundcovers and a variety of nectar-rich flowers, they'll beat a path to your garden and gobble up all the tarnished plant bugs they can find. (You can read all about hit-squad hospitality in Chapter 8.)

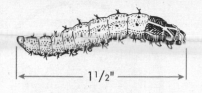

|←——— 1¹/₂" ———→|

The life cycle varies, depending on the species and climate. But generally, in the spring, adult moths lay fluffy, gray, pea-sized egg masses, most often in grassy weeds. The caterpillars hatch, eat for two to four weeks, then burrow into the ground. In another two to four weeks, they emerge, all grown up, and the whole process begins again. In the deep South, there may be as many as six generations per year; up North, usually only one appears.

The fall armyworm (shown in the illustration above) has a big appetite for turf grass, especially Bermuda grass (see Chapter 1 for the lowdown on those lowlifes). Various species, all of whom look very similar to the one shown here, attack seedlings and mature vegetable plants. Favorite menu items include most leaf crops.

Several species of slender, 1- to 2-inch-long caterpillars go by the name of armyworms. And they got that name for a very good reason: They travel in troops, and in years when their population soars, they're like an invading army on the march, gobbling up every plant part in their path. Besides sharing the same battle plan, these vile villains march to the mess hall at the same time, after dark and on overcast days. Their uniform ranges in color from purplish black to dark, shiny brown, usually with contrasting stripes. Armyworms' parents are small, night-flying moths that are usually mottled gray or brown. Fortunately, you don't need to know which battalion your enemy forces are from, because the same tactics will trounce 'em all.

Routine Patrol

In most years, armyworms' natural predators keep the situation well under control. Songbirds, toads, and skunks gobble up all the armyworms they can find, and bats polish off legions of the night-flying moths. In the insect brigade, tachinid flies, spined soldier bugs, and ground beetles go gunnin' for the worms.

Bzzzzz

Two kinds of parasitic wasps, trichogramma and braconid, are lethal to armyworms (but harmless to humans and other critters). The tiny buzzers will generally show up if you plant plenty of flowers that are rich in pollen and nectar.

Into the Drink

If the invasion is too big for your pest-eating posse to handle, give them a hand. Just go out after dark with a flashlight, and handpick the rascals. Then drown them in a bucket of soapy water, and pour the stuff onto the compost pile.

Home on the Range

Armyworms

Choose Your Weapon

Are you a tad squeamish about handling squirmy worms? No problem! Just mix up a batch of my Orange Aid (see page 49), then get out there and take target practice. The citrus oil in the potion will send the pesky pests to you-know-where in a hurry.

Other Scents-able Solutions

Fresh out of citrus fruit? Not to worry! Any of these aromatic sprays will kill armyworms on contact, and the potent aroma will discourage new recruits from moving in. Just check your pantry, mix up whichever weapon you have the ingredients for, and go clobber the creeps!

▶ Ashes-to-Ashes Milkshake (page 176)

▶ Caterpillar Killer Tonic (page 17)

▶ Great-Guns Garlic Spray (page 118)

▶ Knock-'Em-Dead Insect Spray (page 172)

Hired Guns

When you need immediate help in your battle against armyworms, rush down to the garden center and buy either Btk (*Bacillus thuringiensis* var. *kurstaki*) or parasitic nematodes. Both magic bullets deal out death and destruction to armyworms. If you're buying parasitic nematodes, be sure to ask for them by name. You want the kind called *Neoaplectana carpocapsae*—they've been specially bred to polish off armyworms.

DID YOU KNOW?

Here's news for all of you who pooh-pooh the idea of bug-chasing plants. Researchers in England planted sunflowers and corn together. The result: Armyworms stayed away in droves, the corn yield increased, and up to 50 percent fewer bad-guy beetles bugged the sunflowers. So take that!

🍃 Get Rid of Weeds

To an armyworm moth, there's no better maternity ward than a nice, big stand of grassy weeds. So get rid of the weeds, and don't let them grow back! (For one of my best weed-defying tonics, see page 150.)

🍃 Trench Warfare

Armyworms won't invade your vegetable garden if you use this old-time trick. Just dig a steep-sided trench, about 6 inches deep and a few inches wide, all the way around the plot. Then drag a tree branch or other heavy object through the ditch to break up the soil at the bottom. The worms will march in on their way to mess call, but because their feet can't get traction in the loose soil, won't be able to climb out. Then you can choose their method of execution: Either scoop 'em up and drown them in soapy water, or leave 'em there for birds to feast on.

ARMYWORMS
AT A GLANCE

Several species of caterpillars target many vegetables, flowers, and grasses

◆

Populations fluctuate widely from year to year

◆

Most types feed at night and on overcast days

◆

To control them, encourage predators

◆

Handpick and drown in soapy water

◆

Dig a trench around your garden (at left)

◆

Spray with any of my anti-caterpillar tonics

🍃 Two for the Money

Even weeds have their good side. With stinging nettles, make that two good sides. These sometime-pains-in-the-grass give off chemicals that repel armyworms and many other pests; they also pack a load of nitrogen, which is crucial for lush, leafy growth. To deliver this double-barreled firepower, brew up my nettle tea: Put 1 pound of stinging nettle leaves in a bucket, pour in 1 gallon of water, and let the mixture steep for a week. Strain out the leaves, and water your plants with the brew.

🍃 Outsmart 'Em

Did you notice that when the armyworms charged, they ganged up on one kind of plant much more than on others? If so, I'm not surprised: Pests of all types often do that, and it gives you a crackerjack defense tactic for next year. Just sow an early crop of that plant, and when the villains zero in on it, either blast them with one of my anti-caterpillar sprays, or pull up the worm-covered victims and destroy them.

Adult moths emerge in May and lay light green eggs, singly or in groups of two or three, on the undersides of leaves. The larvae hatch in three to four days and immediately sit down (so to speak) to breakfast. They eat like crazy for two to three weeks, then pupate for up to two weeks in silk cocoons attached to stems or the undersides of leaves. In most places, there are three or four generations per year, with the final one pupating through the winter.

Cabbage loopers target all members of the cabbage (Brassica) clan, including broccoli, Brussels sprouts, cauliflower, collards, kale, kohlrabi, mustard, radishes, rutabagas, and turnips. But unlike cabbage maggots and cabbageworms, loopers step outside the family circle to munch on beans, beets, celery, lettuce, peas, potatoes, spinach, and tomatoes.

1¹/₂" – 2" wingspan

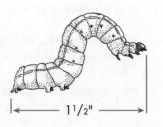

1¹/₂"

Don't let the name fool you. Cabbage loopers do bore into the heads of their namesake plants, but unlike other Brassica pests, they spread their damage far and wide. They munch on the foliage, buds, and flowers of a great many plants, leaving behind ragged holes and masses of brown or green excrement pellets. One or two loopers won't do fatal damage, but in large numbers, they can demolish even mature plants. These gluttons are pale green caterpillars with wavy, lighter green or yellow stripes on their backs and sides. The name looper comes from the critters' habit of "looping" their bodies into the air as they move along, much as inchworms do. The acrobats' parents are mottled, grayish brown moths with a silvery, V-shaped mark in the middle of each forewing. Chances are you won't see them, though, because they do their flying (and egg laying) late in the evening.

Get the Early Worm

If you act fast, you can put a sizable dent in the looper legions before they even hatch, or at least before they can munch on anything more than a dainty appetizer. Just keep a close watch on your plants, and pluck off eggs or caterpillars the minute you see them. Then crush them or toss them into a large pail of soapy water.

An Aromatic Arsenal

Any of these terrific tonics will kill loopers on contact, and the potent aroma will discourage more from moving in. Just check your cupboards, whip up whichever weapon you have the ingredients for, and go get the louses!

▶ Caterpillar Killer Tonic (page 17)

▶ Orange Aid (page 49)

▶ Great-Guns Garlic Spray (page 118)

▶ Cabbageworm Wipeout (page 257)

Staggering Right Along

You can avoid a looper invasion simply by staggering your planting times. Start some seedlings indoors very early, and set them out as soon as you can. That way, by the time the gluttons appear, the plants will be big enough to survive the rascals' advances. After that, sow small batches of seeds, or set out transplants every 10 days, so they won't all be at their most vulnerable stage at the same time.

Fell 'Em in the Fall

As soon as you've harvested your crops, or at least before winter sets in,

Home on the Range

Cabbage Loopers

bury whatever remains of the plants. That way, you'll polish off next spring's egg layers while they're still asleep in their cocoons. Don't compost the stuff unless your bin or pile is very hot.

Send In the Troops

Skunks and toads think cabbage loopers are the tastiest treats in town. So do lacewings, ladybugs, and plenty of songbirds, including Baltimore orioles, bluebirds, chickadees, and flickers. As for the night-flying adult moths, they're a gourmet dinner on the wing for hordes of hungry bats. For tips on laying out the welcome mat for your pest-controlling pals, see Chapter 8.

GRANDMA KNEW BEST

Grandma Putt always planted lots of hyssop in her garden. Looper moths love the old-fashioned herb, so they laid most of their eggs on its leaves and ignored Grandma's other plants. (Of course, as soon as she spotted the eggs, Grandma got that hyssop out of there in a hurry!)

🍃 Turn 'Em Off

Cabbage looper moths will flee fast if you plant plenty of these among their targets:

▶ Garlic

▶ Hot peppers

▶ Onions

▶ Rosemary

▶ Sage

▶ Tansy

▶ Thyme

🍃 Red Means Stop

Or at least proceed with caution. When egg-laying time rolls around, cabbage looper moths tend to zero in on green-leaved varieties and ignore the red or purply types. So when you place your next seed order, consider winners such as 'Violet Queen' broccoli, 'Rubine' Brussels sprouts, 'Giant Red' celery,

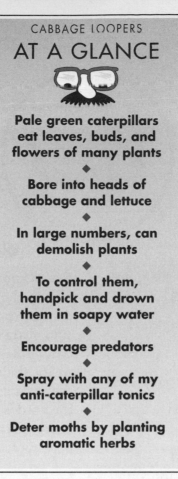

CABBAGE LOOPERS
AT A GLANCE

Pale green caterpillars eat leaves, buds, and flowers of many plants

◆

Bore into heads of cabbage and lettuce

◆

In large numbers, can demolish plants

◆

To control them, handpick and drown them in soapy water

◆

Encourage predators

◆

Spray with any of my anti-caterpillar tonics

◆

Deter moths by planting aromatic herbs

'Red Rookie' cabbage, and 'Purple Head' cauliflower. And there are plenty more where those came from, so peruse catalogs, websites, and heirloom-vegetable books for the latest and greatest, or the oldest and tastiest types.

🍃 Your Backup Plan

There's no guarantee that all of the looper moths will avoid red and purple plants. After all, every crowd has a few non-conformists in it. So cover all of your bases by setting out some traps. In the evening, fill shallow bowls or pans with milk, and set them near your cabbage-family crops. Then shine a light on each bowl. The moths will dive for the light, and that'll be the end of them!

CABBAGE MAGGOTS

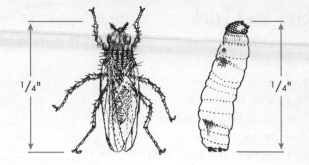

1/4"   1/4"

Adult flies begin appearing in early spring, and females lay eggs in the soil beside plants' roots. The larvae hatch quickly, tunnel into the roots, and feed like crazy for three to four weeks. Then they pupate in the soil for two to three weeks and emerge, all grown up, to continue the vicious cycle. Depending on the climate, there may be from two to four generations per year, with the last bunch of pupae spending the winter several inches deep in the soil.

Cabbage maggots attack only plants in the cabbage (Brassica) family, but it's a big bunch! Besides the head of the household, the group includes broccoli, Brussels sprouts, cauliflower, collards, kale, kohlrabi, mustard, radishes, rutabagas, and turnips.

The cabbage maggot ranks high on any vegetable grower's unwanted list, and for good reason. These vile villains chew their way into the roots and stems of cabbages and their relatives, destroying tissue and leaving the plants wide open to dastardly diseases. And the worst part is that by the time you notice the symptoms—wilting, stunted growth, and dark-spotted leaves—it's often too late to save the victims. When you pull the plant up by its roots, you'll find the culprits: little white, legless worms. Their parents are gray, long-legged flies that look similar to houseflies.

Cabbage maggots cause the most damage early in the season, when the weather is cool and moist, and larvae are hatching by the hordes. During hot, dry summers, fewer eggs survive to become greedy gluttons.

Ashes to Ashes

The end to your cabbage maggot woes is as close as your fireplace. Just spread about 1/4 inch of wood ashes on the soil around each plant, and gently work them in. The ashes'll kill the marauders on contact.

🌿 Give 'Em a Drink

If you don't have a fire-place, or access to a supply of wood ashes, or you simply prefer liquids to powders, give the maggots a shot of Jerry's Lime Rickey (below). It'll perform the same deadly magic.

Home on the Range

Cabbage Maggots

🌿 And Don't Come Back!

Protective coverings will keep the maggot's mommies (flies called *Delia radicum*) from laying their eggs on your cabbage-family plants. Just make sure you bury the edges of the covers in the soil, so the momma flies can't sneak under it.

🌿 One on One

Row covers offer effective protection, all right, but they sure don't offer much in the good-looks department. If appear-ances matter, give each transplant a less obvious security "blanket" in the form of a 4-by-4-inch square of tar paper. Just cut a slit in the paper, slip it around the little tyke's stem, and cover the opening with masking tape. Maggot flies don't like the scent of tar paper, and after one whiff, they'll seek another maternity ward.

🌿 Tea Time

Or maybe you'd prefer a coffee break. Whichever bev-erage you drink, save up your tea bags or coffee grounds through the winter. Then, come spring planting time, work a tablespoon or so into the soil in each hole before you set in your transplants.

THUG BUSTER

Jerry's Lime Rickey

Back in my Uncle Art's day, lime soda rickeys were all the rage. Well, this rickey isn't made with soda or lime juice, but it *will* make the maggots rage!

1 cup of garden lime
1 qt. of water

Stir the lime into the water, and let it sit over-night. Then pour the solution around the rootball of each maggot-plagued plant. Before you can say, "Put another nickel in, in the nickelodeon," those maggots'll be history!

🌿 Cut the Mustard

Cabbage maggot flies flock to wild mustard like bears flock to honey. So if there's a patch of the stuff growing anywhere near your garden, get it outta there!

🍂 On the Other Hand

If you've got a big piece of property, mustard could be your saving grace. Just plant a big crop of the stuff in the spot that's farthest from your garden. The flies will flock to it and leave your cole crops alone.

🍂 The Early Bird Escapes the Worm

There's nothing cabbage maggots like better than radishes. But here's an easy way to foil the felons: Just plant your seeds earlier next year. If you can get a mature crop by June 1, the tangy tubers should be all but free of the slimy squirts.

🍂 Move 'Em Around

Just to be on the safe side, grow your brassicas in a different spot every year. Besides foiling cabbage maggots and other pesky pests, you'll fend off the clan's own private disease: clubroot. It's a foul fungus that invades your garden

---

CABBAGE MAGGOTS AT A GLANCE

Chew into roots and stems of cabbage-family plants

◆

Disease organisms enter through the openings, often killing the plants

◆

Are most damaging early in the season, when weather is cool and moist

◆

To control them, work wood ashes into the soil

◆

Drench the soil with Jerry's Lime Rickey (page 254)

◆

Cover plants to keep egg-laying moths away

---

on infected plants, and it can live in the soil for as long as seven years.

🍂 Just So You'll Know

Many pests cause damage that resembles the symptoms of clubroot: yellowish foliage, stunted growth, and wilting leaves and stems. So to confirm the diagnosis, pull up a plant. If the roots are gnarled and misshapen, you'll know your cole crops have joined the club. There is no cure, so just pull 'em all up and burn them immediately—this stuff spreads like wildfire! And make sure you get out every trace of the roots, because clubroot spends its winter vacation among the decomposing roots.

🍂 No Room at the Inn

If you have no room to rotate your crops, grow them in containers, or simply avoid planting brassicas every other year. Either way, you'll save yourself a whole lot of frustration!

Cabbageworms spend the winter as pupae attached to plant debris. In the spring, the butterflies emerge and lay ribbed, yellow, football-shaped eggs on the undersides of cole-crop leaves. The caterpillars hatch in a week, eat like crazy for another two weeks or so, and then pupate right on their "dining rooms." About 10 days later, they reappear as grown-up, egg-laying butterflies and continue the cycle as long as the weather allows.

Unlike cabbage loopers (page 250), cabbageworms keep their dastardly deeds almost entirely in the family. But the cabbage (Brassica) clan is a *big* one that includes, on the veggie side, broccoli, Brussels sprouts, cauliflower, collards, kale, kohlrabi, mustard, radishes, rutabagas, and turnips. Flower-garden cousins include sweet alyssum, stock, and wallflowers.

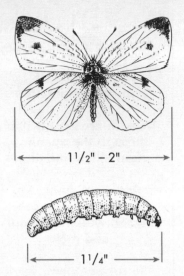

1¹/₂" – 2"

1¹/₄"

The cabbageworm is often referred to as the "imported" cabbageworm, because it came here from Europe eons ago. This Continental customer is part of a very exclusive club: It's one of the few destructive caterpillars that grows up to be a butterfly and not a moth. Of course, the cabbageworm's parents are nowhere near as stunning-looking as the parsleyworm's folks, the black swallowtails. Cabbage butterflies, known in scientific circles as *Artogeia rapae* (formerly *Pieris rapae*), have pure white, black-tipped wings with one or two black spots on the forewings. The youngsters are light green, velvety caterpillars with a thin, light yellow stripe down the back. They chew ragged holes in the leaves of cabbage-family plants and deposit greenish black excrement pellets. You may see the critters resting on the upper surfaces of leaves, but outer foliage is not their prime target. Their real mission in life is eating the hearts out of cabbage, broccoli, and other members of the brassica clan.

🌿 Pick a Peck

At the first sign of trouble, get out there and pick those crawlers off of your plants, and toss 'em into a bucket of soapy water. (I keep an old pair of tongs in the toolshed just for 'pillar pickin' purposes.)

🌿 Dusty Roads

Got no time for pluckin' pesky pests? Here's a faster good-riddance method: Just dust your plants with my Cabbageworm Wipeout (below). Besides routing cabbageworms, it'll deal a death blow to any other caterpillar that tries to turn your garden into his personal salad bar.

🌿 It's an Invasion!

If the cabbageworms are comin' at you right and left, or if you'd simply rather spray than dust, mix up any of the terrific tonics listed in "An Aromatic Arsenal," on page 251. Then

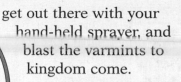

Home on the Range

Cabbageworms

get out there with your hand-held sprayer, and blast the varmints to kingdom come.

🌿 Butter 'Em Up

If you love butter-milk as much as I do, here's a little secret you ought to know: Cabbageworms *hate* the stuff. So every time you empty a carton, rinse it out and pour the milky liquid on your plants. Even well-watered-down, it'll send the 'pillars packin', *pronto!*

🌿 Plant Purple

Cabbage butterflies tend to zero in on green plants and leave purple or red-dish types alone. So use that to your advantage. When you place your next seed order, check out the list in "Red Means Stop," on page 252 for non-green Brassicas.

THUG BUSTER

Cabbageworm Wipeout

When cabbage-crunching crawlers come to call, greet them with this deadly treat.

1 cup of flour
2 tbsp. of cayenne pepper

Mix the ingredients together, and sprinkle the powder on young cabbage-family plants. The flour swells up inside the worms and bursts their insides, while the hot pepper keeps other critters away.

THIS IS THEIR LIFE

The life cycle varies slightly from one species to another. In general, though, adults lay eggs under the surface of a leaf, usually on the underside. The larvae hatch within days and start chowing down on the soft tissue between the leaf ribs. When they've eaten their fill, generally in two to three weeks, they drop off to pupate under the soil or in plant litter. Depending on the species, there may be several generations per year.

ALSO ON THE MENU

Leaf miners can attack anyplace in the vegetable garden. And some species target annual and perennial flowers, including columbine, delphiniums, larkspur, monkshood, and nasturtiums. Others go gunnin' for blackberries, blueberries, and many trees, both ornamental and fruit-bearing. Both boxwood and holly have their own species of leaf miner to contend with.

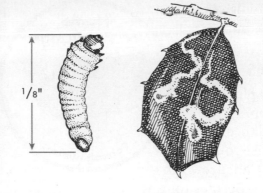

1/8"

When your leaf crops are sporting what look like pale, winding roads, it means just one thing: Leaf miners have arrived on the scene. These critters burrow between the upper and lower surfaces of foliage, eating the inner tissue and leaving nearly transparent tunnels behind. If you hold a stricken leaf up to the light, you'll usually see an itty-bitty worm at the end of the trail. There are many kinds of leaf miners. Most of the species that attack vegetables are the larvae of tiny, black flies with yellow markings. But some of the tiny tunnelers have moths or beetles for parents.

As you'd probably expect, leaf miners cause the most trouble when they dive into leafy edibles, such as lettuce, chard, and spinach. Other plants, including root crops and fruit-bearing vegetables, usually suffer only cosmetic damage—although when the miners strike in huge numbers, they can drain enough chlorophyll to weaken these victims and reduce your harvest.

🌿 Is Your Harvest Doomed?

Maybe. But maybe not. If you reach the crime scene early—or if the victims are not leaf crops—just clip off the damaged foliage and destroy it. If the gods are with you, that may be all she wrote.

On the other hand, if the tiny terrors have invaded a whole head of lettuce, cabbage, or other greens, just bite the bullet and pull it up. Then burn it or send it off with the trash collector. Don't toss it on the compost pile unless you've soaked it in soapy water first, so that you know the miners are good and dead.

Home on the Range

Leaf Miners

Till We Don't Meet Again

At the end of the growing season, get rid of all garden debris where pupae could be settling in for their long winter's naps. Then, if there's time, till your plot thoroughly. That way, you'll destroy many pupae in the soil and bring others to the surface, where hungry birds can gobble them up.

Stick 'Em Up

Like most bugs, leaf miner adults are attracted to the color yellow. So push yellow sticky traps into the soil throughout your garden. You can buy commercial versions, or make your own by coating yellow cardboard with petroleum jelly or a store-bought adhesive such as Tanglefoot®.

Friends in Green Places

Many parasitic (and non-stinging) wasps lay their eggs on leaf miners or near their hatching sites. So do whatever you can to encourage these garden variety heroes. In particular, unless you need to save a valuable shrub or tree, don't try to spray your troubles away. Once the miners have penetrated the leaves, no spray can

THUG BUSTER

Nix 'Em with Nicotine Tea

This potent potion (a variation on my tobacco tea recipe) will polish off leaf miners and other foliage-munching felons, too. It's also just the ticket for soilborne pests, such as root aphids.

1 cup of cigarette or cigar butts
1/2 tsp. of dishwashing liquid
1 gal. of water

Soak the butts in the water for about half an hour (no need to remove any filters or paper). Then strain out the solids, mix in the dishwashing liquid, and pour the tea into a hand-held sprayer. Saturate the undersides of leaves, where leaf miners linger before they tunnel inside. To stop root-munching pests in their tracks, pour the liquid on the soil around the stem and root zone of your troubled plants.

reach them, but it *will* kill off their enemies, i.e., your pals!

Soak 'Em Fast

Several of my Thug Busters will stop leaf miners in their tracks— if you can get to the eggs before they hatch, or if you catch the larvae before they reach their tunnels. That's a tiny window of opportunity; but if the thugs are demolishing, let's say, a beautiful boxwood that your grandma left you, go for it. The minute you spot the first eggs, spray the underside of every leaf with my Nix 'Em with Nicotine Tea (see page 259). It'll stop 'em dead in their tracks.

Clever Cover-Ups

The surest way to protect leafy edibles is to cover your seedlings right from the get-go. Commercial row covers or old, sheer window curtains will do the job; but if you have a small, ornamental kitchen garden or grow your greens in containers, check catalogs for good-looking screen "houses."

Declare War on Weeds

Throughout the growing season, keep after weeds, especially the tall, grassy types, where leaf miners love to lay their eggs. (See "Weed Wipeout" on page 150 for my favorite anti-weed tonic.)

THIS IS THEIR LIFE

Groundhogs are true hibernators. They nap from mid-October until February, when they wake up, enjoy their 15 minutes of fame on the network news, and find a mate. (This is about the only time you'll find two woodchucks together.) About a month later, females give birth to four to six babies. By July, the youngsters are off running roughshod through neighborhood gardens and building living quarters of their own.

ALSO ON THE MENU

Groundhogs love lettuce, spinach, and other leafy greens. But few garden plants are really safe from these little gluttons. Corn, carrot tops, squash, and legumes of every kind are prime menu items. So are many flowers. For a change of pace, they like to snack on fruit-tree bark, and although they rarely climb trees, they snatch up all the fallen fruit they can find.

Groundhogs (a.k.a. woodchucks) do have their share of admirers. And I have to admit it, they *are* cute as all get-out. But they can demolish a whole vegetable patch faster than you can say, "Punxsutawney Phil." If your garden looked just fine when you went to bed, and this morning, everything that hasn't been eaten is trampled, the finger points at these buck-toothed bandits. Besides gobbling up huge helpings of plant material, groundhogs build extensive and surprisingly sophisticated underground living quarters—ruining a lot of lawn and garden area in the process.

To look on the positive side, it's unlikely that your place will be overrun with groundhogs. For the most part, they're loners who'll tolerate a roommate only for as long as it takes to mate in early spring. You can count on their regular habits, too: They tend to go out foraging in the early morning and early evening. In between times, they stay in their burrows snoozing. Or maybe rehearsing for a big television appearance!

🌱 Don't Panic, But...

Like all wild mammals that hang around your yard and garden, groundhogs sometimes carry what scientists call *zoonoses:* diseases that can be transmitted to people and pets. In this case, the potential trouble comes in the form of rabies, distemper, and parvovirus. Now, that doesn't mean you need to call 911 the minute you spot a woodchuck. Just don't let Fluffy or Rover go chasin' after Phil and his pals, and unless you really know what you're doing, think twice before you try to live-trap the critters.

Enemies in Low Places

Badgers, coyotes, and red foxes all prey on groundhogs. So just choose your predator, get some urine, and dribble it around the 'hogs burrow entrances. The furry rascals will hightail it outta there. If your local garden center doesn't carry predator

Home on the Range

Groundhogs

urine, you can order the smelly stuff from many online catalogs.

Help from the Old Jalopy

Even if your car isn't a Cougar, Jaguar, or other feisty beast, it can help you send groundhogs packing. How? Just borrow a little gasoline from the tank (or, better yet, buy an extra gallon at the service station), and set small cans of the fuel at the tunnel openings. The groundhogs will take one whiff and move to less aromatic quarters. They

may not move far, though, so you'll probably have to use this tactic several times before the rascals take off for the far horizons.

Fence 'Em Out

The surest way to keep your veggies out of groundhogs' mouths is with this fence that's designed just for them. You'll need 4½-foot-high metal fence posts, sturdy woven or welded wire fencing that's 6 feet high and long enough to go around your garden, and wire for attaching the fencing to the posts. When you've gathered your

GRANDMA KNEW BEST

Grandma Putt foiled ground-hogs (and pleased all of us humans) by planting bitter-tasting, but great-looking flowers around the perimeter of her garden. She knew that if the furry fellas took one little nibble of marigolds, nasturtiums, wormwood, or yarrow, they'd give up and go elsewhere for dinner. And she was right, too!

supplies, follow this building plan:

1. Dig a trench that's about 2 feet deep and just wide enough so that you can insert the posts and fencing.

2. Sink the posts into the trench about 8 feet apart, and sticking up 2½ feet above the ground.

3. Sink the fencing into the trench and fasten it to the posts so it reaches up 1½ feet above the posts.

4. Bend the top of the fencing outward from your garden at about a 65° angle.

5. Sit back and enjoy the show when the little felons try to get in. The underground part of the fence will keep them from tunneling underneath it. And when they try to climb over, they'll get as far as the floppy top, when their own weight will send them toppling back onto their furry little behinds.

Plant Them a Dining Room

If you'd rather not build a fence to keep pesky groundhogs out of your garden, plant one. (Believe it or not, this tactic has worked for several folks I know.) Here's all you need to do: Around the perimeter of your garden, sow a 3- to 4-foot strip of the groundhogs' favorites, such as lettuce, cabbage, beans, and peas. Then leave about an 8-foot corridor, and plant your own crops. Your resident 'hog will be so busy pigging out in his own private dining room that he probably won't even notice your veggies!

> **DID YOU KNOW?**
>
> How much wood could a woodchuck chuck? I have no idea, but I do know how much soil he can shovel. A single groundhog moves as much as 700 pounds of soil in the course of building his subway system. That's not bad for a critter that tops the scales at 15 pounds!

Say It with Soy

Here's another diversionary tactic that I've tried a time or two, with great success. If you have the space, plant some patches of soybeans here and there in your yard. Those nice-looking legumes are a groundhog's idea of a five-star fine-dining experience. Unless the toothy terrors are *really* hungry, chances are they'll feast on the beans and leave your garden crops alone.

Just in Case

Whether you try to fool 'em or fence 'em out, it pays to have a backup plan. When you need to keep groundhogs in their place—and out of yours—spray their targets with my All-Purpose Varmint Repellent (see page 318).

A Health-Giving Miracle Mix

Manure tea is one of the healthiest drinks a plant could ask for. It delivers a well-balanced blend of nutrients, both major and minor, and fends off diseases at the same time. It also fends off groundhogs! So brew up a batch, and water your garden with the bracing beverage every two weeks throughout the growing season. (For the recipe, see page 361.)

Busy-Day Remedies

When there's no time for brewing teas and tonics, sprinkle any of these wonder workers on the ground among

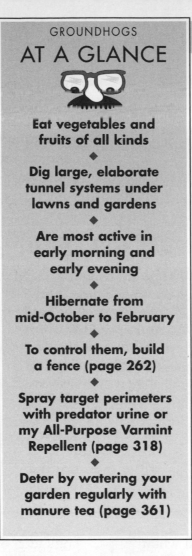

GROUNDHOGS
AT A GLANCE

Eat vegetables and fruits of all kinds

◆

Dig large, elaborate tunnel systems under lawns and gardens

◆

Are most active in early morning and early evening

◆

Hibernate from mid-October to February

◆

To control them, build a fence (page 262)

◆

Spray target perimeters with predator urine or my All-Purpose Varmint Repellent (page 318)

◆

Deter by watering your garden regularly with manure tea (page 361)

your plants. Woodchucks keep their distance from all of them.

▶ Powdered aloe (available in health-food and natural-cosmetics stores)

▶ Red or black pepper

▶ Tobacco

Prime Real Estate

Once you've sent Phil and his pudgy pals packing, their vacant burrows will be prime real estate for other critters. So don't be surprised if you find yourself doing battle with rabbits or skunks.

THIS IS THEIR LIFE

Rabbits breed like, well, rabbits. A female hare produces as many as four litters a year, with up to eight babies (called kits) in each. Cottontails are even more prolific, usually managing to present the world with six annual litters of eight kits each. The youngsters grow up fast, but they don't survive for long. Although pet bunnies commonly live to the ripe old age of 9 or 10, a wild rabbit is lucky to make it past his first birthday, and fewer than 1 percent survive to their third summer.

ALSO ON THE MENU

As Mr. MacGregor found out, there's nothing that pleases bunnies more than a nice, plump head of cabbage. They're crazy about all leaf crops, for that matter. But the ravenous rascals don't stop there. They gleefully gobble up almost any young plants and buds within their reach, and they love shrub and tree bark.

Mother Nature blessed bunnies with the cutest good looks this side of a teddy bear store. Unfortunately, she also equipped them with razor-sharp choppers and an appetite for any plant under the sun. Or so it seems to anyone who's watched a rabbit munch his way from one end of the garden to the other. Scientifically speaking, there are two species of these hoppity critters, and either can show up just about anywhere in the country. In general, rabbits of the Peter Cottontail type prefer places with dense vegetation and plenty of shrubby cover. That way, they can leap into hiding when they're startled or sense danger. Hares, a.k.a. jackrabbits, tend to roam in more open country, and their response to fear is simply to run like blazes. Neither hares nor cottontails hibernate, although they may hole up during periods of severe weather.

🌿 Another Clue

Aside from eyewitness accounts, or tracks left in mud, you'll know the bunny brigade has been at work if the victims (especially young ones) have been nibbled clear down to the ground, or their foliage has been nipped off clean as a whistle. (Unlike deer, these guys don't tear; they slice.)

🌿 Your Fundamental Fence

To protect a small area from the furry fiends, a fence made of hardware cloth or other sturdy wire mesh will do the trick. Just dig a trench around your plot, and install your barrier so that it extends at least 3 feet above the ground and 6 inches below, with another 6 inches bent out underground at a 90° angle from the garden. Then, if looks matter—and if you're enclosing a flower garden, they surely will—disguise the wire with a more decorative fence.

Home on the Range

Rabbits

Take It Out or Put It In

Once you know whether your munchers are jackrabbits or cottontails, you can often get them to move on simply by making your yard less inviting. Here's all you need to do:

▶ Discourage cottontails by removing piles of brush or debris, or clumps of extra-dense plantings where they like to hunker down.

▶ To make jackrabbits feel unwelcome, deprive them of the wide open spaces they crave. Either install "island" beds here and there throughout your yard, or surround your plagued plot with tall shrubs and ornamental grasses.

GRANDMA KNEW BEST

Grandma Putt kept rabbits out of her flower beds by including plenty of Allium-family plants in the crowd. It worked like a charm, and it still does at my place—and not only with the odiferous bulbs like garlic and onions. Bunnies also bounce away from ornamental alliums. One of my favorites is Allium giganteum, a real stunner with softball-sized globes of lilac flowers, and stems that reach to 5 feet high. If your garden can't handle a plant quite that tall, try a shorter variety like A. 'Globemaster', which only grows to about 2¹/₂ feet.

Bribery Might Get You Somewhere

If your yard is large enough, sow a big patch of alfalfa, soybeans, clover, or lettuce well away from the plants the rabbits are gunnin' for. It's not guaranteed protection, but chances are the bunnies will be so busy romping and nibbling in their very own field that they'll give your favorite plants the cold shoulder.

Take It Easy

One of the easiest ways to make your garden plants less tempting to rabbits may just be to slack off a little in your weeding chores. How so? Well, a wildlife biologist with the Missouri Department of Conservation did a three-year study on the food preferences of bunnies in his state, and these were the favorites, paws down:

► Crabgrass

► Daisy fleabane

► Dandelions

► Knotweed

► Lespedeza (the one shrub in this weedy roster)

► Ragweed

Wake Up and Smell the Bacon

If rabbits are targeting your trees and shrubs, smear bacon grease on the trunks. The little guys will take their teeth elsewhere. Just don't try this old-time trick if you've got dogs or cats on the prowl, or they'll descend on your yard in droves!

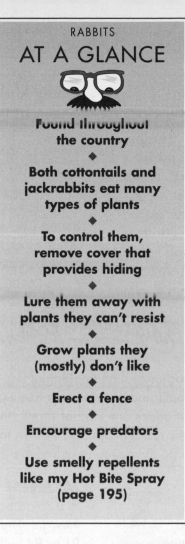

RABBITS

AT A GLANCE

Found throughout the country

◆

Both cottontails and jackrabbits eat many types of plants

◆

To control them, remove cover that provides hiding

◆

Lure them away with plants they can't resist

◆

Grow plants they (mostly) don't like

◆

Erect a fence

◆

Encourage predators

◆

Use smelly repellents like my Hot Bite Spray (page 195)

Boy, That's Hot!

Like any other ornery critter I can think of, rabbits hate like the dickens to bite into anything spicy, especially when it's as powerful as my Hot Bite Spray (see page 195). Just spritz it on your plants, then sit back and enjoy the show: When the bunnies bite down, you'll all but see the smoke rising from their ears!

Run, Rabbit, Run!

Ever wonder why rabbits are timid? Just about every carnivore you can name thinks they make mighty fine eatin'! That list of preferred diners includes cats, coyotes, dogs, foxes, hawks, owls, skunks, and snakes. The presence of any of those predators, or simply their urine or hair (see "Give 'Em a Whiff of Trouble," on page 70), will make your garden less enticing to

Bugs and his buddies. But if the varmints are driving you up the wall, my best advice is to get a ferret. These little guys are the heavyweight champs of the rabbit-hunting world, and the toothy rascals know it. If you'd rather not adopt a ferret of your own, make friends with someone who has, and offer your babysitting services now and then. Take the ferret for a stroll around the yard, and say bye-bye, bunny!

Up Close and Personal

If the plants you love best are also the bunnies' favorite targets, I have a no-muss, no-fuss solution: Grow those flowers (or herbs or veggies) in containers on your deck, or just outside a door that you use frequently. Rabbits have to be awfully hungry and have no other alternatives before they'll dine on your very doorstep!

That's not all, folks!

Most of the bad guys that bug annual and perennial flowers also get up to no good in the vegetable garden. You'll find my tried-and-true tips for fighting those felons in Chapter 4. Also, pests that attack one kind of vegetable usually target other types, too. So if you don't find your resident troublemaker in this chapter, look for him in Chapter 5 or Chapter 7. In addition, you may find these louses in your leaf crops:

ANTS farm root aphids just as they do the terrors' above-ground cousins. You can read all about these cowboys starting on page 36.

JAPANESE BEETLES will belly up to a salad bar any chance they get. The tips on pages 81 to 84 will help you close the chow line.

 FIRE ANTS love nibbling on leaf crops and other vegetables—besides making your garden chores miserable! See pages 8 to 11 for the full story on these vile villains.

LEAFTIERS don't target many vegetables, but they *do* love celery. So if you find your crop all tied up, set it loose using the tactics on pages 101 and 102.

CHAPTER 7

VEGETABLE VILLAINS

What would summer be without tomatoes, corn, peppers, and all those other taste-tempting treasures plucked fresh from your own garden? Well, to my way of thinking, it would be like having Christmas without Santa Claus! It's just too bad that a whole lot of Grinches are itching to steal your harvest before you've even picked your first ripe tomato. Fortunately, whether they're flying, crawling, or scampering over the garden fence, I've got a whole Santa's sack full of tricks for foiling the hungry hellions.

ASIATIC GARDEN BEETLES

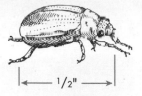

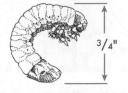

½"

¾"

Adult beetles emerge in late June and early July, and start right in feeding. In the soil near their plant victims, they lay clusters of eggs. Moisture from the soil makes the eggs swell up into pearly white balls that hatch in about 10 days. The grubs dine until October, then tunnel down to their winter homes, 6 to 12 inches underground. They reappear in the spring and go on a brief eating binge before pupating in May and June.

Besides devouring just about any vegetable crop that you care to name, Asiatic garden beetles go after both ornamental and fruit trees, as well as roses and many other shrubs. Favorite targets include asters, cosmos, delphiniums, petunias, zinnias, phlox, salvias, and heucheras. The grubs also target turf grasses. (See Chapter 1 for the lowdown on clearing grubs out of your lawn.)

These imports from Japan and China first showed up in New Jersey in 1921, and since then, they've spread throughout much of the East—munching all the way. They get up to no good at both main stages of their lives, and their damage is often mistaken for the dirty work of other bad-guy bugs. The adult beetles are cinnamon- to velvety-brown, and their shape is similar to that of small Japanese beetles. They snooze in the soil by day, coming out at night to feast on the foliage, flowers, and fruits of a great many garden plants. And I *do* mean feast! In large numbers, these monsters can demolish a garden almost overnight. They can also make first-class nuisances of themselves on hot summer evenings, when they flock to outdoor lights or bang against window screens. The youngsters are C-shaped, grayish grubs with light brown heads. In typical grubby fashion, they munch on roots, causing plants to weaken, wilt, and sometimes die.

Who's There?

When your garden is being eaten alive and you've got brown bugs bouncing off your window screens on hot summer nights, the finger points to Asiatic garden beetles. But before you launch your good-riddance campaign, grab a flashlight, go out to your garden at night, and make a positive I.D.

Get 'Em in Their Sleep

You could go out after dark with a flashlight and handpick the beetles, but there's an easier way to end their fun. In the morning, poke around in the soil at the base of damaged plants. You'll find scores of the foul felons, sound asleep, just below the soil surface. Scoop them up and drop them into soapy water, or spray them with my Peppermint Soap Spray (see page 41).

Home on the Range

Asiatic Garden Beetles

Get Help

If you give them half a chance, scores of songbirds will pluck the snoozing beetles right out of the soil and gobble up the grubs, too. For hints on laying out the welcome mat for your fine-feathered pest-control squad, see Chapter 8.

Dig Deep

Before you plant your spring crops, cultivate your plot thoroughly to a depth of a foot or so. That way, you'll kill many of the overwintering pupae before they have a chance to grow up and lay this year's supply of eggs.

Hired Workers

If you missed your window of opportunity to oust the grubs and they've already hit the chow line, buy some beneficial nematodes and release them into the soil, according to the directions on the package. Those tiny good guys will make quick work of the grubby gluttons.

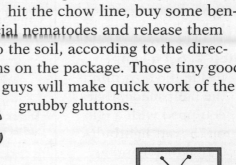

THUG BUSTER

Dead Bug Brew

When you want to keep all kinds of live bugs from dining on your plants, serve them this mulligan stew of dead bugs.

1/2 cup of dead insects (the more kinds, the merrier!)
1 tbsp. of dishwashing liquid
1 tbsp. of cayenne pepper
2 cups of water

Put the ingredients in an old blender (one you'll *never* use again for food preparation), and puree the heck out of 'em. Strain out the pulp, and dilute the remaining brew at a rate of 1/4 cup of brew per 1 cup of water. Apply it to your plants with a hand-held sprayer to the point of run-off.

✒ Let 'Em See the Light

When the beetles are drivin' you batty, trap 'em in this light box. Here's all you need to do:

Step 1. Cut a 3-inch-diameter hole in the top of a cardboard box.

Step 2. Set a lamp inside the box, minus the lampshade, that's equipped with a 60- or 75-watt lightbulb (no higher!) and an outdoor-grade extension cord. Don't let the bulb touch the cardboard. You want to leave at least 6 inches of clearance between the bulb and the top of the box.

Step 3. Make a funnel out of heavy construction paper, with the narrow end just big enough to fit snuggly into the hole in the box. Then tape a piece of stretchy pantyhose over the narrow end, leaving a little slack, but not enough that it touches the

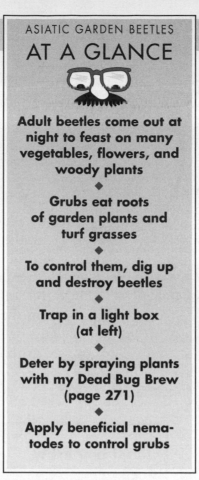

ASIATIC GARDEN BEETLES
AT A GLANCE

Adult beetles come out at night to feast on many vegetables, flowers, and woody plants

◆

Grubs eat roots of garden plants and turf grasses

◆

To control them, dig up and destroy beetles

◆

Trap in a light box (at left)

◆

Deter by spraying plants with my Dead Bug Brew (page 271)

◆

Apply beneficial nematodes to control grubs

bulb. Then shove the funnel into the hole.

Step 4. Set the box on a table or chair in the garden, so that the top is 3 to 4 feet off the ground.

Step 5. About an hour after sunset, turn on the light, and leave it on for 2 hours. The beetles will head for the light and fly into the trap. Then, just pull out the funnel, and dunk the buggy pouch into soapy water. (That job can wait till morning—the beetles won't be going anywhere!)

✒ Knock 'Em Dead

Nothing sends live bugs scurrying away faster than the scent of dead bugs. To make your plants positively repugnant to Asiatic garden beetles and all kinds of other multilegged bad guys, spray the leaves, stems, and crowns with my Dead Bug Brew (see page 271).

Adults spend the winter in garden debris and show up in the spring, just as asparagus shoots begin to sprout. They start munching immediately, and within days, egg laying begins. Just 3 to 8 days later (depending on the temperature), the larvae hatch and chow down on stalks and leaves. Within two weeks, they burrow into the ground, spin silken cocoons, and spend 5 to 10 days growing up. Then a new crew of asparagus aficionados emerges. Depending on the climate, there may be as many as five or six generations per year.

ALSO ON THE MENU

Most bad-guy bugs have preferences for certain kinds of plants, but asparagus beetles carry pickiness to the extreme: Both the common and spotted types eat asparagus and nothing *but* asparagus.

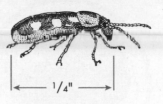

1/4"
1/3"

If you haven't tangled with these terrors a time or two, then you've probably never grown asparagus. The adults chew on the tender, new spears, causing them to grow more slowly and come out of the ground scarred, twisted, or otherwise distorted. Later in the season, both grown-ups and larvae munch on the stems and ferny leaves of the plants. There are two species, both of which can show up anywhere in the country. And they're two of the prettiest, most colorful bugs you'll ever see. The common asparagus beetle *(Crioceris asparagi)* has a shiny, bluish black body, a reddish brown thorax, and wing covers bordered in red with four creamy-white splotches. The spotted asparagus beetle *(C. duodecimpunctata)* is a vibrant red-orange with 12 black spots on its wing covers. The grubs of both, on the other hand, are downright ugly and sluglike in appearance. The common crowd are grayish with dark heads and legs; the spotted youngsters are solid orange.

Give 'Em a Bath

Unless you have a huge plot of asparagus, the simplest way to say, "Bye-bye, beetles," is to brush 'em off of the plants into a pail of hot, soapy water. If you make daily patrols, starting as soon as the first spears poke above the ground, you'll ensure yourself of a tasty crop *and* head off a lot of egg-laying action.

✍ And Then a Shower

A week or so later, when the larvae start to hatch, just blast 'em off with the garden hose. Once the ugly villains are on the ground, they won't climb back up onto the plants, so they'll either starve to death, or

Home on the Range

Asparagus Beetles

become dinner for some hungry birds. Bluebirds, Baltimore orioles, cardinals, and chickadees all love asparagus beetle larvae and the grown-ups, too!

✍ Under the Covers

For the closest thing to guaranteed protection, cover your asparagus plants in the spring, as soon as the spears start to appear, and leave the covers on until fall. Be sure to prop them up on supports that are a few inches taller than the spears will be when you pluck 'em, and hold down the edges with stones or wood strips, so the beetles can't sneak in underneath. If you have an ornamental-edible garden and don't care to look at all that white fabric, cover individual plants with decorative screen enclosures instead. You can find them in many garden centers and catalogs.

✍ An After-Dinner Drink

My Nix 'Em with Nicotine Tea (see page 259) will kill larvae and adult beetles on contact. But don't use it—or any other kind of spray—until after you've harvested all of the spears. Otherwise, you'll damage the sensitive growing tips, and you'll be right back where you started.

Ask Jerry

I read in a gardening book that tomatoes repel asparagus beetles, so last spring, I planted some in my asparagus bed. The beetle population was the lowest it's ever been—but my harvest was the worst ever! The plants yielded up about half the number of spears they normally do. What went wrong?

The tomatoes simply hogged up too much food. Asparagus has a big appetite, and it suffers when any other roots share its nutrient supply. Next year, grow patio tomatoes in containers, and set them around your asparagus bed. Or use pots of nasturtiums or calendulas: Asparagus beetles don't like them, either!

BEAN WEEVILS

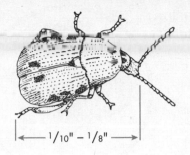

1/10" – 1/8"

It's a real challenge for a home gardener to grow high-quality dry beans and peas for storage, and these teeny monsters are the main reason. They're so small that they often go unnoticed until weeks after harvest, when little holes or pale, circular patches appear on the stored seeds. (The discolored marks show where the larvae have eaten a hole in the seed's cotyledon, a.k.a. seed leaves; the holes are the grown-ups' exit doors.) There are several species of bean and pea weevils. The grown-ups resemble miniature plum curculios (see page 52) and range from just 1/10 to 1/8 inch long. To make detection even harder, their colors—shades of brown or dark camouflage green—blend right in with the legumes' foliage. The fat, whitish grubs are so small that you can hardly see them.

A Pound of Prevention

Once bean weevils have invaded your crop, they're impossible to get rid of, so do everything you can to head 'em off, beginning at seed-shopping time. Buy your seeds from a garden center or catalog you can trust. And examine the seeds carefully before planting. I often use a magnifying glass!

Don't Stock Up

Bean or pea seeds that are just sitting around the garden shed are a mama weevil's idea of a first-

THIS IS THEIR LIFE

In the garden, adult weevils lay eggs on pods, or sometimes manage to get "locked" inside the pods at flowering time. Or they deposit their eggs on dried beans in storage. In any case, the larvae hatch between 5 and 20 days later, tunnel into the beans, and spend another 11 to 42 days eating their way out of a cozy pupal chamber. When they emerge, all grown up, they cut a hole about 1/10 inch in diameter through the bean and crawl into the outside world. Generally, only one or two generations appear in the garden each year, but in stored beans, the weevils breed continually.

ALSO ON THE MENU

Bean weevils target only lima beans, cowpeas, and kidney beans in the garden, but they go for any kind of beans, peas, and lentils that are in storage.

class maternity ward. So don't shop ahead, and don't stock up! Buy only as many seeds as you intend to plant now, and get 'em into the ground as fast as you can.

The Early Bird...

gets fewer weevils. You can put a dent in the weevil population by sowing your beans as early as your climate will allow, and then plowing the plants under immediately after harvest.

Just in Case

Even if you think your harvest is weevil-free, don't take any chances. Before you store your beans or peas, give them this two-step treatment:

Step 1. Lay the cleaned beans or

DID YOU KNOW?

We all know that where bad-guy bugs are concerned, a small problem can quickly turn into a big one. But bean weevils carry that concept to the extreme. Here's an example: As an experiment, scientists at Ohio State University placed a single pair of bean weevils in a bag containing 87 pounds of red kidney beans. Fourteen months later, they opened the bag, and 250,000 adult weevils spilled out!

peas in a shallow pan, and heat them in the oven at 175°F for an hour.

Step 2. Let them cool completely, then bag them and put them in the freezer for a week. The temperature changes will kill any adult weevils or larvae, so after they're frozen, you can safely keep your stash at room temperature.

And to Be Extra-Safe

Before you store dried beans or peas—even if you bought 'em at the supermarket—tuck a bay leaf or two into each container. It's an old-time trick for keeping weevils at bay, and it still works like magic!

CUCUMBER BEETLES

THIS IS THEIR LIFE

In general, adult beetles sleep through the winter in weeds, dense grasses, or garden litter, and emerge in spring to lay eggs in the soil around their host plants. When the larvae hatch, usually in about a week, they tunnel into plants' roots, feed for a few more weeks, then pupate. Depending on the climate, there may be anywhere from one to six generations per year.

ALSO ON THE MENU

Both spotted and striped cucumber beetles dine on the entire cucurbit clan, including melons, squash, gourds, pumpkins, and, of course, their namesake crop. They also target asparagus, early beans, corn, peas, potatoes, radishes, tomatoes, and many flowers. Striped larvae munch on cucurbit roots and sometimes, on fallen fruit. The spotted youngsters, a.k.a. corn rootworms (see page 302), prefer corn and legume roots.

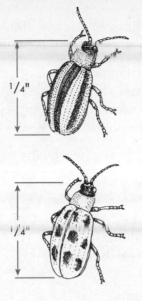

1/4"

1/4"

Several species of these menaces chew ragged holes in the foliage, flowers, stems, and fruits of a whole lot of garden plants. In large numbers, they can quickly demolish a bed of seedlings and make a mess of older plants, too. But that's only part of the problem. Within their digestive systems, cuke beetles carry two of the worst diseases that can strike any garden: fusarium (bacterial) wilt, and cucumber mosaic virus. And, as the beetles feed, they infect their victims.

All cucumber beetles fall into two basic types: striped and spotted. Striped cuke beetles are yellow, orange-yellow, or cream-colored with three broad, black stripes. Their spotted cousins are yellow with 11 or 12 black spots. The larvae of both types are thin, whitish grubs with a black or reddish brown head. These youngsters create their own brand of trouble by munching on the roots of many kinds of plants.

🌿 Act Fast

When you're battling disease spreaders like cuke beetles, there's not a minute to waste! So as soon as they appear in the spring, handpick and drown them in soapy water, vacuum them off of your plants (see page 289), or mix up a batch of my Cuke Beetle Buster (see page 279), and give 'em the old what for.

🌿 Heat Up the Action—Maybe

In the case of a major invasion, go after the varmints with my Hot Pepper Spray (see page 83). But don't use this or any other spray when the flowers are open and good-guy bugs are polli-nating them. Otherwise, you won't get any crop at all.

🌿 Alluring, But...

Garden centers and catalogs sell traps that lure cuke beetles to their death with pheromones, a.k.a. sex hormones. They work like magic, but as with all pow-erful lure traps, you're likely to draw a bigger crowd than you had to begin with. It's your call, though.

🌿 I've Got Enough Already, Thanks

To trap your resident cuke beetles without inviting more to the party, use one of these no-fail alternatives:

▶ Set big, wilted squash leaves on the ground among your plants. The beetles will crawl under the leaves to escape the hot sun. Then you can stroll through the garden, casually step on the leaves, and squash the varmints in the process.

▶ Gather up some cucumber peels, let them dry out, and dust them with diatomaceous earth (DE). The beetles will zero in on the cucumber scent, the DE will punc-ture the villains' skin, and that'll be all she wrote!

DID YOU KNOW?

How do you tell when cuke beetles have infected your plants with their foul germs? Just watch for these telltale signs:

◆ **Fusarium wilt.** Your plants droop, as though they need water NOW. You give them a good, long drink and they perk up, but by the next morning, they're droopy and wilted again. In cool, damp weather, you may see a fluffy, pale pink or white fungus. There is no cure, so pull up and destroy the victims and, in the future, grow resistant varieties (there are many). Then do all you can to keep cuke beetles at bay.

◆ **Mosaic virus.** Leaves are splotched or mottled in yellow, with turned-down edges. If the infection has gone very far, pull up the plants and destroy them. In the earlier stages, pluck off and destroy the infected foliage, and follow up with my Flower and Foliage Flu Shot (see page 361).

▶ Set out shallow bowls of soapy water with strips of melon rind or cucumber peel added. The beetles will dive in for dinner and never get up from the table.

Home on the Range

Cucumber Beetles

soapy water. Or simply pour a pot of boiling water on top of the plants. (It'll kill the radishes along with the beetles, of course, but that crop was never intended for eating.)

🍃 You Are My Sunshine

If cuke beetles have delivered their deadly diseases to your yard (see "Did You Know," on page 278), then solarize your soil before you plant anything else in that space. That way, you'll kill any lingering larvae—and lots of other troublemakers, too. See page 182 for my simple solarizing method.

🍃 Plant a Trap

You might think of a radish as just another tidbit on the relish tray, but to a cuke beetle, it's a fine-dining experience, bar none. Just plant a sacrificial bed of the tangy tubers, and the beetles will beat a path to it. Remember, though, that the key to success with this or any lure crop is fast action. The minute you see the pesky pests ganging up on their victims, toss an old sheet over the plants, pull 'em up, and dump 'em into

🍃 Where the Rubber Meets the Bugs

Cucumber beetles will hit the road if you grow their favorite targets in old tires. There's something in the rubber that the gluttons just can't stand. Whatever the mystery ingredient is, it repels squash bugs, too. I wonder if Mr. Firestone knows about this?

Cuke Beetle Buster

When cucumber beetles are eating their way through your garden, spreading deadly diseases in the process, end their reign of terror with this timely tonic.

½ cup of garden lime
½ cup of wood ashes
2 gal. of water

Mix these ingredients together, and pour the solution into a hand-held sprayer. Then spray your embattled plants from head to toe, and make sure to coat the undersides of leaves. The beetles'll bite the dust!

THUG BUSTER

A Golden Solution

To make cuke beetles scurry in a hurry, move in masses of marigolds. The pretty flowers will also say "Shove off!" to a lot of other veggie-munching villains, including squash bugs, tomato hornworms, and whiteflies.

Make Mine Vanilla

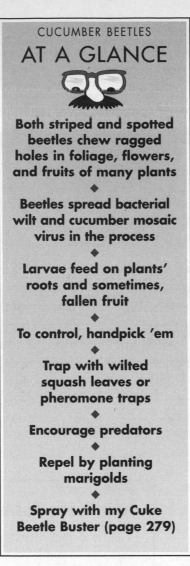

As far as my nose is concerned, there's no more pleasing aroma than vanilla. And what pleases me even more is the fact that cucumber beetles *hate* the stuff. Just mix 2 tablespoons of artificial vanilla flavoring per quart of water in a hand-held sprayer, and spray your plants from stem to stern. The beetles will do their munching and their egg-laying elsewhere. (Genuine vanilla extract works just as well, but why waste the good stuff on your sworn enemy?)

CUCUMBER BEETLES
AT A GLANCE

Both striped and spotted beetles chew ragged holes in foliage, flowers, and fruits of many plants

◆

Beetles spread bacterial wilt and cucumber mosaic virus in the process

◆

Larvae feed on plants' roots and sometimes, fallen fruit

◆

To control, handpick 'em

◆

Trap with wilted squash leaves or pheromone traps

◆

Encourage predators

◆

Repel by planting marigolds

◆

Spray with my Cuke Beetle Buster (page 279)

Mess Call

There's nothing soldier beetles like better than a mess hall full of cucumber beetles! To call up the troops, let some goldenrod or milkweed spring up among your veggies, or set pots of catnip among the plants. Just don't plant it in the ground, or it'll take over the neighborhood! You can read more about soldier beetles and other good guys in Chapter 8.

THIS IS THEIR LIFE

Grasshoppers mate in late summer or fall, and the females lay large clusters of eggs in the soil or on weeds and grasses. The adults die when cold weather sets in, while the eggs stay warm and cozy underground. The baby 'hoppers hatch in the spring and start right in with their life's work: eating, molting, and growing until finally, it's time to make their own contribution to the survival of the species.

ALSO ON THE MENU

When grasshoppers go on a rampage, there's almost nothing they won't eat. They even devour plants such as marigolds and wormwood that send other demons dashing away. Even these greedy gluttons have their favorite snacks, though. Beans, corn, and ornamental grasses are high on the list. And a bed of seedlings of any kind is like a bowl of popcorn to a hungry 'hopper—pure comfort food.

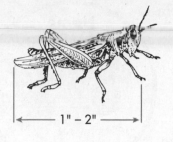

1" – 2"

Some years, grasshoppers just go about their business, not bothering anybody. Then one day, out of the blue, BAM! They descend in swarming masses, and almost before you can blink, every speck of green has vanished from your garden. These scourges appear most often on the hot, dry western plains, but grasshoppers can gang up on any patch of green in the country. When it comes to controlling grasshoppers, there's good news and bad news. The bad news is that they stand up and say "Boo!" to Thug Busters and other sprays that knock most other bugs flat. The good news is that they have hordes of natural enemies, who can usually keep the situation well in hand. That is, except in those years when the population suddenly explodes. Then it pays to have a few extra tricks up your sleeve.

🌿 Mighty Molasses Mixes

Grasshoppers flock to molasses the way bears flock to honey. You can put their craving to work in two ways:

1. Bury a jar up to its rim, and fill it with a mixture of equal parts of molasses and water. The 'hoppers will dive right in, and they won't get out—not alive, that is!

2. Mix 1 part molasses to 9 parts water, and pour the stuff into shallow containers, such as cat-food or tuna-fish cans. Set the cans in your garden and sprinkle bread crumbs or sun-

flower seeds around them. Grasshoppers will zero in on the sweet water, and in the blink of an eye, birds will pounce on them and then hang around to nibble on the seeds and help with your other pest-control chores.

Home on the Range

Grasshoppers

✎ Faster Action

If the birds aren't winging in fast enough to clear out the 'hoppers, don't worry. Just mix up a batch of my Great-Guns Garlic Spray (see page 118), and go gun 'em down. It's one of

GRANDMA KNEW BEST

Grandma Putt knew of a great way to put a dent in the 'hopper population. In the fall or early spring, she'd thoroughly till her garden to bring a lot of 'hopper eggs to the surface, where they'd freeze, dry out, or be gobbled up by hungry birds. And in the tilling process, so many eggs get buried deeper into the soil that when the nymphs hatch, they can't scramble to the top. Now that's a double dose of protection!

the few weapons that really works on these hooligans.

✎ Pray for Help

For reasons I've never quite figured out, praying mantises have gotten a reputation as big-time hero bugs. The fact is, they devour as many good guys as they do villains. (They even eat each other!) But there is one pest-control event at which they've earned a black belt: gobbling up grasshoppers. So in a year when the 'hoppers have hit hard, you might want to call for help from the mantises. Here's how:

▶ In early to mid-spring, find some mantis egg cases in your neighborhood. Look for clusters, about an inch long, covered with a frothy, gummy substance, and stuck to twigs or plant stems. Cut off the whole stem; don't try to scrape off the eggs.

▶ Put the egg case in a paper bag, fasten it with a paper clip, and put it on a sunny windowsill (but don't let it get hot!).

▶ Six to seven weeks later, check every day to see whether any eggs are hatching. As soon as the youngsters start appearing, take 'em outside and let 'em go. (Don't dawdle, or they'll start eating each other for breakfast!)

VEGETABLE VILLAINS

MEXICAN BEAN BEETLES

THIS IS THEIR LIFE

Adult beetles spend the winter in garden litter or wooded areas. In the spring, after some light snacking, females lay clusters of yellowish eggs on the undersides of bean leaves. When the larvae hatch, they feast for two to five weeks, then pupate right on the leaves. When they first emerge, they're plain yellow, but they soon turn reddish, and black spots appear. Depending on the climate, there may be as many as four generations per year, with adults, eggs, and pupae often appearing simultaneously in late summer.

ALSO ON THE MENU

Mexican bean beetles love all kinds of beans, including soybeans; but limas and snap beans are special favorites. They also target cowpeas, and sometimes they depart from their legume menu to chomp on cabbage, kale, collards, and mustard greens, and occasionally, clover and alfalfa.

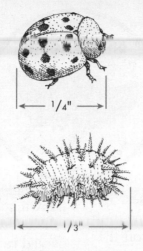

1/4"

1/3"

It seems to me that Mother Nature must enjoy playing practical jokes. Otherwise, why would she make the Mexican bean beetle—one of the vilest villains in the vegetable patch—almost a dead ringer for the ladybug—a true-blue garden hero if there ever was one? Fortunately, when you're not sure which cousin has come to call, there are a few differences you can look for: Bean beetles are a little larger, they lack the white spots that ladybugs have on their heads, and their wing covers have a more bronze or coppery sheen. But the surest clue that these south-of-the-border bandits are on the scene will be in your bean patch: You'll see veiny skeletons where leaves used to be.

Bean beetle larvae start out green and then turn yellow, and they're covered with fuzzy spines. They join the grown-ups in the feeding frenzy, munching on the undersides of leaves and sometimes pods and stems, too. Afflicted plants often die, and even when they survive, pod production is reduced.

🌱 Pounce on 'Em, Pronto!

Mexican bean beetles churn out young'uns as long as the warm weather lasts, so you need to get on 'em the minute they appear in the spring. Otherwise, by midsummer, your bean patch could be as full of skeletons as a Day of the Dead party in Tijuana!

Hand-to-Hand Combat

Unless you're facing a major invasion, the easiest way to control bean beetles is to handpick the larvae and adults, and drown them in soapy water. And, while you're on your search-and-destroy mission, check the undersides of leaves for egg cases. When you find one, either scrape it off into your sudsy bucket, or clip off the whole leaf and drop it in.

Home on the Range

Mexican Bean Beetles

They've Gotten Out of Hand!

When there are just too many beetles or too many plants to make handpicking practical, put old sheets on the ground under your beans, and shake the plants. When the beetles tumble down, gather up the fabric and dump the contents into soapy water. Or, if you'd rather spray than brush, blast the bugs with my Homegrown Daisy Spray (see page 104) or Beetle Juice (see page 53).

Protect the Little Guys

Even a small crowd of Mexican bean beetles can quickly demolish a bed of seedlings. So keep your young beans under wraps until flower buds form. Then take off the covers so birds and good-guy bugs can pollinate the blossoms. Either commercial row covers or old, sheer window curtains will do the trick; but whichever ones you use, bury the edges in the soil, or seal them down with rocks or wood strips, so that the beetles can't crawl under them.

GRANDMA KNEW BEST

Grandma Putt knew that even within the same variety, some individual plants attract more pests than others. So, the minute she saw that a particular plant had too many bean beetles to handpick, she'd throw an old sheet over it, pull it up, and burn it. It's an old technique called "rogueing," and it operates on the theory that getting rid of pest magnets not only gets rid of a lot of troublemakers, but somehow, also improves growing conditions for the remaining plants. It works, too!

Shop Carefully

With just a little savvy shopping in the spring, you can avoid a whole lot of bean beetle trouble down the road.

MEXICAN BEAN BEETLES

AT A GLANCE

Ladybug lookalikes skeletonize the leaves of beans and sometimes, other plants

◆

Pod production is reduced and plants often die

◆

To control them, handpick adults, nymphs, and egg cases

◆

Plant resistant varieties

◆

Spray with my Homegrown Daisy Spray (page 104) or Beetle Juice (page 53)

◆

Use row covers on seedlings

◆

Deter by planting rosemary, summer savory, or potatoes

When you place your seed order, keep the following in mind:

- Look for resistant varieties. There are many, and new ones come out almost every year. Bear in mind, though, that resistance doesn't *guarantee* safe passage for your crop; it simply means that the plants are lower down on the hit list, or better able to withstand some damage.
- Grow varieties that bear beans, or at least get to be big and sturdy, before the local beetle population builds up.
- If you're not sure which plants will work best where you live, check with the folks at your Cooperative Extension Service or your local garden club.

Bye-Bye, Bean Plants

No matter what kind of beans you've grown, plow them under at the end of the season. That way, you'll eliminate the beetles' winter homes and also add valuable nitrogen to the soil.

Enlist the Enemy

Mexican bean beetles have plenty of natural enemies, including parasitic wasps, assassin bugs, spined soldier bugs, and ladybugs. You can order these heroes from catalogs, but you'll have a more stable workforce if you entice them to your garden by planting some of their favorite flowers. See Chapter 8 for the full scoop on posting a "Help Wanted" notice.

Plant Protection

Rosemary and summer savory both send bean beetles bounding away. But for double-dip pest control, plant beans and potatoes together. The spuds chase away the bean beetles, and the beans guard the spuds from their arch enemy, Colorado potato beetles.

SQUASH BEETLES

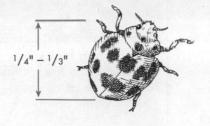

1/4" – 1/3"

THIS IS THEIR LIFE

Adult beetles spend the winter in garden litter, weedy fields, or wooded areas. In the spring, after some light snacking, females lay clusters of yellowish eggs on the leaves of squash and other cucurbit plants. When the larvae hatch, they feast for two to five weeks, then pupate right on the leaves. Depending on the climate, there may be as many as four generations per year, with adults, eggs, and pupae often appearing simultaneously in late summer.

ALSO ON THE MENU

Squash beetles feast on all cucurbit plants, including summer and winter squash, gourds, pumpkins, cucumbers, and every kind of melon under the sun. Their kissin' cousins, Mexican bean beetles, target (surprise!) beans, such as lima, snap, soy, and kidney beans. They also munch on cowpeas. You can read all about those villains beginning on page 283.

These ladybug lookalikes are closely related to Mexican bean beetles, and they perform similar dirty work. Both adults and larvae munch on plants of the cucurbit clan, filling the leaves with holes and sometimes, turning them to mere skeletons. The two generations work as a team: The youngsters feed on the undersides of leaves, while the grown-ups dine on top. The beetles look like pale, orange-yellow ladybugs, with seven black spots on each wing cover. The larvae are plain yellow and are covered with spines. Once these guys set up camp in your garden, they're the dickens to get rid of. They've become resistant to a number of chemical pesticides and, like their cousins from south of the border, they even shrug off many natural remedies. Fortunately, there are a lot of ways to outsmart the rascals!

✐ Snatch 'Em

In a small garden, or when the invasion is light, handpick the larvae and adults, and drop them in a bucket of soapy water. And, be sure to check the leaves for egg cases. When you spot one, either scrape it off into your sudsy bucket, clip off the whole leaf and drop it in, or simply squish the eggs with your (gloved!) fingers.

✐ They're Runnin' Rampant!

When there are just too many beetles, or too many plants to make handpicking practical, make up a batch of my Garden Cure All Tonic (see page 44), and spray the leaves from top to bottom, taking special care to get the undersides. The combination of garlic, onion, and pepper in this Thug Buster is potent enough to thwart even truly tough customers like squash beetles.

Seeing Yellow

Like many bugs, squash beetles are attracted to the color yellow. You can demolish droves of the demons by making sticky traps out of yellow cardboard and standing them among your cucurbit crops. But, because squash beetles are on the job all summer long, here's a better idea: Get some shallow, yellow plastic bowls, fill them with soapy water, and set them on the ground near your plagued plants. The beetles will make a beeline for the bowls, fall in, and drown. Then all you need to do is empty the contents and refill your trap, and you're back in business.

Home on the Range

Squash Beetles

DID YOU KNOW?

Squash beetles and Mexican bean beetles are part of the *Coccinellidae* family—and they're the clan's only two bad-guy members in the entire United States. All the rest of the cousins, including ladybugs, do heroic work in the garden, chowing down on other insects, such as scale, aphids, and even some of their own veggie-eating relatives.

A Variation on the Theme

Here's another way to put the power of yellow to work: As soon as your climate will allow, plant an early crop of squash, and cover the ground under the plants with yellow plastic mulch (available at garden centers). As soon as the beetles descend on the plants—and will they ever!—throw a sheet over the plants, pull 'em up by the roots, and dump 'em into soapy water. If you have the room, you can make staggered plantings of trap (sacrificial) crops throughout the growing season. Just keep these three guidelines in mind:

1. Put the trap crop as far away as possible from the cucurbit plants that you intend to eat.

2. Use the yellow mulch *only* on the lure crop.

3. The minute you see the beetles on the lure plants, pull up and destroy the plants, bugs and all.

SQUASH BUGS

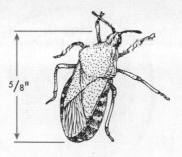

5/8"

THIS IS THEIR LIFE

Squash bugs overwinter as unmated adults in garden litter, weeds, and other protected places. They're slow to get going in the spring, but about the time squash vines take off and start to flower, the bugs wake up and make whoopee. The females lay clusters of yellowish brown to brick-red eggs on the undersides of cucurbit leaves, and about 10 days later, the nymphs hatch and start eating. They mature in four to six weeks, but they forego marital rituals until the following spring.

ALSO ON THE MENU

Squash bugs live up to their name: They prefer to feast on squash (both summer and winter types) and pumpkins, which are, technically speaking, a kind of winter squash. But, like any of us, when these critters are hungry and they can't find their favorite foods, they settle for lesser fare—in this case, cucumbers, melons, and gourds.

Don't confuse squash bugs with squash beetles. Although both of these bad guys go gunnin' for the cucurbit clan, they're not even remotely related to each other. Squash bugs are exactly what their name implies: true bugs with sucking mouthparts that drain the juices out of leaves, often killing whole plants in the process. Your first clue that these villains may be at work will be pale green or yellow specks on the leaves of your cucurbit plants. These specks soon enlarge into brown patches, and other parts of the plant may suddenly wilt and turn brittle. Eventually, the vines turn black and die. It's unlikely that you'll see the bugs right away. The shy little devils generally hide deep in the interior of the plant, under leaves, and on the undersides of fruit. But if you search a little, you'll find brownish black, flat-backed bugs. The nymphs are whitish to greenish gray, with black legs.

Look First

Before you launch your attack on squash bugs, look around and make sure they're really the guilty party. Their sucking produces damage that looks very similar to the symptoms of fusarium and verticillium wilts, two deadly diseases spread by cucumber beetles and squash vine borers.

Surprise!

Squash bugs are, by nature, one of the most secretive pests on the planet—or at least in the average American garden. And this personality trait plays right into your hand. Just put a piece of thin board or heavy cardboard under each of your cucurbit plants, and check back frequently. You'll find hordes of the hellions hunkered down underneath. Then all you need to do is smash them with a hoe or your foot. Or, if you'd prefer, scoop 'em up and drop them into a pail of soapy water.

Home on the Range

Squash Bugs

'em up with your wet/dry vacuum cleaner. (Put an inch or two of soapy water in the reservoir first.) If you don't have a wet/dry model, a hand-held version will work just fine; when the job is finished, just dump the bugs into a bucket of soapy water.

Watch Those Flowers

As soon as your cucurbits begin to bloom, start inspecting leaves for egg cases. Unlike the grownup bugs, they can't run for cover, so all you have to do is clip off the leafy maternity wards and either drop them into a bucket of soapy water, or squash the eggs. Then, just toss the whole mess onto the compost pile.

Swoop 'Em Up

To my way of thinking, squash bugs and vacuum cleaners were made for each other. Just go out early in the morning, before the bugs have rubbed the sleep out of their eyes, and sweep

Movin' On

Next year, foil the felonious fellas by planting your cucurbits as far away as possible from this year's crop. You say the only space you've got is a strip

THUG BUSTER

Super Soil Sandwich Dressing

When you've stacked up all the makings for your new, no-work planting bed (see "Movin' On," above), top off your "super soil sandwich" with this zesty condiment. By the following spring, your super soil will be rarin' to grow!

1 can of beer
1 can of regular cola (not diet)
¹/₂ cup of ammonia
¹/₄ cup of instant tea granules

Mix these ingredients in a bucket, and pour the solution into a 20 gallon hose-end sprayer. Then spray your "sandwich" until all the layers are saturated.

that's covered with weeds? No problem! Here's how to turn any piece of ground into a fertile, fluffy planting bed in four easy steps:

Step 1. Lay a 1- to 2-inch layer of newspapers over the plot, trampling tall weeds as you go. (Just ignore short weeds or turf grass.) Then soak the papers thoroughly with water.

Step 2. Spread 1 to 2 inches of compost over the papers. Then top that with 4 to 6 inches of whatever organic matter is close at hand. (Leaves, grass clippings, or pine needles will all work like a charm.)

Step 3. Add alternate layers of compost and organic matter until the stack reaches 12 to 24 inches high.

Step 4. Saturate the bed with my Super Soil Sandwich Dressing (see page 289), let it "cook" until spring, and then plant.

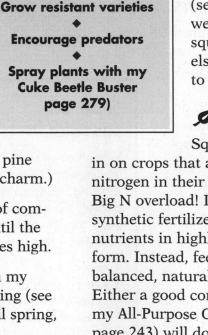

SQUASH BUGS
AT A GLANCE

Brownish black, flat-backed bugs suck juices from the leaves of cucurbit crops

◆

Plants are often killed

◆

Early symptoms resemble those of many diseases

◆

To control them, trap under squares of cardboard or shingles

◆

Grow resistant varieties

◆

Encourage predators

◆

Spray plants with my Cuke Beetle Buster page 279)

🌿 It's Too Late for That!

If spring has sprung and you need to get your squash in the ground soon, don't worry. Just top off your sandwich with 4 to 6 inches of good-quality topsoil, or a half-and-half mix of compost and topsoil. Then add my Super Soil Sandwich Dressing (see page 289), wait two weeks, and plant your squash (or anything else you're hankerin' to grow).

🌿 Feed 'Em Right

Squash bugs zero right in on crops that are getting too much nitrogen in their diet. So beware of Big N overload! In particular, avoid synthetic fertilizers, which deliver nutrients in highly concentrated form. Instead, feed your plants a well-balanced, natural organic fertilizer. Either a good commercial brand or my All-Purpose Organic Fertilizer (see page 243) will do the trick.

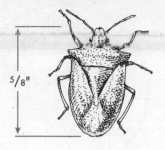

5/8"

Adult stinkbugs spend the winter in garden litter or patches of weeds, or sometimes inside your house. In the spring, females begin laying tiny masses of barrel-shaped eggs on leaves or stems. The nymphs hatch in about a week, crawl to a tasty leaf or fruit, and start feeding. They mature in five to six weeks without pupating. Meanwhile, their mothers keep right on laying more eggs, so as many as four overlapping generations may appear each year.

Stinkbugs attack many vegetables, but some of their favorites are tomatoes, beans, peas, squash, corn, and okra. They're also partial to strawberries, peaches, plums, pears, pecans, and all kinds of bush-grown berries.

Several species of these odiferous rascals attack vegetables and many other plants. Both adults and nymphs sink their razor-sharp mouthparts into leaves, fruits, flowers, and seeds, and suck out the life-giving juices. The grown-ups have five-sided, shield-shaped bodies that may be green, brown, tan, or gray. The youngsters are usually the same color as their parents, but oval-shaped. And, as their name implies, these critters give off a nasty odor when they're disturbed or (heaven forbid!) squashed.

The signs of attack vary from one type of plant to another. In general, though, foliage may develop white or yellow blotches or brown spots, or the leaves may wilt and turn brown. Bean and pea pods drop off, and their seeds are deformed or nonexistent. Tomatoes and other fruits may have either white or yellowish patches under the skin, or numerous discolored, sunken patches known as "catfacing."

🌱 Get 'Em outta There!

Most often, stinkbugs first strike the weakest plants in a garden, then move on to the healthy, robust ones. So don't give the villains the chance! The minute you spot trouble, throw an old sheet or a big trash bag over each bug-bedecked plant, and pull it up by the roots. Then dump it, bugs and all, into soapy water.

Take 'Em Off!

When the bugs target tomatoes or strawberries, remove all damaged fruit before it ripens. Then, the plants may have a chance to churn out a later crop.

Triple Play

If you're really Johnny-on-the-spot, you may be able to catch the mama stinkers before they've laid their first batch of eggs in your garden—in which case, just swoop 'em up with a vacuum cleaner, and then clean out the vacuum immediately to remove their awful stench. More likely, though, you won't notice any plant damage until you've got three generations of troublemakers on the scene: adults, nymphs, and eggs. So just grab your pail of soapy water, and go for it. Brush the grown-ups and babies right into the drink. Then either scrape the egg cases into the bucket, or clip off the leaves and drop them in.

Zap 'Em

In the case of a major invasion, or if you simply don't want to get too close to the odiferous invaders, let 'em have it with my Safe-

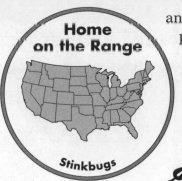

Home on the Range

Stinkbugs

and-Sound Pesticide (see page 238), or Grandma Putt's Simple Soap Spray (see page 86). Either weapon will send the bad-smelling bad bugs to the back of beyond.

Feed 'Em to Your Pals

Songbirds, spiders, tachinid flies, and a lot of other helpful predators will gladly gobble up all the stinkbugs you can give them—even if you don't offer them clothespins for their noses. For the full scoop on hit-squad hospitality, see Chapter 8.

The Diet Squad

Stinkbugs and a lot of other vile villains zero right in on plants that are getting too much nitrogen and too little of the other essential nutrients, including certain trace elements that are crucial for good plant health. So what do you do to keep your veggies in tip-top shape? Every couple of weeks during the growing season, give them a drink of my Compost Tea (see page 179). It supplies all the nutrition that most vegetables need to stay healthy and better able to fend off pests—and deliver a bumper harvest.

WHITEFLIES

THIS IS THEIR LIFE

Adults lay almost invisible eggs on the undersides of leaves. In just a day or two, the nymphs hatch, equipped with legs and antennae. They stroll around, sucking like crazy for a few days, then lose their appendages and transform into fringed, oval, nearly transparent pupae. Shortly thereafter, the winged adults emerge, and the process starts all over again. In cool regions, there is only one generation per year. But in warm climates and greenhouses, the fun goes on nonstop.

ALSO ON THE MENU

Whiteflies are especially fond of anything in the squash and tomato families. They also attack most annual and perennial flowers, as well as many shrubs, trees, and fruit plants. Azaleas, rhododendrons, grapes, and mulberry trees are all high-risk targets. And, no windowsill or greenhouse plant is safe from these problem drinkers.

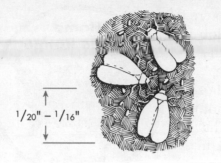

1/20" – 1/16"

If you kneel down to weed your vegetable garden and a white cloud flies up in your face, there's only one possible explanation: Whiteflies are on the rampage! If you look closely at the undersides of the plants' leaves, you'll see their babies: tiny, pearly-white specks that look like scales. Both adults and babies suck the juices from plants' foliage, leaving it covered with yellow speckles. Eventually, leaves may curl up and turn brown, plants lose their get-up-and-grow power, and growth is stunted. When the attack force is great, the victims often keel over and die.

Like other sap-sucking insects, whiteflies excrete a sticky, sugary honeydew, which quickly becomes covered with black, sooty mold that blocks air and light from reaching the leaves. The sweet stuff also attracts ants, who arrive by the droves to "farm" the pesky pests—thereby ensuring themselves a steady supply of their favorite drink. (You can read all about those rascals in Chapter 2.) But worst of all, as whiteflies feed, they often spread viruses from one plant to another.

🌿 Sweep Your Troubles Away

The answer to a major whitefly attack is as close as your garage—or your broom closet. Just grab your vacuum cleaner and sweep your troubles away. Either a wet/dry vacuum with soapy water in the reservoir, or a regular model will do the trick (in the latter case, empty the contents into

soapy water when you're finished). To make the job
even easier, wrap some
yellow electrical tape
around the vacuum hose
nozzle—being sure not to
block it, of course! The
tiny terrors will flock to
their favorite color, and
that'll be all she wrote.

Home on the Range

Whiteflies

stuff. Shove the stake into the
ground so that the sticky
trap is behind your
stricken plants. Then,
spray the foliage with
water from the garden
hose. You'll blast the culprits off of the leaves and
right onto the sticky trap.

✐ Stick 'Em Up!

Here's one of the easiest ways I know of
to send whiteflies to the Great Beyond:
Just get a 24-by-36-inch sheet of yellow
poster board, staple it to a wooden
stake, and coat the poster board with
petroleum jelly or commercial sticky

✐ Lemon Aid

To guard your tomatoes
and make them better-
tasting at the same time,
plant plenty of lemon basil among the
plants. Whiteflies hate the stuff, but
you'll love it! It's a tender annual with
small, pretty flowers, a lemony fra-
grance, and a flavor that's tailor-made
for salads, stir-fries, and
cream-based sauces.
Plus, it's a snap to grow
from seed anyplace in
the country.

THUG BUSTER

Whitefly Wipeout Tonic

Whitefly woes got you down? Don't
cry, just mosey into the kitchen and
mix up a batch of this discomfort food.
It's a meal they'll *die* for!

1 cup of sour milk*
2 tbsp. of flour
1 qt. of warm water

Mix the ingredients in a bowl. Then pour the mixture into
a hand-held sprayer, and coat your plants from top to
bottom. Make sure you get the underside of every leaf!

*If you don't have sour milk on hand, mix 2 tablespoons
of vinegar with enough fresh milk to make 1 cup.

✐ Oh, No—Not Tomatoes!

Once your tomatoes are
safe, borrow some of
their leaves to protect all
of your other plants
from whiteflies. How?
Just use them as the
main ingredient in my
On-Guard Tomato Tonic

(see page 300). Tomato leaves contain chemical compounds called *alkaloids*, which work like guardian angels to fend off whiteflies and a whole lot of other pesky pests, including aphids, asparagus beetles, cabbageworms, corn earworms, and flea beetles (to name just a handful). The jury is still out on whether alkaloids perform their magic by repelling bad bugs or by attracting good ones, who quickly gobble up the villains. But who cares? The bottom line is that this stuff works—so go for it! There's just one minor drawback to this wonder tonic, or any other spray: You have to reapply it after every rain.

✿ A More Permanent Protection Plan

For protection that *won't* wash away, encourage the whiteflies' enemies to settle down in your yard. It's not hard: Whiteflies have scores of predators and parasites champing at the bit to get at 'em. The hit squad includes lacewings, ladybugs, several kinds of parasitic wasps, and songbirds galore. See Chapter 8 for tips that will bring them flocking to your aid.

✿ Shine On, Harvest Mulch

Whiteflies won't land on your crops if you lay aluminum foil on the ground under the plants. The sunlight glinting off of the shiny surface fouls up their navigation system, and they can't tell which end is up. But if you have more than a few plants to protect, leave the foil in the kitchen, and buy some reusable, silver-colored mulch at the garden center. It'll do the same good job and last for years. Just make sure you remove the glittery stuff when the weather gets hot, or the intense sun reflecting off it could burn lower leaves.

WHITEFLIES

AT A GLANCE

Adults and nymphs suck juices from plants, leaving foliage with yellow speckles

◆

Leaves may curl up and turn brown

◆

Plants become weak and stunted

◆

Secrete honeydew, which attracts ants

◆

Often spread viruses among plants

◆

To control them, vacuum off of plants

◆

Catch in yellow sticky traps

◆

Spray with my Whitefly Wipeout Tonic (page 294)

◆

Deter by spraying my On-Guard Tomato Tonic (page 300)

◆

Encourage predators

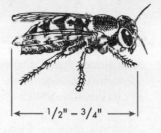

← 1/2" – 3/4" →

THIS IS THEIR LIFE

In the spring, a queen emerges from hibernation and finds a nesting site. She builds a nest made of chewed-up wood fibers, lays eggs that hatch into legless, blind larvae, and tends the brood until they pupate and emerge as unfertile females. Through the summer, these workers cater to the queen and her youngsters. In late summer, some larvae mature into fertile males and females, who mate in early fall. Then, when cold weather comes, everybody dies except the young princesses.

ALSO ON THE MENU

Yellow jackets crave anything sweet, so they often chew holes in ripe or damaged strawberries and other garden fruits. They also make a beeline to plants that are covered in the sugary honeydew produced by aphids, whiteflies, and other insects. And, of course, they love crashing picnics to nibble right off your plate.

Yellow jackets do almost no damage to plants. In fact, these buzzers are some of the best pest-control helpers that money can't buy. For starters, they pull caterpillars (many times their own size) right out of the garden, tear them to bits, and take them back to the nest to feed their young. They perform the same feat with flies, including the kinds that produce plant-devouring offspring. In fact, the workers from a single nest can snag more than 225 flies per hour. And some types of yellow jackets catch their own weight in mosquitoes every single day.

Unfortunately, these predatory dynamos have a dark side. Yellow jackets are mean, short-tempered, and highly protective of their nests. What's more, unlike bees, who implant their barbed stingers only once and then die, these nasty Nellies can shove their smooth weapons into you again and again—and, given half a chance, they will!

Sorry, Your Majesty

The easiest way to head off yellow jacket trouble is to keep your eyes open in the early spring, when young queens are establishing their colonies. When you spot one, you can encourage her to make her home elsewhere by repeatedly knocking down her nest while she's out gathering building material. But if you want to put an end to her reign, just whack her with an old-fashioned fly swatter, or give her a blast of Grandma Putt's Simple Soap Spray (see page 86).

🌿 Gotcha!

To trap yellow jackets in droves, cut the top third off of a plastic soda bottle and spritz it with cooking-oil spray. Then invert the top over the lower part of the bottle—that is, after you've put some tasty bait in the bottom. The yeller fellers will zoom in, and they'll stay there.

🌿 Gotcha—the Sequel

Here's a no-fail yellow jacket trap: Hang a fish or a piece of meat over a bucket of soapy water. The jackets will zoom in and tear off a big chunk to take back to their nest. But before they can fly off, the weight of the bait will make them drop into the drink.

Home on the Range

Yellow Jackets

🌿 'Tis the Season

When you're ready to set out yellow jacket traps, what do you bait your traps with? It all depends on the season. In early summer, yellow jackets are looking for protein to feed their young'uns. Later on, they crave sugar for themselves. So at first, use scraps of meat or bits of canned dog or cat food. When that no longer gets results, switch to honey, sugar water, or soda. But if the sweet stuff starts attracting honey bees, switch back to meat. The jackets will still grab the goods, though maybe not as quickly as they would in the spring.

🌿 Think Twice

Trapping is an effective and generally safe way to handle visiting yellow jackets. But to my way of thinking, removing an active nest is a job for a pro. And if you've ever had an allergic reaction to a bee sting or other insect bite, don't even think about going face-to-face with the foul-tempered hooligans. Instead, call an exterminator or a professional who specializes in relocating wasp and bee

---

GRANDMA KNEW BEST

Whenever I wound up on the wrong end of a yellow jacket, Grandma Putt knew just what to do: She dabbed the spot with water and covered it with salt. Almost before I could say "Ouch!", the pain was gone.

---

colonies. To find one of these brave souls, check the Yellow Pages under "Pest Control Services," or call your Cooperative Extension Service.

✑ If You Insist

If you're bound and determined to remove a nest yourself, try to time your attack for spring, when the yellow jackets are still small and the population hasn't peaked. And before you go anywhere near the nest, deck yourself out in full battle dress, and have any helpers do the same. You'll need a sturdy, long-sleeved shirt and long pants (or better yet, coveralls if you've got 'em), boots, gloves, and a hat. Then, to protect your face and neck, put a beekeeper's veil or an old net curtain over the hat and tuck in the edges all the way around your collar.

✑ Into the Fray

Start your nest attack just after dusk, when the workers have settled in for the night. If you need extra light, take

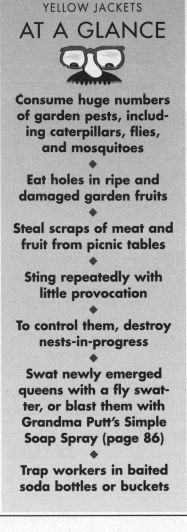

YELLOW JACKETS AT A GLANCE

Consume huge numbers of garden pests, including caterpillars, flies, and mosquitoes

◆

Eat holes in ripe and damaged garden fruits

◆

Steal scraps of meat and fruit from picnic tables

◆

Sting repeatedly with little provocation

◆

To control them, destroy nests-in-progress

◆

Swat newly emerged queens with a fly swatter, or blast them with Grandma Putt's Simple Soap Spray (page 86)

◆

Trap workers in baited soda bottles or buckets

along a lantern or flashlight and set it on the ground, well off to the side. Whatever you do, don't shine any light directly on the nest! It'll get the workers all riled up, and they'll come swarming out at you. Then follow the appropriate procedure, based on the nest's location:

▶ Fastened to a building or tree branch: Put a heavy paper or cloth bag over the nest so it covers the entrance, and scrape or knock the nest into the sack. Then burn it, bury it, or submerge it in a tub of soapy water—quickly!

▶ In a hole in the ground: Set a big, clear plastic or glass bowl upside down over the entrance hole, and push the edges into the soil. In the morning, when the workers see daylight streaming in, they'll try again and again to fly out, but they won't dig an exit hole. Before long, they'll starve to death.

▶ In a spot away from flammable objects: Burn the nest with a torch.

1 1/2" – 2"   1" – 2"

Beginning in early spring in the South and later on up north, female moths lay dome-shaped, white eggs on corn silks or the undersides of leaves. The caterpillars hatch in 2 to 10 days, feed for two to four weeks, then pupate in the soil at the base of their victim. Anywhere from 10 to 25 days later, adult moths emerge to continue the cycle. In warm climates, pupae overwinter in the soil, but they can't survive cold winters. The moths, however, head south for the winter, then migrate north in the spring. There may be as many as seven generations per year.

ALSO ON THE MENU

Corn, tomatoes, and peppers rank highest on the earworms' menu. But they'll also munch on beans, okra, peas, potatoes, cabbage, peanuts, and squash. And on occasion, they'll wander into the flower garden.

If you've ever grown corn, or even bought it at a roadside stand, you've probably come face to face with these creepy crawlers. If you haven't, you've at least seen the results of their mischief: ear tips chewed to bits and riddled with white eggs and trails of excrement. Although corn earworms are best known for munching on their namesake crop, they also target many other flowers and vegetables, including tomatoes (hence their alias, tomato fruitworms) and peppers. In those cases, you'll see holes at the stem end of the fruits, where the villains have chewed their way in. Their other victims (see "Also on the Menu," at left) will have chunks missing from leaves and buds.

Earworms start out as tiny white caterpillars with black heads, and grow to be 1 to 2 inches long and light yellow, green, brown, or pink, with rickrack stripes down their bodies. If you look at one under a magnifying glass, you'll also see hairy warts along their backs. The adults are yellowish tan moths that fly at night and migrate long distances.

The Early Picker Gets the Worm

The easiest way to get rid of corn earworms is to pick 'em off the plant and drop 'em into a bucket of soapy water. When the victims are plants other than corn, you can grab the worms whenever you see them. With corn, though, timing is crucial. You need to wait until the silks (corn's equivalent of flowers) begin to turn brown, which indicates that pollination has occurred. Otherwise, the ears won't develop properly. Then, all you need to do is gently pull back the husk at the tip of each ear, and remove the worm.

Home on the Range

Corn Earworms

🍃 Yuck!

If the thought of touching worms makes you turn greener than your corn husks, here's a more hands-off method: Fill a medicine dropper about halfway with mineral oil, pull back the husk at the tip of each ear, and squirt the oil in. The oil will smother the worms and any eggs that are on the scene, without affecting the flavor of the corn. Again, though, wait until the silks have wilted and begun turning brown.

THUG BUSTER

On-Guard Tomato Tonic

Thanks to potent chemical compounds called *alkaloids* found in tomato leaves, this potion works like an invisible suit of armor to guard plants from some of the hungriest pests on the planet.

2 cups of tomato leaves, chopped
1 qt. of water
¹/₂ tsp. of dishwashing liquid

Put the leaves and water in a pan, and bring the water to a simmer. Then turn off the heat, and let the mixture cool. Strain out the leaves, and add the dishwashing liquid to the brew. Pour the solution into a hand-held sprayer, and spritz your plants' foliage from top to bottom. Then wave good-bye to corn earworms, whiteflies, asparagus beetles, cabbageworms, and many other garden-variety villains. But remember: As with all sprays, you need to renew the supply after every rain.

🍃 Separate Quarters

Whatever you do, never plant corn and tomatoes anywhere near one another. If you do, earworms and fruitworms will leap from one plant to the other, and you'll have double trouble in double-quick time!

🍃 Let's 'Ear It for Tomatoes

Next year, when you plant your corn crop, spray the stalks with my On-Guard Tomato Tonic (at left) to protect it from earworms. It's made with tomato leaves, which contain chemical compounds called *alkaloids* that protect plants from corn earworms and a whole lot of other pesky pests. Try it—you'll like it!

Yes, We Have No Tomatoes

No tomato leaves on hand? No problem! Just spray your corn, or any other earworm targets, with my Orange Aid (see page 49). Caterpillars can't stand the stuff, but you'll love the citrusy aroma.

Long-Lasting Relief

There's just one drawback to spray-on repellents: No matter how well they do their job, they fade away when water hits them, and you have to reapply the stuff after

---

CORN EARWORMS
AT A GLANCE

Feed on corn, tomatoes, peppers, and other vegetables and flowers

◆

Damaged corn ears show chewed kernels, white eggs, and trails of excrement

◆

Tomatoes and peppers have holes at the stem end

◆

Other victims have chunks missing from leaves and buds

◆

To control them, handpick worms

◆

Smother worms and eggs with mineral oil

◆

Plant resistant varieties

◆

Spray with my Orange Aid (page 49) or On-Guard Tomato Tonic (page 300)

◆

Encourage predators

---

every rain. So, for stay-away power that has staying power, round up a permanent posse of earworm predators. It won't be hard. Toads, many songbirds, and scores of good-guy bugs eat earworms by the zillions, and bats feast on the night-flying moths. For the lowdown on these and other heroes, see Chapter 8.

Long and Tight

When seed-shopping time rolls around, look for corn varieties that are resistant to earworms. They owe their Stay Out! power to longer, tighter husks, harder kernels, and lower concentrations of amino acids. You have many winners to choose from, but a few of the best are 'Seneca Chief', 'Silver Cross Bantam', and (Grandma Putt's favorite) 'Country Gentleman'.

CORN ROOTWORMS

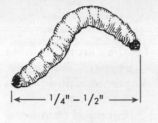

|← ¼" – ½" →|

THIS IS THEIR LIFE

Adult cucumber beetles (corn rootworm parents) start showing up in gardens after the soil has warmed up in the spring. After mating, the females lay eggs in the soil at the base of corn or legume plants. When the larvae hatch, usually in about a week, they tunnel into the soil, spend a few weeks munching on plants' roots, and then pupate. About two weeks later, they emerge to begin families of their own. There may be anywhere from one to six generations per year.

ALSO ON THE MENU

Corn rootworms dine on the roots of corn (of course), but they also devour the underground parts of beans, peas, and other legumes. And every once in a while, they munch on the roots of cucurbit crops, such as cucumbers, squash, gourds, pumpkins, and melons.

If your cornstalks are looking sickly, wilting, and maybe even falling over, dig up a stalk and look at the roots. There's a good chance that you'll find a milling mass of what look like little white maggots. They're corn rootworms, the larvae of spotted cucumber beetles. Early in the season, they can kill newly sprouted seedlings in just a few days. Later on, when their targets are a little bigger, the worms' munching weakens plants, stunts their growth, and over time, can kill them, too.

If you look at the villains closely, you'll see that they're thin, whitish grubs with a black or reddish brown head. Their parents are rounded, yellow beetles with 11 or 12 black spots. You can read all about them and their striped cousins beginning on page 277.

🌿 Have a Look-See

Before you launch an attack on corn rootworms, dig up a stricken plant and examine the roots. You may find rootworms, but then again, you may not. After all, a whole lot of pests and diseases can make plants wilt and lose their get-up-and-grow power. What's more, perfectly healthy cornstalks often fall over—these very tall plants, with only shallow roots to hold them upright, are simply obeying the law of gravity.

🌿 Bye-Bye, Corn Roast?

If the roots of your dug-up cornstalk are crawling with rootworms, your best option may be to simply pull up all of the stricken plants and destroy them. Then till the soil to bring any lingering grubs up to the surface, where birds and good-guy bugs can gobble them up. (Soldier beetles *love* them!) The following spring, plant your corn in fresh ground, and from then on out, rotate your crops every year and do everything you can to control the rootworms' villainous parents (see page 277).

It's Worth a Shot

On the other hand, if your root examination reveals only a dozen or so diners, buy some beneficial nematodes at the garden center, and apply them to the soil according to the directions on the package. (Read the label first to make sure you're getting nematodes that target corn rootworms; not all of them do.)

Other Options

Rootworm relief could be as close as your flower garden, or the florist section at your local supermarket. First, pick (or buy) some painted daisies *(Chrysanthemum coccineum)* and whip up a batch of my Homegrown Daisy Spray (see page 104). But don't spray it. Instead, lightly cultivate the ground at the base of your cornstalks, then drench the soil with the solution. It'll stop the worms dead in their tracks.

Home on the Range

Corn Rootworms

Pile It On

Whichever anti-rootworm weapon you've used, pile up 6 inches or so of soil around the base of the plants. It'll encourage them to grow new roots to replace those that the worms have nibbled away.

Egg 'Em On

To keep the next generation of rootworms from showing up on the job, put out the welcome mat for ladybugs and lacewings. Both of these good guys feast on cuke beetle eggs. You can read all about these and other hero bugs in Chapter 8.

DID YOU KNOW?

Like most insect pests, corn rootworms plague commercial farms—especially the big, one-crop operations—far more than home gardens. In fact, every year, these baby beetles cost U.S. farmers about $1 billion in lost crops and control measures.

EUROPEAN CORN BORERS

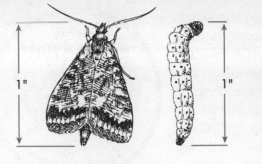

1"   1"

THIS IS THEIR LIFE

Corn borer larvae overwinter in corn stubble or other garden litter and then pupate in early spring. Adult moths emerge in June, and from late June until mid-July, females lay eggs on leaves of corn and other plants. In about a week, the youngsters hatch and start munching on leaves, tassels, and the undersides of husks. As the larvae grow, they burrow into the stalks and ears. Three to four weeks later, they spin delicate cocoons inside stalks and pupate. Depending on the species, there may be one to three generations per year.

ALSO ON THE MENU

Borers crave corn above all else, but they'll cheerfully devour any of more than 200 other plants—most often when the plants are growing near cornfields. Tomatoes, eggplant, peppers, and potatoes rank high on the hit list.

When these lowlifes have invaded your corn, the first sign will be leaves peppered with tiny holes. A little later, you'll see broken tassels, chewed kernels, and stalks riddled with holes surrounded by stuff that looks like gummy sawdust. Although the tasty ears are the corn borers' favorite targets, they're also very partial to peppers, tomatoes, and eggplant. In these cases, besides the telltale openings in the stalks, you'll see holes in the fruit where the stem cap attaches to the stalk, and the fruit may decay or drop before its time. As the borers tunnel downward in all of their victims, the foliage, flowers, and buds above them weaken, wilt, and die.

These terrible tunnelers are small caterpillars with tan, grayish, or pink bodies, darker heads, and spots on each body segment. Their parents are small, night-flying moths with yellowish brown wings.

Send 'Em to the Showers

Often, a good, hard rain will knock borer eggs right off the leaves before they have a chance to hatch. But if Mother Nature isn't forthcoming in your hour of need, just haul out the garden hose, turn the nozzle on full blast, and let 'er rip.

✒ Pick Me!

Once the eggs hatch, handpicking is your best option—that is, if you reach the scene before the larvae have started tunneling into the ears or stalks. Just pluck the borers and any egg cases that you find off the leaves, and drop them into a bucket of soapy water.

✒ They're Taking Over the Place!

If the borer population has escalated beyond the handpicking stage, collect about ½ cup of the larvae, whirl them up into a batch of my Beetle Juice (see page 53), and let 'em have it. The slimeballs'll never know what hit 'em! Or, for a neater way to accomplish the same result, spray the villains with any of these terrific tonics:

▶ Ashes-to-Ashes Milkshake (see page 176)

▶ Caterpillar Killer Tonic (see page 17)

▶ Homegrown Daisy Spray (see page 104)

Home on the Range

European Corn Borers

✒ Too Late

Once the larvae have bored their way into stems, ears, or other fruit, it's too late for any spray to reach them. Then you have only two options:

1. Cut a slit in each stalk, just below the hole, pluck the worm out with tweezers, and polish him off any way you like.

2. Prune off the infested stems. Then, you can squash the creeps while they're still inside their hidey-holes,

THUG BUSTER

All-Season Green-Up Tonic

To put your veggies back on their feet (roots, rather) after a harrowing pest attack, give them a drink of this excellent elixir. It's also a great way to supercharge your whole garden all summer long.

1 can of beer
1 cup of ammonia
½ cup of dishwashing liquid
½ cup of liquid lawn food
½ cup of molasses or corn syrup

Mix the ingredients in a large bucket, pour the solution into a 20 gallon hose-end sprayer, and spray your formerly plagued plants to the point of run-off. Repeat the treat every three weeks throughout the growing season.

soak the stalks in soapy water until you're sure the larvae are dead, or run the stalks through a shredder and toss 'em on the compost pile.

Whichever method you've used, once you've eliminated the borers, give your plants a good, long drink of my All-Season Green-Up Tonic (see page 305) to get 'em growing on the right root again.

Till We Don't Meet Again

Right after the harvest, dig up and destroy all plants that have been infested by the borers. You can burn them if that's allowed in your neighborhood, or better yet, run them through a shredder and toss them onto the compost pile. Or, if you have a tiller, just plow them into the soil. Whichever method you choose, you'll kill the pupae, which are just settling in for the winter.

Got Milk?

To stop trouble before it starts (or at least lessen the damage), set shallow

pans of milk in your garden at night, and shine a light on each one. The borer moths will dive for the bright, white surface and drown. This trick is most effective if you can catch the first generation of egg layers when they emerge in June.

Procrastinate

Borer moths do most of their egg laying early in the season, so if they've plagued your crop in the past, hold off planting as long as your climate will allow. That way, by the time the stalks are up and growing, the worst of the danger will have passed.

Call for Help

To really bid bye-bye to the borer blues, make friends with their enemies. Ladybugs, lacewings, tachinid flies, braconid wasps, assassin bugs, and a whole lot of songbirds are on your side in the borer wars. You'll find the lowdown on these and other heroes in Chapter 8.

THIS IS THEIR LIFE

Adult webworms emerge around midsummer and lay eggs on their target plants. They hatch in 3 to 7 days, and the caterpillars start munching. Anywhere from three weeks to a month later, they drop to the soil, pupate for 7 to 10 days, and appear, all grown up, to start the cycle again. As many as five generations appear each year, with the final batch of pupae spending the winter in the soil.

ALSO ON THE MENU

Garden webworms feed on nearly all vegetables, but beans, peas, and strawberries are special favorites. And, just to show that they do have a good side, they include several weeds on the menu. Similar caterpillars, including fall webworms, sod webworms, and many species of leaftiers, attack trees, shrubs, and both ornamental and turf grasses. You can read about that crowd in Chapters 1 and 3.

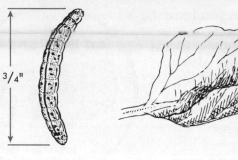

3/4"

These slender caterpillars operate in much the same way as fall webworms (see page 97), but they ransack the vegetable garden, rather than the shrub border. They spin silken webs around leaves, then proceed to eat until there's nothing left but the veins and stems. Usually, native parasitic wasps keep the damage well under control; but in years when the worms' population soars, they can devastate a small garden. The malicious munchers are pale green to nearly black caterpillars, with either a darker or lighter stripe down the back and three black spots on each body segment. Their parents are brown moths with gray and yellowish marks on the wings.

In the Beginning

Once the larvae have spun their protective webs, they're all but impossible to reach with sprays. Early on, though, it's another story. If you're Johnny-on-the-spot, dust your plants' leaves with Btk (*Bacillus thuringiensis* var. *kurstaki*), or spray on the liquid version.

Home Cookin'

Several of my 'pillar-killing Thug Busters will also stop the youngsters dead in their tracks. Just check the contents of your pantry and whip up whichever of these recipes you have the ingredients for:

▶ Ashes-to-Ashes Milk-shake (see page 176)

▶ Caterpillar Killer Tonic (see page 17)

▶ Orange Aid (see page 49)

▶ Homegrown Daisy Spray (see page 104)

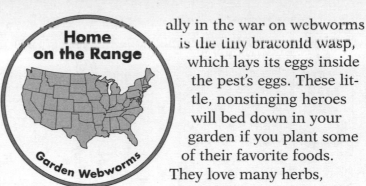

Home on the Range

Garden Webworms

Knock 'Em Off

After the worms are snug inside their webs, your best option is handpicking. And it's a snap, thanks to the fact that when these creepy crawlers are disturbed, they drop from their leaves on strands of silk. So just stroll around the garden with a bucket of soapy water, and knock the diners off the dinner table. They'll land right in the drink. Then, to discourage them and a whole lot of other troublemakers from coming back, spray your plants with my Merry Marigold Marinade (at right).

Winging Right Along

Birds and toads eat garden webworms like there's no tomorrow. But your best

ally in the war on webworms is the tiny braconid wasp, which lays its eggs inside the pest's eggs. These little, nonstinging heroes will bed down in your garden if you plant some of their favorite foods. They love many herbs, including angelica, chamomile, and caraway, and a whole lot of easy-to-grow flowers, such as bee balm, purple coneflowers, yarrow, bachelor's buttons, and black-eyed Susans.

THUG BUSTER

Merry Marigold Marinade

Garden webworms, tomato hornworms, asparagus beetles, and a whole lot of other bad bugs flee from this tangy tonic.

1 cup of pot marigold (*Calendula officinalis*) leaves and flowers
2 cups of water
¼ tsp. of dishwashing liquid
1½ qts. of water

Mash the leaves and flowers in a bowl, mix them with the 2 cups of water, and let the slurry marinate for 24 hours. Strain it through cheesecloth, stir in the remaining 1½ quarts of water, and add the dishwashing liquid. Then pour the solution into a handheld sprayer, and spray the webworms' targets from top to bottom. Reapply after every rain.

SEED-CORN MAGGOTS

THIS IS THEIR LIFE

Pupae spend the winter in the soil and emerge as adult flies in early spring. Then each female lays more than 250 eggs in garden litter or in moist, tilled soil with a lot of fresh organic matter in it. In anywhere from one to nine days—even in soil temperatures as low as 40°F—the eggs hatch and the larvae burrow into seeds, cotyledons, or rotting plant debris. They feed for one to three weeks, then tunnel into the soil and pupate for another one to four weeks. In most places, there are several generations per year.

ALSO ON THE MENU

Although corn, peas, and beans of all kinds are these maggots' prime victims, they have a big list of secondary targets. They'll also attack asparagus, cabbage, turnips, radishes, onions, beets, spinach, squash, melons, and potatoes.

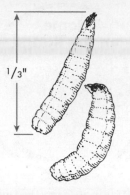

1/3"

When you see a whole lot of gaps in your garden rows where there ought to be brand-new seedlings, the likely suspects are seed-corn maggots (even if the seeds you planted weren't corn). And if the baby plants that *have* poked their heads above the surface sport chewed leaves, or dead or crooked growing tips, you've definitely found the culprit. These malevolent munchers bore into germinating seeds, making holes in the infant stems and cotyledons (those are the first, false leaves that show above the surface). Often, the seedlings are killed before the shoots even poke above the ground. The good news is that the seedlings that *do* appear above ground usually survive, though they may grow slowly at first, especially if the growing tips have been destroyed and the plants must develop new side shoots.

The munchkins responsible for this mischief are yellowish white, legless maggots. They're the larvae of a brownish gray fly, *Delia platura*, which looks like a common housefly, but only grows to about half its size.

Get Ready for Round Two

Unfortunately, once you discover that seed-corn maggots have targeted your crop, it's too late to clobber the villains—they'll already have pupated and flown the coop. So get ready to launch your campaign to prevent the next generation from causing trouble. In the meantime, just be grateful for any seedlings that survived the attack. And be sure to give them regular doses of my Compost Tea (see page 179) to help them fend off all kinds of future trouble.

Home on the Range

Seed-Corn Maggots

Fall in Line

After the harvest, till all crop debris into the soil to deprive the pupae of winter home sites. If you're planning to add manure or other organic matter to the soil, do it now, and let it age through the winter. This will foil the female flies, who lay their eggs only in fresh organic matter.

Don't Rush the Season

Seeds that take their time germinating are sitting ducks for seed-corn maggots, so always wait until the soil has dried out and warmed up before you sow anything. That way, those seeds will be off and runnin' before the creeps can chow down. In the case of corn (and beans, too), the soil temperature should be at least 55°F. (If you're planting one of the super-sweet hybrid corns, the soil needs to be at least 65°F.)

Ready, Set, Grow!

When you do finally get those seeds in the ground, you want them to get up and get growing *fast*. So send them off to a rip-roaring start with this routine: About two weeks before planting time, give your garden a big helping of my Vegetable Power Powder (at left), and work it into the soil. This'll give your seeds a strong start toward keeping seed-corn maggots at bay.

A Coat of Armor

No matter how warm the soil is, before you plant your seeds, put them in a paper

THUG BUSTER

Vegetable Power Powder

This mighty mixture will give all of your crops the get-up-and-grow power they need to fend off seed-corn maggots and all kinds of other pesky pests, too. Use it two weeks before you sow your seeds or set in your transplants.

25 lbs. of organic garden food
5 lbs. of gypsum
2 lbs. of diatomaceous earth
1 lb. of sugar

Mix the ingredients together, and put the blend into a hand-held broadcast spreader. Set the spreader on medium, and apply the mixture over the top of your garden soil. Follow up immediately by over-spraying the area with my Spring Soil Energizer Tonic (see page 361).

bag with ¼ cup or so of diatomaceous earth, and shake it until the seeds are coated. Seed-corn maggots and all kinds of other seed-eating insects will stay away in droves.

No, Mother!

To keep later generations of seed-corn mamas from laying eggs on your newly planted seedbeds, cover them with fine-mesh screening, cheesecloth, or old, sheer window curtains. Just be sure the covers extend at least 6 inches beyond the bed on each side, and weigh the fabric down with rocks or boards so that it doesn't blow away.

Give 'Em a Head Start

One of the best ways to foil seed-corn maggots is simply to deprive them of a target. How? Just start with transplants, rather than seeds. Unfortunately, the maggots' most likely victims—peas, beans, and corn—resent having their roots disturbed, so you probably won't find started plants at any garden center. But you can start your own. Just be sure to

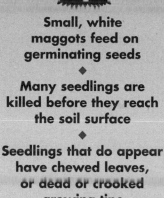

SEED-CORN MAGGOTS
AT A GLANCE

Small, white maggots feed on germinating seeds

◆

Many seedlings are killed before they reach the soil surface

◆

Seedlings that do appear have chewed leaves, or dead or crooked growing tips

◆

Plants that make it above ground usually survive, though they may grow slowly at first

◆

To control them, delay planting until the soil warms up

◆

Dust seeds with diatomaceous earth

give each seed an individual home that can go right into the ground at planting time. You can buy pots made of peat or compressed paper that dissolve in the soil, but it's a snap to make your own. All you need are a soda can or beer can and some sheets of newspaper. Here's the routine:

Step 1. Cut a strip of newspaper about 12 inches long and 6 inches wide.

Step 2. Wrap the paper around the can lengthwise, with about 4 inches covering the side of the can and 2 inches hanging over the bottom.

Step 3. Fold that extra piece onto the bottom of the can, press it tight with your fingers, and pull the can out. Bingo! You've got yourself a travelin' pot.

Step 4. Make as many as you need, fill them with seed-starting mix, and put them into flats with holes in the bottom for drainage. Just be sure to pack 'em in tight so that they don't unravel.

SQUASH VINE BORERS

Borers overwinter in the soil as either larvae or pupae, and the adult moths emerge in early summer to lay clusters of bright red eggs on vines or leaf stems. In a week or two, the larvae hatch and tunnel into the stem, where they eat and grow for the next four to six weeks. Then they burrow into the soil, pupate, and begin the process all over again. In the South, there are two generations each year, but up north, there's only one.

ALSO ON THE MENU

For the most part, squash vine borers live up to their name: They invade summer and winter squash, pumpkins, and gourds (both of which are actually types of winter squash). Sometimes, though, the bad burrowers attack cucumbers and all types of melons.

1" – 1 1/2"

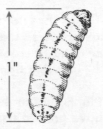

1"

The majority of bad-guy bugs raise their biggest ruckus in farm fields. Squash vine borers are an exception: They cause the most trouble in home gardens that have only a few squash or pumpkin plants. Your first clue that the marauders have arrived on your turf will be when all or part of a vine suddenly wilts. On closer inspection, you'll see small holes with what looks like moist sawdust piled at their base. You may not find many holes: Just two or three of these overachievers can knock a big, strong plant for a loop.

The guilty parties are fat, white caterpillars with brown heads. Their parents are day-flying moths that are easy to mistake for wasps. Their bodies have horizontal rings of red, black, and copper, with dark wings in front and transparent ones in the rear.

Cut It Out

At the first sign of trouble, cut off infested leaf stems and destroy them. Then go after the critters in the vines themselves. Using a sharp knife, slit the stem at each hole site, then reach in with a bent wire and pull out the borer. (Grandma Putt always used a crochet hook for this maneuver.) Drown the culprit in a bucket of soapy water laced with alcohol, and heap soil over the opening in the stem to encourage new roots to form.

Oh, Shoot!

If you'd rather not touch a squirmy caterpillar, even at the end of a wire, don't worry: You have a no-hands-on alternative. Just get a glue injector or a garden syringe, and shoot beneficial nematodes into each hole. The tiny heroes will go charging after the borers, and that'll be the end of them. Then pile soil over the wound, and you're good to go.

Home on the Range

Squash Vine Borers

▶ Use about 1 cc of Btk per injection. If you use less than that, you won't get full coverage; if you use too much, it'll just flow back out of the stem.

▶ Jab the needle into the center of the stem, about 1½ inches above the soil line. This is roughly the spot where the baby borers eat their first meal after hatching. And, if you're lucky, it'll be their last meal, too!

Vaccinate 'Em

If you're quick on your feet, you can head off trouble before it starts. Again, you'll need a syringe; but this time, load it with liquid Btk *(Bacillus thuringiensis var. kurstaki)*, following the directions on the package. The idea is to coat the inside of the hollow stem so that the newly hatched borers eat the lethal poison as they feed. Timing is crucial and so is technique, so follow these guidelines:

▶ Give the plants their first injection just after the first blossoms appear. Then follow up with a booster shot a week to 10 days later.

THUG BUSTER

Double-Punch Garlic Tea

This zesty brew will kill squash vine borer moths and many other pesky pests on contact.

5 unpeeled cloves of garlic, coarsely chopped
2 cups of boiling water
½ cup of tobacco tea*
1 tsp. of instant tea granules
1 tsp. of baby shampoo

Put the chopped garlic in a heatproof bowl, pour the boiling water over it, and let it steep overnight. Strain out the solids, and mix the liquid with the other ingredients in a hand-held sprayer. Then take aim, and fire!

*To make tobacco tea, place half a handful of chewing tobacco in an old nylon stocking and soak it in a gallon of hot water until the mixture is dark brown.

TOMATO HORNWORMS

THIS IS THEIR LIFE

Hornworms spend the winter a few inches underground in shiny, brown, hard-shelled pupal cases. Adult moths emerge in late spring and lay round, pale green eggs on the undersides of leaves (only one egg per leaf). They hatch within days and in less than a month, the caterpillars eat their way to their full, monstrous size. Then they crawl into the soil to start the cycle over again. In the North, there is only one generation per year, but in warm climates, there may be as many as four.

ALSO ON THE MENU

Tomato hornworms love every member of their namesake family, including eggplant, peppers, and potatoes. They're also fond of peas, okra, squash, and grapes, and they're partial to many flowers. Datura, nicotiana, and petunias are special favorites. But more than just about any other plant, hornworms go daffy over dill.

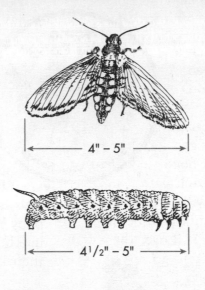

4" – 5"

4½" – 5"

These guys are the Godzillas of the caterpillar world (at least among those normally found in American gardens). They grow to 5 inches long, with a horn on their rear end that makes them look menacing enough to be in a grade-B monster movie. But the horn's just for show. The *really* vicious part is the mouth in front: A few of these rascals can defoliate a tomato plant before the movie's half over. And once they've polished off the leaves, they'll move on to the fruit. In spite of their size, they can be tricky to spot because they usually hang out on the undersides of leaves, and their color—green with white diagonal stripes—blends right in with the foliage. But you can track them down by looking on the ground for dark green or black droppings that are almost the size of rabbit pellets.

A Chip off the Old Block

The hornworms' parents are an impressive sight, too. They're giant, gray or brownish moths with such a rapid wing beat that at first glance you might mistake them for hummingbirds in flight. They're about the same size as hummers, too. Hence, their nickname (can you believe it?)—hummingbird moths.

🌿 Bug Off, Baby!

If you reach the scene while the hornworms are still small, you can put an early end to their criminal careers. Just give 'em a lethal dose of my Caterpillar Killer Tonic (see page 17), Ashes-to-Ashes Milkshake (see page 176), or Orange Aid (see page 49).

Home on the Range

Tomato Hornworms

🌿 Try This, But...

Btk *(Bacillus thuringiensis* var. *kurstaki)* will snuff out young hornworms, too, but you'll get the best results for the least amount of effort (and money) if you get the timing just right. Wait until the caterpillars are just big enough to chew a hole through a leaf. At that stage, they'll be able to gobble up a lethal dose of the bacteria, but they won't have had time to cause much damage to your plants.

🌿 We Have Liftoff

After these big bruisers get to be about 2 inches long, your best option is handpicking. If you don't want to touch 'em with your fingers (and who over the age of 10 would?), just lift 'em off the plants with an old pair of tongs, and drop 'em into a bucket of soapy water with about half a cup of rubbing alcohol added to it for extra penetrating power.

🌿 No Bedtime for You!

Toward the end of the growing season, keep your eyes open, because you'll often find tomato hornworms crawling around the garden, in flower and shrub beds, or even in the lawn. They're not out for a casual stroll; they're looking for a place to bed down for the winter. And you can make sure they don't find one. You can stomp on

GRANDMA KNEW BEST

Every year, a whole lot of volunteer tomato plants would spring up in Grandma Putt's garden, and she'd always transplant several of them to a separate bed. Then anytime she found an already-doomed hornworm with parasitic-wasp eggs on his back (they look like little grains of rice), she'd carefully move him to the bed, otherwise known as her "wasp nursery." That way, the baby buzzers could hatch, kill the worm, and go on to successful careers in pest control.

them with your foot, pick 'em up and drop 'em into soapy-alcohol water, or serve 'em up to your local songbirds.

Foil 'Em in the Fall

After the harvest, cultivate your soil thoroughly to a depth of 5 inches or so. In the process, you'll destroy many of the hornworm pupae and bring even more up to the surface, where they'll be gobbled up by birds or be done in by cold weather.

Been There, Done That

If tomato hornworms have plagued your garden in the past and you expect more trouble this year, don't take any chances. Spray the potential victims with Btk at the time you transplant them, and repeat the process every two weeks until the first blossoms appear.

Set a Trap

As early as you can in the spring, sow a trap crop of dill. When the horn-

---

TOMATO HORNWORMS
AT A GLANCE

Very large caterpillars devour the foliage, buds, flowers, and fruits of many plants

◆

Are harmless to humans and other animals, despite a menacing-looking horn on their rear ends

◆

To control them, spray young worms with Btk or one of my anti-caterpillar tonics

◆

Handpick any that are longer than 2 inches

◆

Encourage predators

◆

Deter by spraying plants with my Merry Marigold Marinade (page 308)

---

worms show up there for an early snack (and they will!), pour boiling water over the whole bed, or blast the crawlers with my Knock-'Em-Dead Insect Spray (see page 172).

Merry Marigolds

Some chemical in pot marigolds (*Calendula officinalis*) makes tomato hornworms hit the road. They'll mosey off if you plant the pretty flowers, but they'll flee faster if you spray their potential victims with my Merry Marigold Marinade (see page 308).

Dinner Is Served

Several mischief makers—namely moles, skunks, and yellow jackets— eat tons of tomato hornworms. So do spiders, assassin bugs, praying mantises, toads, and a whole lot of songbirds, including Baltimore orioles, barn swallows, bluebirds, downy woodpeckers, and sparrows. You can read more about these anti-worm warriors in Chapter 8.

1¹/₂' – 2'

THIS IS THEIR LIFE

Opossums mate anytime from midwinter until the end of summer. Just 13 days later, the female gives birth to as many as 25 babies—about the size of kidney beans—who must find their way to the pouch on her belly (they're marsupials, like kangaroos). Generally, only 7 or 8 of the little tykes make it that far. They stay inside for seven to eight weeks, then ride around on mama's back until they're weaned, six to seven weeks later. They mate during their first year, and in the wild, rarely survive long after they've raised their young'uns.

ALSO ON THE MENU

Opossums will eat almost anything, but corn and tomatoes top their list of favorite vegetables. They love berries and tree fruits of any kind, especially apples, persimmons, and avocados. And they'll gladly munch on whatever they find in the compost pile or garbage can.

As garden-variety pests go, these shy little critters will never make the big leagues. In fact, much of their diet consists of big-time garden pests, with a little roadkill on the side. What annoys us gardeners so much is the critters' crude table manners. If they made off with your harvest, you could almost understand, at least up to a point (after all, everybody's got to eat). But no, the little rascals couldn't be bothered to do that. Instead, more often than not, they just bite chunks out of corn, tomatoes, and other vegetables, and leave the veggies to rot on the vine.

Opossums have earned an unfair reputation for being dull-witted, probably because they're nocturnal, and when they're disturbed during their normal sleeping hours, they do look pretty stupid. But actually, according to the folks who study such things, they rank higher than dogs on animal intelligence tests. (Sorry, Rover!)

Give It Some Thought

Think twice before you send opossums packing. Although they can make nuisances of themselves, they do eat grubs, snails, snakes, and beetles by the bucketful, along with other bad-guy bugs, gophers, mice, and rats. And that kind of pest-control help is hard to come by!

On the Other Hand

Maybe the possums are coming to your place to snack on your snails and grubs and staying on to make bigger mischief. In that case, close the restaurant! You can say *sayonara* to snails, using the tactics in Chapter 4. See Chapter 1 for my good-riddance-to-grubs guidelines.

Home on the Range

Opossums

🍃 Don't Worry

When opossums are frightened, they hiss, growl, and bare all of their 50 sharp, intimidating teeth. But it's all just for show. In reality, these little guys just want to be left alone. And when push comes to shove, they'll prove it by falling into the shocklike state that we call "playing possum."

🍃 There's No Food Here, Bud

When opossums or any other scavengers are prowling around your neighborhood, these simple steps will keep them out of your yard—that is, unless they're *really* desperate:

▶ Feed your pets inside. Dog and cat chow is irresistible to possums and to other critters, too.

▶ Keep trash in tightly closed cans. And if the hooligans are on your doorstep, keep the containers inside until collection day.

▶ When you toss food scraps onto the compost pile, cover them with a thick layer of leaves or grass clippings. Better yet, use a closed composting bin. Besides keeping your "black gold" safe from little (or big) paws, it'll cook the stuff faster.

▶ Get rid of fallen and overripe fruits and vegetables as soon as you can. Leaving them on the ground or on the vine is like shouting, "Come and get it, guys!"

THUG BUSTER

All-Purpose Varmint Repellent

Opossums and other crafty critters will scurry off in a hurry when they take a whiff of this odiferous elixir.

2 eggs
2 cloves of garlic
2 tbsp. of ground hot chili pepper
2 tbsp. of ammonia
2 cups of hot water

Mix these ingredients together, and let the mixture sit for three or four days. Then paint it on fences, trellises, and wherever else unwanted varmints are venturing and/or foraging for food.

▶ Keep your yard and garden well sprayed with my All-Purpose Varmint Repellent (page 318), or my All-Purpose Pest Prevention Potion (see page 73).

🍃 Better Watch Out!

Foxes and coyotes prey on possums. If you don't have either of these big guys on your turf, order some of their urine and spread it around where the pesky pests are prancin'. You can buy predator urine at some garden centers and through many catalogs and websites.

🍃 Give a Hoot

Owls are big-time possum-eaters, and if you have a fair amount of land, you might want to invite some of them to settle in. Just remove some leaves from a branch of a large, tall tree to make a good landing area, or install a pole that's 15 to 20 feet tall with perches on top. The hooters will solve your possum problems lickety-split. Just one word

DID YOU KNOW?

Unlike most wild animals that hang around cities and suburbs, opossums almost never carry rabies, distemper, or other diseases that humans or pets can pick up. In fact, by dining on notorious germ spreaders like mice, rats, and carrion, these gentle little guys actually make our neighborhoods more hygienic.

of warning: Don't try this trick if you let your cats or small dogs roam outdoors, or they could wind up in the big birds' claws.

🍃 It Works Both Ways

Although in the eyes of some critters, opossums are choice prey, to others, they're fearsome predators. If your family includes favorite possum menu items, such as birds, rabbits, guinea pigs, hamsters, or good-guy mice or rats, keep them indoors except when you're close by their side.

🍃 Give 'Em a Hot Foot

If your garden is fenced in, you can possum-proof it with a single strand of electric wire. String it a few inches above the top of the fence and about 3 inches out from it.

🍃 Get Cagey

Give individual plants possum protection in the form of individual, wire-mesh cages that are anchored firmly to the ground. Use screening that has $1/2$- to 1-inch openings so good-guy bugs can get in to pollinate the blossoms. And be sure you make the structures big enough to hold the plant at maturity.

Corny Thoughts

Cages might be fine for protecting bush-type tomatoes and other small plants, but corn, vining tomatoes, and other big crops demand a different approach. Here's a pair of ways to say "Possum, pass by" (they work just as well for raccoons, too):

▶ Prop old window screens or bushel baskets against the cornstalks or tomato supports.

▶ Cover the corn silks with pantyhose toes dabbed with perfume or hot sauce.

No Tree Treats for You!

To keep the little gluttons out of your fruit trees, first prune back any branches that droop within 6 feet or so of the ground. Then wrap a 2-foot-wide sheet of galvanized metal around the trunk and fasten it with bungee

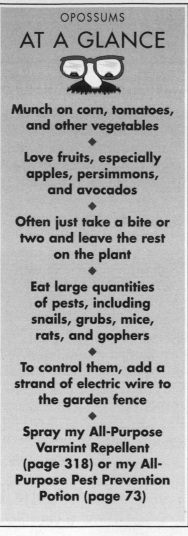

OPOSSUMS
AT A GLANCE

Munch on corn, tomatoes, and other vegetables

◆

Love fruits, especially apples, persimmons, and avocados

◆

Often just take a bite or two and leave the rest on the plant

◆

Eat large quantities of pests, including snails, grubs, mice, rats, and gophers

◆

To control them, add a strand of electric wire to the garden fence

◆

Spray my All-Purpose Varmint Repellent (page 318) or my All-Purpose Pest Prevention Potion (page 73)

cords. Do the same with any nearby shade trees that could serve as launching pads to the fruit tree. And be sure to check back periodically to make sure the trunks aren't outgrowing their collars.

Lighten Up

Because opossums are nocturnal, they cherish their daylight sleeping time. And that desire plays right into your hands. Just find the critters' domicile, which is usually in a tree, and string up some Christmas-tree lights that will blink on and off all day long. In no time flat, they'll pack up and head for more peaceful territory.

Turn 'Em Up

If you don't know where the little night owls are camping out during the day, keep your garden, or if necessary, your whole yard, brightly lit at night. After a few uncomfortable encounters with the lights, the possums will look for a dimmer place to dine, and you can flick off the switch.

THIS IS THEIR LIFE

In February, a polygamous male finds a willing female and moves into her den for a few weeks of fun and frolic. Then he goes off in search of other mates, while she awaits the birth of her babies (usually quadruplets), about 63 days later. After about eight weeks, the babies venture out with mama to learn the ins and outs of mischief making. The youngsters may go off on their own at the end of the summer, or the family may stay together through the winter. Raccoons hole up in their dens during the cold months up north. In the balmy South, however, they're out and about all year-round.

ALSO ON THE MENU

Raccoons will eat just about anything they can get their paws on. But even these gluttons have their favorite menu items, and corn, fruits, and berries of all kinds top the list.

24" – 40"

There's no doubt about it: These masked bandits are some of the cleverest and most conniving critters who ever came down the pike. But the fact that you're reading this paragraph undoubtedly means that you've already learned that the hard way! In the wild, raccoons are top-notch hunters, fishers, and foragers. But in suburbia—and even in the heart of major cities—they prefer the easier pickins in our gardens, garbage cans, bird feeders, and fish ponds. But sometimes, raccoons can be more than garden-variety nuisances: Like most wild mammals that hang around your home, sweet home, raccoons often carry roundworms and what scientists call *zoonoses:* diseases that can be transmitted to people and pets. Now, that doesn't mean you need to panic if you see a 'coon in your yard. But it *does* mean that when you're trying to make the rascals ramble, you want to keep your distance.

🌿 No Picnics Allowed!

There's nothing raccoons love more than pet food. So if you've spotted even one of the masked marauders in your yard, don't feed your dog or cat outdoors. Even a few scraps of leftover grub is a racoon's idea of an invitation to a never-ending dinner party.

✔ A Word to the Wise

If there's one thing I've learned about raccoons over the years, it's this: They're agile, persistent—and *smart*. So whatever ploys you use to make the rascals roll, remember to change your tactics frequently. Otherwise, they'll catch on to your game (probably sooner rather than later), and you'll be right back where you started from.

Home on the Range

Raccoons

✔ Fan-tastic!

When raccoons are eating you out of house and garden, gather up all the electric fans you can beg, borrow, or buy, and set them in place around your garden. (Be sure to use outdoor-grade extension cords.) Then, just before you go to bed, turn 'em all on. The raccoons will hightail it for calmer pastures. Repeat this trick every night for a week or so.

✔ Sure Doesn't Smell like Corn

Raccoons hate the scents of both bleach and ammonia. So fill old margarine tubs or other small bowls with either aromatic liquid, and set them among your vulnerable plants. The greedy gluttons will go elsewhere to eat.

Ask Jerry

I had to take my bird feeder down because the raccoons were coming right up on my deck, opening up the lid, and eating all the birdseed. But I miss the birds so much! Can you think of any way to keep the rascals away from the feeder?

Here's a trick you can try: Rig a motion detector to a lawn sprinkler, and set it at the base of the feeder. The birds will be able to fly in from above, but when the 'coons try to scamper up the pole, boy, will they get a surprise!

✔ Can Do!

To keep raccoons out of a garbage can, dip a large wad of paper towels in ammonia, dowse it with hot sauce, and toss the wad into the can. Then, for good measure, spray the surrounding area—and anyplace else the varmints are venturing—with my All-Purpose Pest Prevention Potion (see page 73) or All-Purpose Varmint Repellent (see page 318). (For best results, alternate the two tonics so the 'coons don't become accustomed to the scent.)

That's Strange

Raccoons have hairless and very sensitive feet, and they don't like to walk on anything that's sticky, slippery, sharp, or just plain strange-feeling. So lay a 3-foot-wide strip of any of these materials around your vegetable patch, and those 'coons'll clear out fast:

▶ Broken pot shards or jagged stones

▶ Leaves with Tanglefoot® sprayed on them

▶ Nylon netting

▶ Plastic sheeting

▶ Smooth, round pebbles

▶ Thorny rose or bramble fruit canes

▶ Wire mesh

Hah—Fooled Ya!

If raccoons have been plaguing your corn crop for more than a couple of years, you can bet they've figured out when it's going to be ripe and tasty. So this year, fool the felons by planting a variety that matures early. Then later, when your old type would have been ready to harvest, keep an eye on the

garden so you can watch the frustrated looks on the rascals' faces.

Get Serious

To a hungry raccoon, a normal garden fence is nothing but a piece of amusing exercise equipment, designed to be scampered over on the way to dinner. But with just a little doctoring, you can turn that plaything into a serious barrier. Depending on how decorative your fence is, here are two ways to say, "Stay out, and I mean it!"

▶ **The looks-matter fence.** Run three strands of electric wire around the base of your existing fence on the outside. (You can buy electrified fencing at most hardware and farm-supply stores.) Put the bottom wire 3 to 4 inches off the ground, then follow with two more, 3 to 4 inches apart. When the 'coons start to scamper over the top, they'll get a hot foot they won't soon forget!

▶ **The no-nonsense fence.** Get some 36-inch-wide sheets of heavy black plastic, and clip them to the fence with clothespins so they reach up about 30 inches above the ground, with the remaining 6 inches spread out below. The raccoons won't be able to get a handhold on the slick stuff to climb over the fence, and they won't dig under to get in. (They'd do that only if they were trapped inside and couldn't get out.) Don't try to economize on the plastic—they'll shred the cheap stuff to bits. Why not use clear plastic? Well, you can if you want to, but it'll deteriorate in the sunlight faster than the black plastic will.

That's not all, folks!

Most of the bugs and bigger bad guys who make mischief in the flower garden also target vegetables. In Chapter 4, you'll find my foolproof (well, *almost* foolproof) methods for making those marauders mosey on. Also, critters who love one kind of vegetable usually hanker for others, too. So if you don't find your particular brand of trouble in this chapter, check Chapters 5 and 6. In addition, you may see these villains vandalizing your veggies:

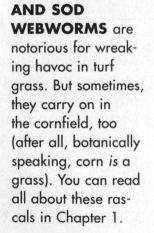

BILLBUGS, CHINCHBUGS, AND SOD WEBWORMS are notorious for wreaking havoc in turf grass. But sometimes, they carry on in the cornfield, too (after all, botanically speaking, corn *is* a grass). You can read all about these rascals in Chapter 1.

SQUIRRELS will gladly grab almost any kind of vegetable that comes their way. See Chapter 2 for my best tips on pulling down the curtain on these cuties.

WHITE GRUBS of many kinds munch on the roots of vegetable plants. Individual types are covered in their parents' sections, but you'll find general anti-grub guidelines in Chapter 1.

CHAPTER 8

GOOD
GUYS

All through this book, you've been reading about the hordes of greedy gluttons who are just waiting to sink their teeth into your treasure trove of trees, shrubs, flowers, fruits, and vegetables. And time after time, I've told you that the best way to counter the bad guys is to enlist an opposing army of good guys. And that's what this chapter is all about. Here, I'll give you the lowdown on nine world-class garden heroes. These good guys would love nothing better than to do battle with your garden's worst enemies.

ASSASSIN BUGS

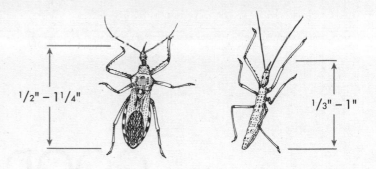

½" – 1¼"   ⅓" – 1"

There are roughly 160 different species of assassin bugs in North America, and their life cycles vary in terms of timing. In general, the adults, nymphs, and eggs overwinter in garden litter or on the soil under perennials and shrubs. In the spring, females lay bundles of barrel-shaped eggs (often rust-colored) on the leaves of plants. These hatch into nymphs that are smaller, darker versions of their parents, but without wings. Depending on the climate, some species produce several generations per year; others take more than a year to complete their life cycle.

Assassin bugs' dining preferences differ from one species to another. Overall, though, the menu includes aphids, leafhoppers, snails, beetles of all kinds (eggs, larvae, and adults), and just about every kind of caterpillar on the planet.

Like all true bugs, these hit men sink their supersharp mouthparts into their victims and suck out the life-giving juices. But in this case, the targets aren't plants—they're bad-guy bugs. You'll know assassin bugs have been at work in your garden if you find the empty, dried-up shells of what were once tomato hornworms, Japanese beetles, Colorado potato beetles, or other plant-plaguing pests. Many species of assassin bugs patrol home gardens and wooded areas throughout the U.S. They range in size from a half inch to more than a full inch long and may be any of numerous colors, including gray, brown, black, or brilliant red. But every assassin bug has long, almost spiderlike legs; even longer, angled antennae; a broad, flat body; large, often reddish eyes; and—appropriately enough—a concealed weapon: a long, curved, piercing beak that stays in a groove on the underside of its body until the moment of truth is at hand.

✿ What's in a Name?

Assassin bugs operate in a manner that's true to their name: They lurk quietly at a hidden observation post and wait for an unsuspecting victim to saunter by. Then ZAP! The assassin reaches out and grabs the victim with its long, bristly front legs, shoves in that razor-sharp beak, and injects an enzyme that liquefies the prey's innards—which it then proceeds to suck out through the same beak. Talk about grisly! Sounds like a low-budget horror movie on late-night television, dooon't it?

Home on the Range

Assassin Bugs

✎ Look at 'Em Ramble

If you only get a passing glance, you could easily mistake an assassin bug for a squash bug. So look before you squash him! In particular, watch how the critter moves when he's disturbed. Squash bugs run like the dickens. Assassin bugs, on the other hand, move with a distinctive, fast crawl, very much like a spider.

✎ Ouch!

Assassin bugs do not go gunnin' for humans or any other mammals. But if you handle them or even touch them accidentally, they *will* deliver a sting that you won't forget anytime soon. So just leave 'em be to do their job. And if by chance you do find yourself on the wrong end of that wicked beak, use one of Grandma Putt's tried-and-true pain-removal remedies (see "Grandma Knew Best," at right). But if you have

an allergic reaction, or if the pain persists for longer than 24 hours, get to a doctor, *pronto!*

✎ Nobody's Perfect

Unfortunately, not all assassin bugs confine their attacks to bad-guy bugs. Sometimes, they bring down good guys, too. In fact, out west, a small species called the bee assassin targets honeybees, which puts those guys in the vile villain category. But most assassin bugs polish off so many truly obnoxious pests that you can overlook the occasional loss of an innocent victim.

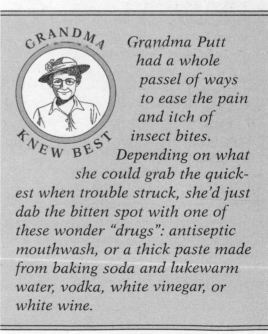

Grandma Putt had a whole passel of ways to ease the pain and itch of insect bites. Depending on what she could grab the quickest when trouble struck, she'd just dab the bitten spot with one of these wonder "drugs": antiseptic mouthwash, or a thick paste made from baking soda and lukewarm water, vodka, white vinegar, or white wine.

BATS

10" wingspan

In warm climates, bats are active year-round, but the ones that live in cool-weather regions either hibernate or migrate elsewhere for the winter. Before they do that, they mate, but the sperm stays dormant in the female until the following spring, when she wakes up or returns to her summer home. She gives birth to a single baby, or sometimes twins. For about three weeks, they drink mama's milk and ride along on her back as she makes her nightly rounds. Then the kids go off to pursue their own careers in pest control.

ALSO ON THE MENU

All but two species of North American bats eat nothing but insects—and plenty of them. Among their prime menu items are mosquitoes and the flying (and egg-laying) adult forms of cabbageworms, cutworms, corn earworms, and corn rootworms.

Like a lot of folks, I used to turn purple at the thought of having a bat anywhere near my house. Then I learned that although they're not the cutest critters on the face of the earth, they are one of the most valuable—and one of the most harmless. These mammals avoid humans and pets like the plague, but they're murder-on-wings to the bad-bug brigade, including mosquitoes and other vile villains that spread nasty human diseases. In fact, every night, a single little brown bat (the most common of the 44 North American species) puts away as many as 1,200 insects an *hour*. When you consider that these guys can live for 30 years or more, that adds up to one *big* bad-bug body count! Bats are also important pollinators of a great many plants. In fact, for a lot of wild plants, bats provide the *only* means of reproduction. These little critters even produce useful waste products: Bacteria that live in bat droppings in caves are being used to clean up toxic wastes, produce antibiotics, and improve detergents.

Home on the Range

Bats

🌿 The Vegetarians

Our country's only two non-insect-eating bats live in the southern reaches of Texas and Arizona, where they flit around sipping nectar from flow-ore, pollinating them and dispersing their seeds in the process. In fact, these bats are almost the sole reproductive mechanism for two of our great national treasures: the giant organ-pipe cactus and saguaro cactus that have been starring in western movies since John Wayne was knee-high to a cowboy boot. These winged wonder workers also ensure the survival of the agave—the plant from which tequila is made. (Margarita drinkers, take note!)

Come On Over, Guys!

The simplest way to attract bats to your place is to order ready-made houses from Bat Conservation International at **www.batcon.org.** For you do-it-yourselfers, they also offer simple building plans on their website. If you're not plugged into the Internet, you can write to BCI at P.O. Box 162603, Austin, TX 78716.

Site It Well

Hang each bat house 10 to 25 feet above the ground in a spot that's sheltered from the wind and faces south or southeast. A tree, a tall post, or a building wall will work. Because bats will fly directly into the bat house through its open bottom, make sure no wires, plants, or other obstacles block the critters' flight path. If you're close to a permanent water source, such as a lake, river, or creek, bats are much more likely to take up residence. But a water garden or small pond will entice them; even several bird baths will give them the H_2O they need.

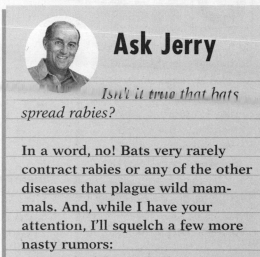

Ask Jerry

Isn't it true that bats spread rabies?

In a word, no! Bats very rarely contract rabies or any of the other diseases that plague wild mammals. And, while I have your attention, I'll squelch a few more nasty rumors:

- Bats *don't* bite people, except in self-defense, and American bats *don't* suck blood. The few vampire bats that live in the tropics target only livestock.
- Bats *don't* fly into people's hair— not on purpose and certainly not by mistake. They have a superb sonar navigation system that makes our Navy and Air Force green with envy.
- Bats are *not* blind. Most have excellent vision.
- Bats are *not* rodents. In fact, they're closely related to us primates.

BIG-EYED BUGS

Depending on the species (there are several in various parts of the country), big-eyed bugs overwinter as either eggs or adults in leaves and garden litter. In the spring, females lay eggs singly or in clusters on leaves and stems of plants, usually in the midst of their prey. The nymphs hatch in about two weeks, and spend another two or three weeks growing up. There may be one to several generations per year, depending on the climate.

If there's one thing you can say for big-eyed bugs, it's this: They're not picky eaters! They chow down on aphids, flea beetles, chinch bugs, tarnished plant bugs (a.k.a. lygus bugs), psyllids, whiteflies, leafhoppers, thrips, mealybugs, and just about any kind of caterpillar you care to name, including armyworms, tomato hornworms, cabbage loopers, and corn earworms.

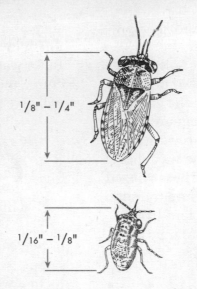

1/8" – 1/4"

1/16" – 1/8"

Like their fellow predators the assassin bugs (see page 326), these good garden helpers polish off bad guys by sucking out their body fluids. But the big-eyed boys don't lie in wait for their victims, as the assassins do. Instead, both adults and nymphs stalk their targets. And I do mean stalk! They'll follow a target up and down stems, around leaves, and even into flower buds until they can get within striking range. Then POW! End of story.

As adults, these patient hunters have small, oval bodies that may be black, brown, tan, or gray, and have (as you might have guessed) big, bulging eyes. The kiddos are almost identical to the adults in appearance, but wingless and a little smaller. Despite their tiny size, both generations have monstrous appetites. Just as an example, studies have shown that the youngsters gobble up an average of 47 spider mites a day, and their parents chow down on 80 or more of the tiny terrors.

What's for Dinner, Honey?

Besides dining on many of the insects that produce honeydew, big-eyed bugs also lap up the sweet, sticky stuff. And they do it in double-quick time, too, thereby relieving you of another common source of plant distress: sooty mold. (You can read all about that nasty nuisance on page 137.)

Jeepers Creepers

Big-eyed bugs bear a striking resemblance to one of their favorite menu items, chinch bugs (see page 5). So before you set out to do battle with these terrors of the turf, make sure you've got the right target. A set of oversized peepers will be your first clue that you're looking at a good guy. But also notice how the bug moves: The big-eyed boys waggle as they walk, while chinch bugs have a more scampering gait. After a careful look-see, if you're still not sure who the critters are,

Home on the Range

Big-Eyed Bugs

catch a few of them and take them to your local Cooperative Extension Service or the entomology department at the closest university. The insect gurus there can give you a positive I.D.

Three Packs of Big-Eyed Bugs, Please

Like many of their fellow good guys, big-eyed bugs are up for sale in catalogs and over the Internet. So should you haul out your credit card and order a posse of the critters? Well, if you're in the throes of an all-out invasion (let's say, for instance, your lawn is being devoured by chinch bugs), it'll give you a good quick fix. But once the goggle-eyed gluttons have gobbled up the bad guys, they'll take off for more bountiful territory—unless you make it worth their while to hang around.

GRANDMA KNEW BEST

Grandma Putt knew that insects need water, just like everyone else. So anytime she came across a teacup with a missing handle, she'd turn it into what she called a "bug bath." She'd bury the cup, almost up to its rim, in the garden and keep it filled with water so that good-guy bugs—and their bad-bug food supply—could mosey on by for a drink anytime they wanted to.

They'll Be Rollin' in Clover

To keep big-eyed bugs close to home, you'll want to give them a place to hang out when they're not busy dogging the heels (so to speak) of their prey. One of their very favorite napping places is in a nice bed of clover. But they'll also cheerfully snooze under any low-growing groundcover, or even hidden among the foliage of lush vegetable plants. (They *love* potatoes!)

Talk about versatile performers! What else but a bird can pack away pests by the peck, pollinate your plants—and give you hours of viewing and listening pleasure at the same time? Now, don't get me wrong: I know that some kinds of birds will snatch your fruits and seeds if they have the chance. But the fact is, most of those tricksters eat so many bad bugs that they'd put a garden full of yellow sticky traps to shame! Even in the dead of winter, birds carry on with their pest-control chores by gobbling up grubs, bug eggs, and hibernating insects. And take it from me: That kind of help is hard to come by!

🌿 Make Their Job Easy

Your resident birds and those that are just passing by are more likely to visit your vegetable garden if you try this neat trick: Put up a tall perch so that they can rest a spell, survey the scene, and then zoom in for the kill. A stake that's 6 to 8 feet tall with a crosspiece attached near the top will work just fine.

🌿 Build Your Nest Here!

Besides putting up feeders and planting trees and shrubs where they can set up housekeeping, you can encourage birds to make your home *their* home in another way: by helping them line their nests in the spring. All you need are wire-basket-type suet feeders and soft, fluffy stuff like combings from a dog's or bunny's soft under-

THIS IS THEIR LIFE

As we all know, birds differ greatly in their routines. Some types migrate hundreds or even thousands of miles twice a year; others stay put. At breeding time, some play the field; others mate for life. Some conduct elaborate courtship rituals first, while others just get the job done. Some species are solitary nesters, and others camp out in huge colonies. But in every case, the basics of reproduction are essentially the same: Birds mate in the spring, mama lays eggs, and one or both parents tend to the youngsters until they're ready to fly off.

ALSO ON THE MENU

In general, birds dine on grubs, caterpillars, beetles, snails, slugs, ants, termites, moths, flies, mosquitoes, and other flying insects, as well as insect eggs by the crateful. The bigger bunch, such as owls, hawks, and jays, also eat mice, voles, and other small mammals.

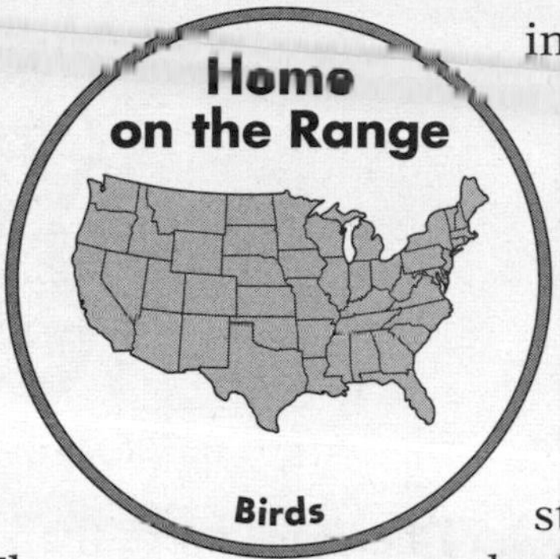

coat, cotton balls or pads (*all*-cotton, not spun-polyester!), and dryer lint from all-cotton fabrics. Pull the cotton and lint into pieces, and put everything loosely into the basket. Make sure some of the material sticks out through the openings. Then offer it up in one of two ways:

Home on the Range

Birds

▶ For hummingbirds, hang the basket about 6 feet off the ground, well away from any kind of bird feeder. That way, the female hummers won't be challenged by other birds when they come to collect the material. (By the way, these little birds don't just sip nectar; they also eat zillions of insects.)

▶ For bigger birds, fasten the basket securely to a board, wall, or fence so that it won't sway when they land on it.

Baby, It's Cold Out There!

Even in the icy-cold North, it's easy to keep your resident birds well fed in the winter—all you need to do is remember to fill the feeder. But supply-

ing them with fresh drinking water is another story. Of course, you could invest in a heated birdbath. But here's another idea: Find a disposable aluminum serving tray (you can buy one at a party-supply store) and set it on top of the birdbath. Using a hammer or a rubber mallet, shape the tray so that it fits neatly inside the bowl. Then, when the water freezes, just lift out the liner and pour warm water over the outside. The ice will slide right out. Refill the tray with warm water, and you're good to go!

Homemade Bird Treats

Just serve up these gourmet goodies, and your fine-feathered friends will flock to your feeder—and hang around to gobble up bad-guy bugs.

THUG BUSTER

1 part cornmeal
1 part wild-bird seed
Bacon grease (room-temperature)
2 pinches of sand or crushed eggshells

Mix the cornmeal and birdseed with enough bacon grease to get a bread-dough consistency. Add the sand or eggshells. Shape the dough into a ball, put it in a mesh onion bag, and hang it from a sturdy tree branch or bird-feeder post. Then get out your binoculars and have fun watching the action!

GROUND BEETLES

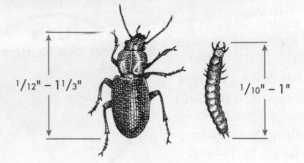

$1/12" - 1 1/3"$ $1/10" - 1"$

Ground beetles emerge in the spring, and females lay eggs in the soil. When the larvae hatch, they tunnel around, gobbling up whatever underground bad guys they encounter. They pupate in the soil, then emerge, grown up, to carry on the good work above ground. There may be anywhere from one to four or more generations per year.

Just name a lawn or garden pest, and you can bet there's a ground beetle that dines on it. The menu choices vary depending on the good glutton's life stage and species, but among the blue-plate specials are ants, aphids, asparagus beetles, cabbage loopers, cabbageworms, Colorado potato beetles, cutworms, flea beetles, flies, grubs, gypsy moth larvae, root maggots, slugs, snails, spider mites, tent caterpillars, termites, and wireworms.

There are more than 3,000 species of ground beetles in North America, and they're just about the fiercest predators you'll find anywhere. They're some of the best pals a gardener could ask for because they target some of the peskiest pests on the planet. They make their deadly rounds at night, going underground or climbing up plants and even tall trees to reach their prey. By day, you'll find ground beetles lurking under rocks, logs, or dense foliage. You'll know them by their hard, shiny bodies that are usually black, but may be either brown or brilliant, iridescent green. They have long, slender legs, distinct "waists," and long antennae. The larvae are slender, with distinct body segments, strong legs that are clustered toward the front of their bodies, and strong jaws.

✍ Caution!

When they're disturbed, ground beetles run away fast, if they can. But if they're cornered, many of them give off a unpleasant odor. Others release a toxic substance that burns or stains (or both) if it touches your skin. And just about any of them will deliver a painful nip if you give them a chance. So don't go asking for trouble! When you're working around a likely ground beetle hangout, like a woodpile, or if you're picking up stones, wear thick, sturdy gloves.

✍ Leave Some Stones Unturned

During the day, ground beetles love hunkering down under nice, cool stones. So do them a favor by leaving some big rocks here and there in your garden. Better yet, make paths out of stepping-stones, concrete pavers, or quarry tile. You'll keep down weeds and please your pest-controlling pals at the same time!

✍ Hit-Squad Hospitality

Ground beetles and all kinds of other helpful critters will flock to your yard and garden if you follow these basic guidelines:

▶ **Lay off pesticides.** They kill off the good guys along with the bad ones.

▶ **Have something for everybody.** Plant as many different kinds of flowers, herbs, vegetables, fruits, and even trees and shrubs as you have room for.

▶ **Give them a drink.** It doesn't have to be a big pond. A few old plant saucers sunk into the ground and filled with pebbles and water will work fine.

▶ **Give them shelter.** Provide shrub borders, perennial flower beds, hedgerows, and a few clumps of

Home on the Range

Ground Beetles

weeds where your allies can set up housekeeping.

▶ **Don't panic.** You can't have good guys unless they have bad guys to munch on. So don't reach for your spray gun (or your baking soda box) at the first sign of a slug or a cutworm.

Ask Jerry

I'm so confused! I want to plant flowers to lure good-guy bugs to my garden, but how do I know who likes what?

I wouldn't worry too much about that. While it is true that a few bugs have very definite tastes, most of them will flock to any flower that's rich in pollen and nectar. The key to keeping the troops on duty is to have *something* in bloom throughout the growing season, and plant a mixed bag of flowers. In particular, look for flowers that have daisy shapes, like black-eyed Susans and purple coneflowers, and ones that have lots of tiny, flat flowers, like yarrow and sweet alyssum.

THIS
IS
THEIR
LIFE

Lacewing adults lay tiny, white, oval eggs one at a time on the end of a threadlike, spun-silk stalk that's attached to a plant stem or tree trunk. The larvae hatch in four to seven days with their appetites turned on full-blast, and scamper off in search of food. They feast for about three weeks, then spin round pupal chambers and attach them with silk to tree trunks or the undersides of leaves. About five days later, they emerge, to mate and continue the process.

**ALSO
ON
THE
MENU**

Adult lacewings dine only on pollen, nectar, and the honeydew produced by sap-sucking insects. But the larvae gobble up pests galore, including aphids, mealybugs, psyllids, scale, spider mites, thrips, whiteflies, and the eggs and larvae of many other pests, including asparagus beetles, cabbage loopers, Colorado potato beetles, and leafhoppers.

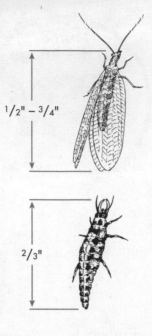

1/2" – 3/4"

2/3"

If you saw a lacewing mama beside one of her youngsters (and you didn't know better), you'd never in a million years take them for relatives. The adult, with her delicate, fragile-looking wings, could pass for the pet of a fairy-tale princess. The kid, on the other hand, looks like a tiny alligator. But the generation gap goes beyond looks. As befits their appearance, grown-up lacewings flit around the garden, sipping nectar and eating pollen from flowers. And the offspring live up to their looks, too. They spend their short childhood tracking and consuming many times their weight in bad-guy bugs, among them hundreds of aphids (hence their nickname, aphid lions). Although it's heroic work, it's not a pretty sight. The little lions suck the juices from their victims, and then travel around with the hollowed-out carcasses on their backs. Yuck!

🌿 Keep Your Laces Straight

Don't confuse lacewings with lace bugs, which are big-time pests of trees, shrubs, and many other plants. The two critters aren't even remotely related. The only thing they have in common is their delicate, lacy wings. You can read all about battling the bad-bug types in Chapter 3.

I Saw an Ad...

Of all the hero bugs that are sold commercially, green lacewings are among the most popular. Should you order some? In my humble opinion, you'll probably be wasting your money. For one thing, they frequently die en route, and those sent as eggs (the more common approach) often hatch along the way or within hours of their arrival. Then, unless you let 'em loose in the garden *pronto*, the larvae start eating each other. To complicate matters further, you need to release them on dry foliage, because the tiny hatchlings can

Home on the Range

Lacewings

drown in a drop of water. Lacewings are a snap to lure to your garden by planting their favorite flowers. So spend your bucks on seeds, instead (see "Dinner!", below).

If You Insist

If you do decide to send away for your predatory helpers, wait until several weeks after your last frost before you place your order. And check the long-range weather forecast first. You want the shipment to arrive when the weather is dry. When you get the package, rush right out to the garden and release the critters, or scatter the eggs on the leaves of your pest-plagued plants. Then, set about implementing my "Hit-Squad Hospitality" plan (see page 335) so that your hired guns will hang around.

Dinner!

Adult lacewings will cheerfully sip nectar and nibble pollen from any flower they can find, but their very favorites are angelica, coreopsis, cosmos, morning glories, oleander, Queen Anne's lace, sunflowers, sweet alyssum, and yarrow. I know that a lot of folks think of Queen Anne's lace as a common weed, but to good-guy bugs of all kinds, it's the equivalent of dinner at a five-star restaurant!

DID YOU KNOW?

If you've glanced at a glossy garden magazine or fancy garden book lately, you know that old-fashioned cottage gardens are all the rage. Well, you should also know that those anything-goes landscapes have a lot more going for them than trendy looks. How so? Just this: When you plant a whole mixed bag of flowers, herbs, vegetables, fruits, and even trees and shrubs, all kinds of good guys automatically show up and sign on for pest-control duty!

For the most part, adult ladybugs over-winter in leaf litter and wake up in the spring to lay clusters of long, upright orange eggs on the under-sides of leaves. The fierce-looking larvae hatch in 3 to 5 days and set right off in search of food. They spend two to three weeks stuffing themselves with bad-guy bugs, then pupate. A week to 10 days later, adults emerge, ready to start the cycle again. Depending on the climate and the species, there may be from one to five generations per year.

ALSO ON THE MENU

Adult ladybugs and their youngsters are best known for devouring aphids like there's no tomorrow. But both generations also chow down on scale, mealybugs, thrips, leafhoppers, mites, and the eggs and larvae of many other villains, including asparagus beetles, chinch bugs, and Colorado potato beetles.

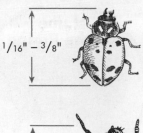

1/16" – 3/8"

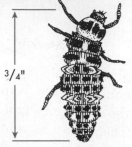

3/4"

Have you ever noticed that even folks who run screaming from a room at the sight of most insects will pick up a ladybug and let her walk all over their hands? I suppose there's just something irre-sistible about a crit-ter that looks like a tiny, red Volkswa-gen. But I'll bet those squeamish types wouldn't touch a *baby* ladybug if you paid them a million dollars. (Well, let's say a hundred dollars.) Except for their color—which in some species is black with orange spots—they could pass for alligators who got caught in a shrinking machine. And there's nothing tiny about their appetite: They hunt down and eat huge numbers of aphids and other soft-bodied bad guys. Not that the grownup ladies are slackers when it comes to pest control. Unlike just-for-show lacewings (see page 336), adult lady-bugs put away their share of bad guys, too.

🌿 That Was No Lady!

If you ordered some ladybugs from a catalog and set them out in your garden only to have them fly the coop, I'm not surprised. The ladybugs most often sold commercially are collected while they're hibernating, and when they wake up, their standard operating procedure is to move on to fresh territory. For long-term protection from bad bugs, you really need to encourage native ladies—as well as other good guys—to settle down in your yard. (See my simple "Hit-Squad Hospitality" plan on page 335.)

Home on the Range
Ladybugs

✒ But I Need Help Now!

I know: It's almost impossible to resist the lure of those ads that claim these cute little ladies will save your garden from aphids. So go ahead and order some, and I'll let you in on a little secret: The key to success with mail-order ladybugs is to get them to hang around long enough to lay eggs. Then it won't matter if they take off, because when the larvae hatch, they'll get right to work and stay on the job as long as you treat them right (which brings us right back to "Hit-Squad Hospitality" on page 335).

✒ Here's the Way to Treat a Lady

When your hired guns arrive in the mail, plan to release them in the evening, because they don't usually fly away in the dark. And here are a

few more helpful hints:

▶ Put the package in the refrigerator for a few hours. That will make the bugs sluggish and less likely to take off.

▶ Handle the little critters *very* gently. If they're agitated or feel threatened, they'll fly away to safety.

▶ Give your garden a thorough sprinkling, from top to bottom, just before you release the bugs. They need humidity and moisture to survive.

▶ When the big moment arrives, put about a tablespoon of the ladies at the base of each plant.

✒ Serve 'Em Breakfast in Bed

After you tuck the ladybugs into their plant-base beds for the night, spray your plants with a solution made of 1 part sugar or honey to 9 parts water. That way, when the little ladies wake up in the morning, they'll have something to snack on right away, and they won't have to fly off in search of breakfast.

SOLDIER BEETLES

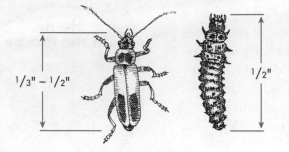

1/3" – 1/2"   1/2"

In general, adult beetles lay eggs in clusters on or just under the soil. When the larvae hatch, they burrow deeper into the soil to feast on whatever underground pests they can sink their choppers into. Then they pupate and emerge to start the process all over again. Soldier beetles overwinter in the soil as either eggs or pupae, and depending on the species and climate, there may be from one to several generations per year.

**ALSO
ON
THE
MENU**

All adult soldier beetles dine on flower pollen and nectar, and some species also gobble up aphids, leafhoppers, mealybugs, caterpillars, and other soft-bodied insects. But all of the larvae eat only underground pests. The menu includes grasshopper eggs, root maggots, corn rootworms, and the larvae of many other villains, such as cucumber beetles and Colorado potato beetles.

At first glance, you could mistake one of these guys for a lightning bug with a burned-out blinker. They have the same long, slender shape; long, angled antennae; and, in most cases, the same blackish body and red head. But if you look closely, you'll see that soldier beetles' wings have a more leathery texture than those of their flashing cousins. Hence their alternate name, leatherwings. The larvae are dark, hairy, flattened grubs, which spend all their time in the soil, feasting on garden-variety lowlifes. In some species, adult soldier beetles also eat bad guys, in this case, above ground.

Different Uniforms

Although the soldier beetles that appear most often in gardens sport the black-and-red suits of their firefly cousins, other types broaden the spectrum. Various species are tan, orange, solid black, bluish gray, or golden with black markings.

Another Lookalike

Fireflies are not the soldier beetle's only doubles. The all-black soldiers also bear a more-than-passing resemblance to blister beetles. The moral here, kids, is before you grab what you think is a lightning bug, wait for the flashing light!

🍃 Mess Call

You can enlist soldier beetles into your pest-control army simply by following my "Hit-Squad Hospitality" plan on page 335. But they'll come running on the double if you include some of their very favorite flowers in your planting scheme. They go gaga for catnip, goldenrod, hydrangeas, and milkweed. To play it safe, though, plant the catnip in containers; otherwise, it'll invade your whole yard and then go on to conquer the rest of the neighborhood!

Home on the Range

Soldier Beetles

🍃 Weeds, Please

When your first dandelions come up in the spring, don't dig 'em out—at least not all of them. Instead, let them bloom. That way, soldier beetles and other good guys will have nectar to nourish their souls while they're waiting for other flowers to bloom. Of course, you *do* want to clip those dandelion heads off before they go to seed!

🍃 Permanent Duty

Because these soldiers spend the winter just under the soil surface as either eggs or pupae, mama beetles look for protected sites to lay their eggs. They're especially fond of permanent beds and shrubs. So if you want your troops to wake up in your vegetable garden, where they'll eat your cuke and tater beetles for breakfast, plant a border of shrubs just outside the garden fence.

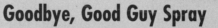

Goodbye, Good Guy Spray

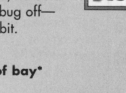

THUG BUSTER

Even good bugs can drive you crazy when they're batting at your windows all evening long. Well, here's a spray that will make them bug off—but it won't hurt them one bit.

**¼ cup of vinegar
8 tbsp. of essential oil of bay*
3 cups of water**

Pour the vinegar, oil, and water in a hand-held sprayer. Tighten the cap and shake until the ingredients are well blended. To keep the bugs from flying at your closed windows, use the potion to clean the outside of the glass in your usual way. If the little guys are bouncing off of the screens, thoroughly spray the mesh. Just make sure you spray from the inside out, so you don't wind up with a puddle on the floor!

*Available in craft-supply and herbal-products stores.

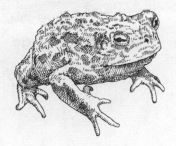

THIS IS THEIR LIFE

As we all learned in school, toads are amphibians, which means that water plays a crucial role in their life cycle. In fact, they're born in it. Mama toads deposit anywhere from 5,000 to 25,000 eggs at a time in a pond or other body of water. These hatch into tadpoles, which swim around for anywhere from 40 to 60 days before turning into teeny-tiny toads. Then the little guys immediately hightail it to dry land.

ALSO ON THE MENU

Toads are carnivores, pure and simple. They eat only protein, and only in the form of live bugs—and plenty of them. The villains they snag on the ends of their long, sticky tongues include beetles, cutworms, maggots, slugs, snails, termites, and weevils, plus all kinds of caterpillars, including armyworms, fruitworms, gypsy moth larvae, and hornworms.

Talk about bug zappers! With the possible exception of bats, these warty guys are the most useful pest-control equipment a homeowner (or renter) could ask for. The folks who study these things say that a single toad will pack away about 15,000 bad-guy bugs in a single year and—for reasons I don't understand, and they probably don't, either—almost none of the good guys. One of the best things about toads is that once you've encouraged a few to take up residence in your yard, they'll stay on the job for years, as long as you keep them supplied with food, i.e., live bad-guy bugs. What's more, toads don't tend to scare the daylights out of people. So you can keep a bunch of the little guys on garden guard duty without having to worry that a guest at your next barbecue will spot one and run, shrieking, from your yard. But that might happen if you had snakes (which are also excellent bad-bug blasters).

🖋 There Is One Thing I Should Mention

Although toads don't bite, sting, or emit foul odors, when they're attacked, their bodies do secrete a substance that irritates mucous membranes. You won't feel it if you pick the critters up in your hands, but if your dog or cat gets one in his mouth, he'll get a taste he won't soon forget. In most cases, the experience will be merely unpleasant. But if you live in the South (especially the southern part of Texas or Florida), look out for a big bruiser called the *Bufo marinus* toad. If your pet bites into one, rush him to a vet IMMEDIATELY, because Bufo toads emit a substance that could actually kill your pal.

The Essentials

For such superstars, toads are pretty easy to please when it comes to living quarters. All they ask for is a place to escape the sun and hide from noisy contraptions, like lawn mowers and loud radios, and predators like snakes, skunks, big birds, and family pets. Any spot that's moist, cool, and shady, with some decent ventilation, suits them just fine. You can buy some mighty fancy "toad abodes" from garden centers and catalogs, but it's simple to make your own. Just find an old clay flowerpot, break a chunk out of the rim to make a door, and then set the pot upside down on top of some loosened soil in a quiet part of your garden.

Water!

Toads don't drink through their mouths; they absorb water

Home on the Range

Toads

through their skin, so they need a body of water that's deep enough to jump into. It doesn't have to be elaborate, though—a big birdbath sunk into the ground will work just fine. Unless, that is, you want your toads to be fruitful and multiply, in which case you'll need a small pond. (This could be the excuse you've been waiting for to install a water garden!)

The Hiring Process

Toads are a lot more likely to stay around if you attract them with choice room and board, rather than kidnapping them from other territory. But it might take a long time for that to happen. If you don't want to bide your time waiting for your prince of pest control to come, your best bet is to find a pond or ditch with tadpoles in it, scoop a few up, take them home, and give them a nice watery place, like a shallow pan or a little pool, to grow up in. Before you'll know it, they'll make your pests' worst nightmares come true!

DID YOU KNOW?

Want to keep your pet toad *really* happy? Then try this trick: Rig up a low-watt light or a footpath lamp near a patch of low-growing vegetation, where the little guy can hide. Bugs will be drawn to the light and...you can guess what comes next!

JERRY'S
THUG BUSTERS

Throughout this book, I've been telling you how my Thug Busters can solve even your peskiest pest problems, *pronto*. In this section, I've gathered all those remarkable recipes together in one place, from A to Z. So when you come upon a critter who won't take "No" for an answer, glance through these pages. Whether you've got beetles bashing your begonias, lace bugs lousing up your lilacs, caterpillars clobbering your carrots, or deer dining on everything in sight, you'll find the solution right here.

Aeration Tonic

To keep your turf grass in the pink of health—and billbugs far away from it—aerate your lawn regularly with the help of this timely tonic.

1 cup of dishwashing liquid
1 cup of beer

Combine these two ingredients in your 20 gallon hose-end sprayer, and fill the balance of the sprayer jar with warm water. Then once a month during the growing season, spray your lawn with this tonic to the point of run-off. (For related text, see page 4.)

All-Purpose Organic Fertilizer

This well-balanced diet will make any plant grow up big and strong, without the risk of a pest-pleasing nitrogen overload.

5 parts seaweed meal
3 parts granite dust
1 part dehydrated manure
1 part bonemeal

Combine these ingredients in a bucket, then sidedress your plants with the mixture, and water it in well. Serve it up two or three times during the growing season. (For related text, see page 243.)

All-Purpose Pest Prevention Potion

Voles, rabbits, and just about any other critter I can think of will run away when they get a whiff of this powerful potion.

1 cup of ammonia
1/2 cup of urine
1/2 cup of dishwashing liquid
1/4 cup of castor oil

Mix all of these ingredients in your 20 gallon hose-end sprayer. Then thoroughly saturate the area around each of your young trees (or anyplace else you don't want hungry varmints venturing). (For related text, see page 73.)

All-Purpose Var...

Opossums and other ... off in a hurry when th... odiferous elixir.

2 eggs
2 cloves of garlic
2 tbsp. of ground
2 tbsp. of ammonia
2 cups of hot water

Mix these ingredients together, and let the mixture sit for three or four days. Then paint it on fences, trellises, and wherever else unwanted varmints are venturing and/or foraging for food. (For related text, see page 318.)

All-Season Clean-Up Tonic

This excellent elixir will kill lingering webworms and just about any other bad-guy bugs that mistake your yard for the local salad bar.

1 cup of dishwashing liquid
1 cup of antiseptic mouthwash
1 cup of tobacco tea*

Mix these ingredients in your 20 gallon hose-end sprayer, and saturate your plagued plants from top to bottom. Repeat as needed until the vile varmints vamoose for good, then apply it every two weeks in the evening for season-long control. (For related text, see page 98.)

*To make tobacco tea, place half a handful of chewing tobacco in an old nylon stocking and soak it in a gallon of hot water until the mixture is dark brown. Pour the liquid into a glass container with a tight lid for storage.

Green-Up Tonic

...veggies back on their
...(rather) after a
...g pest attack,
...om a drink of
...excellent elixir. It's
...o a great way to
supercharge your
whole garden all
summer long.

1 can of beer
1 cup of ammonia
½ cup of dishwashing liquid
½ cup of liquid lawn food
½ cup of molasses or corn syrup

Mix the ingredients in a large bucket, pour
the solution into a 20 gallon hose-end
sprayer, and spray your formerly plagued
plants to the point of run-off. Repeat the treat
every three weeks throughout the growing
season. (For related text, see page 305.)

▶ Amazing Ammonia Antidote

This fabulous formula is a powerful mite killer
and mild fertilizer all in rolled into one.

1 tsp. of dishwashing liquid
2 tsp. of ammonia
2 gal. of water

Mix these ingredients together, and pour the
solution into a hand-held sprayer. Spray your
beleaguered plants every five days for three
weeks, and you'll moan over mites no more!
(For related text, see page 147.)

▶ Ashes-to-Ashes Milkshake

This milky beverage will bid bye-bye to all
kinds of caterpillars and some of the meanest, toughest pests around, including weevils,
cucumber beetles, and stalk borers.

1 tbsp. of wood ashes
1 cup of sour milk or buttermilk
Water

Mix the wood ashes in 1 quart of water, and
let it sit overnight. Strain out the solids, stir
the sour milk or buttermilk into the remaining
liquid, and add 3 quarts of water. Pour the
solution into a hand-held sprayer, and zap
the pesky pests. (For related text, see page
176.)

▶ Beetle Juice

When beetles, weevils, or any
other bugs are driving you to
drink (or just increasing your consumption),
round up a bunch of the culprits and whip
'em up into this potent potion.

½ cup of beetles (adults, larvae, or both,
  either dead or alive)
2 cups of water
1 tsp. of dishwashing liquid

Whirl the beetles and water in an old
blender (one you'll *never* use again for
human or pet food preparation). Strain the
goop through cheesecloth, and mix in the
dishwashing liquid. Pour the liquid into a 2-
gallon bucket, and fill it the rest of the way
with water. Drench the soil around the plant
to kill hibernating adults and larvae in the
ground. **Note:** To use the juice as a spray,
pour ¼ cup of the strained, soapy mixture
into a 1 gallon hand-held sprayer, and fill
the rest of the jar with water. Spritz your
plants from top to bottom, and make sure
you coat both sides of the leaves. (For related
text, see page 53.)

Bug Away Spray

This timely tonic will issue a death warrant to four-lined plant bugs and other foul felons who are fussin' around with your favorite flowers (or any other plants).

1 cup of Murphy's Oil Soap®
1 cup of antiseptic mouthwash
1 cup of tobacco tea*

Mix these ingredients in a 20 gallon hose-end sprayer and soak your plants to the point of run-off. (For related text, see page 133.)

*To make tobacco tea, wrap half a handful of chewing tobacco in an old nylon stocking and soak it in a gallon of hot water until the mixture is dark brown. Pour the liquid into a glass container with a tight lid for storage.

Bug-Off Bulb Bath

This spa treatment will help your spring- or summer-blooming bulbs fend off disease germs, as well as bulb mites and other cunning critters.

2 tsp. of baby shampoo
1 tsp. of antiseptic mouthwash
¼ tsp. of instant tea granules
2 gal. of hot water (120°F)

Mix these ingredients in a bucket. Then drop in your bulbs, and let them soak for 2 to 3 hours (longer for larger bulbs). And don't peel off the papery skins! The bulbs use them as a defense against pests. Then either plant the bulbs immediately or let them air-dry for several days before you store them—otherwise, rot could set in. (For related text, see page 126.)

Cabbageworm Wipeout

When cabbage-crunching crawlers come to call, greet them with this deadly treat.

1 cup of flour
2 tbsp. of cayenne pepper

Mix the ingredients together, and sprinkle the powder on young cabbage-family plants. The flour swells up inside the worms and bursts their insides, while the hot pepper keeps other critters away. (For related text, see page 257.)

Caterpillar Killer Tonic

This potent brew means death on contact to armyworms and any other cantankerous caterpillars.

½ lb. of wormwood leaves
2 tbsp. of Murphy's Oil Soap®
4 cups of water

Simmer the wormwood leaves in 2 cups of the water for 30 minutes. Strain, then add the Murphy's Oil Soap and the remaining 2 cups of water. Pour the solution into a 6 gallon hose-end sprayer, and saturate your lawn in the early evening, when armyworms (and other grass-munching caterpillars) come out to dine. Repeat this treatment until the varmints are history. (For related text, see page 17.)

Chinch Bug Tonic

If problem areas are too big for the flannel-sheet treatment in "How Cozy!" (see page 6), make up a batch of this potent brew.

1 cup of Murphy's Oil Soap®
3 cups of warm water
Gypsum

Combine the soap and water in a 20 gallon hose-end sprayer, and saturate your lawn. After it dries, apply gypsum to the bug-infested areas at the recommend rate. (For related text, see page 7.)

Citrusy Soap Spray

This potent insecticidal soap will go after extra-hard-to-kill pests like foliar nematodes and hard shelled beetles. The secret lies in the super penetrating power of the citrus oil.

½ **bar of Fels Naptha® or Octagon® soap,***
   shredded
2 gal. of water
1 tbsp. of orange or lemon essential oil

Add the soap to the water and heat, stirring, until the soap dissolves completely. Let the solution cool, mix in the essential oil, then pour it into a hand-held mist sprayer and let 'er rip. Test it on one plant first, though—and be sure to rinse it off after the bugs have bitten the dust. (For related text, see page 169.)

*You'll find Fels Naptha and Octagon in either the bath soap or laundry section of your supermarket.

Compost Tea

This health-giving potion dishes up a well-balanced supply of all the essential nutrients your plants need, keeping them healthy, perky, and better able to fend off all kinds of pesky pests—and dastardly diseases, too.

1½ gal. of fresh compost
Burlap sack
10-gal. bucket with lid
4½ gal. of warm water

Scoop the compost into a burlap sack, tie it closed, and put it in a 10-gallon bucket with the water. Cover, and let it steep for three to seven days. Then pour the liquid into a hand-held sprayer, and spritz your plants every two to three weeks. (For related text, see page 179.)

Cuke Beetle Buster

When cucumber beetles are eating their way through your garden, spreading deadly diseases in the process, end their reign of terror with this timely tonic.

½ **cup of garden lime**
½ **cup of wood ashes**
2 gal. of water

Mix these ingredients together, and pour the solution into a hand-held sprayer. Then spray your embattled plants from head to toe, and make sure to coat the undersides of leaves. The beetles'll bite the dust! (For related text, see page 279.)

Dead Bug Brew

When you want to keep all kinds of live bugs from dining on your plants, serve them this mulligan stew of dead bugs.

½ **cup of dead insects**
   (the more kinds, the merrier!)
1 tbsp. of dishwashing liquid
1 tbsp. of cayenne pepper
2 cups of water

Put the ingredients in an old blender (one you'll *never* use again for food preparation), and puree the heck out of 'em. Strain out the pulp, and dilute the remaining brew at a rate of ¼ cup of brew per 1 cup of water. Apply it to your plants with a hand-held sprayer to the point of run-off. (For related text, see page 271.)

Doggone Dogs Tonic

Dogs may be man's best friends, but they sure as shootin' aren't the best pals your lawn ever had! Keep your pooch and other neighborhood dogs where they belong by dousing off-limits areas with this spicy concoction.

2 cloves of garlic, finely chopped
2 small onions, finely chopped
1 jalapeño pepper, finely chopped
1 tbsp. of hot sauce
1 tbsp. of chili powder
1 tbsp. of dishwashing liquid
1 qt. of warm water

Combine the garlic, onions, and pepper with the rest of the ingredients. Let the mixture sit and "marinate" for 24 hours, then strain it through cheesecloth or old pantyhose, and sprinkle it on any canine-problem areas. Repeat after each rain, and before long, the spot makers and hole diggers will get their kicks elsewhere. (For related text, see page 29.)

▶ Double-Punch Garlic Tea

This zesty brew will kill squash vine borer moths and many other pesky pests on contact.

5 unpeeled cloves of garlic,
    coarsely chopped
2 cups of boiling water
1/2 cup of tobacco tea*
1 tsp. of instant tea granules
1 tsp. of baby shampoo

Put the chopped garlic in a heatproof bowl, pour the boiling water over it, and let it steep overnight. Strain out the solids, and mix the liquid with the other ingredients in a handheld sprayer. Then take aim, and fire! (For related text, see page 313.)

*To make tobacco tea, place half a handful of chewing tobacco in an old nylon stocking and soak it in a gallon of hot water until the mixture is dark brown.

▶ Garden Cure-All Tonic

When you need bad-guy bug relief pronto, mix up a batch of this fast-acting remedy.

4 cloves of garlic
1 small onion
1 small jalapeño pepper
1 tsp. of Murphy's Oil Soap®
1 tsp. of vegetable oil
Warm water

Pulverize the garlic, onion, and pepper in a blender, and let them steep in a quart of warm water for 2 hours. Strain the mixture through cheesecloth or pantyhose, and dilute the liquid with about 3 quarts of warm water. Add the Murphy's Oil Soap and vegetable oil, and pour the solution into a hand-held sprayer. Then take aim, and polish off the bugs that are buggin' you! (For related text, see page 44.)

▶ Garlic Oil

Keep a batch of this potent oil in the fridge, and you'll always have ammunition against aphids and other garden thugs.

1 bulb of garlic, minced
1 cup of vegetable oil

Mix the minced garlic and the oil, and pour into a glass jar with a tight lid. Put the jar in the refrigerator and "steep" the oil for a day or two. To see whether it's ready for action, open the lid and take a sniff. If the aroma is so strong that you take a step back, you're ready to roll. If the scent isn't so strong, mince half a bulb of garlic, mix it into the oil, and wait another day. Then strain out the solids and pour the oil into a fresh jar with a lid. Keep it in the fridge, and use it in any Thug Buster that calls for Garlic Oil. (For related text, see page 119.)

▶ God-Sink-the-Queen Drench

When fire ants are driving you up a wall, serve their boss lady this fatal cocktail.

4 cups of citrus peels
3 gallons of water

Toss the peels into a pot with the water, bring it to a boil, and let it simmer for about 10 minutes. Then pour the potion into the hole. (Be sure to follow the procedure described in "Death to the Queen(s)!" on page 9.) The boiling water will polish off any ants it reaches, and the citrus-oil fumes will send more to the gas chamber. Repeat the procedure every two or three days, until there's no sign of life in the mound. (For related text, see page 9.)

Go-Go, Ground Squirrels Tonic

Ground squirrels don't often take "No!" for an answer, but when their tongues touch this firey brew, they usually go looking for a cooler dinner.

6 habanero chili peppers*
1 tsp. of dishwashing liquid
3 gal. of water

Puree the peppers in a blender with about 1 cup of the water. Strain out the solids, add the rest of the water, and stir in the dishwashing liquid. Pour the solution into a hand-held sprayer, and spray the ground all around the squirrels' target plants. Spray the plants, too, but *only* after testing a few leaves, because this hot stuff could burn them. And the peppers *will* burn your skin, so wear rubber gloves when you're working with them! (For related text, see page 230.)

*Available in some specialty markets, or in catalogs that specialize in southwestern and Mexican food.

Goodbye, Good Guy Spray

Even good bugs can drive you crazy when they're batting at your windows all evening long. Well, here's a spray that will make them bug off—but it won't hurt them one bit.

1/4 cup of vinegar
8 tbsp. of essential oil of bay*
3 cups of water

Pour the vinegar, oil, and water in a hand-held sprayer. Tighten the cap and shake until the ingredients are well blended. To keep the bugs from flying at your closed windows, use the potion to clean the outside of the glass in your usual way. If the little guys are bouncing off of the screens, thoroughly spray the mesh. Just make sure you spray from the inside out, so you don't wind up with a puddle on the floor! (For related text, see page 341.)

*Available in craft-supply and herbal-products stores.

Gopher-Go Tonic

When gophers just won't give up, reach for this remarkable recipe.

4 tbsp. of castor oil
4 tbsp. of dishwashing liquid
4 tbsp. of urine
1/2 cup of warm water
2 gal. of warm water

Combine the oil, dishwashing liquid, and urine in 1/2 cup of warm water, then stir the solution into 2 gallons of warm water. Pour the mixture over any problem areas, and the gophers will gallop away! (For related text, see page 227.)

Grandma Putt's Simple Soap Spray

This old-fashioned solution kills off lace bugs and just about any other soft-bodied insect you can name, including rose midges, mealybugs, thrips, and aphids.

1/2 bar of Fels Naptha® or Octagon® soap,*
**   shredded**
2 gal. of water

Add the soap to the water and heat, stirring, until the soap dissolves completely. Let the solution cool, then pour it into a hand-held sprayer, and let 'er rip. Test it on one plant first, though—and be sure to rinse it off of the plants after the bugs have bitten the dust, because lingering soap film can damage leaves. (For related text, see page 86.)

*You'll find Fels Naptha and Octagon in either the bath soap or laundry section of your supermarket.

▶ Great-Guns Garlic Spray

This fragrant concoction will halt an aphid invasion faster than you can say, "Please pass the dish soap!" In the process, it'll also kill any foul fungi that might be lingering on your plants, fixin' to cause dastardly diseases.

1 tbsp. of my Garlic Oil (see page 349)
3 drops of dishwashing liquid
1 qt. of water

Mix these ingredients together in a blender, and pour the solution into a hand-held sprayer. Then take aim and fire. Within seconds, those bugs'll be history! (For related text, see page 118.)

▶ Hit-the-Trail Mix

When cats are cuttin' capers in your flower beds or gunnin' for your fine feathered friends, put up a "Keep Out!" sign in the form of this zesty potion.

4 tbsp. of dry mustard
3 tbsp. of cayenne pepper
2 tbsp. of chili powder
2 tbsp. of cloves
1 tbsp. of hot sauce
2 qts. of warm water

Mix all of the ingredients, and sprinkle the solution around the perimeter of your yard, or anyplace where Puffy isn't welcome. She'll get her kicks elsewhere! (For related text, see page 191.)

▶ Homegrown Daisy Spray

If you grow painted daisies *(Chrysanthemum coccineum)*, you've got the makings of one powerful pesticide. It'll deal a death blow to lilac borers and just about any other bad-guy bug you can think of. And the recipe couldn't be simpler.

¹⁄₈ cup of rubbing alcohol
1 cup of packed, fresh painted-daisy
   flower heads*

Pour the alcohol over the flower heads and let it sit overnight. Strain out the flowers, then store the extract in a sealed, labeled container. When you need it, mix the extract with 3 quarts of water, and pour the solution into a hand-held sprayer. (For related text, see page 104.)

*If you don't grow painted daisies, look for them in the florist section of a large supermarket or, in the summertime, at your local farmers' markets.

▶ Homemade Bird Treats

Just serve up these gourmet goodies, and your fine-feathered friends will flock to your feeder—and hang around to gobble up bad-guy bugs.

1 part cornmeal
1 part wild-bird seed
Bacon grease (room-temperature)
2 pinches of sand or crushed eggshells

Mix the cornmeal and birdseed with enough bacon grease to get a bread-dough consistency. Add the sand or eggshells. Shape the dough into a ball, put it in a mesh onion bag, and hang it from a sturdy tree branch or bird-feeder post. Then get out your binoculars and have fun watching the action! (For related text, see page 333.)

Homemade Btk

When caterpillars are crawling out of the woodwork and you're fresh out of Btk, don't waste time running to the garden center for a new supply. Instead, make your own with this simple recipe.

1 cup of Btk victims*
2 cups of milk
Water

Mash the caterpillars slightly with an old fork, or chop them coarsely in a blender (one that you never plan to use again for human or pet food prep). Put them in a tight-lidded glass jar with the milk, and let it stand at room temperature for three days, well out of reach of children or pets. Strain out the solids, and add enough water to make a gallon of liquid. Then pour the solution into a hand-held sprayer, and go kill those 'pillars! (For related text, see page 162.)

*Caterpillars that have been sprayed with Btk and are dead or dying.

Hooray-for-Horseradish Tonic

This tangy tonic is instant death to some of the vilest villains in gardendom, including blister beetles, aphids, Colorado potato beetles, whiteflies, and any caterpillar that ever crept down the pike.

2 cups of cayenne pepper, finely chopped
1-inch piece of horseradish root, finely chopped*
3 qts. of water

Bring the water to a boil, add the pepper and horseradish, and let the mixture steep for an hour or so. Let it cool to room temperature, then strain out the solids. Pour the liquid into a hand-held sprayer, and blast those bugs to you-know-where! (For related text, see page 122.)

*Or 2 tablespoons of bottled, pure horseradish.

Hot Bite Spray

When chipmunks or other furry felons are feeding on your flowering plants, whip up a batch of this timely tonic.

3 tbsp. of cayenne pepper
2 cups of hot water
1 tbsp. of hot sauce
1 tbsp. of ammonia
1 tbsp. of baby shampoo

Mix the cayenne pepper with the hot water in a bottle, and shake well. Let the mixture sit overnight, then pour off the liquid without disturbing the sediment at the bottom. Mix the liquid with the other ingredients in a hand-held sprayer. Keep a batch on hand, especially when tender shoots and new buds are forming, and spritz the plants as often as you can to keep them hot, hot, *hot!* No critter who tastes the stuff will come back for a second bite! (For related text, see page 195.)

Hot Bug Brew

This potent beverage will deal a death blow to mole crickets, maggots, flies, and any other bug that's buggin' your plants.

3 hot green peppers (canned or fresh)
3 medium cloves of garlic
1 small onion
1 tbsp. of dishwashing liquid
3 cups of water

Puree the peppers, garlic, and onion in a blender. Then pour the mixture into a jar, and add the dishwashing liquid and water. Let stand for 24 hours. Strain out the solids, pour the liquid into a spray bottle, and blast the mole crickets to kingdom come. **Note:** You probably won't get all the varmints on the first try, so you may need to repeat the process a few times. (For related text, see page 19.)

Hot Pepper Spray

This hot toddy will say a loud, strong "Get lost!" to any Japanese beetle who starts to sink his chops into your shrubs (or any other plants). And recipes don't come any simpler than this one!

½ cup of dried cayenne peppers
½ cup of jalapeño peppers
1 gal. of water

Add the peppers to the water, bring it to a boil, and let it simmer for half an hour. (Make sure you keep the pan covered, or the peppery steam will make you cry a river of tears!) Let the mixture cool, then strain out the solids, pour the liquid into a spray bottle, and spritz your plagued plants from top to bottom. You'll have to repeat the process after every rain, but that's a small price to pay for a beetle-free summer! (For related text, see page 83.)

Instant Insecticide

When there's no time to fumble with fancy formulas, mix up this potent pest potion.* It's instant death to almost any bad bug in the book.

1 cup of rubbing alcohol
1 tsp. of vegetable oil
1 qt. of water

Mix all of the ingredients in a hand-held sprayer, take aim, and give each pest a direct hit. (For related text, see page 152.)

*See "Test First" on page 144.

Jerry's Lime Rickey

Back in my Uncle Art's day, lime soda rickeys were all the rage. Well, this rickey isn't made with soda or lime juice, but it *will* make the maggots rage!

1 cup of garden lime
1 qt. of water

Stir the lime into the water, and let it sit overnight. Then pour the solution around the rootball of each maggot-plagued plant. Before you can say, "Put another nickel in, in the nickelodeon," those maggots'll be history! (For related text, see page 254.)

Knock-'Em-Dead Insect Spray

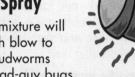

This potent mixture will deal a death blow to geranium budworms and other bad-guy bugs.

6 cloves of garlic, finely chopped
1 small onion, finely chopped
1 tbsp. of cayenne pepper
1 tbsp. of dishwashing liquid
1 qt. of warm water

Mix all of these ingredients, and let the mixture sit overnight. Strain out the solids, pour the liquid into a hand-held sprayer, and knock those pesky pests dead! (For related text, see page 172.)

Lawn Saver Tonic

When bad things happen to good grass, reach for this liquid safety net.

½ can of beer
½ can of regular cola (not diet)
½ cup of ammonia

Combine these ingredients in your 20 gallon hose-end sprayer. Then saturate your grass to the point of run-off. (For related text, see page 28.)

Lethal Leafhopper Spray

Even hard-to-get bugs like leafhoppers will kick the bucket when you hit 'em hard with this stuff.

½ cup of liquor (any kind will do)
2 tbsp. of dishwashing liquid
1 gal. of warm water

Mix all of these ingredients together, and pour the solution into a spray bottle. Then saturate your plants from top to bottom, especially the undersides of leaves, where leafhoppers love to hide. (For related text, see page 213.)

Lethal Weapon Tonic

If ants have turned your favorite tree into an aphid ranch, don't pull any punches. Reach for your trusty hose-end sprayer, and load it with this magic bullet.

3 tbsp. of garlic and onion juice*
3 tbsp. of skim milk
2 tbsp. of baby shampoo
1 tsp. of hot sauce
1 gal. of water

Mix all of these ingredients in a bucket, and pour the solution into a 20 gallon hose-end sprayer. Then spray your tree every 10 days until the aphids are lyin' 6 feet under on Boot Hill. (For related text, see page 37.)

*To make garlic and onion juice, put 2 cloves of garlic, 2 medium onions, and 3 cups of water in a blender, and puree. Strain out the solids, and pour the remaining liquid into a jar. Use this mixture whenever it's called for in a Thug Buster. When you're done, bury the solids in your garden to repel aphids and other pesky pests.

Merry Marigold Marinade

Garden webworms, tomato hornworms, asparagus beetles, and a whole lot of other bad bugs flee from this tangy tonic.

1 cup of pot marigold (*Calendula officinalis*) leaves and flowers
2 cups of water
¼ tsp. of dishwashing liquid
1½ qts. of water

Mash the leaves and flowers in a bowl, mix them with the 2 cups of water, and let the slurry marinate for 24 hours. Strain it through cheesecloth, stir in the remaining 1½ quarts of water, and add the dishwashing liquid. Then pour the solution into a hand-held sprayer, and spray the webworms' targets from top to bottom. Reapply after every rain. (For related text, see page 308.)

Mighty Fine Miticide

This excellent elixir will eliminate mites and give your yews—or any other mite-plagued plants—a dose of valuable nitrogen at the same time.

1 tbsp. of ammonia
1 tsp. of dishwashing liquid
2½ gal. of water

Mix these ingredients in a bucket, and pour the solution into a hand-held sprayer. Spray your afflicted plants every five days for three weeks. Then sit back and admire your pest-free greenery! (For related text, see page 95.)

Mite-Free Fruit Tree Formula

Mites might be teeny, but they can do BIG damage to shrubs as well as fruit trees. When these pests attack, protect your prize plants with this easy recipe.

5 lb. of white flour
1 pt. of buttermilk
25 gal. of water

Mix the ingredients together, and keep the potion in a tightly closed garbage can. Stir before each use, and spray shrubs and trees weekly until the mites are history. (For related text, see page 92.)

Mole-Chaser Tonic

Moles will pack up and head outta town (or at least out of your yard) when they get a taste of this potent potion.

1½ tbsp. of hot sauce
1 tbsp. of dishwashing liquid
1 tsp. of chili powder
1 qt. of water

Mix all of these ingredients in a bucket, and pour a little of the mix into each mole hole. The little guys will get a taste they won't soon forget! (For related text, see page 33.)

Mosquito Lemon Aid

There's nothing mosquitoes hate more than the scent of lemon. So what are you waiting for? Give 'em a whiff of this fragrant potion!

1 cup of lemon-scented ammonia
1 cup of lemon-scented dishwashing liquid

Put these ingredients into your 20 gallon hose-end sprayer, and hose down everything in your yard three times a week, preferably early in the morning or late in the evening. (For related text, see page 15.)

Move On, Moles Tonic

When you want to clear out a mole-tunnel system in a hurry, mix up a batch of this tonic, and let 'er rip!

1 cup of dishwashing liquid
1 cup of castor oil
2 tbsp. of alum, dissolved in hot water

Mix these ingredients in your 20 gallon hose-end sprayer, and saturate the problem areas. (For related text, see page 32.)

Mulch Moisturizer Tonic

Serve up this tasty drink in midsummer to keep your organic mulch fresh as a daisy, your plants happy as clams—and potato tuberworms absolutely miserable!

1 can of regular cola (not diet)
½ cup of ammonia
½ cup of antiseptic mouthwash
½ cup of baby shampoo

Mix these ingredients in your 20 gallon hose-end sprayer, and give your mulch security blanket a nice long, cool drink. (For related text, see page 221.)

Nix 'Em with Nicotine Tea

This potent potion (a variation on my tobacco tea recipe) will polish off leaf miners and other foliage-munching felons, too. It's also just the ticket for soilborne pests, such as root aphids.

1 cup of cigarette or cigar butts
½ tsp. of dishwashing liquid
1 gal. of water

Soak the butts in the water for about half an hour (no need to remove any filters or paper). Then strain out the solids, mix in the dishwashing liquid, and pour the tea into a hand-held sprayer. Saturate the undersides of leaves, where leaf miners linger before they tunnel inside. To stop root-munching pests in their tracks, pour the liquid on the soil around the stem and root zone of your troubled plants. (For related text, see page 259.)

No Mo' Nematodes Tonic

This simple elixir will polish off nasty nematodes lickety-split.

1 can of beer
1 cup of molasses

Mix these ingredients in your 20 gallon hose-end sprayer, and thoroughly soak any area where the nematodes are doin' their dirty work. (For related text, see page 182.)

▶ No Way! Garlic Spray

Use this aromatic concoction to make your plants a no-munching zone for leaftiers and other garlic-phobic gallivanters. Because this repellent contains no soap, which can damage young, tender plant parts, it's safe to use even on brand-new buds.

¹/₂ cup of garlic, finely chopped*
2 cups of water

Mix the ingredients, then strain out the solids. Pour the liquid into a hand-held sprayer, and spray your plants once a week, paying special attention to new leaf and flower buds. Repeat after every rain. (For related text, see page 102.)

*Or substitute onion or chives.

▶ On-Guard Tomato Tonic

Thanks to potent chemical compounds called *alkaloids* found in tomato leaves, this potion works like an invisible suit of armor to guard plants from some of the hungriest pests on the planet.

2 cups of tomato leaves, chopped
1 qt. of water
¹/₂ tsp. of dishwashing liquid

Put the leaves and water in a pan, and bring the water to a simmer. Then turn off the heat, and let the mixture cool. Strain out the leaves, and add the dishwashing liquid to the brew. Pour the solution into a hand-held sprayer, and spritz your plants' foliage from top to bottom. Then wave good-bye to corn earworms, whiteflies, asparagus beetles, cabbageworms, and many other garden-variety villains. But remember: As with all sprays, you need to renew the supply after every rain. (For related text, see page 300.)

▶ Orange Aid

You'll love the aroma of this citrusy spray—and you'll love its firepower even more. It'll deliver a death blow to any caterpillar who comes within shooting range of your spray gun. It also works like a charm on other soft-bodied insects, including whiteflies and aphids.

1 cup of chopped orange peels*
¹/₄ cup of boiling water

Put the orange peels in a blender or food processor, and pour the boiling water over them. Liquefy, then let the mixture sit overnight at room temperature. Strain the slurry through cheesecloth, and pour the liquid into a hand-held sprayer. Fill the balance of the bottle with water, then take aim, and let 'er rip. (For related text, see page 49.)

*Or substitute lemon, lime, or grapefruit peels.

▶ Peppermint Soap Spray

This brew is a nightmare-come-true for hard-bodied insects like beetles. The secret weapon: peppermint. It cuts right through a bug's waxy shell, so the soap can get in and work its fatal magic.

2 tbsp. of dishwashing liquid
2 tsp. of peppermint oil
1 gal. of warm water

Mix the soap and water together, then stir in the peppermint oil. Pour the solution into a hand-held sprayer, take aim, and fire! Those beetles'll never know what hit 'em! (For related text, see page 41.)

▶ Pop Off, Pillbugs Tonic

This simple solution will send pillbugs and sowbugs searching elsewhere for supper.

3 medium-sized onions
1 qt. of water

Puree the onions and water in a blender or food processor, and strain out the solids.

Then pour the liquid into a hand-held sprayer, and spritz the soil around any plants that need protection from those crafty crustaceans. (For related text, see page 241.)

▶ Quack-Up Slug Cookies

Slugs will think it's time to party when they get a beer-scented whiff of these tasty treats. But after a couple of bites, they'll have a killer of a hangover!

1 part dried quackgrass blades, finely chopped
1 part wheat bran*
1 can of beer

Mix the quackgrass and bran in a bowl, then slowly add the beer, stirring until the mixture has the consistency of cookie dough. Run the dough through a meat grinder, or chop it into small bits (roughly 1/8 to 1/4 inch thick). Let the "cookies" air-dry overnight, sprinkle them on the ground among your plants, and let the good times roll! (For related text, see page 187.)

*Available in supermarkets and health-food stores.

▶ Safe-and-Sound Pesticide

Looking for a bad-bug killer that you know is harmless? Look no further! This one comes right out of your kitchen cupboard, but it's lethal to some of the peskiest pests that ever came down the pike.

1/3 cup of vegetable oil (any kind will do)
1 tsp. of baking soda
1 cup of water

Mix the oil and baking soda together. Then combine 2 teaspoons of the mixture with the cup of water in a hand-held sprayer, and go get those bad guys! (For related text, see page 238.)

▶ Skunk Odor-Out Tonic

When a skunk comes a-callin' and leaves some fragrant evidence behind, reach for this easy remedy.

1 cup of bleach or vinegar
1 tbsp. of dishwashing liquid
2 1/2 gal. of warm water

Mix all of these ingredients in a bucket and thoroughly saturate walls, stairs, or anything else your local skunk has left his mark on. **Caution:** Use this tonic only on non-living things—not on pets, humans, or plants. (For related text, see page 113.)

▶ So Long, Sucker Spray

This fabulous formula is just the ticket for tiny insects, like thrips and aphids, that are too small for you to handpick and whirl in a blender all by themselves.

2 cups of thrip-infested flowers or leaves*
2 cups of warm water plus 1 gal. of water
Cheesecloth

Put the plant parts in an old blender, and whirl 'em with the 2 cups of warm water (tiny bugs and all). Strain the goop through cheesecloth, dilute with 1 gallon of water, and pour the juice into a hand-held sprayer. Then spray your plants from top to bottom, on both sides of leaves and stems, and along all runners. Repeat the treatment after rain. If you have any extra juice, freeze it right away before bacteria can get a toehold. Be sure to label it clearly—you don't want to have this stuff for dinner! Two notes of caution: Once you've used a blender to make this spray, don't use it again for either human or pet food preparation—ever! And don't make this spray (or any other) from mosquitoes, ticks, or other blood-sucking insects that transmit human and animal diseases. (For related text, see page 155.)

*Substitute whatever pests are sucking the life out of your plants.

Spiked Soap Spray

When you've got a tree-sized pest invasion on your hands, this simple soapy spray, spiked with alcohol, is just the remedy to reach for.

2 cups of dishwashing liquid
1 cup of isopropyl (rubbing) alcohol

Mix these ingredients in your 20 gallon hose-end sprayer, then saturate your bug-infested trees from top to bottom. If necessary, repeat the process once or twice at one-week intervals until the culprits are history. (For related text, see page 56.)

Squeaky Clean Tonic

This is a more powerful version of my All-Season Clean-Up Tonic (see page 345), and it deals a mighty blow to cutworms and other bad guys who are buggin' your lawn.

1 cup of antiseptic mouthwash
1 cup of tobacco tea*
1 cup of chamomile tea
1 cup of urine
½ cup of Murphy's Oil Soap®
½ cup of lemon-scented dishwashing liquid

Mix all of these ingredients in a large bucket. Then pour the solution into your 20 gallon hose-end sprayer, and apply it to your lawn to the point of run-off. (For related text, see page 166.)

*For the recipe, see "Winterizing Tonic" on page 360.

Squirrel Beater Tonic

To keep pesky squirrels from making off with your crop, spray your fruit and nut trees with this spicy potion.

2 tbsp. of cayenne pepper
2 tbsp. of hot sauce
2 tbsp. of chili powder
1 tbsp. of Murphy's Oil Soap®
1 qt. of warm water

Mix all of these ingredients together. Then pour the mixture into a hand-held sprayer, and coat your trees from top to bottom. Just make sure you rinse your fruit thoroughly before you bite into it, or you'll get a taste "treat" you won't soon forget! (For related text, see page 69.)

Super Scale Spray

This double-barreled potion works two ways: The soap kills the unprotected scale babies (a.k.a. crawlers), and the alcohol cuts right through the grown-ups' waxy shells.

1 cup of rubbing alcohol
1 tbsp. of dishwashing liquid
1 qt. of water

Mix these ingredients in a hand-held sprayer, and treat your scale-stricken plants every three days for two weeks. The scale will sail off into the sunset. (For related text, see page 144.)

Super Soil Sandwich Dressing

When you've stacked up all the makings for your new, no-work planting bed (see "Movin' On," on page 289), top off your "super soil sandwich" with this zesty condiment. It'll kick-start the cooking process, and by the following spring, your super soil will be rarin' to grow!

1 can of beer
1 can of regular cola (not diet)
½ cup of ammonia
¼ cup of instant tea granules

Mix these ingredients in a bucket, and pour the solution into a 20 gallon hose-end sprayer. Then spray your "sandwich" until all the layers are saturated. (For related text, see page 289.)

Thatch Blaster Tonic

This excellent elixir will help keep your lawn free of nasty thatch all season long.

1 cup of beer or regular cola (not diet)
½ cup of dishwashing liquid
¼ cup of ammonia

Mix all of these ingredients in your 20 gallon hose-end sprayer. Fill the balance of the sprayer jar with water, and saturate the entire turf area starting in spring. Repeat once a month during the summer, when the grass is actively growing. (For related text, see page 21.)

Tomato-Leaf Tonic

Our ancestors thought tomatoes were poisonous, so they avoided them like the plague. Fortunately for us, flea beetles still do. Just spray your plants' leaves with this timely tonic, and kiss your flea-beetle battles good-bye!

2 cups of tomato leaves, chopped
1 qt. of water
½ tsp. of dishwashing liquid

Put the leaves and water in a pan, and bring the water to a simmer. Then turn off the heat, and let the mixture cool. Strain out the leaves, and add the dishwashing liquid to the water. Pour the solution into a hand-held sprayer, and spritz your plants from top to bottom. This potent potion also repels whiteflies, asparagus beetles, and cabbageworms. Like all repellent sprays, though, you need to reapply this tonic after every rain. (For related text, see page 130.)

Toodle-oo, Tick Spray

Ticks can make life miserable for both humans and pets. If these germ-totin' terrors are hanging out in your flowers or ornamental grasses, cook their goose with this spray. (The rubbing alcohol is the secret weapon here: It penetrates the rascals' protective, waxy covering so the soap can get in to do its deadly work.) Just make sure you wait until evening to blast the culprits; otherwise, the combination of sunshine and alcohol will burn your plants.

1 tbsp. of Ivory® liquid soap
1 gal. of rainwater or soft tap water
2 cups of rubbing alcohol

Mix the Ivory liquid with the water in a 6 gallon hose-end sprayer jar, then add the alcohol. With the nozzle pressure turned on high, spray your plants from top to bottom— and make sure you get under all the leaves. Repeat whenever necessary. (For related text, see page 158.)

Tree Protection Potion

Use this mild, but potent oil to keep insect eggs from hatching into tree-eating monsters.

1 cup of corn oil or olive oil
1 tbsp. of dishwashing liquid
1 gal. of water

Combine the ingredients together thoroughly, and pour the mixture into a hand-held sprayer. Shake well, and spray the trunk of your tree until it's well covered. Shake the sprayer every now and then to keep the oil and water mixed. (For related text, see page 62.)

Vegetable Power Powder

This mighty mixture will give all of your crops the get-up-and-grow power they need to fend off seed-corn maggots and all kinds of other pesky pests, too. Use it two weeks before you sow your seeds or set in your transplants.

25 lbs. of organic garden food
5 lbs. of gypsum
2 lbs. of diatomaceous earth
1 lb. of sugar

Mix the ingredients together, and put the blend into a hand-held broadcast spreader. Set the spreader on medium, and apply the mixture over the top of your garden soil. Follow up immediately by overspraying the area with my Spring Soil Energizer Tonic (see page 361). (For related text, see page 310.)

Weed Wipeout

When you've got weeds that won't take no for an answer, knock 'em flat on their backs with this potent potion.

1 tbsp. of gin
1 tbsp. of vinegar
1 tsp. of dishwashing liquid
1 qt. of very warm water

Mix all of these ingredients, and pour the solution into a hand-held sprayer. Then drench the weeds to the point of run-off, taking care not to spray any nearby plants. (For related text, see page 150.)

Whitefly Wipeout Tonic

Whitefly woes got you down? Don't cry, just mosey into the kitchen and mix up a batch of this discomfort food. It's a meal they'll *die* for!

1 cup of sour milk*
2 tbsp. of flour
1 qt. of warm water

Mix the ingredients in a bowl. Then pour the mixture into a hand-held sprayer, and coat your plants from top to bottom. Make sure you get the underside of every leaf! (For related text, see page 294.)

*If you don't have sour milk on hand, mix 2 tablespoons of vinegar with enough fresh milk to make 1 cup.

Wild Mustard Tea

Potato beetles, cabbage moths, and cabbage loopers will give your garden a wide berth if you spray your plants with this tangy tea.

4 whole cloves
1 handful of wild mustard leaves
1 clove of garlic
1 cup of boiling water

Steep the first three ingredients in the boiling water for 10 minutes. Let the elixir cool, then pour it into a hand-held sprayer, and let 'er rip! (For related text, see page 210.)

Winterizing Tonic

To stop trouble before it starts, give bad-guy bugs a fatal drink of this bedtime beverage.

1 cup of Murphy's Oil Soap®
1 cup of tobacco tea*
1 cup of antiseptic mouthwash

Mix these ingredients in a 20 gallon hose-end sprayer, filling the balance of the jar with warm water. Then, after you've done your fall clean-up, saturate your carrot patch and the rest of your lawn and garden, too. Come spring, your plants will be pest-free and rarin' to grow! (For related text, see page 207.)

*To make tobacco tea, place half a handful of chewing tobacco in an old nylon stocking and soak it in a gallon of hot water until the mixture is dark brown. Pour the liquid into a glass container with a tight lid for storage.

More Great Bug-Busting Formulas!

▶ Flower and Foliage Flu Shot

There's no cure for plant viruses, but this vaccine could help fend off their onset.

2 cups of leaves from a healthy, sweet green pepper plant
½ tsp. of dishwashing liquid
2 cups of water

Put the leaves and the water in a blender and liquefy. Then dilute the mixture with an equal amount of water, add the dishwashing liquid, pour the solution into a spray bottle, and have at it!

▶ Manure Tea

This enriching elixir offers up a full menu of plant nutrients, fends off diseases—and sends groundhogs scurrying.

1½ gal. of well-cured manure
4½ gal. of warm water

Scoop the manure into a burlap sack, tie it closed, and put it in a tub or big bucket with the water. Cover, and let it steep for three to seven days. Pour the solution into a watering can, and water your garden with the brew every two weeks throughout the growing season.

▶ Oil's-Well-That-Ends-Well Mix

This oily potion is just the ticket for wipin' out scale, aphids, and other little pests.

1 tbsp. of basic oil mixture*
2 cups of water

Combine these ingredients in a hand-held sprayer, and mist-spray your plants from top to bottom. (Shake the bottle now and then to make sure the oil and water stay mixed!) Repeat the process in seven days.

▶ Rhubarb Pest-Repellent Tonic

Here's a potent plant tonic that'll say "Scram!" to just about any kind of pest you can think of.

3 medium-sized rhubarb leaves
¼ cup of dishwashing liquid
1 gal. of water

Chop up the rhubarb leaves, put the pieces in the water, and bring it to a boil. Let the mixture cool, then strain out the solids and mix in the dishwashing liquid. Apply with a hand-held sprayer.

▶ Spring Soil Energizer Tonic

Use this elixir on its own or as a follow-up to my Vegetable Power Powder (see page 310). It'll get your plants growin' so they'll be better able to fend off pesky pests.

1 can of beer
1 cup of dishwashing liquid
1 cup of antiseptic mouthwash
1 cup of regular cola (not diet)
¼ tsp. of instant tea granules

Mix these ingredients in a bucket and pour the solution into a 20 gallon hose-end sprayer. Overspray the soil in your garden to the point of run-off. Then let the plot sit for two weeks before you start planting.

*To make basic oil mixture, pour 1 cup of vegetable oil and 1 tablespoon of Murphy's Oil Soap® into a plastic squeeze bottle (an empty ketchup or mustard bottle is perfect). Then measure out whatever you need for a Thug Buster recipe, and store the rest for later use.

INDEX